GEORGE WASHINGTON
BICENTENNIAL EDITION

THE WRITINGS OF
GEORGE WASHINGTON

FROM A RARE MEZZOTINT MADE BY CHARLES WILLSON PEALE FROM HIS PORTRAIT
FROM LIFE IN 1787

THE *WRITINGS OF*

George
Washington

from the

Original Manuscript Sources
1745–1799

Prepared under the direction of the UNITED STATES
GEORGE WASHINGTON BICENTENNIAL COMMISSION
and published by authority of CONGRESS

JOHN C. FITZPATRICK, *Editor*

Volume 29
September 1, 1786–June 19, 1788

United States
Government Printing Office
Washington

PRINTED

JANUARY, 1939

32459

UNITED STATES GEORGE WASHINGTON BICENTENNIAL COMMISSION

(The Commission expired December 31, 1934)

President of the United States
Chairman

Vice President of the United States
Speaker of the House of Representatives

United States Senate	House of Representatives
SIMEON D. FESS,* *Vice Chairman* Ohio	WILLIS C. HAWLEY Oregon
ARTHUR CAPPER Kansas	JOHN Q. TILSON Connecticut
CARTER GLASS Virginia	JOSEPH W. BYRNS* Tennessee
MILLARD E. TYDINGS Maryland	R. WALTON MOORE Virginia

Presidential Commissioners

MRS. ANTHONY WAYNE COOK Pennsylvania	C. BASCOM SLEMP Virginia
MRS. JOHN DICKINSON SHERMAN * Colorado	WALLACE McCAMANT Oregon
HENRY FORD Michigan	ALBERT BUSHNELL HART Massachusetts
GEORGE EASTMAN* New York	JOSEPH SCOTT California

Executive Committee

THE SENATE AND HOUSE
COMMISSIONERS
C. BASCOM SLEMP
MRS. ANTHONY WAYNE COOK
JOSEPH SCOTT

Historian

PROF. ALBERT BUSHNELL HART

Director

REPRESENTATIVE SOL BLOOM

Executive Secretary
WILLLIAM TYLER PAGE

---

*Deceased.

ADVISORY COMMITTEE
ON THE WRITINGS

DR. J. FRANKLIN JAMESON, *Chairman**
Chair of American History and Chief of Manuscripts Division
Library of Congress

PROFESSOR RANDOLPH G. ADAMS
Librarian William L. Clements Library
University of Michigan

PRESIDENT J. A. C. CHANDLER*
William and Mary College

PRESIDENT TYLER DENNETT
Williams College

DR. CHARLES MOORE
Chairman United States Commission of Fine Arts

GEORGE W. OCHS-OAKES, ESQ.*
Editor New York Times

BRIGADIER GENERAL JOHN M. PALMER
United States Army, Retired

DR. VICTOR H. PALTSITS
Chief of American History Division
and Chief of Manuscripts Department
New York Public Library

---

* Deceased.

TABLE OF CONTENTS

1786

TABLE OF SYMBOLS

The following symbols have been used to denote the place of deposit of Washington letters not found in draft or letter-book form in the *Washington Papers* in the Library of Congress:

Indicating that the letter is in Washington's own handwriting	*
Chicago Historical Society	[CH.H.S.]
Clements Library, University of Michigan	[C.L.]
Connecticut Historical Society	[C.H.S.]
Harvard College Library	[HV.L.]
Haverford College	[HD.C.]
Historical Society of Pennsylvania	[H.S.P.]
Huntington Library	[H.L.]
John Carter Brown Library, Rhode Island	[J.C.B.]
Maine Historical Society	[M.H.S.]
Maryland Historical Society	[MD.H.S.]
Massachusetts Historical Society	[MS.H.S.]
J. P. Morgan Library	[M.L.]
New Hampshire Historical Society	[N.H.H.S.]
New York Historical Society	[N.Y.H.S.]
New York Public Library	[N.Y.P.L.]
New York State Library	[N.Y.S.L.]
Rhode Island Historical Society	[R.I.H.S.]
Rhode Island Society of the Cincinnati	[R.I.S.C.]
Society of the Cincinnati	[S.C.]
University of Chicago Library	[U.C.L.]
University of Pennsylvania Library	[U.P.]
Virginia Historical Society	[V.H.S.]
Virginia State Library	[V.S.L.]

THE WRITINGS OF
GEORGE WASHINGTON

THE WRITINGS OF
GEORGE WASHINGTON

———◆———

To GEORGE GILPIN AND JOHN FITZGERALD

Mount Vernon, September 1, 1786.

Gent: Nothing but sickness would have prevented my attending at the Seneca Falls on Monday next agreeably to appointment. On Sunday last (occasioned by an imprudent act) I was seized by an ague and fever. Whether the Doctors efforts will baffle them tomorrow, remains to be determined; but at any rate he thinks it would be improper for me to leave home. The fevers moreover, have made such havock of my mouth, nose and chin that I am unable to put a razor to my face. Thus circumstanced, I have given up all idea of meeting the Board the 4th. instant.

Besides the business which is the immediate occasion of this meeting, it might be well, as we are every day thrown back in our operations on the bed of the River, to prepare the draft of a Petition which will be necessary to hand to the respective Assemblies for prolongation of the time for that part of the undertaking; and, as there may be difficulties in the way yet unforeseen, I should incline to enlarge it to the greatest extent it is thought we can obtain. I submit for consideration also, the propriety (if the waters should get low enough in the course of the Fall) of a thorough investigation of the River, by a skilful person, from the Shannondoah falls to Fort Cumberland at least; that by having the matter fully before us, we may be enabled to form some precise judgment of the difficulties which lie in the way, and prepare for them accordingly.

As I cannot do greater justice to the sentiments of the Company respecting its approbation of the conduct of the Directors, than is conveyed by the address of the Committee, I have the honor of forwarding a copy of that letter to me, which I beg the favor of you, Gentn. to lay before the Board at the Meeting which is about to take place. With great esteem and regard, I am, etc.[1]

To DAVID HUMPHREYS

Mount Vernon, September 1, 1786.

My dear Humphreys: Enclosed are all the documents Mr. Lear could find respecting the confinement, and treatment under it, of Captain Asgill. For want of recurrence to them before I wrote to Mr. Tilghman,[2] I perceive that a bad memory had run me into an error in my narrative of the latter, in one particular. For it should seem by that, as if the loose and unguarded manner in which Captn Asgill was held, was sanctioned by me; whereas one of my letters to Colo. Dayton condemns this conduct, and orders Asgill to be closely confined. Mr. Lear has given all the letters at length. Extracts might have answered. But I judged it better that the whole tenor of the Correspondence should appear, that no part might seem to be hidden.

---

[1] From the "Letter Book" copy in the *Washington Papers*.
On September 1 Washington wrote to William Hartshorne, sending him the address from a committee of the Potomac company, which "will convey the sense of that Company on the fidelity and accuracy with which your accots. have been kept, in the fullest and clearest manner. I have great pleasure in communicating these sentiments, and with very great esteem and regard, I am etc." A copy of this is in the "Letter Book" in the *Washington Papers*.
[2] See Washington's letter to James Tilghman, June 5, 1786, *ante*.

I well remember Major Gordon's attending Asgill; and by one of my letters to Dayton it is evident that Gordon had written to me; but my letter-books have registered no reply. In what manner it would be best to bring this matter before the Publik eye I am at a loss, and leave it to you to determine under a consideration of the circumstances which are as fully communicated as the documents in my hands will enable me to do. There is one mystery in the business which I cannot develop, nor is there any papers in my possession which explain it. Hazen was ordered to send an unconditional prisoner. Asgill comes. Hazen or some other must have given information of a Lieutenant Turner, (under the former description). Turner is ordered on, but never came. Why? I am unable to say; nor is there any letter from Hazen (to be found) that accounts for a noncompliance with this order. If I had not too many causes to distrust my memory I should ascribe it to there having been no such Officer, or that he was also under capitulation, for Captn. Shaack seems to have been held as a proper victim after this.

I will write as soon as I am able to Mr. Tilghman, requesting him to withhold my first acct of Asgill's treatment, from his corrispondent in England, promising an authentic one from original papers. It may however have passed him, in that case, it will be necessary for me to say something to reconcile my own Accts.

I write to you with a very aching head, and disordered frame, and Mr. Lear will copy the letter. Saturday last, by an imprudent act, I brought on an ague and fever on Sunday, which returned with violence Tuesday and Thursday; and if Doctor Craik's efforts are ineffectual, I shall have them again this day. The family join me in every good wish for you. It is unnecessary to assure you of the friendship and affection with which I am &c.

P. S. We have found Gordon's letters. They contain [a remonstrance and de]mand of Asgill as an officer protected by the Capitulation of York-Town. This I suppose is the reason they were never answered.[3]   [N.Y.P.L.]

To JAMES TILGHMAN

Mount Vernon, September 2, 1786.

Dr. Sir: If the Account I handed to you respecting the treatment of Captn. Asgill (in confinement) has not passed from you, I should be obliged to you for withholding, and suffering no copies to be taken from it; to counteract such an injurious and ill founded calumny which obtains credit as it rolls on.

I have it in contemplation to inspect my registers, and to give something from authentic documents relative to this matter. The former being drawn up in a hasty manner, and from memory, may contain something inconsistent with the latter, which will be substantiated. With great esteem etc.[4]

To JOHN FITZGERALD

Mount Vernon, September 9, 1786.

Dear Sir: Have you heard from Annapolis since Monday? Have the Commercial Commissioners met?[5] Have they proceeded to business? How long is it supposed their sessions will last? and is it likely they will do anything effectual?

---

[3] In the writing of Tobias Lear. The words in brackets are in the writing of Washington.

[4] From the "Letter Book" copy in the *Washington Papers*.

[5] Otherwise known as "the Annapolis Convention."

Is Colo. Gilpin[6] returned? Was there a meeting of the Board? What was the result of the enquiry into the charges exhibited against Stuart?[7]

I hope Mrs Fitzgerald and yourself are quite recovered. I am tolerably well again,[8] but obliged to make use of Scissars instead of a Razor, for part of my face, when shaving. I am, etc.[9]

To JOHN FRANCIS MERCER

Mount Vernon, September 9, 1786.

Dr. Sir: Your favor of the 20th ulto. did not get to my hands 'till about the first of this month. It found me in a fever from which I am now but sufficiently recovered to attend to business. I mention this as the reason why your propositions have not been attended to before.

With respect to the first, I never mean (unless some particular circumstance should compel me to it) to possess another slave by purchase; it being among my first wishes to see some plan adopted, by which slavery in this country may be abolished by slow, sure, and imperceptible degrees. With respect to the second, I never did, nor never intend to purchase a military certificate. I see no difference it makes with you, (if it is one of the funds allotted for the discharge of my claim) who the purchaser is. If the depreciation between them and specie is three for one; you will have it in your power whilst at the receipt of Custom, Richmond, where it is said the great regulator of this business (Graves) resides, to convert them

---

[6] Col. George Gilpin, of Alexandria, Va. He was a director of the Potomac Company.

[7] Richardson Stewart (Stuart). He was assistant manager of the Potomac Company. James Rumsey had preferred charges against him and Stewart's managership was terminated at the end of the year 1788.

[8] Washington had an attack of fever and ague on August 31, apparently of a rheumatic character.

[9] The text is from a typed copy kindly furnished by G. A. S. Wieners, of College Point, N. Y., who owns (1934) the original.

into specie at that rate. If the difference is more, there would be no propriety (if I inclined to deal in them at all) in my taking them at that exchange.

I shall rely upon your promise of £200 in five weeks from the date of your letter. It will enable me to pay the workmen which have been employed about this House all the Spring and Summer (some of whom are yet here): but there are two debts which press hard upon me, one of which, if there is no other method left, I must sell Land or Negroes to discharge. It is owing to the Govr. of New York, Clinton, who was so obliging as to borrow the sum of £2000 to answer some calls of mine; to be paid in 12 months after the conclusion of Peace.

For this sum he became my security, and for what remains due (about £800 York Curry.) I am now paying an interest of 7 pr. Ct. but the high interest, tho' more than any estate can bear, I should not regard if my credit was not at stake to comply with the conditions of the loan. The other debt, tho' I am anxious to discharge it, and the person to whom I owe it, I know wants it, yet it might I believe, be put off a while longer; this sum is larger than the other. I am, &c.[10]

To SAMUEL VAUGHAN

Mount Vernon, September 12, 1786.

Dr. Sir: A few days ago I had the honor to receive your favor of the 22d. ulto.

At the same time that I regret not having had the pleasure of testifying under my own roof the respect and regard I had imbibed for your Lady and family before their departure from this Continent, I beg you to be assured that every wish which

---

[10] From the "Letter Book" copy in the *Washington Papers.*

I can offer for a short and agreeable passage, and happy meetings with their friends in England, attends them. Although
I can now no longer look for the pleasure of the Ladies companies at this seat of my retirement, I will not despair of seeing you at it, when it can be made to comport with your other
pursuits. It is unnecessary I persuade myself to repeat the assurances of the pleasure it would give me you, or such of your
family as remain in this country, here, or of the sincere esteem
and respect with which I have the honor, etc.[11]

To CHARLES SIMMS

Virginia, September 22, 1786.

Dear Sir: I now sit down to avail myself of your friendly
offer of serving me, whilst you are on your Western tour.

I give you the trouble of some letters: that to Mr. Smith I
leave open for your perusal, please to seal before delivering it.
Mr. Smith has my Patent. Posey's Bond on which my military
right was founded, and on which the warrt. for surveying
issued, together with every other public and private document
which could be obtained in evidence of the regularity and le-
gality of my claim. The plea of the Defendants will be, I
know, that I cannot trace any steps of regular and authentic
proceedings, back to their occupancy. For say they, you can
find no entry in the Surveyor's books, nor on the records of
Council, previous to the Survey; which is the first legal process
you can adduce, and this is not dated 'till Feby. when our settlement of the Land was in the month of Octr. preceeding,
nay more, your warrant of Survey, which was laid upon this
Land, received date in Novr. subsequent by a month to our
settlement. The latter (under the rose) I believe is fact, and

---

[11] From the "Letter Book" copy in the *Washington Papers*.

is as unaccountable, as it may be unlucky, as my purchase from Posey (for the express purpose of covering this tract) was made, as will appear by the Bond, if my memory has not deceived me, in the year 1770; this difference, if it is not founded in mistake, is altogether incomprehensible, as the land was explored and surveyed for me the first time in the fall of 1770, or early in the following year; and this right, as I have before observed, was intended as the legal security of it.

The first and second surveys, or in other words, the legal return of the first differing in dates, were both made by Captn. (afterwards Colonel) Crawford. The first was made whilst his commission was local; given for the express purpose of surveying 200,000 acres granted by Mr. Dinwiddie's Proclamation, to the officers and soldiers of the *first* Virgia. Regiment. The second, or, as I have before mentioned, the return, was made after he had received a deputation under Mr. Thos. Lewis for Augusta, in which County the land was supposed to lie, and this I believe did not happen 'till Feby. 1774; consequently the date was made subsequent to the date of the deputation.

Upon these grounds, my *legal title* I am convinced will be disputed, with a view to establish *their occupancy;* but there is an act (an authentic copy of which I have sent Mr. Smith) which legalizes the surveys of Crawford from the period he first held a commission from the College.[12] But for Arguments sake, supposing my Patent, and every thing which led to the attainment of it, were mere nullities, and my military claim out of the question, had I not an equal right with any other Citizen or subject, to obtain land in that Country? It cannot be laid to my charge that I have been either a monopolizer, or

---

[12] William and Mary College.

land-jobber, for I never sold a foot of Land in the Country, nor am I possessed of an acre west of the Alleghaney (and the quantity comparatively speaking is small) that I do not hold under military rights; except the tract at what is called Washington's bottom, and about 2 or 300 acres at the Gt. Meadows, both of which I purchased: the latter at a high price. And that I surveyed this land before the defendants ever saw it; built one or more Cabins thereon before they came into the Country; hired people to live on it; gave them repeated notices of my right afterwards of the consequences of their usurpation, are facts. But whether evidence can *now* be obtained in support of all of them, is questionable; as the two Crawfords who were my principal Agents in that Country are both dead, others knowing to the transactions, removed, and a third sett unwilling, I have no doubt to come forward. Yet under all these disadvantages, Charles Morgan will be able, or I am mistaken, to prove that the survey was made a year or two before the Defendants pretend any claim to occupancy (the date of which requires better proof than their own assertion). And I think he is the most likely person to prove also that there were cabbins erected thereon for my benefit, claims antecedent to those of the Defendts. purchased by Crawford on my accot. to avoid disputes, a man hired to live on the land to keep others off it, and that frequent notices were given to them of the lands being mine, and admonishing them to quit it.

Marcus Stephenson must be knowing to many if not all of these circumstances, but a spell of sickness, I have been told, has impaired his memory, and may have rendered him an unfit evidence. Major Lite[13] and George McCormick, or the brother who married Colo. Crawfords daughter, cannot, I shou'd think,

---

[13] Jacob Hite(?).

be unacquainted with many of these facts. There can be no question of Colo. Cannon's[14] testifying to what I have recited in my letter to Mr. Smith, because I had the information from his own mouth and he is a Gentn. of credit. I should think it strange indeed, if Colo. Jno. Stephenson from his connexion and intimacy with Colo. Crawford is not privy to most of these things. Possibly Mrs. Crawford may be as strong an evidence to some points as any one. Captn. Swearingin[15] also seemed to have knowledge of them.

The reason of my being so particular with you, my good Sir, is, that if any of these people should fall in your way, and upon enquiry it shall be found that they possess the knowledge I conceive of these transactions, but are unwilling to come forward, that effectual steps may be taken to compel them. There is reason to apprehend that an oath *only* will extort from *some of them* all they do know. Colo. Cannon, Chas. Morgan, Marcus Stephenson (if he has recollection enough), and perhaps Majr. Lite, must be more intimately acquainted with Colo. Crawfords proceedings on my behalf in the early stages of this business, than any others. Morgan or Lite surveyed the Land; M: Stephenson carried the chain, and, I believe made the improvements. What G: McCormick and Captn. Swearingin can say in the case, I know not, both I believe would willingly serve me, and would point out if they are acquainted with them, the evidences that may be essential on the tryal if it shall be found necessary for me to attack on this ground.

The enclosure No. 2 contains some queries which were put to Mr. Smith, but not answered, tho' touched upon by him as appears by his letter No. 3. I will thank you for doing what shall seem necessary in this business. There is an open Accot.

---

[14] Col. John Cannon.
[15] Van Swearingen.

between Vale. Crawford and me, by which it appears that he is about £100, in my debt. Conscious of this, and of my engagements for him, unsollicited, he wrote me the letter and sent me the Bill of sale referred to in my letter to Mr. Smith of the 8th. of May last, and now in his trust.

My Lands in Pennsylvania (west of the Laurel-hill) have been so unproductive of every thing but vexation and trouble, that I am resolved to sell them at long or short credit, as may best suit the purchaser, provided I can get near the value of them. The tract where the Mill is, lying in Fayette County, and commonly called Washington's bottom, contains about 1650 acres. The one in dispute, lying in Washington County, contains about 2,800 acres. The defendants were a long time deliberating on eligibility of giving me 25/ pr. acre, rather than to engage in a Law suit; but finally chose the latter: they must give more now if I cost [*sic*] them. Should you hear of any purchasers, or if you could discover the price it is probable to obtain from them, you would render me a service by the communication. Inclosed are several advertisements,[16] one of which I pray you to have set up at the Court houses of the County in which the Lands lie, at Pittsburgh, and at such other places as you may think best.

I give you the trouble of proving (I believe before a Magistrate) the power of Attorney which I have executed before you, and to send it with my letter inclosed to Major Thomas Freeman who does business for me in that County.

I paid Mr. Smith, at the time the Ejectments were brought, some where about £20 If you could by indirect or other means, discover what would be proper compensation for his trouble in this business, I should be much obliged by it. I have

---

[16] See Advertisement, Sept. 22, 1786, *post*.

had in the course of my life, so little to do with Law and Lawyers, that I feel myself extreamly awkward in these matters.

With sentiments of great esteem, etc.[17]

ADVERTISEMENT

Virginia, September 22, 1786.

The Subscriber would sell his land in Fayette County, State of Pennsylvania, containing about 1650 acres, distinguished, commonly, by the name of Washington's Bottom

Also,

About 2800 acres on Miller's-run, a branch of Shirtee, in Washington Coty. and State aforesaid, if the Ejectments now depending are decided in his favor.

The credits may be long or short according to the price given.

To describe these Lands is needless, as the presumption, and wish of the proprietor is, that those who incline to purchase, would examine them well.

Majr. Thos. Freeman will shew the land in Fayette County; and Majr. Geo: McCormick the other tract.

To THOMAS SMITH

Mount Vernon, September 22, 1786.

Sir: the letter which you did me the favor of writing to me from Philada. the 9th. ulto. came duly to hand.

A fever, of which I am but just well recovered, makes me fearful of encountering the bad roads and disagreeable accommodations between this and the Western Country at this season: other circumstances too, rendering it inconvenient for me to be from home at this time, have combined to set aside the

---

[17] From the "Letter Book" copy in the *Washington Papers*.

journey I had it in contemplation to make to the Court of Nisi prius to be holden in Washington county State of Pennsylvania, on the 23d. of next month. Nor, upon a revision of the notes with which I have furnished you, do I see wherein I could add aught to them, were I to be present at the trial. The summoning of a Jury so long before the merits of the cause will come *legally* before it, is, in my opinion, very much against me; for there can be no doubt but that every indirect (if not direct) means, which the Defendants and their friends can adopt, will be used to impress the members who constitute it, with all the circumstances favourable to their claim. However, if it is an event to be regretted, it is equally unavoidable, as it is constitutional.

There were Proclamations (as I have observed on a former occasion) and orders of Council in this State previous to the Revolution, which, could they have been adduced, might have subserved my cause, in as much as it would have appeared from them, that tho' military rights were recognized, and warrants of Survey were actually issued by the Executive previous, to the occupancy of the Defendants; yet, that their settlement of the Lands which were considered as appertaining to the State of Virga. was expressly contrary to a pointed Proclamation, consequently must not only have been illegal, but highly unwarrantable, as it was an invasion of private right (for the Defendants do not deny having been informed that the land was surveyed for me) as well as a contempt of public authority; however, the records of these proceedings are lost, as you will find by the authenticated Certificate, which has been heretofore sent you.

My opinion of the case, as I have mentioned in a former letter, is, that the legal title ought to be insisted upon strenuously; and that the Deed, as it was the last solemn act of the Government, shou'd be considered as conclusive evidence of the regularity of the antecedent proceedings; it being a fact well known in this Country, that by the removal of the Records from Williamsburgh whilst the enemy were manoeuvering in the State, many of them were lost or destroyed. To argue otherwise, is to arraign the conduct of the Government in the management of its own internal policy; and I do not know under, or by what authority the State of Pennsylvania can *now,* after having made a solemn compact with this State, by which she engages to confirm all legal established titles, go into such an enquiry. But if, notwithstanding, from the complexion of matters it should be conceived that the plea of pre-occupancy is likely to have weight; I would *then* as if to shew that *even on that ground* the defendants stand hindmost, call evidence to prove that the land was surveyed for me before they came into the Country; that a cabbin if no more (for one remain'd there in 1784) was built on the land before they ever saw it; that Colo. Cannon had fixed himself thereon before them; but discovering traces of a regular Survey, and upon enquiry finding it was made for me, quit it after having done some work thereon; that the Defendants were also told that the land belonged to me, whilst they were in the act of settling upon it, and were repeatedly informed of it afterwards, and admonished by public notices and private intimations of the hazard they run, as I was determined (as soon as my public duty would allow me to attend to private concerns) to assert my right to the land. These all are indubitable facts; but where the evidences are, or by what means they can be drawn forward to prove them, are questions which I am not able to solve; unless Colo. Crawfords letters will be admitted, and those persons whom I have named in the notes formerly sent you, will make them appear.

As I have confided this cause entirely to your management, I should, if Mr. Ross's abilities had not spoke so powerfully in his favour, have been perfectly well pleased at your choice of him as a coadjutor. With talents such as you describe, I cannot but be highly satisfied therewith.

My friend Colo. Simms, who will do me the favor of presenting this letter to you, is called to the Western Courts in your State on some business of his own. He perfectly understands the Laws of this State, the practices of our Courts, and the principles of our Land Office, and may be able to communicate much useful information. You may place entire confidence in him, safely trusting him with all the communications I have to you and with a sight of the papers if he should incline to see them.

I am much obliged to you for the information respecting the Bill of Sale from Vale. Crawford. At the time of my writing to you on this business, I was quite ignorant of the agency you had in the matter, on behalf of another, the declaration of which will, I hope, be an apology for my application to you in a case where you were Counsel for another. I have requested the favor of Colo. Simm to do, or cause to be done what shall appear just and proper in this case. To secure my debt is all the inducement I have for resorting to the Bill of Sale.

I ought my good Sir, to have recollected the trouble you have had in this business 'ere this, and I intended to have compensated it out of the funds I had in that country, but in truth they have been very unproductive, but if you will be so obliging as to inform me by Colo. Simm with what sum can equal your expectations, I will resort to other means to lodge it in Philadelphia for you. With very great esteem, etc.[18]

---

[18] From the "Letter Book" copy in the *Washington Papers*.

To CLEMENT BIDDLE

Mount Vernon, September 23, 1786.

Dr. Sir: It is sometime since my window curtains were sent to you to get dyed; I should be glad to have them back as soon as an opportunity offers of forwarding them to me. Let me beg you to send by Mr. Porter,[19] (who will deliver you this letter) if he can bring it, or with the curtains if he cannot, 16 yards of Stuff of the same kind and colour of the curtains, to cover two dozen chairs, the front of which will require cloth near 2½ feet wide, and the hinder part near two feet; this I fear is wider than that kind of Stuff generally is, but it is to be hoped that the gores which come off the latter, will be sufficient for the former.

Do the prices of the articles mention'd in my former letter still keep up? I pray you to cause the enclosed Advertisement to be published three weeks in one of your Gazette's which has the most general circulation. With great esteem, I am, etc.[20]

To WILLIAM TRIPLET

Mount Vernon, September 25, 1786.

Sir: If Mr. Lund Washington has not misconceived the conversation which passed between you and me the day you lay ill in bed; or if you understood the matter in the same light he seems to have done, I find there is another mistake between us respecting Mrs. French's[21] land, which it behooves me to clear up as soon as possible.

---

[19] Of Alexandria, Va.
[20] From the "Letter Book" copy in the *Washington Papers*.
[21] Mrs. Penelope French.

He thinks you asked me if I meant to take the land for the term of Robinson's[22] lease; and that I answered yes. If such a question and such an answer passed, we must some how or other have been at cross purposes; for clear and evident it must be, even to yourself, that I could have no intention of being concerned with the land at all, unless it was for Mrs. French's life. You may well recollect Sir, that I declared this in explicit terms in the conversation I had with you at my own house, and assigned reasons for it to you, namely, that if I got this and Mr. Manley's Land it was my intention to blend them and my other plantations together, and to form entire new ones out of the whole; that I meant to go into an entire new course of cropping, and would lay off my fields accordingly in a permanent and lasting form by Ditches and Hedges; and that it was for this reason I was desirous of knowing this fall (before I went into such arrangement and expence) whether I had any chance of getting these places or not, because it might be too late afterwards to make any change in my plan. With this object in view, I must have been insane to have taken the plantation for the remainder of Robinson's lease only; first, because it is uncertain whether I could get possession of the Land or not, never having exchanged a word with Robinson on the subject, nor never intending to do it unless I had got the place to myself entirely; and, secondly, if I did, because I should not probably be able to compleat the plan of enclosures by the time the Lease would expire. What situation should I be in then? A new bargain under every disadvantage to make, or go back to my former grounds? In the latter case all my labour and expence would have been thrown away and my whole plan defeated. In the former

---

[22] John Robertson (Robinson). His agreement with Washington, dated Oct. 24, 1786, is in the *Washington Papers*.

(that is supposing Robinson could not be got off by fair means, and Mr. Lee is of opinion, which opinion I had in my pocket at the time I call'd upon you in expectation of meeting Mrs. French that without a regular demand of rent and reentry, which might be a tedious and expensive process in Courts, the Lease cannot be set aside) under these circumstances I say, I should have made myself liable for the payment of Robinson's rent, without deriving a single advantage. Will any body think this reasonable; or suppose that whilst I retain my senses, I would do it?

As I do not recollect that in the course of my life I ever forfeited my word, or broke a promise made to any one, I have been thus particular to evince (if you understand the matter in the same light that Lund Washington did) that I was not attending to or did not understand the question.

I am sorry any mistake has happened and to convince you and Mrs. French that through the whole of this business, I meant to act upon fair, open and honorable grounds, I will, as mistakes have taken place, and as there is a difference of opinion respecting the annual value of the Lands and negroes,[23] leave it to any person of her own choosing (Major Little if she pleases) to say, whether the rent after the expiration of Robinson's lease shall be £136, or £150 pr. ann: if he thinks one too much and the other too little, any sum between. Mrs. French has declared that she neither wanted, nor would take more than the intrinsic worth of the place. I on the word of a man of honor declare that I do not desire it for a farthing less than the value; for to make money by it was never my

---

[23] An undated press copy of "A list of Negros the property of Mrs. French, in possession of George Washington, by virtue of a Contract which terminates with the life of the former" is in the New York Public Library. It was drawn up by Washington, presumably, during the negotiations.

object; but we differ in our sentiments of this. Is there any mode then so fair, as for an impartial person to see the place, and to hear what Mrs. French, or you in her behalf and my-self will say on the subject, and then to decide according to this judgment from the facts? and can there be any thing more favourable to her wishes than to have this determined by her friend in whom she places, I presume, implicit confidence? I never exchanged a word directly nor indirectly with Majr. Little on the subject, but believing him to be a gentleman who will decide according to the dictates of his judgment, I am not afraid to entrust the matter to him, notwithstanding the family connexion between him and Mrs. French. In a word, I am so conscious of the rectitude of my intentions in the whole of this business, that it is a matter of the most perfect indiffer-ence to me, to whom it is left; and tho' it may be supposed I have some sinister views in saying it, yet without the gift of prophecy, I will venture to pronounce, that if Mrs. French misses me as a Tenant, she will repent, long before Robinson's Lease expires, for having done so: for I can assure her from an experience of more than twenty five years that there is a very wide difference between getting Tenants and getting rents. She may get a dozen of the first (and I have not the smallest doubt but she may); but if there is one among them who (having no other dependence than the produce of the Plantation) will pay her the latter without hard working and pinching her negroes, and a great deal of trouble and vexa-tion to her, I shall be more mistaken than I ever was in any thing of the kind in my life.

This may not appear so to her at first view; because it is but too common to compare things without attending enough to the circumstances of them.

I have no doubt but that Mrs. French thinks it very strange that I should receive £120 a year rent from Mr. Dulaney, and scruple to give her £150 for rather more land, and twenty odd negroes; but has she considered that the one is accompanied by no charge except the land tax, and the other with many and heavy ones? And do not every body who have meadows, and have ever made an estimate of their value, know that an acre of tolerable good grass will pay all the expences of cutting, curing and stacking, and will put at least 40/ in the owner's pocket annually? What then has Mr. Dulaney to do more than to keep up his fences to pay the rent? By his Advertisement of pasturage for Horses at 3/ pr. week he has   acres. Suppose it   only the meadow alone without a single hand will yield him at least   pr. ann: Is there a single acre of land on Mrs. French's plantation from which, (besides cropping, so precarious) this is to be expected? Is there a single acre which can be converted into meadow? Is not the Land much worn, greatly exhausted and gullied in many places? None can deny it. But why need I enumerate or dwell on these things? Have I not put the matter upon as fair a footing as a man possibly can do? If Mrs. French wants no more than the value, as she has declared, what objection can she have to Majr. Little's saying what that value is? If this proposition is acceded to the sooner it is communicated to me the better. I have never yet opened my mouth to Robinson on the subject of his Lease, nor never intended to do it unless I had got the Plantation for Mrs. French's life. When I sent the papers to Mr. Lee to draw the writings, I asked his opinion of the lease, which he gave, to the effect already mentioned.

It was for my private satisfaction I asked it, for as I told you before and now repeat, I never had an intention to get him off otherwise than by fair means, this year or any other. This year will convince him or I am mistaken, that his inevitable ruin (if he has any thing to loose) will follow his holding it another year, if it is not the case already. I am, &c.[24]

To WILLIAM JACKSON

Mount Vernon, September 28, 1786.

Dr. Sir: I have received your letter of the 20th. ulto. together with the pamphlets enclosed. I consider your sending the latter to me as a mark of attention wch. deserves my warmest acknowledgments.

I cannot join with you in thinking that the partiality of your friends in assigning to you so honorable a task,[25] prejudiced their discernment. The subject is noble, the field extensive, and I think it must be highly satisfactory, and indeed flattering to a man that his performance upon such an occasion, is approved of by men of taste and judgment. I am, etc.[24]

To BUSHROD WASHINGTON

Mount Vernon, September 30, 1786.

Dear Bushrod: I was from home when your servant arrived, found him in a hurry to be gone when I returned; have company in the House, and am on the eve of a journey up the river to meet the Directors of the Potomac Company; these things combining, will not allow me time to give any explicit answer to the question you have propounded.[26]

---

[24] From the "Letter Book" copy in the *Washington Papers*.

[25] Jackson's oration before the Pennsylvania Society of the Cincinnati on July 4, 1786.

[26] Bushrod Washington's letter to Washington, stated by Sparks, to have been dated Sept. 27, 1786, is quoted by him as follows: "We have lately instituted a society in these lower counties, called the 'Patriotic Society.' As it is something new, and there are a few men both good and sensible who disapprove of it, it will be a high

Generally speaking, I have seen as much evil as good result from such Societies as you describe the Constitution of yours to be; they are a kind of imperium in imperio, and as often clog as facilitate public measures. I am no friend to institutions except in local matters which are wholly or in a great measure confined to the County of the Delegates. To me it appears much wiser and more politic, to choose able and honest representatives, and leave them in all national questions to determine from the evidence of reason, and the facts which shall be adduced, when internal and external information is given to them in a collective state. What certainty is there that Societies in a corner or remote part of a State can possess that knowledge which is necessary for them to decide on many important questions which may come before an Assembly? What reason is there to expect, that the society itself may be accordant in opinion on such subjects? May not a few members of this society (more sagacious and designing than the rest) direct the measures of it to private views of their own? May not this embarrass an honest, able Delegate, who hears the voice of his Country from all quarters, and thwart public measures?

---

gratification to me to know your sentiments of it, if you will be so kind as to communicate them. The object of the institution is to inquire into the state of public affairs; to consider in what the true happiness of the people consists, and what are the evils which have pursued, and still continue to molest us; the means of attaining the former, and escaping the latter; to inquire into the conduct of those, who represent us, and to give them our sentiments upon those laws, which ought to be or are already made.

"It will also be a considerable object to instil principles of frugality into the minds of the people, both by precept and example. If any real good should result from such a society, we hope similar ones will be generally instituted through the State; and, if so, they may establish a very formidable check upon evil-disposed men, who, clothed with power, make interested motives, and not public good, the rule of their conduct. These are the general outlines of the institution; and, whether in the event it may be beneficial or not, I think that it has taken its rise in virtuous motives. We have had a considerable meeting of the most sensible and respectable gentlemen in this part of the country, and another is to be held on Tuesday next, previous to the meeting of the Assembly. Our design is to hold another as soon as the Assembly has risen; the first to instruct our delegates what they ought to do, the next to inquire what they have done." This letter is not now found in the *Washington Papers*.

These are first thoughts, but I give no decided opinion. Societies nearly similar to such as you speak of, have lately been formed in Massachusetts: but what has been the consequence? Why they have declared the Senate useless; many other parts of the Constitution unnecessary; salaries of public officers burthensome &c. To point out the defects of the constitution (if any existed) in a decent way, was proper enough; but they have done more: they first vote the Court of Justice, in the present circumstances of the State, oppressive; and next, by violence stop them; which has occasioned a very solemn Proclamation and appeal from the Governor to the people. You may say no such matters are in contemplation by your Society: granted: a snow-ball gathers by rolling; possibly a line may be drawn between occasional meetings for special purposes, and a standing Society to direct with local views and partial information the affairs of the Nation, which cannot be well understood but by a large and comparative view of circumstances. Where is this so likely to enter as in the general Assembly of the people? What figure then must a Delegate make who comes there with his hands tied, and his judgment forestalled? His very instructors, perhaps (if they had nothing sinister in view) were they present at all the information and arguments, which would come forward, might be the first to change sentiments.

Hurried as this letter is, I am sensible I am writing to you upon a very important subject. I have no time to copy, correct, or even peruse it; for which reason I could wish to have it or a copy returned to me.[27] George and his wife set off yesterday

---

[27] In answer to this letter from Washington, Bushrod stated: "The motives which gave birth to the Society, were these. We conceived, that in a government where the voice and sentiments of the people are delivered by representation, the few who are elected to speak these sentiments are the servants of the electors; that in grand points of national concern, the people are the best judges of their wants, their own interests,

for the races at Fredericksburg; the rest of the family are well
and join in love and good wishes for all at Bushfield. I am, &c.[28]

and can more sensibly feel those evils, which they wish to be corrected; that upon
these two principles they have a right to instruct their delegates; and that silence at a
time when they had reason to apprehend a conduct in these servants contrary to their
wishes would be highly criminal. We thought that an appearance of corruption was
discoverable in the mass of the people, or, what is as bad, a total insensibility to their
public interest. Persuaded of this, and equally convinced that this inattention proceeded more from the want of information than from want of real virtue, a number
of the principal gentlemen in these four counties determined to assemble, for the
purpose of inquiring and deliberating upon such subjects as were of the most interesting consequence, and to communicate their sentiments to the people in the form
of instructions; which, if approved by them, are signed and sent to their delegates; if
otherwise, they continue only the opinion of a few, and can have no weight.

"The people's attention being thus awakened to their public concerns, they are led
to investigate the causes of those evils which oppress them, and to endeavor by some
method to relieve them. The most uninquiring mind must, when put in action, perceive that the defect is either in the manners of the people, or in the misconduct of
those, who, being intrusted to form salutary laws, have adopted the most destructive
measures. The evil when seen may easily be removed; and unless the majority of
the people are vitiated, which can hardly be the case, they would certainly be led to
apply the only two possible remedies; the one, to exert more zeal in making a judicious
choice of delegates; the other, to reform their manners. I am fully convinced that
nothing could be more effective of the prosperity of this country, than the method
you have pointed out of electing honest and able representatives. To recommend
this to the attention of the people is a principal object with this Society.

"Thus you will perceive, that this institution assumes no other power, than that of
recommending to the people an attention to their own interests, and of furnishing
them with the sentiments and opinions of a few, which they may either reject or
adopt. It is true, that a few designing men might creep into these societies; but I
should hope that a majority will be virtuous. If this should be the case, their recommendation may have happy consequences; if the majority should unhappily be
vicious, they are but the opinions of a few expressed collectively. In this, however, I
am resolved, that as soon as I perceive that other motives than those of the public
good influence their conduct, I will quit them." This letter is not now found in the
Washington Papers, but is quoted as given by Sparks.

[28] From the "Letter Book" copy in the *Washington Papers.*
In the "Letter Book," page 186, in the *Washington Papers* at the end of September,
1786, occurs another indefensible piece of carelessness, in entering a letter to
William Heth, dated November 8. Following it is a letter to Edmund Randolph,
of which the following is all that survives, pages 187 to 190 having been torn from
the "Letter Book" at some unknown time in the past: "By Doctr. Stuart I return the
books you were so obliging as to allow me the reading of: by him also I send you
the Travels of the Marqs. de Chastellux for your perusal.
"I felt for your disappointment the day you left this, and hope no accidents inter-
vened afterwards to give further interruption to your journey. Unknowing of the
quantity of rain which had fallen in the course of the night, I was never more surprized than in a ride I took to some of my plantations an hour or two after you
went away, to find every place deluged. I"
Randolph left Mount Vernon Sept. 18, 1786, so this letter probably should be dated
some time between September 18 and September 30. According to the "Letter
Book" index, a letter to Betty Lewis, dated some time between October 1 and
October 22, was entered on the missing pages.

*To JEREMIAH WADSWORTH

Mount Vernon, October 22, 1786.

Dear Sir: I have received and thank you for the communications in your letter of the 1st. instt. It has given me much satisfaction, to find that the letter [29] I had written to my much lamented friend Genl. Greene (respecting his affair with Captn. Gun) had reached his hands. Had the case been otherwise, and he had harboured a suspicion of my inattention or neglect, the knowledge of it, would have given me real pain.

Persuaded as I always have been of Genl. Greene's integrity and worth, I spurned those reports which tended to columniate his conduct in the connection with Banks; [30] being perfectly convinced that whenever the matter should be investigated, his motives for entering into it would appear pure and unimpeachable. I was not without my fears though that he might suffer in a pecuniary way by his engagement with this man. I would fain hope however that the case may, ultimately, be otherwise; and that upon a final settlement of his affairs there will be a handsome competency for Mrs. Greene and the Children. But should the case be otherwise, and Mrs. Greene, yourself, and Mr. Rutlidge would think proper to entrust my namesake G: Washington Greene to my care, I will give him as good an education as this Country (I mean the United States) will afford and will bring him up to either of the genteel professions that his frds. may chuse, or his own inclination shall lead him to pursue, at my own cost and expence.

I Condole very sincerely with Mrs. Greene (to whom please to tender my respects) and the rest of General Greenes friends on the loss the public, as well as his family, has sustained by

---

[29] Of May 20, 1785.
[30] John Banks.

the death of this valuable character, especially at this crisis, when the political machine seems pregnant with the most awful events.

My compliments if you please to Mrs. Wadsworth, and any of my old acquaintance who may happen to compose your circle. With much esteem and regd. I am etc.[31]

To DAVID HUMPHREYS

Mount Vernon, October 22, 1786.

My Dr. Humphreys: Your favor of the 24th. ulto. came to my hands about the middle of this month. For the enclosures it contained I pray you to receive my warmest acknowledgments and thanks. The Poem, tho' I profess not to be a connoisseur in these kind of writings, appears pretty in my eye, and has sentiment and elegance which must I think render it pleasing to others.

With respect to the circular letter,[32] I see no cause for suppressing or altering any part of it, except as to the place of meeting. Philadelphia, on three accots. is my opinion must be more convenient to the majority of the delegation, than New York. 1st. as most central. 2dly. because there are regularly established packet-boats, well accommodated for Passengers, to it from the Southern States; and 3dly. because it appears to me that the seat of Congress would not be so well for this meeting. When you have digested your thoughts for publication, in the case of Captn. Asgill, I would thank you for a copy of them; having arrested the account I had furnished Mr. Tilghman, with an assurance of a more authentic one for his friend in England.

---

[31] From a photostat of the original kindly permitted by Hon. James W. Wadsworth, of New York City.

[32] See Washington's letter to the State societies of the Cincinnati, Oct. 31, 1786, *post.*

I am pleased with the choice of Delegates which was made at your State meeting; and wish the Representatives of all the State societies may appear at the Genl. Meeting, with as good dispositions as I believe they will. It gives me pleasure also to hear that so many Officers are sent to your Assembly: I am persuaded they will carry with them more liberality of sentiments, than is to be found among any other class of Citizens. The speech of our friend Cobb was noble, worthy of a patriot and himself; as was the conduct of Genl. Sullivan. But for God's sake tell me what is the cause of all these commotions:[33] do they proceed from licentiousness, British-influence disseminated by the tories, or real grievances which admit of redress? If the latter, why were they delayed 'till the public mind had become so much agitated? If the former why are not the powers of Government tried at once? It is as well to be without, as not to live under their exercise. Commotions of this sort, like snow-balls, gather strength as they roll, if there is no opposition in the way to divide and crumble them. Do write me fully, I beseech you, on these matters; not only with respect to facts, but as to opinions of their tendency and issue. I am mortified beyond expression that in the moment of our acknowledged independence we should by our conduct verify the predictions of our transatlantic foe, and render ourselves ridiculous and contemptible in the eyes of all Europe. My health (I thank you for the enquiry) is restored to me; and all under this roof join me in most affectionate regards, and in regretting that your letter has held out no idea of visiting it again this winter, as you gave us hope of doing when you left us. To all the gentn. of my acquaintance who may happen to be in your circle, I beg to be remembered with sincere regard. To assure you of the

---

[33] Shay's rebellion in Massachusetts.

sincerity of my friendship for you, would be unnecessary; as you must I think be perfectly satisfied of the high esteem and affection with which, I am, etc.[34]

To GEORGE AUGUSTINE WASHINGTON

Mount Vernon, October 25, 1786.

Dear George: It is natural for young married persons (who are launching into life) to look forward to a permanent establishment. If they are prudent, they will be *reasonably* sollicitous to provide for those who come after, and have a right to look to them for support.

It is also natural for those who have passed the meridian of life, and are descending into the shades of darkness, to make arrangements for the disposal of the property of which they are possessed. The first of these observations will apply to you, and the second to myself. I have no doubt but that you and Fanny are as happy and contented in this family as circumstances will admit. Yet, something is still wanting to make that situation more stable and pleasing.

It is well known that the expensive mansion in which I am, as it were, involuntarily compelled to live, will admit of no diminution in my income; nor could it be expected if I now had, or ever should have descendants, that I either would, or ought in justice to deprive them of what the laws of nature, and the laws the land (if left to themselves) have declared to be their inheritance. The first however is not the case at present, and the second, not likely to be so hereafter.

Under this statement then I may add that, it is my present intention to give you, at my death, my landed property in the neck; containing by estimation, between two and three thou-

---

[34] From the "Letter Book" copy in the *Washington Papers*.

sand acres (by purchases from William Clifton and George Brent) and that the reasons why I mention the matter to you at this time are, that you may, if you choose it, seat the negroes which Colo. Bassett has promised you, upon that part of the tract, on which Samuel Johnson formerly lived. And under this expectation and prospect, that you may, moreover, when it perfectly suits your inclination and convenience, be preparing for, and building thereon by degrees.

You may say, or think perhaps, that as there is a contingency tacked to this intimation, the offer is too precarious to hazard the expence of building; but if Mrs. Washington should survive me there is a moral certainty of my dying without issue, and should I be the longest liver, the matter in my opinion is almost as certain; for whilst I retain the reasoning faculties I shall never marry a girl; and it is not probable that I should have children by a woman of an age suitable to my own, should I be disposed to enter into a second marriage. However, that their may be no possibility of your sustaining a loss, the matter may rest on the footing of compensation. I do therefore hereby declare it to be, and it is my express meaning, that if by the event above alluded to, or any other, by which you may be deprived of the fee simple in the land herein mentioned (unless a full equivalent is given in lieu thereof) that I will pay the cost of any buildings which you may erect on the premises.

The use of the plantation, it is presumed, will be adequate for the fences with which it may be enclosed, and for the labour arising from the cultivation; nothing therefore need be said on that head.

Here then, the prospect of a permanent inheritance is placed in the opposite scale of possible disappointment, and you are to judge for yourself.

I have been thus particular because I would be clearly understood. because it is not my wish to deceive. and because I would not [35] raise an expectation not warranted from the premises, by fair deduction.

Johnson's plantation as I believe, you know, is destitute of fencing; but there is timber at hand. The cleared land, whatever may have been the original quality of it, now is, by use, and more so by abuse, much gullied and in bad condition; but as there is a sufficiency of it for the hands you will get, it may soon by care, good management, and a proper course of cropping be recovered.

One thing more and I will close this letter. Do not infer from my proposing it to you to build, that I meant it as a hint for you to prepare another home. I had no such idea. To point you to a settlement which you might make at leizure, and with convenience, was all I had in view. More than once I have informed you that in proportion as age and its concomitants encrease upon me, I shall stand in need of some person in whose industry and integrity I can confide, for assistance. The double ties by which you are connected with this family (to say nothing of the favourable opinion we entertain of you) in the marriage union which has placed you differently from any other of my relations for this purpose; because no other married couple could give, or probably would receive, the same satisfaction by living in it that you [36] do. But whether you remain in the same house, or at a future day may remove to the place proposed, your services will be convenient and essential to me; because with your aid I shall be able to manage my concerns without having recourse to a Steward,

---

[35] The "Letter Book" copy has "even raise."
[36] The "Letter Book" copy has "and Fanny."

which comports neither with my interest nor inclination to employ.

With very affe. regard I am &c.[37]

*To THE STATE SOCIETIES OF THE CINCINNATI

(Circular)

Mount Vernon, in Virginia, October 31, 1786.

Sir: I take this early opportunity, in my character of President of the Cincinnati, of announcing to you, that the triennial General Meeting of the Society is to be convened at the City of Philadelphia on the first Monday of May in the year 1787.

As it will not be in my power (for reasons which I shall have the honor of immediately communicating) to attend the next General Meeting; and as it may become more and more inconvenient for me to be absent from my Farms, or to receive appointments which will divert me from my private affairs; I think it proper also to acquaint you, for the information of your Delegates to the General Meeting, that it is my desire not to be reelected to the Presidency, since I should find myself under the necessity of declining the acceptance of it.

The numerous applications for information, advice, or assistance which are made to me in consequence of my military command; the multiplicity of my correspondencies in this Country as well as in many parts of Europe; the variety and perplexity of my own private concerns, which, having been much deranged by my absence through the war, demand my entire and unremitting attention; the arduousness of the task, in which I have been as it were unavoidably engaged, of superintending the

---

[37] From a copy of the original kindly furnished by Stephen Decatur, jr., of Garden City, N. Y.

opening of the navigation of the great rivers in this State; the natural desire of tranquility and relaxation from business, which almost every one experiences at my time of life, particularly after having acted (during a considerable period) as no idle spectator in uncommonly busy and important scenes; and the present imbecility of my health, occasioned by a violent attack of the fever and ague succeeded by rheumatick pains (to which till of late I have been an entire stranger); will, I doubt not, be considered as reasons of sufficient validity to justify my conduct in the present instance. Although the whole of these reasons could not have before operated; yet, in conformity to my determination of passing the remainder of my days in a state of retirement, I should certainly have refused to accept the office of President with which I was honored in 1784, but from an apprehension that my refusal, at that time, might have been misrepresented as a kind of dereliction of the Society on my part, or imputed to a disapprobation of the principles on which it was then established. To convince the opposers of the Institution, should any such remain, that this was not the fact; and to give no colourable pretext for unreasonable attacks; I prevailed upon myself to accept the appointment with a view of holding it only until the next election: before which time I expected the jealousy that had been excited, would subside; and this, I am happy to be informed, has universally taken place.

Highly approving as I do, the principles on which the Society is now constituted; and pleased to find, so far as I have been able to learn from reiterated enquiries, that it is acceptable to the good people of the United States in general; it only remains for me to express the sense I entertain of the honor conferred by the last General Meeting in electing me their President, and too implore in future the benediction of Heaven on the virtuous Associates in this illustrious Institution.

During the residue of my continuance in Office, I shall be constantly ready to sign such *Diplomas* as may be requisite for the members of your State Society, being sincerely desirous of giving every possible proof of attachment, esteem, and affection for them; as well as of demonstrating the sentiments of perfect consideration and respect with which I have the honor etc.

P. S. I have thought it expedient to forward a transcript of this circular address to Majr. Genl. Gates, Vice President of the Society: In order that the General Meeting may suffer no embarrassment for want of an Official character to preside at the opening of it.[38]   N. Y. H. S.]

To HENRY LEE

Mount Vernon, October 31, 1786.

My Dr. Sir: I am indebted to you for your several favors of the 1st. 11th. and 17th. of this instt: and shall reply to them in the order of their dates; but first let me thank you for the interesting communications imparted by them.

The picture which you have exhibited, and the accounts which are published of the commotions, and temper of numerous bodies in the Eastern States, are equally to be lamented and deprecated. They exhibit a melancholy proof of what our trans-Atlantic foe has predicted; and of another thing perhaps, which is still more to be regretted, and is yet more unaccountable, that mankind when left to themselves are unfit for their

---

[38] This text is from the letter sent to Horatio Gates, as vice president of the General Society and president of the Virginia State Society.

On November 8 Washington wrote a brief note to Gates that this letter would be handed to him in Richmond, Va. The original of this note is in the New York Historical Society.

On this same day (November 8) Washington also wrote to William Heth, asking him to deliver the preceding note and the circular to Gates. A copy of this letter is in the "Letter Book" in the *Washington Papers*.

own Government. I am mortified beyond expression when I view the clouds that have spread over the brightest morn that ever dawned upon any Country. In a word, I am lost in amazement when I behold what intrigue, the interested views of desperate characters, ignorance and jealousy of the minor part, are capable of effecting, as a scourge on the major part of our fellow Citizens of the Union; for it is hardly to be supposed that the great body of the people, tho' they will not act, can be so short-sighted, or enveloped in darkness, as not to see rays of a distant sun thro' all this mist of intoxication and folly.

You talk, my good Sir, of employing influence to appease the present tumults in Massachusetts. I know not where that influence is to be found; and if attainable, that it would be a proper remedy for the disorders. Influence is no Government. Let us have one by which our lives, liberties and properties will be secured; or let us know the worst at once. Under these impressions, my humble opinion is, that there is a call for decision. Know precisely what the insurgents aim at. If they have *real* grievances, redress them if possible; or acknowledge the justice of them, and your inability to do it in the present moment. If they have not, employ the force of government against them at once. If this is inadequate, *all* will be convinced that the superstructure is bad, or wants support. To be more exposed in the eyes of the world, and more contemptible than we already are, is hardly possible. To delay one or the other of these, is to exasperate on the one hand, or to give confidence on the other, and will add to their numbers; for, like snow-balls, such bodies increase by every movement, unless there is something in the way to obstruct and crumble them before the weight is too great and irresistible.

These are my sentiments. Precedents are dangerous things; let the reins of government then be braced and held with a steady hand, and every violation of the Constitution be reprehended: if defective, let it be amended, but not suffered to be trampled upon whilst it has an existence.

With respect to the navigation of the Mississippi, you already know my sentiments thereon: they have been uniformly the same, and as I have observed to you in a former letter, are controverted by one consideration *only* of weight, and that is the operation the occlusion of it may have on the minds of the western settlers, who will not consider the subject in a relative point of view or on a comprehensive scale, and may be influenced by the demagogues of the country to acts of extravagance and desperation, under a popular declamation that their interests are sacrificed. Colo. Mason, at present, is in a fit of the gout; what [his] sentiments on the subject are, I know not, nor whether he will be able to attend the Assembly during the present Session. For some reasons, however, (which need not be mentioned) I am inclined to believe he will advocate the navigation of that river. But in all matters of great national moment, the only true line of conduct, in my opinion, is, dispassionately to compare the advantages and disadvantages of the measure proposed, and decide from the balance. The lesser evil, where there is a choice of them, should always yield to the greater. What benefits (more than we now enjoy) are to be obtained by such a [Treaty as you have delineated with Spain, I am not enough of a Commercial man to give any opinion on. The China [39] came to hand without much damage; and I thank you for your attention in procuring and forwarding of it to me. Mrs. Washington joins me in best wishes for Mrs. Lee and yourself and I am &c.][40]

---

[39] This was the well known "Cincinnati China," in which each piece was marked with the figure of Fame bearing the eagle emblem of the Society. Lee purchased this set, of about 306 pieces, in New York City, for Washington, at a cost of £45: 5: o.

[40] From the "Letter Book" copy in the *Washington Papers*. The portion within brackets is from the original fragment in the New York Public Library.

To GOVERNOR WILLIAM MOULTRIE

Mount Vernon, October 31, 1786.

Dr. Sir: As soon as your Excellency's favor of the 7th. of Augt., came to my hands, I forwarded the enclosure therein, to Mr. Brindley under cover to Saml. Hughes Esqr. Herewith you will receive their answers.

Presuming that your Excelly. is President of the Society of the Cincinnati in the State of South Carolina, I have the honor of addressing the enclosed circular letter to you. If I am mistaken, I pray you to forward it to the right person. Mrs. Washington joins me in every good wish for Mrs. Moultree and yourself, and with sentiments of great regard and respect, I have the honor, etc.

P. S. Permit me to request the favor of you to direct the blank cover herewith sent, to the President of the Georgia Society of the Cincinnati, and cause it to be forwarded by the first safe conveyance that may offer.[41]

*BIOGRAPHICAL MEMORANDA [42]

[October, 1783]

REMARKS

Page 1st. (1) It was rather the wish of my eldest brother (on whom the general concerns of the family devolved) that this shd. take place and the matter was contemplated by him. My father died when I was only 10 years old.

---

[41] From the "Letter Book" copy in the *Washington Papers*.

[42] After David Humphreys returned from Europe, he revived the matter of writing a life of Washington, which he had broached in 1785. He apparently made a start and submitted some fourteen (or more) pages of his effort to Washington for criticism and revision. Washington returned the manuscript with the "Remarks," which are of considerable value, even though Humphreys's manuscript to which they refer, does not seem to have survived.

(2) He [Lawrence Washington] was not appointed Adjutant General of the Militia of Virginia untill after his return from the expedition to Cathageua. Nor did he Command the Colonial troops on that occasion. these were under the Orders of Sir Wm. Gouch Lt. Govr. of Virginia. He was no more than the Senior Officer of those which were raised in this Colony and wch. with those of the other Colonies formed what was called the American Brigade, under Sir William Gouch; he was scarcely of age when he went on this expedn.

(3) And from whom he had received many distinguished marks of patronage and favor.

(4) Not all, for the second Son (Augustine) left many childn., sevl. of whom are now living; and inherit a very large portion of his Fathers Estate. perhaps the best part.

Page 2. (1) Before he was 20 years of age.

(2) He was then more than 21 years, as will appear from dates.

Page 3. (1) At a most inclement Season, for he travelled over the Apalacheon Mountains, and passed 200 miles thro an uninhabited Country (except by a few tribes of Indians settled on the Banks of the Ohio) to Presque Isle within 15 miles of Lake Erie in the depth of winter while the face of the Earth was covered with snow and the waters covered with Ice; The whole diste. from Wmsburgh the then seat of Governmt. at least 500 miles.

(2) It was on this occasion he was named by the half-King (as he was called) and the tribes of Nations with whom he treated, Caunotaucarius (in English) the Town taker; which name being registered in their Manner and communicated to other Nations of Indians, has been remembered by them ever since in all their transactions with him during the late War.

Page 4th (1)[43] This is a task to which G W. feels himself very incompetent (with any degree of accuracy) from the badness of his memory, loss of Papers, mutilated state, in which those of that date were preserved, and the derangement of them by frequent removals in the late war and want of time to collect and methodize them since. However accordg. to the best of his recollection: By the indefatigable Industry of the Lt. Colo. and the Officers who seconded his measures the Regiment was in great forwardness at Alexandria (the place of general rendezvous) early in the spring of 1754. and without waiting till the whole should be compleated, or for a detachment from the Independant Companies of regulars in the Southern Provences (which had been reqsd. by the Executive of Virginia for this Service) or for troops which were raising in North Carolina and destined in conjunction to oppose the Incroachment of the French on our Western frontiers. He began his march in the Month of May in order to open the Roads; (and this he had to do almost the whole distance *from Winchester* (in the County of Frederick, not more than 80 miles from Alexandria to the Ohio). Form deposits, &ca., and for the especiall purpose of siezing, if possible, before the French shd. arrive at it, the important Post at the conflux of the Alligany and Monangahela; with the advantages of which he was forcibly struck the preceeding year; and earnestly advised the securing of, with Militia, or some other temporary force. But notwithstanding all his exertions, the New, and uncommon difficulties he had to encounter (made more intolerable by incessant Rains and swelled waters of which he had many to cross) he had but just ascended the Laurel Hill 50 M: short of his

---

[43] Note 1 to page 4 of Humphreys's effort was published in *Scribner's Magazine* in May, 1893, under the title of "The Braddock Campaign," where the text is not accurately followed, and the explanatory note advances a theory of the genesis of the manuscript which is not substantiated by a critical study of the entire document.

object: after a March of 230 Miles from Alexa. when he received
information from his Scouts that the French had, in force,
siezed the Post he was pushing to obtain; having descended
from Presque Isle by the Rivers Lebeauf and Alligany to this
Place by Water with Artillery &ca. &ca. The object of his
precipitate advance being thus defeated. The detachmt. of
Regulars, wch had arrived at Alexa. (by Water) and under
his orders being far in his rear, and no Acct. of the Troops
from No. Carolina, it was thought advisable to fall back a few
miles; to a place known by the name of the great Meadows.
abounding in Forage more convenient for the purpose of forming a Magazine and bringing up the Rear, and to advance
from (if we should ever be in force to do it) to the attack of
the Post which the enemy now occupied; and had called Du
Quesne. At this place, some days after we were joined by the
above detachment of Regulars; consisting (before they were
reduced on the march by desertion, Sickness &ca.) of a Captn.
(McKay a brave and worthy Officer), three Subalterns, and
100 Rank and file. But previous to this junction the French
sent a detachment to reconnoitre our Camp and obtain intelligence of our Strength and position; notice of which being
given by the Scouts G W marched at the head of a party, attacked, killed 9. or 10; and captured 20 odd. This, as soon as
the enemy had assembled their Indian Allies, brought their
whole force upon him; consisting, according to their own compared with the best accts. that could be obtained from others
of about 1500 Men. His force consisted of the detachment
above mentioned, and between two and 300 Virginians; for
the few Indians which till now had attended him; and who
by reconnoitering the enemy in their March had got terrified
at their numbers and resolved to Retreat as they advised us to
do also but which was impracticable without abandoning our

Stores, Baggage, &ca. as the horses which had brought them to this place had returned for Provision had left us previous to the Attack. About 9 Oclock on the 3d. of July the Enemy advanced with Shouts, and dismal Indian yells to our Intrenchments, but was opposed by so warm, spirited, and constant a fire, that to force the works in *that way* was abandoned by them; they then, from every little rising, tree, stump, Stone, and bush kept up a constant galding fire upon us; which was returned in the best manner we could till late in the Afternn. when their fell the most tremendous rain that can be conceived, filled our trenches with Water, Wet, not only the Ammunition in the Cartouch boxes and firelocks, but that which was in a small temporary Stockade in the middle of the Intrenchment called Fort Necessity erected for the sole purpose of its security, and that of the few stores we had; and left us nothing but a few (for all were not provided with them) Bayonets for defence. In this situation and *no* prospt. of bettering it terms of capitulation were offered to us by the enemy wch. with some alterations that were insisted upon were the more readily acceded to, as we had no Salt provisions, and but indifferently supplied with fresh; which, from the heat of the weather, would not keep; and because a full third of our numbers Officers as well as privates were, by this time, killed or wounded. The next Morning we marched out with the honors of War, but were soon plundered contrary to the Articles of capitulation of great part of our Baggage by the Savages. Our Sick and wounded were left with a detachment under the care, and command of the worthy Doctr. Craik (for he was not only Surgeon to the Regiment but a lieutt. therein) with such necessaries as we could collect and the Remains of the Regimt., and the detachment of Regulars, took up their line for the interior Country. And at Winchester met 2 Companies from

No. Carolina on their March to join them. These being fresh, and properly provided, were ordered to proceed to Wills's Creek and establish a post (afterwards called Fort Cumberland) for the purpose of covering the Frontiers. Where they were joined by a Company from Maryland, which, about this time, had been raized, Captn. McKay with his detachment remd. at Winchester; and the Virginia Regiment proceedd. to Alexandria in order to recruit, and get supplied with cloathing and necessarys of which they stood much in need. In this manner the Winter was employed, when advice was recd. of the force destined for this Service under the ordrs. of G. B. and the arrival of Sir Jno. St. Clair the Q: Mastr. Genl with some new arrangement of Rank by which no Officer who did not *immediately* derive his Comn. from the *King* could command one *who did*. This was too degrading for G. W to submit to; accordingly, he resigned his Military employment; determining to serve the next campaign as a Volunteer; but upon the arrival of Genl. Braddock he was very particularly noticed by that General; taken into his family as an extra-Aid; offered a Captns. Comn. by *brevet* (which was the highest Grade he had it in his power to bestow and had the compliment of several blank Ensigncies given him to dispose of to the Young Gentlemen of his acqe. to supply the vacancies in the 44 and 48 Regts. which had arrived from Ireland.

In this capacity he commenced his second Campaign; and used every proper occasion till he was taken Sick and left behind in the vicinity of Fort Cumberland to impress the Genl., and the principal Officers around him, with the necessity of opposing the nature of his defence, to the mode of attack which, more than probably, he would experience from the *Canadian* French, and their Indians on his March through the Mountains and covered Country but so prepossessed were they in favr. of *regularity* and *discipline* and in such absolute contempt were *these people held,* that the admonition was suggested in vain.

About the middle of June, this Armament consisting of the two Regiments from Ireland, some Independant Companies and the Provincial troops of Virga. Maryld. and North Carolina, began to move from Fort Cumberland whither they had assembled. After several days March; and difficulties to which they had never been accustomed in regular Service, in Campaign Countries; and of whh. they seemed to have had very little idea. the Genl. resolved to divide his force, and at the head of the first division which was composed of the flower of his Army, to advance; and leave Colo. Dunbar with the second division and the heavy Baggage and Stores, to follow after. By so doing, the first division approached the Monongahela 10 miles short of Fort Duquesne the 8th. of July; and which time and place having so far recovered from a severe fever and delerium from which he had been rescued by James's powder, administed by the positive order of the Genl. as to travel in a covered Waggon, he joined him and the next day tho' much reduced and very weak mounted his horse on cushions, and attended as one of his aids.

About 10 Oclock on the 9th., after the Van had crossed the Monongahela the *second time,* to avoid an ugly defile (the season being very dry and waters low) and the rear yet in the River the front was attacked and by the unusual Hallooing and whooping of the enemy, whom they could not see were so disconcerted and confused as soon to fall into irretrievable disorder. The rear was forced forward to support them, but seeing no enemy, and themselves falling every moment from the fire, a general panic took place among the Troops from which no exertions of the Officers could recover them. In the early part of the Action some of the Irregulars (as they were called) without direcns. advanced to the right, in loose order, to attack; but this, *unhappily* from the unusual appearance of the movement being mistaken for cowardice and a running away was discountenanced. and before it was *too late,* and the confusion became general an offer was made by G. W to head the Provincials and engage the enemy in their own way; but the propriety of it was not seen into until it was too late for execution. After this, many attempts were made to dislodge the enemy from an eminence on the Right but they all proved ineffectual; and fatal to the Officers; who by great exertions and good examples endeavourd to accomplish it. In one of these the Genl. recd. the Wd. of which he died; but previous to it, had several horses killed and disabled under him. Captns. Orme and Morris his two Aids de Camp. having received wounds which rendered them unable to attd. G W. remained the sole Aid through the day, to the Genl.; he also had one horse killed, and two wounded under him. A ball through his hat, and several through his clothes, but escaped unhurt. Sir Peter Halket (secd. in Command) being early killed, Lieutt. Colo. Burton and Sir Jno. St. Clair (who had the Rank of Lt. Colo. in the Army) being badly wounded, Lieutt. Colo. Gage (afterwards Genl Gage) having recd. a contusion. No person knowing in the disordered State things were, who the surviving Senr. Officer was. and the Troops by degrees going off in confusion; without a ray of hope left of further opposition from those that remained; G W. placed the Genl. in a small covered Cart, which carried some of his most essential equipage, and in the best order he could, with the best Troops (who only contind. to be fired at) brought him over the *first* ford of the Monongahela; where they were formed in the best order circumstances would admit on a piece of rising ground; after wch., by the Genls. order, he rode forward to halt those which had been earlier in the retreat: Accordingly, after crossing the Monongahela the *second time* and ascending the heights, he found Lieutt. Colo. Gage engaged in this business to whom he delivered the Genls order and then returned to report the situation he found them in. When he was again requested by the Genl. whom he met coming on, in his litter with the first halted troops, to proceed (it then being after sundown) to the second division under the command of Colo. Dunbar, to make arrangements for covering the retreat, and forwarding on provisions and refreshments to the retreating and wounded Soldiery. To accomplish this, for the 2d. division was 40 odd miles in the rear it took up the whole night and part of the next Morning, which from the weak state in which he was, and the fatigues, and anxiety of the last 24 hours, rendered him in a manner wholly unfit for the execution of the duty he was sent upon when he arrived at the Dunbars Camp. To the best of his power however he discharged it, and remained with the secd. division till the other joined it. The shocking Scenes which presented themselves in this Nights March are not to be described. The dead, the dying, the groans, lamentation, and crys along the Road of the wounded for help (for those under the latter descriptions endeavoured from the first commencement of the action, or rather confusion to escape to the 2d. divn.) were enough to pierce a heart of adamant. the gloom and horror of which was not a little increased by the impervious darkness occasioned by the close shade of thick woods which in places rendered it impossible for the two guides which attended to know when they were in, or out of the track but by groping on the ground with their hands.

Happy was it for him, and the remains of the first division that they left such a quantity of valuable and enticing baggage on the field as to occasion a scramble and contention in the seizure and distribution of it among the enemy for had a pursuit taken place, by passing the defile which we had avoided; and they had got into our rear, the whole, except a few woodsmen, would have fallen victims to the merciless Savages. Of about 12 or 13 hundred which were in this action eight or 9 hundd. were either killed or wounded; among whom a large proportion of brave and valuable Officers were included. The folly and consequence of opposing compact bodies to the sparse manner of Indian fighting, in woods, which had in a manner been predicted, was now so clearly verified that from hence forward another mode obtained in all future operations.

As soon as the two divisions united, the whole retreated towards Fort Cumberland; and at an Incampment near the Great Meadows the brave, but unfortunate Genl. Braddock breathed his last. He was interred with the honors of war, and as it was left to G W. to see this performed, and to mark out the spot for the reception of his remains, to guard against a savage triumph, if the place should be discovered, they were deposited in the Road over which the Army, Waggons &ca. passed to hide every trace by which the entombment could be discovered. thus died a man, whose good and bad qualities were intimately blended. He was brave even to a fault and in regular Service would have done honor to his profession. His attachments were warm, his enmities were strong, and having no disguise about him, both appeared in full force. He was generous and disinterested, but plain and blunt in his manner even to rudeness. After this event, the Troops continued their March for, and soon arrived at Fort Cumberland without molestation;

and all except the Pr[ovinci]als immediately resolved to proceed to Philadelphia; by which means the Frontiers of *that* State but *more especially* those of Virginia and Maryland were laid *entirely* open by the *very avenue* which had been prepared. Of the direful consequences of this measure G W, in a visit wch. he immediately made to Williamsburgh for the purpose brought the Govr. and Council of Virga. acquainted. But in vain did they remonstrate against the March of the B. Troops to that place of the officer Comg. them. They n[ext] proceeded to augment their own; the command of which under a very enlarged and dignified Commission, to Command *all* the Troops now raised, or to be raised in the Colony, was given to him with very extensive powers, and blank Commissions to appoint all new Officers. About this time also or soon after it the discontents and clamours of the Provincial Officers, and the remonstrance of G W. in person, to Genl. Shirley, the then Comr. in chief of the British Forces in America and through the Govr. and Council to the King's Minister with respect to the degrading Situation in which they were placed a new arrangement took place by the Kings Order, by which every Provincial Officer was to rank according to the Comn. he bore, but to be Junrs. to those of the same grade in the established Corps.

As G W foresaw, so it happened, the frontiers were continually harrassed, but not having force enough to carry the war to the gates of Du Quesne, he could do no more than distribute the Troops along the Frontiers in the Stockaded Forts; more with a view to quiet the fears of the Inhabitants than from any expectation of giving securities in so extensive a line to the settlements. During this interval in one of his tours along the frontier posts, he narrowly escaped, according to the acct. afterwards given by some of our People who were Prisoners with them, and eye witness at the time, [undecipherable] falling by an Indian party who had waylaid (for another purpose) the communication along which with a small party of horse only he was passing, the road in this place formed a curve, and the prey they were in weight for being expected at the reverse part, the Captn. of the party had gone across to observe the number and manner of their movemt. &ca. in order that he might make his disposition accordingly, leaving orders for the party not to take notice of any passengers the other views [*sic*] till he returned to them, in the meantime in the opposite direction I passed and escaped almt. certain destruction for the weather was raining and the few Carbines unfit for use if we had escaped the first fire. This happened near Fort Vass. Never ceasing in the meantime in his attempts, to demonstrate to the Legislature of Virga., to Lord Loudoun, &ca. that the only means of preventing the devastations to which the middle states were exposed, was to remove the Cause. But the war by this time raging in another quarter of the Continent all applications were unheeded till the year 1758 when an Expedition against Fort Du Quesne was concerted, and undertaken under the conduct of Genl. Forbes; who tho a brave and good Officer, was so much debilitated by bad health, and so illy supplied with the means to carry on the expedition, that it was November before the Troops got to Loyal hanning 50 or 60 miles short of Du Quesne and even then was on the very point of abandoning the Expedition when some seasonable supplies arriving the Army was formed into three Brigades took up its March, and moved forward; the Brigade Commanded by G. W. being the leading one.

Previous to this and during the time the Army lay at Loyal haning a circumstance occurred wch. involved the life of G W in as much jeopardy as it had ever been before or since the enemy sent out a large detachment to reconnoitre our Camp, and to ascertain our strength; in consequence of Intelligence that they were within 2 Miles of the Camp a party commanded by Lt. Colo Mercer of the Virga. line (a gallant and good Officer) was sent to dislodge them between whom a severe conflict and hot firing ensued which lasting some time and appearing to approach the Camp it was conceived that our party was yielding the ground upon which G W. with permission of the Genl. called (for dispatch) for Volunteers and immediately marched at their head to sustain, as was conjectured the retireing troops. led on by the firing till he came within less than half a mile, and it ceasing, he detached Scouts to investigate the cause and to communicate his approach to his friend Colo. Mercer, advancing slowly in the meantime. But it being near dusk and the intelligence not having been fully dissiminated among Colo. Mercer's Corps, and they taking us, for the enemy who had retreated approaching in another direction commenced a heavy fire upon the releiving party which drew fire in return in spite of all the exertions of the Officers one of whom and several privates were killed and many wounded before a stop could be put to it. to accomplish which G W never was in more imminent danger. by being between two fires, knocking up with his sword the presented pieces.

When the Army had got within about 12 or 15 Miles of the Fort the enemy dispairing of its defence, blew it up having first embarked their Artillery, Stores and Troops, and retreated by water down the Ohio to their Settlements below. Thus ended that Campaign, a little before Christmas in very inclement weather and the last one made during that War by G W whose health by this time (as it had been declining for many months before, occasioned by an inveterate disorder in his Bowels) became so precarious as to induce him (having seen quiet restored by this event to the Frontiers of his own Country

which was the principal inducement to his taking arms) to re-
sign his Military appointments. The sollicitation of the Troops
which he commanded to Continue, their Affecte. farewell address to him, when they found the Situation of his health and
other circumstances would not allow it. affected him exceedingly and in grateful sensibility he expressed the warmth of his
attachmt. to them on that, and his inclination to serve them on
every other future occasion.

Page 8 (1). I believe about 7,000 Bushls. of Wheat and 10000
bushels of Indn. Corn which was more the staple of the farm

Page 11 (2) Whether it be necessary to mention that my
time and Services were given to the public without compensation, and that every direct and indirect attempt afterwards, to
reward them (as appeared by the Letter of G. Mifflin, and the
vote of 50 shares in each of the Navigations of Potomack and
James River by the State of Virga. who knew that I would refuse anything that should carry with it the appearance of
reward, you can best judge.

Page 14 (1). Once a week is his fixed hunts tho sometimes
he goes oftner.

(2) And many others in this Country

(3) remarking the state of the Weather, nature of the Soil
&ca.

The information given in these sheets, tho related from
Memory, Is it is believe[d] to be depended upon. It is hastily
and incorrectly related; but not so much for these reasons, as
some others, it is earnestly requestd. that after Colo. Humphrey, has extracted what he shall judge necessary, and given it
in his own language, that the *whole* of what Is here contained
may be returned to G W, or committed to the flames. some of
the enumerations are trifling; and perhaps more important circumstances omitted; but just as they occurred to the memory,

they were committed. If there are any grains among them Colo. H can easily separate them from the chaff.[44]

To PRESIDENT BENJAMIN FRANKLIN

Mount Vernon, November 3, 1786.

Dr. Sir: The letter, of which I have the honor to enclose your Excellency an extract, and the Addresses, came to my hands a few days since. Whether the latter are originals or copies, and whether any steps have been taken in compliance with Sir Edwd. Newenham's wishes, you can better decide than I. Also, if there has not, what is best to be done with the application.

If I mistake not, this case militates with a resolve of Congress, which declares that none but Citizens of these United States shall hold Consular appointments under it; but how far the singularity of the application, from such a character and under such an enumeration of circumstances, may occasion a departure therefrom (if my belief is founded) is not for me to determine.

This letter to you, My good Sir, is the first move I have made in this business; and I will await your sentiments before I make another. I am, as I hope you will always believe me to be, with the greatest respect and regard, Dr. Sir, etc.[45]

*To JAMES MADISON

Mount Vernon, November 5, 1786.

My dear Sir: I thank you for the communications in your letter of the first instt. The decision of the House on the question respecting a paper emission, is portentous I hope, of an

---

[44] The text is from a photostat of the original kindly furnished by John Pickering, of Salem, Mass.
[45] From the "Letter Book" copy in the *Washington Papers*.

auspicious Session. It may certainly be classed among the important questions of the present day; and merited the serious consideration of the Assembly. Fain would I hope, that the great, and most important of all objects, the fœderal governmt., may be considered with that calm and deliberate attention which the magnitude of it so loudly calls for at this critical moment. Let prejudices, unreasonable jealousies, and local interest yield to reason and liberality. Let us look to our National character, and to things beyond the present period. No morn ever dawned more favourably than ours did; and no day was ever more clouded than the present! Wisdom, and good examples are necessary at this time to rescue the political machine from the impending storm. Virginia has now an opportunity to set the latter, and has enough of the former, I hope, to take the lead in promoting this great and arduous work. Without some alteration in our political creed, the superstructure we have been seven years raising at the expence of so much blood and treasure, must fall. We are fast verging to anarchy and confusion!

A letter which I have just received from Genl Knox, who had just returned from Massachusetts (whither he had been sent by Congress consequent of the commotion in that State) is replete with melancholy information of the temper, and designs of a considerable part of that people. Among other things he says,

there creed is, that the property of the United States, has been protected from confiscation of Britain by the joint exertions of *all,* and therefore ought to be the *common property* of all. And he that attempts opposition to this creed is an enemy to equity and justice, and ought to be swept from off the face of the Earth.

again

They are determined to anihillate all debts public and private, and have Agrarian Laws, which are easily effected by the means of unfunded paper money which shall be a tender in all cases whatever.

32459

He adds

The numbers of these people amount in Massachusetts to about one fifth part of several populous Counties, and to them may be collected, people of similar sentiments from the States of Rhode Island, Connecticut, and New Hampshire, so as to constitute a body of twelve or fifteen thousand desperate, and unprincipled men. They are chiefly of the young and active part of the Community.

How melancholy is the reflection, that in so short a space, we should have made such large strides towards fulfilling the prediction of our transatlantic foe! "leave them to themselves, and their government will soon dissolve." Will not the wise and good strive hard to avert this evil? Or will their supineness suffer ignorance, and the arts of self-interested designing disaffected and desperate characters, to involve this rising empire in wretchedness and contempt? What stronger evidence can be given of the want of energy in our governments than these disorders? If there exists not a power to check them, what security has a man for life, liberty, or property? To you, I am sure I need not add aught on this subject, the consequences of a lax, or inefficient government, are too obvious to be dwelt on. Thirteen Sovereignties pulling against each other, and all tugging at the fœderal head will soon bring ruin on the whole; whereas a liberal, and energetic Constitution, well guarded and closely watched, to prevent incroachments, might restore us to that degree of respectability and consequence, to which we had a fair claim, and the brightest prospect of attaining. With sentiments of the sincerest esteem etc.[46]

*To GOVERNOR GEORGE CLINTON

Mount Vernon, November 5, 1786.

Dear Sir: Not having heard, or not recollecting who the President of the Society of the Cincinnati in the State of New

---

[46] From a facsimile in the *Washington-Madison Papers* sales catalogue (The McGuire Collection), 1892.

York is, I take the liberty of giving you the trouble of the enclosed.

I am endeavouring by the sale of Land, to raise money to pay for my Moiety of the purchase on the Mohawk River. So soon as this is effected I will write your Excellency more fully. In the meantime, with every good wish for Mrs. Clinton and the rest of your family, in which Mrs. Washington cordially unites, I am etc.[47]

To DAVID STUART

Mount Vernon, November 5, 1786.

Dr. Sir: Enclosed is a Petition from the Directors of the Potomac Company, which they request you to present; and to use your endeavours to obtain the prolongation which is prayed for therein. The Assembly need be under no apprehension of unnecessary delay. Interest and inclination equally prompt the Company to dispatch. To shorten the time required may occasion a contrariety in the acts of the different assemblies, and would create confusion, trouble and delay in the business. We hope therefore, no attempt will be made to do this.

As the Petition recites the causes which have given rise to the application, and the facts are notorious, I shall add nothing in support of it.

I also give you the trouble of a small matter which concerns myself only. It is, if you shall see no impropriety from the lapse of time, (which is injurious only to myself) to offer the enclosed accounts when you shall find a fit opportunity, for payment. The circumstances are these.

In the year 1774, I bought a number of servants, hired many freemen, and sent negroes to the Ohio for the purpose of

---

[47] From a photostat of the original through the kindness of Judge E. A. Armstrong, of Princeton, N. J.

saving, seating and improving my military Lands agreeably to the Laws then existing. The Indian disturbances which obliged Lord Dunmore to embody and march the Militia into that Country, checked my operations; and the seizure of part of my goods (as will appear by these certificates) compelled me the next year, to encounter the same expence, trouble and difficulty, and no Assembly happening that could or wou'd take cognizance of such claims, before my departure from this State, in May 1775; the Certificates during my absence, and the frequent removal of my papers, (to keep them from the hands of the enemy) got so intermixed as not to be found till very lately. If these circumstances, which are truly related, are insufficient to obtain compensation without subjecting the question to much disputation, I had rather undergo the loss, than the mortification of an opposition to a measure which is merely personal.

As we are to be made rich by the maggoty-bay Pease; might it not be well for you to enquire how, in what manner this great good is to be accomplished; particularly, when they are to be sowed, the quantity to the acre, preparation of the ground and nature of the soil best adapted to them, whether they are to be ploughed in as a manure, and in what stage of their growth; or whether the fall of the leaf alone is sufficient to answer this purpose, how the seed is sowed, and the quantity to be obtained from an acre, &c. &c. Mr. Savage,[48] or some of the Gentn. from the Eastern shore, can no doubt give full information on all these heads.

Will you be so good as to enquire if Spring barley can be had, in what quantity, at what price, and how it could be got here. The family all join me in best wishes for you. Mrs. Stuart who is here and will put a letter under cover with this,

---

[48] George Savage, of Northampton County, Va.

will tell you I presume that she and the Children are all well. I am, etc.

P. S. If you could inform me what sum, and at what time I may depend upon the Estate of Mr. Custis for it, it would be obliging. My want of money presses. I must sell something if I cannot receive part of what is owing to me.[49]

*To ELIAS DAYTON

Mount Vernon, November 6, 1786.

Dear Sir: Presuming you are Presidt. of the Society of the Cincinnati in the State of New Jersey, I give you the trouble of the enclosed address. If I am mistaken, you will be so good as to hand it to the right person.

Months ago, I received a number of blank Diplomas for my Signature, which was affixed and held in readiness for Mr. Peck [50] or his order. No call has yet been [made] for them. If a good conveyance should offer, I will forward them; but I am not much in the way of meeting this. With great esteem and regard. I am etc.   [H.L.]

To THOMAS WEST

Mount Vernon, November 6, 1786.

Sir: From the *last* application which was made to you, I expected the papers so long promised, a fortnight ago. If you have any objection to my receiving them in order to effect a final settlement of the Admn. of Colo. Thos. Colvill's Estate, I beg you will have candour enough to declare it; that I may know what further steps are necessary for me to take to bring this business to a close.

---

[49] From the "Letter Book" copy in the *Washington Papers*.
[50] John Peck.

I think I have been ungenteely treated, to be put off seven months in obtaining what was promised in three weeks, and reiterated several times since. I have had repeated applications made to me, as well from the Debtors to, as the Creditors of that Estate, for settlements, and could do no more than assure the applicants that the moment I was furnished with the necessary documents, I shou'd be ready to proceed to the business. I am anxious to do this on many accots.; one of which is, that unfavorable suspicions will result from these delays. My wish is to avoid them. I am, etc.[51]

To JOHN FRANCIS MERCER

Mount Vernon, November 6, 1786.

Dr. Sir: It was not 'till after you had left this place, that I received your letter of the 4th. ulto. Altho' I have great repugnance to encreasing my Slaves by purchase; yet as it seems so inconvenient to you to make payment by other modes than those you have proposed, and so injurious as not to be accomplished at a less loss than fifty or more Pr. Ct. I will take six, or more negroes of you, if you can spare such as will answer my purpose; upon the terms offered in your former letter. The negroes I want are males: three or four young fellows for Ditchers; and the like number of well grown lads for Artificers. It is for you to determine whether you can supply me with such negroes. If you agree to do it, and will appoint a time, I would send for them, relying on your word, that the whole are healthy, and none of them addicted to runing away. The latter I abominate; and unhealthy negroes, woman, or children would not suit my purposes on *any terms*.

---

[51] From the "Letter Book" copy in the *Washington Papers*.

If you accede to this proposition I will extend it. I will take all the good and merchantable wheat and indian Corn you may have for sale, at a reasonable price (the first immediately, the latter at a proper time), and Military Certificates of this State for the balance of my claim, at the difference which *really* exists between them and specie; altho' I never intended to possess one of them on *any terms whatever* in a depreciated state. If these proposals are agreeable to you in all their parts, I should be glad to receive a decided and speedy answer; because in that case I will no longer look to you for the means of discharging those Debts I have enumerated to you, and to do which I am exceedingly anxious, but will endeavour without more delay, to sell land to enable me to pay them.

I had written thus far, when Colo. Simms called, on his way from Charles Coty. Court, to obtain some information respecting your suit against Combs. I was naturally led by the interest I thought I had in this business, to enquire into the state of it; and was told, if Mr. Ellzey's absence did not impede the sitting of Loudoun Court, he expected next week to obtain judgments for more than a thousand pounds: but guess Sir, what my surprize must have been, when he added that every shilling of this money was assigned to a Mr. Colston, and authority given to receive it as fast as it could be recovered. I had flattered myself that my forbearance for near fifteen years, and the disposition I have discovered (since the negotiation of the business seems to have got into your hands) to accommodate my wants as much as I possibly could to your convenience, merited more candid treatment. You cannot, I think, have forgotten the repeated assurances you have given me, that the monies arising from this fund should be sacredly appropriated to the discharge of my claim, whilst any of it remained. If this was possible, your letters in my possession would explicitly remind you of them. A conduct so extreamly unfair, ungenerous, and disingenuous, I cou'd not suffer to pass over unnoticed.

I send herewith the remainder of the blank Deeds which were formerly put into my hands by your brother James Mercer Esqr., as also the survey and partition of the Shannandoah tract, into the Lotts by which the land was sold, that you may fill them up as occasion may require. If it is *absolutely* necessary for me to sign the Deeds for conveyance of these Lotts, now the business by a decree of [the high Court of Chancery is taken out of my hands and put into yours, I will do it; otherwise, having stronger reasons than ever against resuming any agency in this business I would wish to decline it. I am etc.

Your letter of the 21st. Ulto. requesting me to execute a Deed to Mr. Rawleigh Colston, for the lott No. 7, has been delivered to me. You now will receive the only Deeds in my possession, and the Survey of the Shanondoah tract; and can do with them as circumstances may require. If it is indispensably necessary for me to convey the title, and you shall accompany the return of the Deed with authority for me to do so, I will go to Alexa. and execute it before evidences who will prove it in Fredk. Ct.][52]

To BENJAMIN LINCOLN

Mount Vernon, November 7, 1786.

My Dr. Sir: I have seen, I think, your name as President of the Society of the Cincinnati in the State of Massachusetts. I therefore give you the trouble of the enclosed Address.

---

[52] From the "Letter Book" copy in the *Washington Papers*. The portion in brackets is from a facsimile in a sales catalogue, 1936.

See note on p. 24, *ante*, regarding a letter dated Nov. 8, 1786, addressed to William Heth.

I hope your wishes were perfectly accomplished by your Eastern trip. Are your people getting mad? are we to have the goodly fabrick we were nine years raising, pulled over our heads? What is the cause of all this? When and how is it to end?

I need not tell you how much I am, etc.[53]

*To JAMES McHENRY

Mount Vernon, November 11, 1786.

My dear Sir: I met your favor of the 5th., in Alexandria yesterday. Today I dispatched one of my Overseers and two Servants for the Jack and mules which are arrived at Baltimore.

The Pheasants and Patridges, I pray you to procure a passage for them by Water, in the Packet. To bring them by Land would be troublesome, and might perhaps be dangerous for them. Be so good as to let me know the expence of these importations, and the cost of their detention in Baltimore. It shall be immediately paid, with many thanks to you, for your obliging attention to the business.

If you have particular information from my good friend the Marquis de la Fayette respecting the above things, I shall be obliged to you for it; his letter to me takes no notice of them, altho' I had for sometime been expectating one Jack and two she Asses through his medium; but by no means as a present.

One of the Servants who accompany's my Overseer, belongs to the Honble. William Drayton of Charleston So. Ca. This Gentn. Spent a day or two here on his return from New York,

---

[53] From the "Letter Book" copy in the *Washington Papers*.

On November 9 Washington wrote again to Lincoln, forwarding bills of exchange for Doctor Gordon. "I am sorry the Doctrs. Commission has given his friends so much trouble; tho' it can not be imputed to him, but must be considered as one of the lightest evils resulting from a paper currency." A copy of this letter is in the "Letter Book" in the *Washington Papers*.

and at Dumfries (proceeding on) the above fellow run away from him and came here. He goes to Baltimore under the impression of assisting in bringing the Jack and Mules home, but the real design of sending him there is to have him shipped for Charleston, if the Packet (which I am informed is regularly established betwn. that place and Baltimore,) or any other vessel is on the point of sailing for the former. Mr. Drayton will readily pay the Captn. for his passage, and other incidental expences, having intimated this in a letter to my Nephew; but if any doubt is entertained of it, I will see it done. Under this relation of the Circumstances attending [mutilated] way I would beg of you, my good Sir, (if an opportunity presents) to have him shipped, and previously secured.

The fellow *pretends* a willingness to return to his master, but I think it would be unsafe to trust to this, especially as he has discovered a great inclination to get back to Philadelphia (with a view *he says* of taking a passage from thence)

Why will you not make a small excursion to see an old acquaintance. It is unnecessary I hope to assure you of the pleasure it would give. Yr. etc.

PS. Engage the Master of the Packet Boat to drop the Birds at this place as he passes by, otherwise I shall have to send to Alexandria for them.[54]

To THOMAS JOHNSON

Mount Vernon, November 12, 1786.

Dr. Sir: On a supposition that you are now at Annapolis, the Petition of the Directors of the Potomac Company, is enclosed to your care. A Duplicate has been forwarded to the Assembly

---

[54] From a photograph in the photostats of the *McHenry Papers* in the Library of Congress.

of this State. The fate of it I have not heard, but entertain no doubt of its favorable reception, as there are many auspicious proofs of liberality and justice already exhibited in the proceedings of it this Session.

I hope the same spirit will mark the proceedings of yours. The want of energy in the fœderal government; the pulling of one State, and parts of States against another; And the Commotion among the Eastern people, have sunk our national character much below par; and have brought our politics and credit to the brink of a precipice. A step or two more must plunge us unto inextricable ruin. Liberality, justice and unanimity in those States, wch. do not appear to have drank so deep of the cup of folly, may yet retrieve our affairs; but no time is to be lost in essaying the reparation of them.

I have written to no gentlemen in your Assembly respecting the Potomac business but yourself, the justice of the case and your management of it, will ensure success. With great regard and respect, I am, etc.[55]

To ROBERT ALEXANDER

Mount Vernon, November 14, 1786.

Sir: Fifteen months ago I informed you in as explicit language as I was master of, of my want of the money you are indebted to me. I have waited (considering the urgency of my call) with patience to see if you would comply with the demand. But no disposition having yet appeared in you to do this; I find myself under the disagreeable necessity of informing you, that unless you name a time not far distant for payment, and secure the same to me without delay, that I shall

---

[55] From the "Letter Book" copy in the *Washington Papers.*

(tho' very reluctantly, as I think you have abundant reason to conclude from my long forbearance) have recourse to the most effectual mode the Law will give me to obtain justice.

It will avail nothing Sir, for you to repeat to me the claim you have upon Mr. Custis's Estate. This, independent of the Law suit, is, I am told, very trifling; but were it otherwise, his Affairs and mine now are, and have long been as distinct as yours and mine. If justice is denied you there, seek it; but let it be no plea for withholding my money which ought to have been refunded to me twelve or fifteen years ago, before your dealings with Mr. Custis came into existence. I am, etc.[56]

To MRS. ANNE ENNIS

Mount Vernon, November 15, 1786.

Madam: Your letter, or Memorial dated the 12th. of July, in Dublin, came to my hands yesterday under cover of a letter from Mr. Peter Trenor of the 8th. inst:

The Memorial mis-states several facts, one of them materially; for I have not, nor never had one shilling of the late Mrs. Savage's property in my hands: on the contrary, merely to relieve that Lady from the distress she represented herself to be in, I sent her in the year   [57] a Bill for £   [57] which sum is yet due to me. The circumstances attending that unfortunate Lady and her Estate are these. Her first husband, the Revd. Chas. Green, left all his property real and personal to her, estimated at about £5000 current money of this State: not in trust, as you set forth, but at her absolute disposal. When she was about to enter into her second marriage, with Doctr. Savage, she previously thereto made this Estate over to him, securing an

[56] From the "Letter Book" copy in the *Washington Papers*.
[57] Left blank in the "Letter Book" in the *Washington Papers*.

annuity of £100 currency, for the term of her life, if it should be demanded: And it was this sum, which was secured to her by a trust bond to Bryan Fairfax Esqr. and myself. The unhappy differences which soon arose and occasioned a separation between the Doctor and her, obliged Mr. Fairfax and myself, in order to obtain support for Mrs. Savage, to put the Bond in suit. The Doctor (who I believe might very properly be classed among the worst of men) made use of every subterfuge, and practiced all the chicanery of the Law to postpone the payment; which he was well enabled to do, as there was a suspension of our Courts of justice consequent of the dispute with Great Britain. However, when no longer able to stave off judgment at Common Law, he threw the matter into the high Court of Chancery of this State, where it now is. We are encouraged by our Lawyer to expect a final issue of the business in a term or two more; but what reliance is to be placed on these assurances, is not for me to decide.

As soon as the money is finally recovered, and in the hands of Mr. Fairfax and myself, we have neither the power nor inclination to withhold it one moment from the Executors of the deceased Mrs. Savage; but it will readily occur to you Madam, that for our security, there must be an attested Copy of the Will, under the Seal of the Corporation where it is recorded, annexed to a regular power of Attorney (to be proved in this Country) from the Exors. to some person here, to receive the money from us. It is the business of the Exors, not of the Trustees, to settle the accounts and pay the legacies of the Testator.

I have never seen any *authentic* copy of the Will. In the one which was shewn to me by a Mr. Moore of Baltimore I was not named as an Executor; If I had, it would not have been agreeable to me to have acted. I am, etc.[58]

---

[58] From the "Letter Book" copy in the *Washington Papers*.

*To ARTHUR YOUNG

Mount Vernon in Virginia, November 15, 1786.

Sir: The enclosed is a duplicate of the letter I had the honor of writing to you the 6th. of August. The evil genius of the Vessel by which it was sent (which had detained her many weeks in this Country after the letters intended to go by her were ready, agreeably to the owners appointment) pursued her to Sea, and obliged the Captain (when many days out) by the leaky condition in which she appeared, to return to an American Port. The uncertainty of his conduct with respect to the letters, is the apology I offer for giving you the trouble of the enclosed.

Since the date of it, I have had much satisfaction in perusing the Annals of Agriculture which you did me the favor to send me. If the testimony of my approbation, Sir, of your disinterested conduct and perseverence in publishing so useful and beneficial a work (than which nothing in my opinion can be more conducive to the welfare of your Country) will add aught to the satisfaction you must feel from the conscious discharge of this interesting duty to it, I give it with equal willingness and sincerity.

In addition to the articles which my last requested the favor of you to provide for me, I pray you to have the goodness of forwarding what follows.

Eight bushels of what you call velvet (The Books being at a Bookbinders, I may have miscalled this Wheat) Wheat, of which I perceive you are an admirer.

Four bushels of Beans of the kind you most approve for the purposes of a Farm.

Eight bushels of the best kind of Spring Barley.

Eight bushels of the best kind of Oats, and

Eight bushels of Sainfoin Seed: all to be in good Sacks.

My Soil will come under the description of **Loam**; with a hard clay, or (if it had as much the properties as the appearance, might be denominated) marl, from eighteen Inches to three feet below the Surface. The heaviest Soil I have would hardly be called a stiff or binding Clay in Engld.; and none of it is a blowing Sand. The sort which approaches nearest the former, is a light gray; and that to the latter, of a yellow red. In a word the staple has been good, but by use and abuse it is brought into bad condition.

I have added this information, Sir, that you may be better able to decide on the kind of Seed most proper for my Farms. Permit me to ask one thing more. It is to favor me with your opinion, and a plan, of the most compleat and useful Farm yard, for Farms of about 500 Acres. In this I mean to comprehend the Barn, and every appurtenance which ought to be annexed to the yard. The simplest and most œconomical plan would be preferred, provided the requisites are all included. Mr. Welch will answer your draught for the cost of these articles, as before. He is advised of it. I have the honor etc.[59]

To WAKELIN WELCH

November 15, 1786.

Sir: I take the liberty of giving you the trouble of forwarding the enclosed letters to their Addresses. I have again requested the favor of Mr. Young to send me a few Seeds: the cost may be about Ten pounds, more or less; for the amount of which, and other small matters, (should he think proper to add them) I pray you to honor his Draft.

You would do me a singular favor by engaging the Captain who has charge of the vessel by which they may be sent, to put

---

[59] From a photostat of the original through the kindness of Dr. A. S. W. Rosenbach, of New York City.

them in the cabbin or steerage. If they go into the hold of the vessel, the destruction of the seeds will be followed by a disappointment which would be of infinitely more importance to me than the cost of them.

Messrs. Forrest and Stoddard have Ships which pass by my door: so have Messrs. Drusina Ridder and Clark. I persuade myself the masters of any of these would so far oblige me as to be attentive to your recommendation of them: Captn. Johns of the Potomac Planter I am sure would.

I have a Farmer [60] who was sent to me from Gloucestershire in England by a friend of mine at Bath. He has now written for his wife to come to him, with her children, and to bring with her some seeds, implements of Husbandry &ca., to this Country. Bristol is their nearest Port, but opportunities from thence to this river rarely happening, I have recommended it to their friend and patron Mr. Peacy, to open a correspondence with you, or the House of Messrs. Forrest and Stoddard of London, that she may be advised of the sailing of a vessel from that place to this river as a more speedy and certain mode of conveyance; your compliance therein would be very pleasing to me, and very serviceable to an honest, old English farmer. I am, etc. [61]

To BUSHROD WASHINGTON

Mount Vernon, November 15, 1786.

Dear Bushrod: Your letter of the 31st. of October in reply to mine of the 30th. of Septr. came safe to hand. It was not the intention of my former letter either to condemn, or give my voice in favor of the Patriotic Society, of which you have now, but not before, declared yourself a member; nor do I mean to do it

---

[60] James Bloxham.
[61] From the "Letter Book" copy in the *Washington Papers*.

now. I offered observations under the information I had then received, the weight of which was to be considered. As first thoughts, they were undigested, and might be very erroneous.

That representatives ought to be the mouth of their Constituents, I do not deny, nor do I mean to call in question the right of the latter to instruct them. It is to the embarrassment, into which they may be thrown by these instructions in *national matters* that my objections lie. In speaking of national matters I look to the fœderal Government, which in my opinion it is the interest of every State to support; and to do this, as there are a variety of interests in the union, there must be a yielding of the parts to coalesce the whole. Now a County, a District, or even a State might decide on a measure which, tho' apparently for the benefit of it in its unconnected state, may be repugnant to the interests of the nation, and eventually to the State itself as a part of the confederation. If then, members go instructed, to the Assembly, from certain Districts, the requisitions of Congress repugnant to the sense of them, and all the lights which they may receive from the communications of that body to the Legislature, must be unavailing; altho' the nature and necessity of them, when the reasons therefor are fully expounded; which can only be given by Congress to the Assembly thro' the Executive, and which come before them in their legislative capacity, are as clear as the sun. In local matters which concern the District; or things which respect the internal police of the State, there may be nothing amiss in instructions. In national matters also, the *sense,* but not the *Law* of the District may be given, leaving the Delegates to judge from the nature of the case and the evidence before them.

The instructions of your Society as far as they have gone, meet my entire approbation, except in the article of commutables. Here, if I understand the meaning and design of the clause, I must disagree to it most heartily; for if the intention of it is to leave it optional with the person taxed to pay any staple commodity (Tobo. would be least exceptionable) in lieu of specie, the people will be burthened, a few speculators enriched, and the public derive no benefit from it. Have we not had a recent and melancholy proof of this during the war in the provision tax? Did not the people pay this in some way or other, perhaps badly; and was not the army almost starved? Can any instance be given where the public has sold Tobacco, Hemp, Flour or any other commodity upon as good terms as individuals have done it? Must not there be places of deposit for these commutables; Collectors, Storekeepers &c. &c. employed? These, rely on it, will sink one half, and a parcel of Speculators will possess themselves of the other half. It was to these things that we owe the present depravity of the minds of so many people of this Country, and filled it with so many knaves and designing characters.

Among the great objects which you took into consideration at your meeting at Richmond, how comes it to pass, that you never turned your eyes to the inefficacy of the Fœderal Government, so as to instruct your Delegates to accede to the propositions of the Commrs. at Annapolis; or to devise some other mode to give it that energy, which is necessary to support a national character? Every man who considers the present constitution of it, and sees to what it is verging, trembles. The fabrick which took nine years, at the expense of much blood and treasure, to rear, now totters to the foundation, and without support must soon fall.

The determination of your Society to promote frugality and industry by example, to encourage manufactures, and to avoid dissipation, is highly praise-worthy: these, and premiums for the most useful discoveries in Agriculture within your

district, the most profitable course of cropping, and the best
method of fencing to save timber &c. would soon make us a
rich and happy people. With every good wish for you and
yours, in which your aunt joins. I am, &c.[62]

To WILLIAM PEACEY

Mount Vernon, November 16, 1786.

Sir: Enclosed I give you the trouble of receiving the copy of
a letter I had the honor of writing to you in behalf of Mr.
James Bloxham. Since the date of it he has agreed to remain
another year with me, and has written (as he informs me) in
decided terms for his wife and family to come to him, and
bring with them the seeds and implements which are enumerated in the enclosed letters.

As Vessels from Bristol (tho' the nearest shipping Port to
her) do not often come to this River, or to any convenient place
of debarkation, it wou'd be better, I conceive, for her to resolve
on a passage from London at once; and if you Sir, in her behalf
would open a correspondence with either Messrs. Forrest &
Stoddard, or with Wakelin Welch Esqr. of that City, to the last
of whom I have written on the subject, I am persuaded a passage cou'd be obtained and the time fixed for her to be there.
Mr. Bloxham places so much confidence in your friendship for
him, and patronage of his family, that I have no scruple in suggesting these ideas to you, tho' it is a liberty I should not have
taken under any other circumstances.

If his wife brings seeds, it cannot be too strongly impressed
upon her, to keep them out of the Ship's hold; for they will
certainly heat and spoil if put there. Mr. Bloxham informs me
that there is a young man of the name of Caleb Hale who is

[62] From the "Letter Book" copy in the *Washington Papers*.

desireous of coming to this Country. I have mentioned to the old man the terms on which I would employ this Hale. I have no doubt of his finding the country answerable to his expectation, and his coming might be very satisfactory and serviceable to Mrs. Bloxham and her children on the passage, and previous to their embarkation. I have the honor, etc.[63]

To SAMUEL VAUGHAN

Mount Vernon, November 18, 1786.

My Dr. Sir: The obligations you are continually laying me under, are so great that I am quite overwhelmed and perfectly ashamed of myself for receiving them, notwithstanding your politeness leaves me without a choice. The picture of a battle in Germany, and the Jarrs came very safe. The first is fine: the latter is also fine and exceedingly handsome, they shall occupy the place you have named for them.

May I hope Sir, that you have heard of the safe arrival of your Lady and family in England. Every occasion which informs me of your health and happiness, is pleasing to me; but none would equal that of testifying under my own roof the sentiments of perfect esteem and regard, with which I have the honor, etc.[64]

To JAMES MADISON

Mount Vernon, November 18, 1786.

My Dr. Sir: Not having sent to the Post Office with my usual regularity, your favor of the 8th. did not reach me in time for an earlier acknowledgment than of this date. It gives

---

[63] This "Letter Book" copy varies in minor verbal details from a Toner transcript, in the Library of Congress, made from the original, which was said to be in the Historical Society of Pennsylvania in 1892.

[64] From the "Letter Book" copy in the *Washington Papers.*

me the most sensible pleasure to hear that the acts of the present session are marked with wisdom, justice and liberality. They are the palladium of good policy, and the sure paths that lead to national happiness. Would to God every State would let these be the leading features of their constituent characters: those threatening clouds, which seem ready to burst on the Confederacy, would soon dispel. The unanimity with which the Bill was received, for appointing Commissioners agreeably to the recommendation of the Convention at Annapolis; and the uninterrupted progress it has met with since, are indications of a favourable issue. It is a measure of equal necessity and magnitude; and may be the spring of reanimation.

Altho' I had bid adieu to the public walks of life in a public manner, and had resolved never more to tread that theatre; yet, if upon an occasion so interesting to the well-being of the Confederacy it should have been the wish of the Assembly that I should have been an associate in the business of revising the fœderal System; I should, from a sense of the obligation I am under for repeated proofs of confidence in me, more than from any opinion I should have entertained of my usefulness, have obeyed its call; but it is now out of my power to do this with any degree of consistency,[65] the cause I will mention.

I presume you heard Sir, that I was first appointed, and have since been rechosen, President of the Society of the Cincinnati; and you may have understood also, that the triennial Genl. Meeting of this body is to be held in Philada. the first Monday in May next. Some particular reasons combining with the peculiar situation of my private concerns; the necessity of

---

[65]Madison's letter of Nov. 8, 1786, in the *Washington Papers,* stated that Washington's name was mentioned as the head of Virginia's delegation to the convention to revise the Federal Constitution. One of the broadside acts of the Virginia Legislature, dated Nov. 23, 1786, to appoint deputies to the convention to be held in Philadelphia in May next, is in the *Washington Papers.*

paying attention to them; a wish for retirement and relaxation from public cares, and rheumatic pains which I begin to feel very sensibly, induced me on the 31st ulto. to address a circular letter to each State society informing them of my intention not to be at the next meeting, and of my desire not to be rechosen President. The Vice President is also informed of this, that the business of the Society may not be impeded by my absence. Under these circumstances it will readily be perceived that I could not appear at the same time and place on any other occasion, without giving offence to a very respectable and deserving part of the Community, the late officers of the American Army. I feel as you do for our acquaintance Colo. Lee;[66] better never have delegated than left him out, unless some glaring impropriety of conduct had been ascribed to him. I hear with pleasure that you are in the new choice. With sentiments of the highest esteem and affectn. I am &c.[67]

To THEODORICK BLAND

Mount Vernon, November 18, 1786.

Dr. Sir: Several matters in which I have been pretty closely engaged, having prevented my sending to the Post office with my usual regularity, is the cause of my not having got, and of course acknowledged, the receipt of your obliging favors of the 4th. and 9th. inst:[68] earlier than I now do. By ascribing this delay to the true cause, I shall stand acquitted of all seeming inattention.

Permit me now, Sir, to thank you for the interesting communications in your letters, and to express to you the sincere

---

[66] Col. Henry Lee, who was not chosen a Delegate to the Continental Congress.
[67] From the "Letter Book" copy in the *Washington Papers*.
[68] Not now found in the *Washington Papers*.

pleasure with which I am filled at hearing that the acts of the present Session are marked with wisdom, justice and liberality. The critical situation of our affairs calls for the most vigorous display of these virtues, and it is much to be wished that so good an example from so respectable a State will be attended with the most salutary consequences to the Union.

No man entertains a higher sense of the necessity of revising the fœderal System, and supporting its government, than I do; nor would any man more readily depart from a prescribed line of conduct to effect this, than myself, in any matters I am competent to. With these sentiments and under such impressions, notwithstanding my having bid adieu to the public walks of life in a public manner, I should if the partiality of my Country had called to me to the service you allude to in your letter of the 9th., have yielded assent, not from an opinion that I could have answered their purposes better, or with equability to many that might have been named, but to evince my gratitude for the numberless instances of the confidence they have placed in me, and my obedience to their call. . . .[69]

I thank you for the Cutting-box. The Drill-plough I promised to have made for you has been ready sometime, and wou'd have been sent to the care of Mr. Newton 'ere this; but the hourly expectation of receiving the Timothy seed I promised to obtain for you, induced me to keep it (as I did not imagine you would apply it to any use 'till the Spring) 'till both should go together. My best respects to Mrs. Bland. I am, etc.[70]

---

[69] The omitted portion is practically the same as that found in Washington's letter to James Madison, Nov. 18, 1786, *q. v.*

[70] From the "Letter Book" copy in the *Washington Papers.*

On November 18 James Lawson agreed with Washington to work as a ditcher. This agreement, in the writing of George Augustine Washington, is in the *Washington Papers.*

To JAMES MERCER

Mount Vernon, November 19, 1786.

Dr. Sir: I was informed by your brother, Colo. Jno. Mercer, who with his family called here on their way to Annapolis, that by some discovery which had been lately made, it appears that Blair and McCool had not a legal right to dispose of the moiety of the 4 Mile run tract, which belonged to Colo. Geoe: Mercer. This defect I presume, can easily be remedied, as you are his Executor and heir at Law.

It is the same to me to whom I pay the purchase money, if I am properly acquitted and assured of the title. I shall be obliged to you therefore to pass such a Deed of Confirmation for the moiety of the Land purchased from the above named persons, as to you shall seem proper. You drew the Deed from them to me, and have, I doubt not, the necessary documents for the one now asked: if not, I would furnish such papers as are in my possession. My wish is to have these matters made clear before I go hence, that no dispute may arise hereafter. With very great esteem, etc.[71]

To MARQUIS DE LAFAYETTE

Mount Vernon, November 19, 1786.

My Dr. Marqs: On thursday last I received in very good order, from Baltimore, under the care of Monsr. Compoint, the most valuable things you could have sent me, a Jack [72] and two she Asses, all of which are very fine. The Pheasants [73] and partridges are coming round by water, for these also I pray you to accept my thanks. Words, my dear Marquis, will not do justice

---

[71] From the "Letter Book" copy in the *Washington Papers*.
[72] This Jack was named by Washington "The Knight of Malta."
[73] Chinese pheasants.

to my feelings, when I acknowledge the obligation I am under for the trouble and pains you have taken to procure, and forward these valuable animals to me.

Monsr. Compoint having brought no letter from you to me; having no instructions or orders to produce, and having lost with his pocket book a letter from your old aid Mr. McHenry to me, which might have contained some information; I am left entirely in the dark with respect to the cost of the Asses in Malta, and the expences attending them since. I therefore pray you My Dr. Marquis, to furnish me with an accot. of them as soon as possible, that I may delay no time in remitting you the amount.

As this letter is only intended to give you the earliest advice of the safe arrival of Monsr. Compoint and his charge, I shall as the Vessel by which it goes is now passing my door, add no more than those assurances, which you will ever believe me sincere it, of being with the most Affectionate regard, Yrs. etc.[74]

*To DAVID STUART

Mount Vernon, November 19, 1786.

Dear Sir: I have been favoured with your letters of the 8th. and 13th. Inst.; but not having sent to the Post Office with my usual regularity, I did not receive them so soon as I might have done from the date of the former.

I thank you for the interesting communications in both. It gives me sincere pleasure to find that the proceedings of the present Assembly are marked with wisdom, liberality and Justice. These are the surest walks to public, and private happiness. The display of which by so respectable a part of the Union, at so important a crisis, will, I hope, be influencial, and attended with happy consequences.

---

[74] From the "Letter Book" copy in the *Washington Papers*.

However delicate the revision of the federal system may appear, it is a work of indispensable necessity. The present constitution is inadequate. The superstructure totters to its foundation, and without help, will bury us in its ruins. Although I never more intended to appear on a public theatre, and had in a public manner bid adieu to public life; yet, if the voice of my Country had called me to this important duty, I might, in obedience to the repeated instances of its attention and confidence, have dispensed with these objections, but another now exists which would render my acceptance of this appointment impracticable, with any degree of consistency. It is this. The triennial General Meeting of the Society of the Cincinnati is to be holden in Philadelphia the first Monday in May next. Many reasons combining, some of a public, some of a private nature, to render it unpleasing, and inconvenient for me to attend it; I did on the 31st. ulto. address a circular letter to the State Societies, informing them of my intention not to be there, and desiring that I might no longer be rechosen President. The Vice Presidt. (Gates) has also been informed thereof, that the business of the Meeting might not be impeded on acct. of my absence. Under these circumstances, I could not be in Philadelphia precisely at the same moment on another occasion, without giving offence to a worthy and respectable part of the American community, the late Officers of the American Army.

I will do as you advise with respect to the Certificates, and trouble you with them again. Colo. Mason, it is said, expresses an inclination to give his attendance but I question much his leavg. Gunston this Winter.

Pray what is become of that Superlative Villain, Posey?[75] It has been reported here, that he is run off to Georgia. By a letter I have just received from Mr. Hill, I find that the whole

---

[75] Price Posey.

produce of my Estate below from the year 1774 together with
the monies which Hill received from others on my acct., has got
into that abandoned wretchs hands, not one shilling of which
I presume, will ever got out of them. All here join me in sincere good wishes for you, and I am etc.   [H.S.P.]

To GOVERNOR EDMUND RANDOLPH

Mount Vernon, November 19, 1786.

Dr. Sir: It gave me great pleasure to hear that the voice of the
Country had been directed to you as chief Magistrate of this
Commonwealth, and that you had accepted the appointment.

Our affairs seem to be drawing to an awful crisis: it is necessary therefore that the abilities of every man should be drawn
into action in a public line, to rescue them if possible from impending ruin. As no one seems more fully impressed with the
necessity of adopting such measures than yourself, so none is
better qualified to be entrusted with the reins of Government.
I congratulate you on this occasion, and with sincere regard
and respect am, Dr. Sir, etc.[76]

To COMTE D'ESTAING

Mount Vernon, November 19, 1786.

Sir: I have had the honor of receiving your letter of the 9th.
of May, by the hands of Genl. Duplissis[77] who did me the honor
to spend a few days with me on his way to Georgia. I am highly
obliged to you for introducing to my acquaintance a Gentleman of so much worth and merit: his own personal qualifica-
tions are sufficient to ensure to him the regard and affection

---

[76] From the "Letter Book" copy in the *Washington Papers*.
[77] Brig. Gen. Jean Baptiste Vigournere Du Plessis, formerly Governor of St. Vincent,
West Indies.

of all good men; but when to these are added his being the intimate friend and companion, and having preserved the life of Count d'Estaing, he will be doubly esteemed by every one who has the honor of knowing you. I sincerely wish that he may find the Country answerable to his expectation, and be induced to reside among us; if he should, America will make the valuable acquisition of a useful and worthy Citizen.

I need not tell you, Sir, how happy I should be to have the honor of paying my respects to you in this Country. Every person who tastes the sweets of American liberty, must esteem and revere you, and those other great characters among our good allies, who by your noble and generous exertions, were highly instrumental in procuring it. I have the honor, etc.[78]

To WILLIAM DRAYTON

Mount Vernon, November 20, 1786.

Sir: I wish it was in my power to give you a more favorable accot. than the following, of your Servant Jack.

After absenting himself from you at Dumfries (as I believe my nephew has already informed you) he came here and remained quietly 'till the 12th.; when being informed by some gentlemen from Baltimore that a Packet from that place was on the point of sailing for Charleston, I sent him under the care of a very trusty Overseer to be shipped from that place, requesting a friend of mine in the Town to engage a passage and to provide everything for him on Ship board, that was necessary. When they arrived at Baltimore, unfortunately, the vessel was hove down. It became necessary therefore to commit him to Goal for security; but before this could be effected, he took advantage of a favorable moment and made his escape.

---

[78] From the "Letter Book" copy in the *Washington Papers*.

Diligent, but ineffectual, search was instantly made, and it is supposed his object is Philadelpa.

The Gentleman to whose care I sent him has promised every endeavor in his power to apprehend him, but it is not easy to do this where there are numbers who had rather facilitate an escape than apprehend a run-away. I hope your journey was not much incommoded by this untoward step of your waiter. With sentiments of great esteem etc.[79]

To SAMUEL PURVIANCE

Mount Vernon, November 20, 1786.

Sir: Your letter of the 12th. instant came duly to hand. I should be very happy if it was in my power to render your friend Majr. Smith[80] any service by giving him the information which he desires; but as I do not remember to have received any recommendatory letter which he alludes to, nor have any knowledge of the payment of the officers of the Continental Army, much less of those who were in the pay of their respective States, I cannot do it, however desirous I may be of obliging the deserving soldier or worthy citizen.[81] I am, etc.[82]

To SAMUEL BRANTON[83]

Mount Vernon, November 20, 1786.

Sir: I have received by Captn. Bartlet, your letter of the 27th. of July. The ass arrived safe, and the other articles agreeably to the Bill of lading. I am much obliged to you Sir, for your

---

[79] From the "Letter Book" copy in the *Washington Papers.*
[80] Maj. Nathaniel Smith. He had been, in 1776, captain of a Baltimore independent artillery company.
[81] On November 20 Washington wrote practically this same letter to Major Smith, a copy of which is in the "Letter Book" in the *Washington Papers.*
[82] From the "Letter Book" copy in the *Washington Papers.*
[83] Branden(?).

attention in executing my commn., and the polite manner in which you offer me your future services. The ass is undoubtedly one of the best kind that could be procured at Surinam; but I do not find it charged in your accot. If you will be so good as to let me know the price of it by the first opportunity, the money shall be remitted to you. I am, etc.[84]

To RICHARD HARRISON

Mount Vernon, November 20, 1786.

Sir: I have received your Letter of the 10th. of July together with the two Toledo Blades[85] sent by Captn. Sullivan.[86]

I am much obliged to Mr. Carmichael for this polite mark of attention to me; but hope I shall have no occasion to use them. I should have been happy Sir, to have received them from you in person; but as your business will not yet permit you to return to your native Country, I must postpone the pleasure of seeing you to a future day, tho' I hope not a very distant one. I am, etc.[84]

To WILLIAM HULL

Mount Vernon, November 20, 1786.

Dear Sir: I have received your letter of the 25th. of October.[87] I only write now to acknowledge the receipt of it, and to inform you that I shall be happy to do anything in my power to forward the settlement which you mention, or to oblige, in any way, any of my Compatriots in the field.

---

[84] From the "Letter Book" copy in the *Washington Papers*.
[85] The swords were a gift from William Carmichael, then in Madrid.
[86] Merchant captain, of the ship *Union*.
[87] In the *Washington Papers*. In it Hull informed of an association of parties in Massachusetts to emigrate to the Northwest Territory.

As soon as I have collected all the necessary and useful information I can respecting the matter, (which I will endeavour to do) I will with pleasure communicate it to you; for at present my knowledge of the Western Country is more general, than particular, especially in the parts of it to which I presume you have turned your eyes. From Fort Pitt, downwards as low as the Great Kanhawa I have a pretty accurate knowledge of the climate, Soil &c.; but below this river, and west of the Ohio my ideas are borrowed. I am, etc.[88]

To WILLIAM HANSBOROUGH

Mount Vernon, November 22, 1786.

Sir: I have just received your letter of the 20th. inst: and can only inform you that I have nothing to do with respect to the collection of my Rents in your part of the Country. I have given it wholly to Mr. Muse, to act as he shall think proper; but have directed him to distress no one without sufficient cause. He will be able to judge of the validity of your reasons for not paying the Rent wch. is due from you, and will act accordingly. I am, etc.[88]

To JOHN FRANCIS MERCER

Mount Vernon, November 24, 1786.

Sir: Your servant having this moment put your letter of the 20th. inst: into my hands, and appearing to be in a great haste; I shall not detain him, especially as it is neither my wish nor intention to enter on the justification of my last to you.

---

[88] From the "Letter Book" copy in the *Washington Papers*.

On November 21 Gilbert Simpson, of Truro Parish, Fairfax County, Va., signed a bond to Washington, to surrender the tenement he held on lease from William Clifton on or before Dec. 25, 1786. This bond, in the writing of Washington, is in the *Washington Papers*.

The evidence, on which the charge of unfairness &ca. was grounded, you have enclosed in Colo. Symm's own hand writing, (the amount of the other bonds in his possession appeared to me to be very trifling). The propriety, or impropriety of this charge, after this transcript and information is given, you are to judge; and whether Combs's bond is not among those assigned to Mr. Colston. Hickmans, a considerable debt, must also have been under this predicament, or Colston's application to me for a Deed was very improper.

I would fain hope that there is not a greater impropriety in my receiving interest on a bonded debt, which lay years without having any part of the principal or interest paid, than is to be found in others; especially when the very fund you assured me should be applied to the payment thereof, you are recovering with interest. But I will have done with this subject, and never more shall give you the trouble of hearing any further observations of mine thereon. What rough expression of mine to you at Richmond has been industriously reported, is for me yet to learn. Your letter conveys the first most distant hint I have ever heard of the matter; I certainly ought therefore to stand acquitted of having any agency in the circulation of it, if I was so ungenteel as to have offered any.

I profess an entire ignorance of the real difference between military Certificates and specie; for never having had inclination or intention to deal in them, and rarely going from home, I have not been in the way of obtaining information on this subject. Nevertheless, I will take two thousand pounds of *Virginia military Certificates* at the price you offer, viz: four for one, so as to discharge five hundred pounds of my claim, and I will take 400 or more barrels of Indian Corn, provided a price is now *fixed* that I can obtain it at. and for your information I add that any quantity, I am told, may be had at 10/ Maryland

Curry. per barrel. Colo. Hooe thinks less. If this price accords
with your ideas, in order to ascertain the point decidedly, I
will give it; but assure you at the same time that your disposing of it to any other and paying the amot. in money to me,
would be quite as agreeable to me. Your accomodation was all
I had in view, my own crop is, I presume, adequate to my consumption. With respect to the negroes, I conclude it is not
in my power to answer your wishes, because it is as much against
my inclination as it can be against your's, to hurt the feelings
of those unhappy people by a separation of man and wife, or of
families; because no others than such as I enumerated in my
last will answer my purposes, and because the price exceeds
what I *supposed* negroes would sell for in ready money; for,
in this as with Certificates, having had no intention to buy, I
have made no enquiry into the price they sold at; but conceived that for ready money the best labouring negroes (which
are the kind I wanted) might have been had for £60, £70,
or at most £75. Upon the whole then, for the balance, I must
take payment in the manner formerly mentioned by you at
this place, unless you should think that young Bob, (who has
only a father without a wife) Tom the baker, Nessey and
David, and James and Valentine (if of sufficient size to go to
trades) could be separated without much uneasiness, and the
prices of them, if not really the ready money prices, cou'd be
abated.

Your reply to this letter soon would be satisfactory, for I
have just hired a compleat Ditcher with a view of putting several hands under him, and wish to know my prospects for it.
I am, etc.

P. S. I rece'd, enclosed in your letter, 2 half Joes, and 7 guineas,
£   in part payment, I presume, of the 15 guineas lent you.[89]

---

[89] From the "Letter Book" copy in the *Washington Papers*.

To ROBERT TOWNSEND HOOE

Mount Vernon, November 27, 1786.

Dr. Sir: The plank I want is to floor a room 24 by 32 feet. It must be 24 feet long and 1½ inches thick, all of a colour, and entirely free from Knots and sap. More than the nett quantity is requisite, for allowances. If it were seasoned, so much the better; but this is hardly to be expected in plank of this particular kind.

If Mr. Swift can supply me, it will be better than to send to the Eastern shore; if he cannot, I then beg the favor of you to engage Messrs. Peterson and Taylor (I think the names are) to furnish me agreeably to the above Memom., as soon as possible. With much esteem, I am, etc.[90]

To PHILIP MARSTELLER

Mount Vernon, November 27, 1786.

Sir: I send my Barge for the German family[91] with which I agreed on Saturday last, and for their necessaries if they have any to bring. As I have no body about me who can converse with them in their own language, I pray you to inform them that it will be necessary they should exert themselves to learn English; that their residence in the room into which they will be first introduced may be temporary, as they probably will be removed from it as soon as I can conveniently provide another place (on *this Estate*) for them to live in; that they will have provisions given to them to dress in the manner they like best; that they may obtain vegetables, out of my Garden by applying to the Gardner, to eat with their meat, and lastly, that I wish to impress upon them in strong terms the propriety of diligent

[90] From the "Letter Book" copy in the *Washington Papers*.
[91] Daniel, Margaret, and Anna Overdonck.

attention to their duty, as I shall expect this of them, and shall myself be hurt if their idle conduct obliges me to remind them of a breach of their contract.

As there is no hurry in the case, I will take a more leisure moment to write to you on the matter hinted to you already. I am, etc.

P. S. Please ask, and let me know if the man understands thatching houses with straw.[92]

To PRESLEY NEVILLE

Mount Vernon, November 27, 1786.

Dr. Sir: Accept my thanks for the information given me in your letter of the 25th. ulto. from the Court House of Washington, respecting the decision of one of my Ejectments. I have, since, been informed by Mr. Smith, of the favorable issue of the whole, and of the necessity there is of my paying immediate attention to the Tenements to prevent the waste and damage which otherwise will follow.

Consequent of this advice I send Mr. Lear, a young gentleman who lives with me, into that Country to take such measures for the preservation of my property as the exigency of the case, when investigated, may require. As it is more than probable he will see you, your friendly information of matters respecting this business, and advice to him would highly oblige me; as also your civilities to him.

Altho' the present occupants have little right to look to me for indulgences, and were told not to expect them; yet, as they are now in my power, it is neither my wish nor intention to distress them further than the recovery of my property from their usurpation, must unavoidably involve them in. They may

---

[92] From the "Letter Book" copy in the *Washington Papers*.

therefore become Tenants upon terms equitable between man and man, or purchasers, it being my intention to dispose of the Land, from a conviction that property at the distance that is from the proprietor of it, never can be converted to uses so beneficial as the money arising from the sales; because those in whose fidelity and care we can depend, are too independent, and generally have too much business of their own to attend to smaller matters; and others who are less qualified, and more ready to accept trusts of this sort, are too apt to abuse them: this I have found to my cost.

As Pittsburgh is a point to which emigrants from the northern and Eastern States, and foreigners almost universally, direct their first steps, you would do me a favor to let those who may enquire for cultivated places in your presence, know that that tract, as well as the other (commonly called Washington's bottom) in Fayette county, are for sale. I would sell them altogether, or in parcels; but not, by the latter mode, in such a manner as to injure the sale of the rest. I would also give credit for the whole or greatest part of the purchase money, provided the principal is well secured, and the interest arising therefrom regularly paid at my own house without trouble or delay. You would oblige me too, my good Sir, by giving me your candid opinion of the value, or in other words, what these Lands ought to sell for upon the terms here mentioned.

If your Father is in that country now, I beg to be remembered to him and to Mrs. Neville. With esteem and regard, I am, etc.[93]

To GEORGE McCARMICK

Mount Vernon, November 27, 1786.

Sir: I have received your letter of the 31st. of October, and thank you for the information contained therein. Since which

---

[93] From the "Letter Book" copy in the *Washington Papers*.

I have obtained a full account of the decisions in my favor against the settlers of my Land on Miller's run, from Mr. Smith.

Altho' those people have little right to look to me for favor or indulgences, and were told, if they run me to the expence of a Law suit, that they were not to expect any; yet, as they are now in my power, it is not my wish or intention to distress them more than the recovery of my property obliges me. They may therefore continue on their respective places either as Tenants at an equitable rent which shall be deemed reasonable between man and man, or as purchasers, if the terms can be agreed on between us; but they, nor no others will ever get it for 20/ pr. acre, this is five shillings less pr. acre, than these people would have given whilst the matter was in dispute, could we have agreed on the security and times of payment. It will be a matter of indifference to me whether I sell the Land altogether, or in parcels of 2, 3, 4 or 500 acres, provided in the latter case the price is proportioned to the quality of the Land and the improvements thereon; and provided also that it is laid off in regular form and in such a manner as not to injure the rest. Nor should I be very sollicitous about the payments, if the principal is well secured and the interest regularly paid at my house without giving me any trouble in the collection of it. For if this should be the case I would immediately put the Bond or Bonds in suit. A part of the purchase money I should require down, or at a short period, perhaps one fourth. On these terms also I would dispose of my land in Fayette county, near Yohoghaney.

If I had known that you had removed from your former place of abode near my Land, to Cat-fish, I should not have taken the liberty of referring those who might wish to become purchasers of it, to you to shew them the land, as it was too inconvenient for you to do it; but would have requested this favor of Colo. Cannon, who lives more convenient. The same cause prevents my requesting you to have an eye to it now. It could only suit a person who lives near, and can know almost every day, what is doing on the places, to take charge of them if the present occupants are determined to remove. But if your Jersey friends or others should want to become purchasers, you might oblige them and me too by letting them know that my lands are for sale.

If it was really necessary to have the outlines of the Tract run, in order to ascertain the boundaries of it, I am very willing to pay the expence, but the course by which this was done ought to have been taken from the Patent as the final act.

I am much obliged to you for the information respecting the expeditions of Genl. Clarke[94] &c., and for the account from Detroit. I wish, most sincerely, that the first may answer the purpose of giving Peace to the Western Settlements.

Mr. Lear, a young gentleman who lives with me and who is the bearer of this letter, will probably deliver it. If he should stand in need of your advice or assistance, I pray you to give it to him. I am, etc.[95]

To RICHARD BUTLER

Mount Vernon, November 27, 1786.

Dr. Sir: I have been requested by the Marqs. de la Fayette, in behalf of the Empress of Russia, to obtain a vocabulary of the languages of the Ohio Indians.

Previous to my hearing of your appointment as superintendant of Indian affairs in that District, I had transmitted to Captn. Hutchins[96] a copy of the Marquis's letter, containing the above

---

[94] George Rogers Clark. He led an expedition against the Wabash Indians in the summer of 1786.
[95] From the "Letter Book" copy in the *Washington Papers*.
[96] Thomas Hutchins.

request; conceiving that it would be much in his power, from the opportunities which would present themselves whilst he was surveying the Western Lands, to do this; and praying him to lend his aid to effect the work for this respectable character.

Since I have heard of your appointment to the above trust, and know to what intercourse with the Indians it must lead, I have resolved to ask the favor of your assistance also. If Capt. Hutchins is on the Ohio, he will shew you the paper which was transmitted to me by the Marquis, and which I forwarded to him. If he is not, it may be sufficient to inform you that it was no more than to insert English words and the names of things in one column, and the Indian therefore in others on the same line, under the different heads of Delaware, Shawanees, Wiendots &c. &c.

Your appointment gave me pleasure, as everything will do wch. contributes to your satisfaction and emolument, because I have a sincere regard for you. In your leisure hours, whilst you remain on the Ohio in discharge of the trust reposed in you, I should be glad to know the real temper and designs of the Western Indians, and the situation of affairs in that Country together with the politics of the people. And as I am anxious to learn with as much precision as your indubitable information goes to, the nature of the navigation of Beaver Creek; the distance, and what kind of portage there is between it and Cayahoga, or any other nearer navigation of the Muskingum, the distance and sort of portage across to the navigable waters of Cayahoga or Sandusky, and the kind of navigation therein, you would do me an acceptable favor to hand them to me, with the computed distances from the River Ohio by each of these routs, to the lake itself.

If you should not write to me by the return of the Bearer, I would beg leave to add that there is no way so certain of conveying letters to me, as to enclose them to your correspondent in Philadelphia, 'till a more direct Post is established with this part of the Country, accompanied by a request to him to put them in the Post office. Private conveyances, (unless by a person coming immediately to my house) I have always found the most tedious and most uncertain: from Philada. letters will reach me, frost permitting, in three or four days.

If you are at Pittsburgh, this letter will be presented to you by Mr. Lear, a deserving young gentleman who lives with me, and whom I beg leave to recommend to your civilities. He is sent by me to see the situation of my property on Miller's Run (lately recover'd) and to adopt some measures for the preservation and security of it. With sincere esteem and regard, I am, etc.[97]

To JOHN CANNON

Mount Vernon, November 28, 1786.

Sir: I have just been advised by Mr. Smith, my Counsel, of the favorable issue of the Ejectments I was compelled to bring for the recovery of my land in your neighbourhood; and of the necessity there is for me to appoint an Agent to take care of my interest therein.

As I am not acquainted with anyone, who lives near the land, in whom I could place such entire confidence as yourself, permit me to ask if you could make it convenient to take charge of this Tract, so far as to see that each tenement, for the preservation of it, has some person living thereon, upon the best terms you can get them. And that you may not conceive, Sir, that I mean to give trouble without compensation, I beg leave to inform you, that whatever you may think adequate to the former, I will readily allow.

---

[97] From the "Letter Book" copy in the *Washington Papers.*

Altho' the present occupants of it have little reason to expect favor or indulgences at my hands, yet as they are now in my power, I do not wish to distress them further than the repossession of my Land, and common justice to myself naturally tends to. I am willing therefore they should remain on their respective places at such a rent as shall appear reasonable and just between man and man; and this I am perfectly willing you should fix, without considering, or in any degree attending to the loss I have sustained by being kept out of my property for more than twelve years. If you should incline to undertake this trust in my behalf, I shall be well satisfied with these or any other Tenants, for the ensuing year; a longer term, I do not at present incline to let the Tenements for, as it is my intention to sell the land if I can obtain what I conceive it is worth, and would not encumber it with Leases.

From the present scarcity of money I know it would sell low for ready cash, or on short credit; but permit me to ask your candid opinion of its real worth, and what you think it would sell for if credit was given for three fourths of the purchase money, three, four, or five years, with interest to be regularly and punctually paid at my own house during that term; and whether you conceive it would be most advantageous for me to sell it by the tract, or in parcels of one, two, three, four, or five hundred acres, as may be most convenient to the purchasers?

Mr. Lear who lives with me, and who I expect will deliver this letter to you, will, if it is necessary, explain any matter that I may be deficient in.

I beg leave to recommend him to your civilities, and friendly advice what steps he had best take in this business, if you should be disinclined to engage in it yourself. With esteem, I am, etc.[98]

---

[98] From the "Letter Book" copy in the *Washington Papers*.

To JOHN STEPHENSON

Mount Vernon, November 28, 1786.

Dr. Sir: This Letter will be handed to you by Mr. Lear a young gentleman who lives with me, and who will pass a receipt in discharge of any money you may pay him on my account. I hope it will be convenient for you to discharge the whole, for it should be remembered that I have lain a long time out of what you are owing me, and that I can no more do without than another. My expences are high, and my calls great, or I should not have reminded you so often of what I had hoped you would have paid without any intimation of my wants. With best wishes for you and yours, I am, etc.[99]

To THOMAS FREEMAN

Mount Vernon, November 28, 1786.

Sir: Mr. Smith having advised me of the decisions in my favor at the Nisi prius Court held for the county of Washington; and of the necessity there is for my sending, or appointing some person on the spot to attend to my interest in the recovered lands; I have, as you appeared fixed on a removal to Kentuckey in the Spring, and with difficulty could be induced to continue the management of my business in your neighbourhood 'till now, sent Mr. Lear, who lives with me, to examine into the situation of the Tenements, views of the present occupants, and on the spot to make such arrangements in my behalf, as the exigency of the case may require, He will call upon you in his way out, or in; and by him I should be glad to know what has been done with my Negroes: if sold, to whom, on what credit and for what sum. I wish also to know whether you

---

[96] From the "Letter Book" copy in the *Washington Papers*.

have received any more of my money; and in that case, how it has been applied: if any is coming to me Mr. Lear will afford a safe conveyance for it. I want also to know, in what situation, under whose occupation, and what the expectations are from my land near you, especially the place lately occupied by Simpson; and in what condition the mill is. I would not wish to have any of the places not already under leases, engaged for more than one year; because, as I am determined to sell the land if I can obtain a price adequate to what I conceive to be the worth of it, it might be considered as an incumbrance. To keep the buildings and fences in good repair may be essential, even if I gain nothing by the Rents.

Considering the present scarcity of money, I am sensible it would not answer to sell for ready Cash; but what do you suppose the tract near you would fetch if three, four, or five years credit (paying interest) should be given for three fourths of the purchase money? And what difference do you think there would be in the amount of the sales, between selling the tract entire, or by the Lotts as now laid off, or in three, four, or five hundred acre parcels? If any person should apply to you for information respecting this Land and the terms, I would accomodate them in this manner; and with respect to price, I want no more pr. acre than such kind of land, with such credit sells at in the same part of the country. I am, etc.[1]

*To JAMES McHENRY

Mount Vernon, November 29, 1786.

Dear Sir: Your letters of the 18th. by the Packet, and 19th. by the Post, are both at hand. The Birds were landed yesterday. A Partridge died on the passage.

---

[1] From the "Letter Book" copy in the *Washington Papers*.

If Monsr. Campion's information is to be depended on, he had no letter from the Marquis de la Fayette or any other character in France for me; nothing confidential therefore could have been disclosed by the loss of his pocket book, unless it was deposited in your letter. His acct. is, that he was ordered to repair to L'Orient with the Asses and Birds, from whence *he* and *they* were to be Shipped by Messrs. Barauds. That the Marquis told him, letters should follow, and he supposes they will arrive in the French Packet. By Monsr. Campion I send the Guinea you paid for his board; if there are any other charges yet behind, I wish to be informed of them that they may be immediately paid. My sincere thanks are due to you, My dear Sir, for your kind attention to this business. Having received no intimation at, or previous to the arrival of Monsr. Campion respecting the light in which he ought to be viewed, I thought it best to err on the safe side, and therefore took him to my table, where he has conducted himself with modesty and propriety.

Under full conviction that the Asses were never intended as a present, and that the Chinese Pheasants (instead of costing 16 Gus. a pair as the Baltimore paragraphist has anounced to the public) came from the King's Aviary as a present to the Marquis for me, (for so says Monsr. Campion) I am concerned that such information should have been exhibited in a public gazette as appeared in the B. Papr. for it may be viewed as a contrivance to bespeak, what I should industriously have endeavoured to avoid, had I supposed it was so meant; a present. Was this publication confined to Maryland, or even to the United States, there would not be so much in it; but as these paragraphs for want of other matter to fill a Paper, are handed from one to another, and ultimately get into the British and French Gazettes; the Marquis will entertain a queer idea of it,

if nothing more is meant than what was promised, and expected; that is, to be the instrument through the Medium of
Adml. de Suffran (Govr. of the Island of Malta, or head of the
Order) of procuring and forwarding them from that place to
me. That he should have paid all the expences which attended
the getting, and shipping them is beyond a doubt. It could not
well be otherwise, as their procuration was a doubtful essay.
As I have not however received a single line respecting these
Animals, I do not undertake to contradict the report, but think
the evidence of it, the cost, &ca. appears to have been too slight,
to hand it in such a dress to the public. With sincere esteem, etc.[2]

*INSTRUCTIONS TO TOBIAS LEAR

Mount Vernon, November 30, 1786.

You will proceed to Pittsburgh by the following route. Lees-
burgh, Keyes' ferry, Bath, Old Town and Fort Cumberland.
From the latter pursue the New Road by the Turkey foot to
Colo. Jno. Stephensons, whh. is in the Road to Pittsburgh.

When you are at Bath, enquire the way to a piece of Land
I have on the River, about 14 miles above the Town, in the way
to old Town; and see if it is in the occupation of any one, and
on what term they hold it. A Colo. Bruin[3] at Bath, or one
McCracken near the Land, will, I expect, be able to give you
information on this head.

When you arrive at Colo. Stephenson's (commonly called
Stinson) you will deliver the letter to him, and receive what
money he may be in circumstances, or inclination to pay you,
on my acct.

---

[2] From a photograph of the original in the photostats of the *McHenry Papers* in
the Library of Congress.
[3] Peter Bryan Bruin (?).

At Pittsburgh, I expect you will find Genl. Butler, to whom you have a letter, and from whom it is probable you may receive an answer. If he is not there, leave the letter for him in care of his Brother (who lives there) or some other.

Colo. Nevill lives at a place called Shirtee's, Six miles below Pittsburgh, and not much out of the way, I believe, to my Land on Millers run (lately recovered) or to Colo. Cannons in the vicinity of it.

You will converse fully, and freely with the Gentleman on the points touched on in my letter, hear his sentiments on them, and find out, if you can, how far, and with what sincerity he is disposed to serve me in providing Tenants and securing the Rents of the newly recovered Lands. You will be able to learn from him also whether Colo. Cannon is at home, or in the Assembly at Philadelphia; probably Colo. Nevill will ride there with you in the former case, or to the Land in the latter one, who it is I have appointed agent, and who [the Tenants] or the residents thereon have little right to expect favor from.

As Colo. Cannon lives near my Land, and is esteemed worthy, and of respectable character, it would be more convenient, and perhaps better, every thing considered, that he should superintend my Tenements than any other person; but if he declines it, and Colo. Nevill discovers an inclination to serve me in this business he would be my next choice, and Majr. McCarmick the third. In case either of the first (in the order they are named) should incline to accept this trust, there will be no necessity for you to deliver the letter to the latter in person.

The name of the person accepting the trust, must be inserted in the blank power herewith given you.

You will endeavor to discover from those to whom you have letters as also of others what is likely to be the highest price I can obtain for the two tracts I wish to dispose of, viz: that

on Millers run, in Washington County containg. 80 acres and
that on Yohiogany (commonly called Washingtons bottom)
in Fayette County of 1650 Acres giving the credits, and receiving the payments, in the manner mentioned in my letters, and
if you should find that none are of opinion that the first will
exceed 30/. pr. Acre and the other 40/ both Pensa. Curry. you
may give it out that altho I have not named the prices of these
tracts in my letters yet you have good reasons to believe, and
indeed know, that if these prices could be averaged (in case
the Lands are sold in parcels) that I would be content therewith and assurances might be given of my disposing of them
on these terms.

After having finished the business which takes you to Washington County return home by the way of my other Land in
Fayette County; the condition of which I wish you to examine
over and above the acct. you will receive from Majr. Freeman
and then return in by Braddocks Road, at the Great Meadows
on which, I have a small tract which sometimes has, and at other
times has not a tenant, (though no rent has ever yet been paid
me for it), see in what State and condition this Tenement is in.

Your Road from hence will cross the No. Branch of Potomack above Fort Cumberland, and pass through Romney, and
thence to Winchester, where you will deliver the letter to Mr.
White and receive the money due from Genl. Lees Estate to
me if he inclines to pay it.

In this trip you will have an opportunity of satisfying yourself fully with respect to Colo. Hulls enquiries, which I wish
you to do. and also what the legal fees of my Lawyers in the
Ejectments lately decided in my favor are, that I may know
better how to add to them.

If Majr. Freeman can give any acct. of the Suit (an ejectment
I believe it is) brot. by my Brothr. Colo. Jno. Washington in

Fayette Court I should be glad if you would obtain, that I may communicate it, to him.

Wishing you good health, and as pleasant journey as can be expected from the Season I am etc.

To DIEGO DE GARDOQUI

Mount Vernon, December 1, 1786.

Sir: I have had the honor to receive the letter which your Excellency did me the favor of writing to me on the 18th ulto. together with the enclosure from the Prime Minister of Spain, for which, and the translation, I pray you to accept my grateful thanks.

Besides the pleasure I feel in making these acknowledgements, one object that prompts me to them at this early period, is, to beg that your Excely. will not take the trouble of being instrumental in procuring for me a She Ass (by means of which I might preserve the breed of the valuable Jack I received as a present from his Catholic Majesty). At all times and under any circumstances, I shou'd have been perfectly ashamed if an unguarded expression of mine should have been the cause of giving you trouble, but more so in the present. When I had the honor of addressing you last, I had actually sent to Surinam, where I was informed very good, though not of the first race of these animals, were to be had, for a she one; and besides, thro' the medium of my good friend the Marqs. de la Fayette, I had assurances and the further prospect of obtaining one or two from the Island of Malta. I am quite unhappy therefore lest the information in my former letter, that "I am endeavouring to provide a female that the advantages which are to be derived from this Jack may not end with his life", should have been construed an expression of a wish that your Excely. would employ your influence to effect this purpose, and it is the inducement which has hastened me to an explanation and correction of the indigested manner in which information was communicated.

Rheumatic pains, with which of late I have been a good deal afflicted, and some other causes, will render it inconvenient for me to be in Philada. in May next as seems to be expected, and where one of my first pleasures would have been to have paid my respects to your Excellency.

It will be to be regretted if a contrariety of sentiments respecting the navigation of the Mississippi, should impede that harmony and mutual intercourse of interests so essential between nations whose territories border on each other. I would fain hope therefore that the true and reciprocal benefits of Spain and the United States, in this case, as well as in all others which may arise between them, will be cooly and dispassionately considered before the ultimatum on either side is fixed. There is no ground on which treaties can be formed that will be found permanent or satisfactory, unless they have these for their basis: but however necessary it may be to inculcate this doctrine upon others, your Excellency I am sure is too much of a politician to need the remark, and too much a friend to these States to insist upon any measure, which the essential interests of your Nation, or the orders of your Court, may not have dictated, incompatible therewith. With very great consideration and respect. I have the honor etc.[4]

To BATTAILE MUSE

Mount Vernon, December 4, 1786.

Sir: As the fifty bushels of wheat stands as an article of charge at 5/6 in your accot. against me, it may remain so, as a final

---

[4]From the "Letter Book" copy in the *Washington Papers*.

settlement of the matter. Altho' I have no flour at present for sale, and have made no enquiry into the price of this article, I do not suppose I shall either loose or gain much in so small a quantity by fixing the wheat at this price.

With respect to the persons[5] named in your letter of the 26th. ulto. (which is just come to hand) I can only repeat what I have often done before, in substance, and that is, that it is my wish to obtain justice to myself, but not to act with that rigor in effecting it, as to bring ruin, or even considerable distress upon poor families. Rather than do this, I would relinquish my claim; but in all cases of this kind, I would endeavor to draw a line between inability and dishonesty; where the former appears with good dispositions to industry and honesty, I would wish lenient means may be used; but where the intention appears fraudulent, no indulgencies should be given. These being my sentiments, you can apply them to the cases of Rector and Thompson as your own judgment, under the circumstances as related, shall dictate, keeping the old proverb in view, not to "sue a beggar and catch a louse." This adage may apply also to Colo. Kennedy, otherwise if he will not give you security for paying the balance in six, nine, or even twelve months, (as he has assumed the payment, for without this he might have plead the act) I would sue him without further delay.

All these difficulties and losses have arisen from Rents lying over, unpaid from year to year; for which reason I am determined that my Rents in future shall be punctually discharged, unless there is some interposition of Providence which calls for forbearance. The best Landlord, I am perfectly convinced, is he who never suffers two rents to become due on the same tenement.

---

[5] Charles Rector and John Thompson.

In the enclosed (which I request you to forward) I have consented to Fielding Lewis's getting timber, if the tenants having leases are willing, to build him a house in Rector-town; but what use he means to put it to afterwards, will, I dare say, puzzle him to tell. I am, etc.[6]

To FIELDING LEWIS[7]

Mount Vernon, December 4, 1786.

Sir: Your letter of the 11th of Octor. never came to my hands 'till yesterday. Altho' your disrespectful conduct towards me, in coming into this country and spending weeks therein without ever coming near me, entitles you to very little notice or favor from me; yet I consent that you may get timber from off my Land in Fauquier County to build a house on your Lott in Recter town. Having granted this, now let me ask you what your views were in purchasing a Lott in a place which, I presume, originated with and will end in two or three Gin Shops, which probably will exist no longer than they serve to ruin the proprietors, and those who make the most frequent applications to them. I am, &c.[6]

To JAMES TILGHMAN

Mount Vernon, December 4, 1786.

Dr. Sir: Your favor of the 14th. ulto. is but just come to hand, or an earlier reply shou'd have been made to it.

The inscription intended for the Tomb of my deceased friend meets my entire approbation;[8] for I can assure you Sir, with

---

[6] From the "Letter Book" copy in the *Washington Papers.*
[7] Nephew of Washington.
[8] A copy of this epitaph for Tench Tilghman is with James Tilghman's letter to Washington, Nov. 14, 1786, in the *Washington Papers.*

much truth, that after I had opportunities of becoming well acquainted with his worth, no man enjoyed a greater share of my esteem, affection and confidence than Colo. Tilghman.

I now transmit you, for the satisfaction of the friend of your deceas'd son, a statement of the conduct which was observed towards Capt: Asgill during his confinement, by which his illiberality and want of candour will fully appear. These extracts are taken from authentic records, and contain every sentence wherein the name of that officer is mentioned according to my best knowledge and belief.

At length, with much difficulty, I have got all the papers which are to be found, respecting the affairs of the deceased Colo. Thos. Colvill, from the son of the principal acting Executor of the Will of that Gentleman, I have put them into the hands of a skilful lawyer to make, if possible, a proper statement of them for final settlement, and as soon as I can speak to any good purpose you shall again hear from me respecting the claim of Miss Anderson. With great esteem etc.[9]

* To THOMAS PETERS [10]

Mount Vernon, December 4, 1786.

Sir: Your Letter of the 18th. Ulto. came duly to hand. From the number of fruitless enquiries I had made for *Spring* Barley before I applied to you, and the intervention between the date of my letter and your answer being pretty considerable I despaired of obtaining any of this grain, and therefore seeded the ground which was at first designated for this Crop with Wheat and Rye.

I have also since heard that many Gentlemen who have tried it (especially some on West River where I know the Lands

---

[9] From the "Letter Book" copy in the *Washington Papers*.
[10] Of Baltimore, Md.

are very fine and such as I conceived were well adapted for this grain) do not find it answerable to their expectation. Nevertheless as I wish to divide my Seed time and am desirous of sowing Clover and other grasses with Barley in preference to other grain I would gladly take fifty bushels of it and will depend *absolutely* upon *you* for this quantity which I pray may be sent me as soon as it can be procured, by the Packet. With respect to the latter I am anxious because having the seed in my possession I can lay out and prepare accordingly and not postpone my Oat Season in expectation of a Barley one and be disappointed at last of the latter as was the case last year.

If I find this essay likely to answer my expectations I shall be better able to talk with you on a Contract. The Barley may be accompanied by the machine you spoke of as eligable for cleaning it; and I shall thank you for sending one accordingly. Let me know decidedly if you please whether I may depend upon the above quantity of Barley in the manner mentioned. I have it now in my power (for it is offered to me) to get what I want from a Brewer in Philadelphia but I may even fail here if my engagement with him is delayed long for your answer.

Can *good* Clover Seed (not imported Seed for that rarely is so) be bought at Baltimore? In what quantity, and at what price? There is not, I believe, a bushel of Barley of any kind in this neighbourhood for sale. A Mr. Wales who Brews in Alexandria procures all of this he can. I am etc.   [N.Y.P.L.]

To RAWLEIGH COLSTON

Mount Vernon, December 4, 1786.

Sir: Your favor of the 10th. of Novembr., (which did not reach me 'till within these three days) as well as the former by Mr. Ireland, came safe to hand.

Mr. Wright, whom I saw at Alexandria, will have informed you, that as the business respecting the affairs of the deceased Colo. *George* Mercer was transferred by a decree of the high Court of Chancery from me to Colo. *John* Mercer; and the Bonds and other papers assigned over to the latter, that it lay with him to settle the accounts and to decide on the propriety of making conveyances. The Deeds were only withheld 'till payment of the consideration money should be made, or satisfactory security should be given for the doing of it, and that (if it was necessary for me to do it at all) I could make no conveyance without his express direction; this being necessary for my justification and this I also repeated to Mr. Ireland in emphatical terms.

Since these conversations I have received a line from Colo. John Mercer requesting me to execute a Deed to you for one of the Lotts sold Mr. Hickman;[11] but as the Deeds for conveyance of these lands are much out of the usual form, (there being many parties to them) and all the papers respecting the business now out of my possession, I have, in answer to this request, desired him if it is *indispensably* necessary for me as the seller to convey, to have the deed (for there were some blank ones left) filled up and sent to me with authority for me to sign, and no delay should be found on my part. Having thus explained my sentiments of, and agency in this business, you will readily perceive to what quarter your future applications are to be directed. Considering the light in which Mr. Ireland stood, I gave him a statement of the case in writing, that Mr. Stone might act in it agreeably to the dictates of his own judgment. or the orders of Colo. Mercer, with respect to the execution. I am, etc.[12]

---

[11] Joseph Hickman.
[12] From the "Letter Book" copy in the *Washington Papers*.

To CLEMENT BIDDLE

Mount Vernon, December 5, 1786.

Dr. Sir: Your letters of the 15th of Octor. and 5th. of Novr. are both before me, and I shall reply to them in their order.

For your trouble in negotiating my Certificate I thank you. If it is necessary, in order that you may receive the half yearly interest thereon, I would wish you to keep it; if you can draw this without, it may be returned to me. In the mean time, inform me if you please if this Certificate can be converted into cash, and upon what terms, that if I should have occasion to make any purchases in Philada., I may know the amount of this fund. The Indents, to the amount of 84 50/90 Dollars, I have received, and note the credit given me for the year and half interest.

The Curtain stuff and nails are at hand safe, and will answer very well. The uncertainty of getting good *Spring* Barley (for I had made many fruitless enquiries in this State, and the parts of Maryland bordering on it, before I wrote to you) induced me to put the ground which I had first allotted for this grain, into Wheat and Rye; but if you could secure and send to me by one of the first vessels bound from your Port to Alexanda. fifty bushels, I will yet find as much ground as will receive this quantity of Seed; or if you have engaged 100 bushels of this grain from Reuben Haines as the expression of your letter seems to import, I will readily take it, but would not chuse to be under any promise of supplying him with the produce of it: first, because being uncertain of the yield, and inclining to go pretty largely upon it if I find it likely to answer my purpose, I shall want a good deal for Seed, and 2dly because the freight around, it is to be feared, would sink too deep in the sales to render me any profit upon a small quantity.

The Clover Seed (as I conceived this had been a productive year of it) is high; yet I would beg you to send me 300 weight. As soon as I know the precise cost of this, and the Barley; the money shall be remitted, or if you have any dealings in Alexandria, and an order on me will answer your purposes equally as well, it shall be immediately paid.

If it is the same thing to Mr. Haines whether I take fifty or an hundred bushels, I shall, under the circumstances already mentioned, prefer the former quantity. It is so essential to every farmer to have his seeds by him in time, that I would urge in strong terms that these now required be sent to me by the first good *water* conveyance.

The uncertainties and disappointments of last Spring, will always make me anxious of obtaining all my Seeds long before the seasons for sowing them shall have arrived. At any rate let me know by Post what it is I have to expect.

Best wishes attend Mrs. Biddle. I am, etc.

P. S. Are the Artichoke of Jerusalem to be had in the neighbourhood of Philada? Could as much of the root, or the seed, be got as would stock an acre? I want to bring it in with my other experiments for the benefit of stock.[13]

To JOHN FRANCIS MERCER

Mount Vernon, December 5, 1786.

Sir: As I have not yet received a reply to my last letter, but, since the date of it, have made some enquiry into the prices of negroes at the ready money sales of them, I take the liberty of informing you, previously to your writing, or my receiving an answer to the above letter, that as it is not likely we shall agree

---

[13] From the "Letter Book" copy in the *Washington Papers*.

on a price, (in case you should be disposed to spare such negroes as would have answered my purposes) it is my wish to save you the trouble of adding anything more on the subject of them. Such as I pointed at might have been useful to me; but as I have no desire of adding to my present number by purchase, to accomodate you was the object I had principally in view; but I cannot think of allowing more to effect this, than the same kind of negroes would command at a sale of ready money, because in fact it is a discount of ready money, and for that species of property which I have no inclination to possess. I mention the matter now lest the intimation of such sentiments after an acquiescence with my purposal, should you have been thereto disposed, might be construed a disposition to take advantage of circumstances to reduce the price; rather than a thought of this kind should be entertained, my choice is to await the money in any manner you shall please to offer it.

It was Mr. Hunter, not Colo. Hooe, that gave the information respecting the price of Corn, as mentioned in my last. I correct the mistake therefore, then made, that there may be no representation suspected in the accot.

As I assured you in my last that I had bid adieu to the altercation respecting the appropriation of the money arising from the Bonds in suit, so I can assure you I have no other motive for enclosing Mr. Colston's letter, which only came to my hands the day before yesterday than to let you see his sollicitude to obtain a Deed for the land for which he has paid the consideration money, and to repeat the assurances of my last, that if it is essential for me to execute the Deed, I am ready to do it when it is presented, and I am properly authorised by you so to do. I am, etc.[14]

---

[14] From the "Letter Book" copy in the *Washington Papers*.

* To DAVID STUART

Mount Vernon, December 6, 1786.

Dear Sir: If Mr. Newton of Norfolk should offer you money on my acct. I wd. thank you for bringing it.

I have a tenant, one Edward Williams, who I want to punish, because I believe him to be a bad man. I pray you therefore to send me a General Court Writ for him. The case I shall relate, and leave the nature of the Writ, and quantum of damages to be filled up by better judges than myself. to frighten, not really to hurt him, is my object.

The case is.

He pulls down my fences which are good, and adjoining to him, to let *his stock* into my Inclosures for the benefit of better pastures than his own. The consequence is, that besides the injury I sustain by having my pastures a common, *my stock* go out and get into his fields, which have not lawful fences, and are there maimed and killed. One Hog of near 200 weight his people were caught in the act of killing; several others of equal size are missing, and no doubt is entertained of their having shared this fate. My wish therefore is to lay the damages high to scare him. I pray you to pay Mr. Hopkins ten or 15/. wch. I owe him for some service rendered me in the payment of a fee for recording a Deed in the General Ct. What are you about below? we hear nothing from you now! The Maryld. Session will be warm. Paper money the cause! The disturbances in Massachusetts have not subsided, on the contrary are growing more systematic. They are alarming, and the evils, if possible, should be averted. To suppose, if they are suffered to go on, they can be kept at the distance they now are, from us, is idle. Fire, where there is inflamable matter, very rarely stops;

and nothing is more certain than that, it is better to prevent misfortunes, than to apply remedies when they have happened. I am etc.[15]

To JOSIAH WATSON

Mount Vernon, December 15, 1786.

Sir: I am exceedingly anxious, to bring the Administration of Colo. Colvill's Estate to a close. To do this, and to discharge some claims on it, (one of which is very pressing) it is become indispensably necessary that the Bond in which you are joined with the late Major Moody, should be paid off. I persuade myself there will be no further delay in doing it when the indulgencies which have already been given and when the circumstances attending this transaction are, moreover, recurred to. Tho' Majr. Moody stands for most in the Bond, he was not at the time it was taken, nor has he at any period since been considered as the principal. It will be remembered, I am certain, that I was assured on that occasion, (tho' a credit of twelve months was given) the Bond should not remain unpaid so long: five years have since elapsed. More than a year ago when application, thro' Mr. Lund Washington, was made for this money, he was referred, as he informed me, to the heir or Exor. of the deceased Mr. Moody; but under the circumstances of this case, I beg leave to add that I must look to you for

[15] From a photostat of the original through the kindness of Judge E. A. Armstrong, of Princeton, N. J.

On December 6 an agreement was signed by Thomas Green to act as an house carpenter and joiner for Washington for three years. This agreement, in the writing of George Augustine Washington, is in the *Washington Papers*. An additional article was added by Tobias Lear, and signed by Green, Mar. 6, 1789, that provided in case Green "addicts himself to drink, idles his time, or becomes in any manner negligent of, or inattentive to his duty that it shall and may be lawful to discharge him . . . at any time without infracting the letter or spirit of this Contract."

On December 12 Washington wrote, briefly, to Gov. Edmund Randolph in Richmond, introducing John Anstey, who had been introduced to Washington by George William Fairfax and John Jay. A copy of this letter is in the "Letter Book" in the *Washington Papers*.

payment. I would have waited yet longer in expectation of having this money tendered to me, but for the reasons above; and which I pray you to receive as the apology for my being so urgent and so explicit now. With esteem, I am, etc.

P. S. If it is convenient to you, the price of the redemptioners, and the cost of the Osnabrigs may go in payment; if it is not, I will send you the money. In   last the son of Mr. Moody paid me £   .[16]

To PHILIP MARSTELLER

Mount Vernon, December 15, 1786.

Sir: To the severity of the weather, wch. has in a manner shut every thing up, and put a stop to all intercourse; and to some other circumstances unnecessary to mention, is to be ascribed my silence 'till now; and even now, when I recollect how fully I have already explained my ideas to you on what is intended to be the subject of this letter, I find that I have hardly anything to trouble you with by way of illucidation.

I will just observe, however, that having been well informed that seasons and circumstances *have occurred* and probably *will arrive again,* when goods by vendue have sold considerably below the Sterlg. cost of them; nay, that they have even been bought for the nominal sum currency, which they cost sterling in the countries from whence they were imported; and having found from experience, that I derive little or no advantage from the ready money payments I make for such articles as are requisite for the use of my Estate, (when I go to the Stores in Alexandria) I had determined to make the proposition to you which was pretty fully explained in the conversation I had with you

---

[16] From the "Letter Book" copy in the *Washington Papers.*

at our last interview as has been already mentioned, and which in a word is as follows:

To allow you a Commission of 2½ pr Ct. (which you yourself declared was sufficient) upon all purchases you shall make for me at Vendue, of articles which may from time to time be enumerated to you. It is your interest, I know to sell high; it is mine to buy low; but there is nothing incompatible that I can conceive, in your agency in both these cases; for when the former is the case, I mean not to become a purchaser; when the latter happens, which no skill or exertion of your's can at all times prevent, is the moment of which I mean, thro' your attention to the business, to avail myself for supplies. To your knowledge of the goods which are intended for sale; the circumstances of the sale, and to your honor, of which I entertain a very favourable opinion from the good report made of it by others, I entirely confide for the management. The payments shall always keep pace with the purchases; you have nothing more to do therefore than to give intimation of the latter by a line lodged at the post office, to receive the former: and were you now and then to add a concise list of the principal articles which are for sale, it would be obliging.

To particularize all the articles which are necessary for the use of a large family, would be as tedious as unnecessary. Every merchant who retails, and every man who provides for one, can be at no loss for them. The heavy articles, and such as at present occur to me are enumerated in the enclosed list: in which you will perceive no mention is made of coarse Woolens; because of these I manufacture a sufficiency to clothe my out-door negroes; nor have I said any thing of wines, because I import my own; but of the latter, if *good* Claret should at any time go cheap, I would take two or three Boxes. I have been obliged to buy about 200 ells of Ticklenburg for present use; perhaps the 2 or 300 more enumerated in the enclosed, may suffice; possibly more may be wanted. The Blankets will not be wanted before next autumn. Of Sugars my demand (as a private family) is great and constant; but of Coffee and Molasses, I have on hand a large stock.

It is scarcely necessary to impress on you the idea that it is the prospect of *very* cheap buying which has induced me to adopt this mode of obtaining my supplies; and that unless the end is accomplished, my purposes will not be answered, nor my inclination gratified by it; but to prevent mistakes, I explicitly declare it. Few of the enumerated articles am I in present want of; those for which I shall soonest have a call, are marked thus (*) in the margin; many of the others I may dispense with a year, or two years. They stand in the List as a memento only, in case *very* favorable moments present, for the purchase of them.

I am told it sometimes happens that Goods which come under the imputation of being damaged, tho' in fact they have received little or no real injury, are frequently sold uncommonly low indeed; particularly Bale blanketing, and other Bale goods. To embrace such opportunities is recommended, but in this, judgment and a close inspection are necessary; for it is not the lowest priced goods that are always the cheapest; the quality is, or ought to be as much an object with the purchaser, as the price.

I pray you to accept my thanks for the trouble you had with the German redemptioners which were purchased for me; the expence my Nephew the bearer of this, will pay. I am, &c.[17]

---

[17] A copy of the "Invoice of Goods wanted by George Washington" follows this letter in the "Letter Book" in the *Washington Papers;* but the copyist has neglected to mark any of the items therein as mentioned by an asterisk in the margin.

To JAMES MADISON

Mount Vernon, December 16, 1786.

My dear Sir: Your favor of the 7th. came to hand the evening before last.[18] The resolutions which you say are inserted in the Papers, I have not yet seen.[19] The latter come irregularly, tho' I am a subscriber to Hay's Gazette.[20]

Besides the reasons which are assigned in my circular letter to the several State Societies of the Cincinnati, for my non-attendance at the next General meeting to be holden at Philadelphia the first Monday of May, there existed one of a political nature, which operates more forceably on my mind than all the others; and which, in confidence, I will now communicate to you.

When this Society was first formed, I am persuaded not a member of it conceived that it would give birth to those Jealousies, or be chargeable with those dangers (real or imaginary) with which the minds of many, and some of respectable characters, were filled. The motives which induced the Officers to enter into it were, I am confident, truly and frankly recited in the Institution: one of which, indeed the principal, was to establish a charitable fund for the relief of such of their compatriots, the Widows, and descendants of them, as were fit objects for their support; and for whom no public provision had been made.

---

[18] "I am entirely convinced from what I observe here, that unless the project of Congs. [for ceding the Mississippi to Spain for 25 years] can be reversed, the hopes of carrying this State into a proper federal system will be demolished. Many of our most federal leading men are extremely soured with what has already passed. Mr. Henry, who has been hitherto the Champion of the federal cause, has become a cold advocate, and in the event of an actual sacrifice of the Missisipi. by Congress, will unquestionably go over to the opposite side."—*Madison to Washington*, Dec. 7, 1786. A photostat of this letter is in the *Washington Papers*.

[19] The resolutions of the Virginia House of Delegates on the memorial of the western members and some of the officers, on the Mississippi question.

[20] James Hayes, jr.'s, *Virginia Gazette, or The American Advertiser*, of Richmond, Va.

But the trumpet being sounded, the alarm was spreading far and wide; I readily perceived therefore that unless a modification of the plan could be effected (to anihilate the Society altogether was impracticable on acct. of the foreign officers who had been admitted), that irritations wd. arise which would soon draw a line betwn. the Society, and their fellow Citizens.

To prevent this. To conciliate the affections. And to convince the world of the purity of the plan, I exerted myself, and with much difficulty, effected the changes which appeared in the recommendation from the General Meeting to those of the States; the accomplishment of which was not easy; and I have since heard, that whilst some States acceded to the recommendation, others are not disposed thereto, alledging that, unreasonable prejudices, and ill founded jealousies ought not to influence a measure laudable in its institution, and salutary in its objects and operation.

Under these circumstances, there will be no difficulty in conceiving, that the part I should have had to have acted, would have been delicate. On the one hand, I might be charged with dereliction to the Officers, who had nobly supported me, and had treated me with uncommon marks of attention and attachment. On the other, with supporting a measure incompatible (some say) with republican principles. I thought it best therefore without assigning this (the principal reason) to decline the Presidency, and to excuse my attendance at the meeting on the ground, which is firm and just; the necessity of paying attention to my private concerns; to conformity to my determination of passing the remainder of my days in a state of retirement; and to indisposition; occasioned by Rheumatic complaints with which, at times, I am a good deal afflicted. Professing at the sametime my entire approbation of the institution as altered, and the pleasure I feel at the subsidence of those Jealousies which yielded to the change. *Presuming,* on the general adoption of them.

I have been thus particular to shew, that under circumstances like these, I should feel myself in an aukward situation to be in Philadelphia on another public occasion during the sitting of this Society. That the prest. œra is pregnant of great, and *strange* events, none who will cast their eyes around them, can deny; what may be brought forth between this and the first of May to remove the difficulties which at present labour in my mind, against the acceptance of the honor which has lately been conferred on me by the Assembly, is not for me to predict; but I should think it incompatible with that candour which ought to characterize an honest mind, not to declare that under my present view of the matter, I should be too much embarrassed by the meetings of these two bodies in the same place, in the same moment (after what I have written) to be easy in the situation; and consequently, that it wd. be improper to let my appointment stand in the way of another.[21] Of this, you who have had the whole matter fully before you, will judge; for having received no other than private intimation of my election, and unacquainted with the formalities which are, or ought to be used on these occasions, silence may be deceptious, or considered as disrespectful; The imputation of both, or either, I would wish to avoid. This is the cause of the present disclosure, immediately on the receipt of your letter, which has been locked up by Ice; for I have had no communication with Alexandria for many days, till the day before yesterday.

My Sentiments are decidedly against Commutables; for sure I am it will be found a tax without a revenue. That the people will be burthened. The public expectation deceived, and a few

---

[21] Madison had stated in his letter of Dec. 7, 1786, that it was the opinion of many judicious friends that Washington's name could not be spared from the Virginia delegation to the convention to meet in Philadelphia in May.

Speculators *only,* enriched. Thus the matter will end, after the morals of *some,* are more corrupted than they now are; and the minds of *all,* filled with more leaven, by finding themselves taxed, and the public demands in full force. Tobacco, on acct. of the public places of deposit, and from the accustomed mode of negotiating the article, is certainly better fitted for a Commutable than any other production of this Country; but if I understand the matter rightly (I have it from report only) will any man pay five pound in Specie for five taxables, when the same sum (supposing Tobo. not to exceed 20/. per Ct.) will purchase 500 lbs. of Tobo. and this, if at 28/. will discharge the tax on Seven? And will not the man who neither makes, nor can easily procure this commodity, complain of the inequality of such a mode, especially when he finds that the revenue is diminished by the difference be it what it may, between the real and nominal price? and that he is again to be taxed to make this good. These, and such like things, in my humble opinion, are extremely hurtful, and are among the principal causes that present depravity and corruption without accomplishing the object in view for it is not the shadow, but the substance with which Taxes must be paid, if we mean to be honest. With sentiments of sincere esteem etc.[22]

To JOHN FRANCIS MERCER

Mount Vernon, December 19, 1786.

Sir: I received your favor of the 10th., last night. The letter I addressed to you about fourteen days ago, I was in hopes would have reached you before your reply to my former, would have been dispatched, and thereby have saved you the trouble of again touching on the subject of negroes.

[22] From a photostat of the original through the kindness of Dr. A. S. W. Rosenbach, of New York City.

I can have no idea of giving eighty or ninety pounds a head for slaves when I am well informed that for ready money the best common labouring negroes in this State, may be bought for less than sixty, and others in proportion. For this species of property I have no predilection nor any urgent call, being already over stocked with some kind of it; consequently can have no inducement to give 50 pr. Ct. more than the like property is offered for and doth actually sell at. A payment in negroes, if this was to take place, can be considered in no other light by either of us, than as ready money; it stops the payment of it, and is I presume a convenience. But to supercede the necessity of enforcing these observations, and to remove every suspicion which might have arisen in your mind, of a desire in me to beat you down in the price of your slaves, was the cause of my last address to you.

As the design however has not been accomplished; and it is necessary both for your information, and for my satisfaction and government that something decisive should be resolved on, I will, in one word, fix my ultimatum with respect to the negroes proposed for sale. Which is to allow you three hundred pounds for young Bob (or another fellow of his age and appearance), Tom the baker. Nessey, David, James and Valentine; but this I do on the proviso that they answer your description in their ages, sizes and qualities; for unless the two last named boys are of sufficient size to be put to trades, they would not answer my purpose; because the persons with whom I should place them are Servants in this family whose terms will expire in less than three years. In making you this offer I have exceeded by at least 25 pr. Ct. the ready money prices which have been reported to me. That you may have given more I by no means question, but possibly your purchases were on credit, or probably the prices have since fallen. My information of the present selling prices is from very well informed characters.

With respect to the corn, it is perfectly agreeable to me, that you should sell it to any person you please, and instead of ten, I wish you may be able to get fifteen shillings pr. barrl. for it. But as Mr. Petit is a gentleman with whom I have no acquaintance, I shall not look to him for the purchase money; I do not wish however to deprive you of the price he offers, by making it a ready money sale to him, altho' it would have been so to me. I am also perfectly willing to allow whatever is due on my Bond (with interest thereon) which passed to Messrs. Blair and McCoul, provided that Bond is got in; but you would not I am persuaded request me to allow this sum on one accot., and be exposed to the claim of it from another quarter.

When I agreed to take two thousand pounds of Certificates, it was my intention, and still is that it shall comprehend every [thing] which relates to this species of property. And you may be assured, Sir, that in whatever light this matter from first to last may have appeared to you, I distress myself exceedingly by these accommodations; because nothing but the money, and that in a lump, would have answered any valuable purposes of mine, for by receiving this debt in driblets, I am actually sinking one sum, without discharging those debts of my own which press upon me and which are accumulating by a heavier interest than I receive. I do not mean however to go over this ground again. I am willing to abide by the propositions now made, and wish to be explicitly resolved on them, because if they are acceded to, I shall endeavour to raise money by the sale of some part of my property, for the purposes alluded to, and do not expect I shall have less difficulty, or sustain less loss in the accomplishment of it than others. I will enquire of Mr. Lund Washington about the Bond you speak of, and am, etc.[23]

---

[23] From the "Letter Book" copy in the *Washington Papers.*

*To LEVIN POWELL

Mount Vernon, December 21,1786.

Dear Sir: Your favor of the 18th. came to hand last night. I by no means wish you to put yourself to the smallest inconvenience in hastening the Buck Wheat down. If you have it *secured,* so as that I may rely upon it, in due Season, it is all I want. The disappointments I sustained last year, in Seeds that were expected, made me anxious to obtain, long before Seed time, all I should want; because having them in hand I hazarded nothing.

I will thank you for the information promised, respecting this Grain when the other load is sent. which I again desire may not be till it suits your convenience. With great esteem etc.[24]

To GOVERNOR EDMUND RANDOLPH

Mount Vernon, December 21, 1786.

Sir: I had not the honor of receiving your Excellency's favor of the 6th, with its enclosures,[25] till last night. Sensible as I am of the honor conferred on me by the General Assembly, in appointing me one of the Deputies[26] to a Convention proposed to

[24] From a photostat of the original kindly furnished by Lieut. Colo. F. W. Manley, United States Army.

[25] Sparks prints the following extract from Randolph's reply to Washington's letter, but the letter itself (Jan. 4, 1787) is not now found in the *Washington Papers:* "Although compelled, by duty to lay before the Council your answer to my notification of your appointment to Philadelphia, I was happy to find them concurring with me in the propriety of entreating you not to decide on a refusal immediately. Perhaps the obstacles now in view may be removed before May; and the nomination of a successor, if necessary at all, will be as effectually made some time hence as now. Perhaps too (and indeed I fear the event) every other consideration may seem of little weight, when compared with the crisis, which may then hang over the United States. I hope, therefore, that you will excuse me for holding up your letter for the present, and waiting until time shall discover the result of the commotions now prevailing."

[26] The other deputies were Patrick Henry, Edmund Randolph, John Blair, James Madison, George Mason, and George Wythe. Henry did not attend and James M'Clurg was appointed in his place.

be held in the City of Philadelphia in May next, for the purpose of revising the Fœderal Constitution; and desirous as I am on all occasions, of testifying a ready obedience to the calls of my Country; yet, Sir, there exists at this moment, circumstances, which I am persuaded will render my acceptance of this fresh mark of confidence incompatible with other measures which I had previously adopted; and from which, seeing little prospect of disengaging myself, it would be disengenuous not to express a wish that some other character, on whom greater reliance can be had, may be substituted in my place; the probability of my non-attendance being too great to continue my appointment.

As no mind can be more deeply impressed than mine is with the awful situation of our affairs; resulting in a great measure from the want of efficient powers in the fœderal head, and due respect to its Ordinances, so, consequently, those who do engage in the important business of removing these defects, will carry with them every good wish of mine which the best dispositions towards the attainment can bestow. I have the honr. etc.   [H.S.P.]

*To GOVERNOR EDMUND RANDOLPH

Mount Vernon, December 25, 1786.

Sir: To promote industry and œconomy, and to encourage manufactures, is certainly consistent with that sound policy which ought to actuate every State. There are times too, which call loudly for the exercise of these virtues; and the present, in my humble opinion, may be accounted a fit one for the adoption of them in this Commonwealth.

How far the proposition which I have the honor to enclose merits Legislative encouragement, your Excellency will determine. As it came to me, you will receive it. The writer is unknown to me; of him, or his plan, I had not the smallest intimation till the papers were handed to me from the Post Office. The document in the hand writing of Mr. Jefferson (with which it is accompanied) entitles the latter to consideration, but as an individual it is not convenient for me to afford Mr. de la Vallee the aids he requires, or to have him upon my hands till he can be properly established; nor indeed is Alexandria, in my opinion, so proper a situation as a more southern one for the Manufacture of Cotton. However, if your Excellency should think his plan not worthy of public attention, or judgg. otherwise, it should not find encouragement from the Assembly, I would thank you for returning the letter and papers to me, that I may give Mr. de la Vallee an answer as soon as possible; his circumstances seeming to require one. With sentiments of grt. esteem etc.   [H. S. P.]

*To HENRY KNOX

Mount Vernon, December 26, 1786.

My dear Sir: Nothing but the pleasing hope of seeing you under this roof in the course of last month, and wch. I was disposed to extend even to the present moment, has kept me till this time from acknowledging the receipt of your obliging favor of the 23d of October. Despairing now of that pleasure, I shall thank you for the above letter, and the subsequent one of the 17th. instt., which came to hand yesterday evening.

Lamentable as the conduct of the Insurgents of Massachusetts is, I am exceedingly obliged to you for the advices respecting

---

On December 23 Washington wrote briefly to De la Dalle, that his "letter, Plan and Estimate for establishing a manufacture of cotton &ca." had been sent to the Governor to be laid before the assembly, "if he shall think proper." A copy of this letter is in the "Letter Book" in the *Washington Papers*.

them; and pray you, most ardently, to continue the acct. of their proceedings; because I can depend upon them from you without having my mind bewildered with those vague and contradictory reports which are handed to us in Newspapers, and which please one hour, only to make the moments of the next more bitter. I feel, my dear Genl. Knox, infinitely more than I can express to you, for the disorders which have arisen in these States. Good God! who besides a tory could have foreseen, or a Briton predicted them! were these people wiser than others, or did they judge of us from the corruption, and depravity of their own hearts? The latter I am persuaded was the case, and that notwithstanding the boasted virtue of America, we are far gone in every thing ignoble and bad.

I do assure you, that even at this moment, when I reflect on the present posture of our affairs, it seems to me to be like the vision of a dream. My mind does not know how to realize it, as a thing in actual existence, so strange, so wonderful does it appear to me! In this, as in most other matter, we are too slow. When this spirit first dawned, probably it might easily have been checked; but it is scarcely within the reach of human ken, at this moment, to say when, where, or how it will end. There are combustibles in every State, which a spark might set fire to. In this State, a perfect calm prevails at present, and a prompt disposition to support, and give energy to the fœderal System is discovered, if the unlucky stirring of the dispute respecting the navigation of the Mississippi does not become a leaven that will ferment, and sour the mind of it.

The resolutions of the prest. Session respecting a paper emission, military certificates, &ca., have stamped justice and liberality on the proceedings of the Assembly, and By a late act, *it* seems very desirous of a General Convention to revise and amend the fœderal Constitution. Apropos, what prevented

the Eastern States from attending the September meeting at
Annapolis? Of all the States in the Union it should have
seemed to me, that a measure of this sort (distracted as they
were with internal commotions, and experiencing the want of
energy in the government) would have been most pleasing to
them. What are the prevailing sentiments of the one now proposed to be held at Philadelphia, in May next? and how will
it be attended? You are at the fountain of intelligence, and
where the wisdom of the Nation, it is to be presumed, has con-
centered; consequently better able (as I have had abundant
experience of your intelligence, confidence, and candour to
solve these questions.

The Maryland Assembly has been violently agitated by the
question for a paper emission. It has been carried in the House
of Delegates, but what has, or will be done with the Bill in the
Senate I have not yet heard. The partisans in favor of the measure in the lower House, threaten, it is said, a secession if it is
rejected by that Branch of the Legislature. Thus are we advancing. In regretting, which I have often done with the
deepest sorrow, the death of our much lamented frd. General
Greene, I have accompanied it of late with a quære, whether he
would not have prefered such an exit to the scenes which it
is more than probable many of his compatriots may live to
bemoan.

In both your letters you intimate, that the men of reflection,
principle and property in New England, feeling the inefficacy
of their present government, are contemplating a change; but
you are not explicit with respect to the nature of it. It has been
supposed, that, the Constitution of the State of Massachusetts
was amongst the most energetic in the Union; May not these
disorders then be ascribed to an endulgent exercise of the powers of Administration? If your laws authorized, and your

powers were adequate to the suppression of these tumults, in the first appearances of them, delay and temporizing expedients were, in my opinion improper; these are rarely well applied, and the same causes would produce similar effects in any form of government, if the powers of it are not enforced. I ask this question for information, I know nothing of the facts.

That G. B will be an unconcerned Spectator of the present insurrections (if they continue) is not to be expected. That she is at this moment sowing the Seeds of jealousy and discontent among the various tribes of Indians on our frontier admits of no doubt, in my mind. And that she will improve every opportunity to foment the spirit of turbulence within the bowels of the United States, with a view of distracting our governments, and promoting divisions, is, with me, not less certain. Her first Manœuvres will, no doubt, be covert, and may remain so till the period shall arrive when a decided line of conduct may avail her. Charges of violating the treaty, and other pretexts, will not then be wanting to colour overt acts, tending to effect the grt. objects of which she has long been in labour. A Man is now at the head of their American Affairs[27] well calculated to conduct measures of this kind, and more than probably was selected for the purpose. We ought not therefore to sleep nor to slumber. Vigilance in watching, and vigour in acting, is, in my opinion, become indispensably necessary. If the powers are inadequate amend or alter them, but do not let us sink into the lowest state of humiliation and contempt, and become a by-word in all the earth. I think with you that the Spring will unfold important and distressing Scenes, unless much wisdom and good management is displayed in the interim. Adieu; be assured no man has a higher esteem and regard for you than I have; none more sincerely your friend, and more Affecte. etc.

---

[27] Foreign Secretary Francis Osborne, Fifth Duke of Leeds.

P. S. Mrs. Washington joins me in every good wish for you and Mrs. Knox, and in congratulatory Compts. on the late addition to your family. Will you be so obliging as to give the enclosed a safe conveyance. I have recd. one or two very obliging letters from Genl. Tupper[28] whilst he was in the Western Country and wish to thank him for them; but know not in what part of Massachusetts he lives.   [MS.H.S.]

To DAVID HUMPHREYS

Mount Vernon, December 26, 1786.

Mr Dr. Humphreys: I am much indebted to you for your several favors of the 1st. 9th. and 16th. of Novr. the last came first. Mr. Morse, having in mind the old proverb, was determined not to make more haste than good speed in prosecuting his journey to Georgia, so I got the two first lately.

For your publication respecting the treatment of Captn. Asgill,[29] I am exceedingly obliged to you. The manner of making it is the best that cou'd be devised; whilst the matter will prove the illiberality, as well as the fallacy of the reports which have been circulated on that occasion, and which are fathered upon that officer as the author.

It is with the deepest and most heartfelt concern, I perceive by some late paragraphs extracted from the Boston papers, that the Insurgents of Massachusetts, far from being satisfied with the redress offered by their general Court, are still acting in open violation of law and government, and have obliged the chief Magistrate in a decided tone to call upon the Militia of the State to support the Constitution. What, gracious God, is

---

[28] Benjamin Tupper.
[29] Humphreys's publication of the Asgill case was printed in the *Columbia Magazine*, January and February, 1787, pp. 205–9, 233–35. It was reprinted by The Holland Club, New York, in 1859.

man! that there should be such inconsistency and perfidious-ness in his conduct? It is but the other day, that we were shedding our blood to obtain the Constitutions under which we now live; Constitutions of our own choice and making; and now we are unsheathing the sword to overturn them. The thing is so unaccountable, that I hardly know how to realize it, or to persuade myself that I am not under the illusion of a dream.

My mind, previous to the receipt of your letter of the 1st. ulto., had often been agitated by a thought similar to the one you have expressed respecting an old friend[30] of your's; but Heaven forbid that a crisis should come when he shall be driven to the necessity of making choice of either of the alternatives there mentioned.[31] Let me entreat you, my dr. Sir, to keep me advised of the situation of affairs in your quarter. I can depend upon your accounts. Newspaper paragraphs un-supported by other testimony, are often contradictory and bewildering. At one time these insurgents are spoken of as a mere mob; at other times as systematic in all their proceedings. If the first, I would fain hope that like other Mobs it will, how-ever formidable, be of short duration. If the latter there are surely men of consequence and abilities behind the curtain who move the puppets; the designs of whom may be deep and dangerous. They may be instigated by British counsel; actu-ated by ambitious motives, or being influenced by dishonest principles, had rather see the Country in the horror of civil discord, than do what justice would dictate to an honest mind.

---

[30] Washington.

[31] Humphreys had written (Nov. 1, 1786): "In case of civil discord, I have already told you, it was seriously my opinion, that you could not remain neuter, and that you would be obliged in self defense to take part on one side or the other: or withdraw from the Continent. Your friends are of the same opinion; and I believe you are convinced, it is impossible to have more disinterested and zealous friends than those who have been about your person." Humphreys's letter is in the *Washington Papers*.

I had scarcely despatched my circular letters to the several State Societies of the Cincinnati, when I received letters from some of the principal members of our Assembly expressing a wish that they might be permitted to name me as one of the Deputies of this State to the Convention proposed to be held at Philadelphia the first of May next. I immediately wrote to my particular friend Mr. Madison (and gave similar reasons to the others) the answer is contained in the extract No. 1; in reply I got the extract No. 2. This obliged me to be more explicit and confidential with him on points which a recurrence to the conversations we have had on this subject will bring to your mind and save me the hazard of a recital in this letter. Since this interchange of letters I have received from the Governor the letter No. 4 and have written No. 5 in answer to it. Should this matter be further pressed, (which I hope it will not, as I have no inclination to go) what had I best do? You as an indifferent person, and one who is much better acquainted with the sentiments and views of the Cincinnati than I am; (for in this State where the recommendations of the General Meeting have been agreed to hardly any thing is said about it) as also with the temper of the people and state of politics at large, can determine upon better ground and fuller evidence than myself; especially as you have opportunities of knowing in what light the States to the Eastward consider the Convention, and the measures they are pursuing to contravene, or to give efficiency to it.

On the last occasion,[32] only five States were represented; none East of New York. Why the Nw. England Governments did not appear, I am yet to learn; for of all others the distractions and turbulent temper of these people would, I should have thought, have afforded the strongest evidence of the *necessity*

---

[32] The Annapolis Convention.

of competent powers somewhere. That the Fœderal Government is nearly, if not quite at a stand, none will deny. The first question then is, shall it be annihilated or supported? If the latter, the proposed convention is an object of the first magnitude, and should be supported by all the friends of the present Constitution. In the other case, if on a full and dispassionate revision thereof, the continuance shall be adjudged impracticable or unwise, as only delaying an event which must 'ere long take place; would it not be better for such a Meeting to suggest some other, to avoid if possible civil discord or other impending evils? I must candidly confess, as we could not remain quiet more than three or four years in time of peace, under the Constitutions of our own choosing; which it was believed, in many States at least, were formed with deliberation and wisdom, I see little prospect either of our agreeing upon any other, or that we should remain long satisfied under it if we could. Yet I would wish any thing, and every thing essayed to prevent the effusion of blood, and to avert the humiliating and contemptible figure we are about to make in the annals of mankind.

If this second attempt to convene the States for the purposes proposed by the report of the partial representation at Annapolis in September, should also prove abortive, it may be considered as an unequivocal evidence that the States are not likely to agree on any general measure which is to pervade the Union, and of course that there is an end of Fœderal Government. The States therefore which make the last dying essay to avoid these misfortunes, would be mortified at the issue, and their deputies would return home chagrined at their ill success and disappointment. This would be a disagreeable circumstance for any one of them to be in, but more particularly so for a person in my situation. If no further application is made to me, of course I do not attend; if there is, I am under no obligation to do it, but as I have had so many proofs of your friendship, know your abilities to judge, and your opportunities of learning the politics of the day, on the points I have enumerated, you would oblige me by a full and confidential communication of your sentiments thereon.

Peace and tranquillity prevail in this State. the Assembly by a very great majority, and in very emphatical terms, have rejected an application for paper money, and spurned the idea of fixing the value of military Certificates by a scale of depreciation. In some other respects too the proceedings of the present Session have been marked with justice and a strong desire of supporting the fœderal system. Altho' I lament the effect, I am pleased at the cause which has deprived us of the pleasure of your aid in the attack of Christmas pies: we had one yesterday on which all the company, tho' pretty numerous, were hardly able to make an impression. Mrs. Washington and George and his wife (Mr. Lear I had occasion to send to the Western Country) join in affectione. regards for you, and with sentiments, &c.[33]

To THOMAS JOHNSON

Mount Vernon, December 28, 1786.

Dr. Sir: It gave me pleasure to find by your letter of the 7th. that the petition of the Directors of the Potomac Company had met so ready and favorable a reception in the Assembly of Maryland. I am informed that an act similar to the one you sent me has passed the Legislature of this State, but I have received no official advice of it.

Permit me, my good Sir, to ask if there would be a probability of your Assembly's (if the matter should be laid before it) doing anything to good effect in the case stated in the

---

[33] From the "Letter Book" copy in the *Washington Papers*.

enclosed letter from Mr. Wilson to me. I am one of the Executors, indeed the only surviving one, of Colo. Thomas Colvill; and am exceedingly anxious to have the administration of that Estate closed. I know nothing of the facts mentioned in Mr. Wilson's letter respecting the confiscations, sales, and the motives which led to them, in the instance alluded to, but would be thankful for your opinion and advice thereon.

Mr. Brindley[34] promised me by letter in Octor. that he would call upon me in his way to So. Carolina, but I have not seen or heard from him since the date of his letter We ought undoubtedly to avail ourselves of all the aids we can derive from experimental knowledge in our reach. I concur readily therefore in sentiment with you and Mr. Lee that it would be proper to see what lights Mr. Brindley can afford us in conducting the navigation thro' the little Falls, and the idea of a model for the Locks at the great Falls, I think good for the reasons you offer, the expence will be trifling and the saving may be great.

The lesson you seem fearful of learning will most assuredly be taught us. The strides we have already taken, and are now making, to corruption are inconceivably great; and I shall be exceedingly, but very agreeably disappointed if next Spring does not display scenes which will astonish the world. Nothing, I am certain, but the wisest councils and the most vigorous exertions can avert them.

With sentiments of very great esteem etc.[35]

To GEORGE DIGGES

Mount Vernon, December 28, 1786.

Dr. Sir: Will you allow me to give you the trouble of enquiring among your friends of the Eastern shore, now at Annapolis,

---

[34] James Brindley, son or nephew of the builder of the Bridgewater Canal.
[35] From the "Letter Book" copy in the *Washington Papers*.

if I could be furnished with one thousand feet of the best pine plank, precisely 24 feet long when dressed, to be without knots or sap. It is for the floor of my new room. Many years ago I provided for this, and thought myself secure of that which was perfectly seasoned. It had been dressed and laid by; but when I was about to make use of it, behold! two thirds of it was stolen, and the other 1/3 will match no plank I can now get.

I do not expect to get seasoned plank of this description; but on whom I cou'd depend for the length and quality, I would wish to know, for if I cannot be supplied with certainty, I shall immediately write to Norfolk. I would thank you for an answer by the Post. I am, etc.[36]

To THEODORICK BLAND

Mount Vernon, December 28, 1786.

Dr. Sir: I am now about to fulfill my promise with respect to the Drill plough and Timothy seed; both accompany this letter to Norfolk, to the care of Mr. Newton. The latter I persume is good, as I had it from a Gentleman (Colo. Levin Powell) on whom I can depend. The former, it is scarcely necessary to inform you, will not work to good effect in Land that is very full either of stumps, stones or large clods; but where the ground is tolerable free from these and in good tilth, and particularly in light land, I am certain you will find it equal to your most sanguine expectation for Indian Corn, wheat, Barley, Pease or any other tolerably round grain that you may wish to sow, or plant in this manner. I have sowed Oats very well with it, which is among the most inconvenient and unfit grains for this machine.

To give you a just idea of the use and management of it, I must observe, that the barrel at present has only one set of

---

[36] From the "Letter Book" copy in the *Washington Papers*.

holes, and those adapted for the planting of Indian Corn only eight inches apart in the row: but by corking these, the same barrel may receive others of a size fitted for any other grain. To make the holes, observe this rule, begin small and encrease the size 'till they emit the number of grains, or thereabouts, you would chuse to deposit in a place. They should be burnt, done by a gage, (that all may be of a size) and made widest on the out side to prevent the seeds choking them. You may, in a degree, emit more or less through the same holes, by encreasing or lessening the quantity of seed in the barrel. The less there is in it, the faster it issues. The compressure is encreased by the quantity and the discharge is retarded thereby. The use of the band is to prevent the seeds issuing out of more holes than one at a time. It may be slackened or braced according to the influence the atmosphere has on the leather: the tighter it is, provided the wheels revolve easily, the better. By decreasing or multiplying the holes in the barrel, you may plant at any distance you please. The circumference of the wheels being six feet or 72 inches, divide the latter by the number of inches you intend your plants shall be asunder, and it gives the number of holes required in the barrel.

The sparse situation of the teeth in the harrow, is designed that the ground may be raked without the harrow being clogged, if the ground should be clody or grassy. The string, when this happens is to be the case, will raise and clear it with great ease, and is of service in turning at the ends of rows; at which time the wheels, by means of the handles, are raised off the ground as well as the harrow to prevent the waste of seed. A small bag, containing about a peck of the seed you are sowing, is hung to the nails on the right handle, and with a small tin cup the barrel is replenished with convenience whenever it is necessary without loss of time, or waiting to come up with the seed bag at the end of the row. I had almost forgot to tell you, that if the hole in the leather band (thro' which the seed is to pass when it comes in contact with the hole in the barrel) should incline to gape, or the lips of it turn out, so as to admit the seed between the band and barrel, it is easily, [*sic*] and must be remedied by rivitting a piece of sheet tin, copper, or brass the width of the band, and about four inches long with a hole through it the size of the one in the leather, I found this effectual. Mrs. Washington joins me in presenting the compliments of the season to Mrs. Bland and yourself, and with great esteem, etc.[37]

To JOHN ARMISTEAD

Mount Vernon, December 29, 1786.

Sir: Many months having elapsed since I informed you in explicit terms of my want of the money which is due to me from the Estate of your deceased Father, without having received any acknowledgment of the letter, I presume it has miscarried. To avoid the like accident, I have taken the liberty of putting this letter under cover to Mr. Holmes, at the Bowling-green, who I persuade myself, will do me the favor of seeing that it gets safe to your hands.

It will serve to assure you, Sir, that I was disposed to hope, considering the long standing and nature of the debt, that you would not have laid me under the necessity of so often reminding you of it, and at length to inform you that however disagreeable it will be to me, I must have recourse to a Court of Justice if the money is not paid me without more delay; for you may believe me when I assure you I am really in want of it. I am, etc.[37]

---

[37] From the "Letter Book" copy in the *Washington Papers*.

To GEORGE WEEDON

Mount Vernon, December 29, 1786.

Dear Sir: I have been favored with your official letter of the ulto. in answer to my circular one of the 31st. October; but will you permit me, in a private and friendly manner, to ask if my letter or a copy of it has been sent to the Vice President, General Gates? You would have perceived that that letter was intended to have met him in the double capacity of President of the State Society, and Vice President of the Genl. Meeting. In the former case, as he did not attend the State Meeting in Richmond, it was unnecessary that he should be furnished with a copy of it; but as Vice President he ought to be made acquainted with my intention of not attending the latter, the reason therefore of this enquiry is, that if it has not been [done] by the State Society, I may do it from hence.

I should be glad to know the names of the Delegates from this State to the general Meeting to be held in May next at Philada.

I shall be ready at all times between this and the appointment of my Successor,[38] to sign any Diplomas which may be presented to me; but it will readily occur to you that after this event takes place my powers wou'd cease, and the signature would be invalid. With great esteem, etc.[39]

To WILLIAM HULL

Mount Vernon, December 29, 1786.

Dear Sir: I informed you in my last, that my own knowledge of the Western Country was rather general than otherwise, but promised to lose no opportunity of collecting every

---

[38] Washington was president of the Society of the Cincinnati until he died.
[39] From the "Letter Book" copy in the *Washington Papers*.

information which I thought might facilitate your intended settlement. Since which time I have had occasion to send Mr. Lear out as far as Pittsburg to transact some business for me in that quarter; I directed him to make such enquiries and to gain such information respecting the points touched upon in your letter as would enable me to answer it with more precision than my own knowledge would permit me to do. He has just returned, and I take the earliest opportunity of conveying to you such information as I hope will be satisfactory.

Cattle of every kind may be purchased in the neighbourhood of Pittsburg very reasonably and in any numbers. Iron castings, bar iron &c. may be bought there, and perhaps cheaper than they can be carried out by families that are removing. The prices of the following articles at and near Pittsburgh, will enable you to determine whether it wou'd be best to carry them out or purchase them there.

Cows (The Cows are not so large nor so good as those in Nw. England) £4 d £4:10. Pennsa: Cury.; Sheep 16/; Hogs 18/ Cwt; Beeves 25/ Cwt; Corn 2/6 d 2/8 pr. bushl; Wheat 3/6. d 4 Do; Flour 15/ Cwt; Salt 20/ and 25/ pr. bushl; Iron Castings 1/ pr lb; Bar iron 8d do; Wrought do 2/ do; Whiskey 3/ pr. gallon; Dry goods 40 pr. Ct. from their cost at Philada.

There is no furnace in the western Country, the nearest to those parts is on the Potomac, sixty miles below Fort Cumberland. Salt may be purchased at Kentucky cheaper than at Pittsburgh, as they have salt Springs in that Country from which they can supply themselves with that article.

You desired my advice respecting the best mode of effecting your plan; but as you did not point out to me the part of the Country where the settlement is intended to be made; I can only give you my opinion as to the best plan of getting over the Alleghany mountains to the Western waters.

I should think it would be well (if the Settlers intend going out in large bodies) to send some person into that Country to make proper arrangements previous to their going; such as to procure Cattle and provisions, provide boats to go down the River &c. The familes could come to Alexandria by water: from thence to Fort Cumberland which is 150 miles there is a good waggon road. From the latter place it would be best to pursue Braddocks road (which is well settled and has good accomodations upon it) to Red Stone 75 miles from Cumberland, where boats are built for the purpose of going down the Ohio, and which is the general rendezvous for people going into the Western Country. These Boats are flat, very large and capable of carrying forty or fifty Tons: they cost from twenty to thirty pounds Pennsylvania currency, according to their size. They generally stop at Pittsburgh in their way down, to procure any Articles they may have occasion for: or boats may be procured at that place which is 50 miles from Red Stone old Fort, and the people can embark there. I am, etc.[40]

To PIERRE CHARLES L'ENFANT

Mount Vernon, January 1, 1787.

Sir: The Letter which you did me the honor of writing to me the 6th. ulto. together with the Memorial which accompanied it[41] came safe, after some delay.

Without entering into the merits of the latter, which I could only do as an individual, I shall regret that your zeal for the honor, and your wishes to advance what you conceived to be the interests of the Society of the Cincinnati, should have led you into difficulties which are attended with such embarrassing

---

[40] From the "Letter Book" copy in the *Washington Papers*.
[41] In the Society of the Cincinnati Deposit in the Library of Congress.

circumstances, and from which none but the general Meeting (to be held at Philada. in May next) can afford you relief. It shall be my care to hand the Memorial to that body for consideration.

In the meantime, if my resources were adequate, it would afford me much pleasure to advance the sum for which you are engaged; but altho' there is no legal obligation upon me to disclose the state of my own finances, and in prudence it might perhaps be better to avoid it; yet Sir, as a testimony of my disposition to serve you if I had the means, I will assure you that what with the losses I sustained during the war, in having, almost without exception the monies which were due to me paid in at a depreciated value, (some at less than 6d. in the pound), my own Debts now to pay at their intrinsic value, with interest thereon, and other circumstances which are unnecessary to enumerate, I find it exceedingly difficult, without the weight of extraneous matters, to make my funds and expenditures accord with each other.

I can only repeat to you the pleasure I should have had, and shall have in seeing you at this seat of my retirement, if circumstances had permitted, or would permit you to visit it, and the assurances of esteem with which, I am, etc.

P. S. Not knowing that the picture mentioned in the postscript to your letter had been sent to this Country; I wrote to the Gentn. who did me the honor of offering it (as soon as I received his letter) declining the acceptance, under conviction that it would not have justice done it in any situation I could place it in my house. Since it is arrived I am at a loss what further to say on the subject, as my letter has long since been dispatched, and if I recollect rightly was addressed to your care. Perhaps it would be best now to await a reply.[42]

---

[42] From the "Letter Book" copy in the *Washington Papers*.

To DOCTOR JOHN LEIGH

Mount Vernon, January 9, 1787.

Sir: I received your letter of the 30th. of October, together with your Dissertation on opium. You will please Sir, to accept my thanks for the honor which you did me in the dedication of your work. Altho' I am not desireous of compliments of this kind, and have put off several applications which have been made to dedicate literary productions to me, yet I should always wish to encourage every useful and beneficial performance as much as is in my power. I am, etc.[43]

To JABEZ BOWEN

Mount Vernon, January 9, 1787.[44]

Dear Sir: I have received your letter of the 23d. of Novr. I should have been happy to have seen you at Mount Vernon agreeable to your intention had you proceeded as far as Annapolis. The Convention at that place would undoubtedly have been productive of some benefit to the Union had it taken place, but the tardiness of the Commissioners from several States rendered abortive every advantage that was expected from it. It is surprising to me that a due punctuality cannot be observed in meetings of this nature, the time is fixed and known, and every Gentleman when he accepts the appointment should consider the business of the meeting as depending upon him, and should determine not to retard its proceedings by a want of punctuality in his Attendance; it is a public duty to which every private consideration should give way.

I have been long since fully convinced of the necessity of Granting to Congress more ample and extensive powers than

[43] From the "Letter Book" copy in the *Washington Papers*.
[44] Entered in the "Letter Book" as 1789.

they at present possess; the want of power and energy in that Body has been severely felt in every part of the United States. The disturbances in new England, The declining state of our Commerce, and the general languor which seems to pervade the Union are in a great measure (if not entirely) owing to the want of proper Authority in the supreme Council. The extreme jealousy that is observed in vesting Congress with adequate powers has a tendency rather to destroy than confirm our liberty's the wisest resolutions cannot produce any good unless they are supported with energy, they are only applauded, but never followed.

Paper money has had the effect in your State that it ever will have, to ruin commerce, oppress the honest, and open a door to every species of fraud and injustice.

I am entirely in sentiment with you Sir, of the necessity there is to adopt some measures for the support of our national peace and honor, the present situation of our public affairs demands the exertion and influence of every good and honest Citizen in the Union, to tranquilize disturbances, retrieve our Credit and place us upon a respectable footing with other Nations.

The Death of our worthy friend General Greene must be sincerly regretted by every friend to America, and peculiarly by those whose intimacy with him gave them a full knowledge of his Virtues and merits. I am etc.[45]

To CHARLES WILLSON PEALE

Mount Vernon, January 9, 1787.

Sir: Your letter of the 31st. of Decemr. came duly to hand. I cannot say that I shall be happy to have it in my power to comply with your request by sending you the bodies of my

---

[45] From the "Letter Book" copy in the *Washington Papers*.

Pheasants; but I am afraid it will not be long before they will compose a part of your Museum, as they all appear to be drooping. One of the Silver Pheasants died sometime before the receipt of your letter, and its body was thrown away, but whenever any of the others make their exit they shall be sent to you agreeably to your request. I am etc.[46]

To SEDDON & COMPANY[47]

Mount Vernon, January 9, 1787.

Gentn: I have received the 10th. of your letter of Decemr. together with the several numbers of the Columbian Magazine. I thank you for your attention to me in sending the several numbers which have been published, and wish you to consider me a subscriber; as I conceive a publication of that kind may be the means of conveying much useful knowledge to the community which might otherwise be lost, and when it is properly conducted, it should, in my opinion be properly encouraged. I am, etc.[48]

*To DANIEL CARROLL

Mount Vernon, January 9, 1787.

Sir: [Your letter of the 26th. Ult. did not reach me till within these 3 days, or it should have received an earlier acknowledgment.

The land I advertised for Sale in Fayette County containing 1650 acres or thereabouts, by the Patents, may, as a tract, be considered as equal to any in the County, or Country; but as it

---

[46] In the writing of Tobias Lear. From a photostat of the original kindly furnished by Judge E. A. Armstrong, of Princeton, N. J.
[47] Consisted of T. Seddon, W. Spotswood, C. Cist, J. Trenchard, and others, in Philadelphia, Pa.
[48] From the "Letter Book" copy in the *Washington Papers*.

is my wish that the purchaser should examine it, I will say no more than that there is an appearance of a rich Iron Ore at the door of the Mill, which is now much out of repair.

Small tracts of land in the vicinity of this, of the same quality have sold for three pounds and upwards Pensa. Curry. an Acre. But if one person will take the whole of mine, I would let it go for Forty shillings that money an Acre (payable in Specie) one fourth down, the other three fourths in annual payments, with interest from] the date of the Bonds; perhaps a longer time might be allowed.[49]

To BUSHROD WASHINGTON

Mount Vernon, January 10, 1787.

My Dear Bushrod: I condole most sincerely with you, my Sister and family, on the death of my Brother.[50] I feel most sensibly for this event; but resignation being our duty, to attempt an expression of my sorrow on this occasion would be as feebly described, as it would be unavailing when related.

If there are any occasional services which I can render my Sister[51] or any of you, I shall have great pleasure in the execution. If I could discharge the duties of an Executor, I would undertake the trust most chearfully; but in truth I am not in a situation to do this. Already I am so much involved in, and so perplexed with other peoples affairs, that my own are very much unattended to. Happily, there is not the least occasion of my assistance in the administration of your deceased Father's Estate. Your competency *alone* is sufficient for this purpose, when joined by that of my Sister and your brother, the task

---

[49] From a facsimile in a sales catalogue, 1920. The portion in brackets is from the "Letter Book" copy in the *Washington Papers.*
[50] John Augustine Washington.
[51] Hannah Bushrod Washington.

will be easy. It may be an alleviating circumstance of my brother's death, that his affairs fall into such good hands, and that each of you have dispositions and capability to do what is proper.

I hope this letter will find my Sister in a better situation than when your's left her. Every good wish of this family is offered for it, and the sincerest regard for you all. With unfeigned Affection I am, etc.

P. S. Mr. Lear is returned from the Western Country. In consequence of my request to Majr. Freeman, to advance Mr. Smith's fees for the Suit depending on accot. of your Lands in Fayette Coty., he had sent me the enclosed, which I forward that you may know how that matter stands.[52]

To CHARLES CARTER

Mount Vernon, January 10, 1787.

Dear Sir: I should have presented you with an earlier acknowledgement of your favor of the 4th. ulto., but expecting to meet the Directors of the Potomac Company, I delayed writing 'till it was over, that I might give you the trouble of receiving one letter *only,* in answer to the several parts of it.

Having laid before the Directors that part of your letter which respects the opinions of Mr. Yates and Captn. Harris on inland navigations unincumbered with Locks, I am authorized to say that any information on this head from Captain Harris, containing the principles of the substitutes for Locks, by which so considerable a saving as you speak of can be made, would be most thankfully received; and if upon the investigation or practice on them, they shall be found of such œconomy and utility as is mentioned, the Board would cheerfully give a

---

[52] From the "Letter Book" copy in the *Washington Papers.*

further proof of their sense of the obligation they would feel themselves under for such important advice.

When you shall have received Mr. Yates's observations on the comparison of the Orchard and New River grasses, I shall be obliged to you for a transcript of them, as I am persuaded they have been made with attention, accuracy and judgment. I have never seen, nor do I remember ever to have read or heard of any grass, denominated Egyptian grass. Whence comes it? From the Country of that name? If so, may it not in fact be our Blue grass, not yet perfectly assimilated by the Climate and soil of this meridian?

I am much obliged by the offer of your farm for the accommodation of my lately arrived Jack Ass; (which I think an exceeding fine one) but as he is too young to cover, being only two years old, and females came along with him, the same attendance does for all of them. And besides as they seem (if I was to form an opinion of the two Jacks from present appearances) to be designed for as different purposes as a Courser and Dray, there will be no propriety in separating them hereafter. The one will suit the strong heavy draft, and the other the light and active one for the road.

I pray you to offer my best respects to Mrs. Carter, in which Mrs. Washington unites. I am, etc.[53]

To PRICE POSEY

Mount Vernon, January 12, 1787.

Sir: It will not be difficult for you to conceive my surprise when I inform you that after waiting near three years since my return home in expectation that an account would be rendered me of the management of my Estate below; and calling, with

---

[53] From the "Letter Book" copy in the *Washington Papers.*

some degree of astonishment, on Mr. Hill for this neglect, to find by his answer lately received, that the accounts had been settled years ago with you, and not only the produce of that Estate paid into your hands, but that other considerable sums of money which he had collected for me from Mr. Newton of Norfolk, for Flour, Fish &c. sent him from my Estate in this County to dispose of on commission had gone this way also.

If it had been inconvenient for you to have delivered me my money, would it not have been right to have given me the accot. and to have informed me of the circumstances which had occasioned the detention of it? Strange and unaccountable as this conduct is, I shall for the present (as I am entirely in the dark with respect to this business) content myself with requesting that the accounts and papers which were put into your hands for my use by Mr. Hill, may be returned either to him or me, with a statement of any transactions of your own on my account, previously or subsequent thereto, that I may know how to come to a final settlement with Mr. Hill.

This request, I expect will meet no denial or delay: reason, Justice and every other consideration call upon you for a compliance therewith. I am, etc.[54]

To JAMES HILL

Mount Vernon, January 12, 1787.

Sir: Your Letter of the 24th. of September in answer to mine of the 20th. of August was a long time in getting to my hands, and very unsatisfactory when it arrived. If you were ever directed by me to settle your accounts with, and pay the produce of my Estate under your management into the hands of Mr. Posey, I should be glad to receive a copy of the order. My memory, nor any paper in my possession does not furnish me with

---

[54] From the "Letter Book" copy in the *Washington Papers*.

the least trace of my having ever given such an order; yet I will not say the fact is otherwise, because the busy scenes in which I was engaged during my continuance in public life, and the multiplicity of things which were constantly pressing on my mind in those days, may have driven the remembrance of it from me. It is for this reason I ask for a copy of the authority under which that matter was transacted. The last letter I can find any copy of, to you, was written from a place called Fredg. in the State of New York and dated the 27th. of Octor.[55] in answer to one from you of the 5th. of September. In this letter I inform you that I had rented my whole Estate, under your care, to Mr. Custis, and requested in the most explicit terms, "that all the money you now possess, or may hereafter receive of mine, before you quit Mr. Custis's business, may be sent to Mr. Lund Washington by him or some other safe hand. And before you remove from your present employment, I must further beg that you will furnish me with an exact accot. of every thing sold from, and purchased for my Estate under your care, in short, the exact state of all expenditures and sales for my use since the last account I settled with you myself; and as letters are subject to miscarriage, I shall be obliged to you to leave a copy thereof with a list of the balances due me (if any there should be), with Mr. Custis, that I may in case of accidents be provided with another copy from him. When I speak of a list of balances, I hope and trust there will be few or none, first from your care in making your collections, and next from the plenty of money, which leaves every person without even the shadow of excuse to withold payment of debts, at this time. But if the case should be otherwise, a list of those debts first properly settled and reduced to specialties (to avoid disputes in the collection by a new hand unacquainted with

---

[55] See Washington's letter to James Hill, Oct. 27, 1778, *ante* (vol. 13).

the transactions, and unable to account for things which would not be disputed with you) left with Mr. Custis, will enable him, or some other person in my behalf to receive payment of the money, with such interest as may be due on the Bonds or Bills".

In a P. S. to this letter, you are desired to put the Tobacco Notes into Colo. Bassett's hands, to be disposed of for my benefit. If subsequent to these you received orders from me to pay my money, and surrender your accots. into the hands of Mr. Posey, I should be glad to be informed of it, as it is my desire to act with candour and fairness in this as well as in every other business. To me it seems exceedingly strange, however, that you should have no copies of the accounts you gave up, common prudence I should have thought would have dictated a measure of this kind to any man.

In your letter of the 24th. of September last, you say you never received any money from Mr. Newton except £180, from one Jacob Williams by his order; but by a letter of your own, in my possession, dated the 10th. of May 1777, you not only acknowledge the receipt of the above sum, but of £120, more from Mr. Willm. Holt in consequence of an order from the same Gentleman, and besides these two sums, I am charged in Mr. Newton's account with £100 paid you the 12th. of September 1776 at the time you received these orders.

It is indispensably necessary that these matters between you and me shou'd be settled, and it is much my wish that it could be done in an amicable and friendly way. I hope you will therefore pursue the necessary modes to do this and without delay which will be exceedingly pleasing to, Sir, Yr. etc.

P. S. I have just written to Mr. Posey to surrender your Accots. to you or me.[56]

---

[56] From the "Letter Book" copy in the *Washington Papers*.

*To THOMAS PETERS

Mount Vernon, January 20, 1787.

Sir: It is now more than six weeks since I begged to be informed in decided terms, if you would furnish me with 50 Bushls. of Barley, that I might know whether to depend upon that quantity from *you,* or resort to *Philadelphia* for it, where it had been offered to me.

I informed you too, that unless the latter was seasonably embraced I might, in case of failure with you, be disappointed altogether. To this momt. (when arrangements should not only have been made, but the ground had in full preparation) I am left in uncertainty, a wish to be relieved from it, must be my apology for giving you the trouble of another letter on this subject. I am etc.[57]

*To DAVID HUMPHREYS

Mount Vernon, January 23, 1787.

My dear Humphreys: Since I have heard of the robbery of the mail at New Ark, on the 4th. Instt., I have been under great apprehension that a long and confidential letter which I wrote to you on the 26th. Ulto. was in it. My only hope is, a strange one you will say, that the inattention to, and practice of *bringing back,* instead of *exchanging mails,* which frequently happens, and did actually happen about that time may have been the means of its preservation, without this interposition it most assuredly would have been in that mail, to relieve me from this state of disagreeable suspence, I pray you to write me by the first Post after you receive this letter.

All here join me in offering every good wish for you, and with sentiments of the greatest friendship and regard I am etc.

[M.L.]

---

[57] From a facsimile kindly furnished by J. D. B. Peters, of Tampa, Fla.

To JOHN HENRY

Mount Vernon, January 23, 1787.

Sir: Your letter of the 26th. of October,[58] and the piece of Antiquity accompanying it, I received by the hands of Doctr. Stuart on the 13th. inst:

You will be pleased to accept of my thanks for your politeness in sending me the latter which, on account of its antiquity and having been once the property of so remarkable a character as Oliver Cromwell, would undoubtedly render it pleasing to almost anyone, and to an antiquary, perhaps invaluable. I am, etc.[59]

To JOHN NICHOLSON[60]

Mount Vernon, January 23, 1787.

Sir: Your letter of the 9th. instant, together with a statement of the Finances of the State of Pennsylvania, came duly to hand. You will accept of my best thanks for your attention and politeness in transmitting to me the above Statement.

The prosperity of any part of the Union gives me a singular pleasure, and I cannot but express the satisfaction I feel at the happy situation of your Finances. I am, etc.[59]

To ALEXANDER SPOTSWOOD

Mount Vernon, January 23, 1787.

Dear Sir: Your favor of the 13th. came to my hands a few days after my Nephew G: Washington left this for New Kent, which, and his not seeing you on his way down, were unlucky circumstances as he could, and no doubt would have arranged

---

[58] Not now found in the *Washington Papers*.
[59] From the "Letter Book" copy in the *Washington Papers*.
[60] Comptroller general and receiver of taxes of the State of Pennsylvania.

matters so as that a Vessel which is sent from Colchester to York River for Negroes which Colonel Bassett has given him, might have stopped at the mouth of Potomac creek for the Oats and other articles you have been so obliging as to provide for me.

Immediately upon the receipt of your letter, I wrote to George informing him, of the contents of it, requesting him to order the Vessel to stop at the above place for the purpose mentioned; but the chances, I fear, are against the letter's getting to his hands. Nevertheless, I pray you to desire Mr. Young[61] to get his Oats ready without delay as the Vessel will not, indeed ought not to be detained a moment longer on her passage, than is indispensably necessary to transport the Oats and other things across, which will be done at one trip if waggons can be hired. To this end my nephew (if the letter reaches him) is instructed. If this vessel should not stop, another shall be sent to Potomac creek, it will be proper therefore that no time should be lost in preparing the Oats.

For the different kinds of seeds, you have promised me of your own growth, I pray you to accept my thanks. I shall be attentive to make the most of them, and shall be obliged to you for letting me know whether the Barley, or bear (as your farmer calls it) is a Spring or Winter grain; and at what time it ought to be sown. Your bunch-bean accounts for the mistake of asking for bunch peas. George led me into it, for I had never heard of them before. The Beans must be valuable, and I shall esteem them an acquisition. When ought they to be planted? Is your field pea subject to the bug, as the garden peas are? How did your field beans turn out? If you have any of these to spare I would thank you for some. They are (if of the proper sort) highly esteemed in the present husbandry of England as a preparatory crop for wheat.

------

[61] Who had rented Col. Burges Ball's place called "Traveller's Rest."

Mrs. Washington and Fanny join me in offering every good wish for you, my niece and the family; and with sentiments of great regard and affection, I am, etc.[62]

*To BATTAILE MUSE

Mount Vernon, January 24, 1787.

Sir: It would seem by your letter of the 3d. instt. that you had not received my last; in which I desired that whatever money you had, or could command of mine, might be sent to me; or an order drawn on some responsible person in Alexandria; as I was much in want of it. This request I now repeat, as I have, since that time been disappointed of other sums wch. I thought myself sure of receiving. and shall be a good deal distressed if I can receive none from you till the late periods mentioned in your letter. I am etc.   [H. L.]

To JOHN FRANCIS MERCER

Mount Vernon, February 1, 1787.

Sir: I am perfectly satisfied with your determination respecting the Negroes. The money will be infinitely more agreeable to me than property of that sort. It will too, if I should want any of those people, procure them on more advantageous terms than I offered.

I beg that the Certificates may be no longer delayed. I have already sunk one hundred pounds specie by consenting to take them at 4 for 1 at the moment I did this, as appeared by the Richmond Gazette which came to my hands a day or two afterwards the price of them was 4½ and five. Now Doctr. Stuart tells me the latter is with difficulty obtained. I wish

---

[62]From the "Letter Book" copy in the *Washington Papers.*

therefore to do something with these before my loss becomes greater.

The money sent by Mr. Diggs came safe. I am, etc.[63]

*To HENRY KNOX

Mount Vernon, February 3, 1787.

My dear Sir: I feel myself exceedingly obliged to you for the full, and friendly communications in your letters of the 14th. 21st. and 25th. ult; and shall (critically as matters are described in the latter) be extremely anxious to know the issue of the movements of the forces that were assembling, the one to support, the other to oppose the constitutional rights of Massachusetts. The moment is, indeed, important! If government shrinks, or is unable to enforce its laws; fresh manœuvres will be displayed by the insurgents, anarchy and confusion must prevail, and every thing will be turned topsy turvey in that State; where it is not probable the mischiefs will terminate.

In your letter of the 14th. you express a wish to know my intention respecting the Convention, proposed to be held in Philada. in May next. In *confidence* I inform you, that it is not, at this time, my purpose to attend it. When this matter was first moved in the Assembly of this State, some of the principal characters of it wrote to me, requesting to be permitted to put my name in the delegation. To this I objected. They again pressed, and I again refused; assigning among other reasons my having declined meeting the Society of the Cincinnati at that place, about the same time, and that I thought it would be disrespectfull to that body (to whom I ow'd much)

---

[63] From the "Letter Book" copy in the *Washington Papers*.

The volume of the Washington "Letter Books," which commences with Feb. 1, 1787, is in an unidentified handwriting. The copying is so inaccurately and carelessly done as to render palpable corrections not only advisable but necessary.

to be there on any other occasion. Notwithstanding these intimations, my name was inserted in the Act; and an official communication thereof made by the Executive to me, to whom, at the sametime that I expressed my sense for the confidence reposed in me, I declared, that as I saw no prospect of my attending, it was my wish that my name might not remain in the delegation, to the exclusion of another. To this I have been requested, in emphatical terms, not to decide absolutely, as no inconvenience would result from the non-appointment of another, at least for sometime.

Thus the matter stands, which is the reason of my saying to you in *confidence* that at present I retain my first intention, not to go. In the meanwhile as I have the fullest conviction of your friendship for, and attachment to me; know your abilities to judge; and your means of information, I shall receive any communications from you, respecting this business, with thankfulness. My first wish is, to do for the best, and to act with propriety; and you know me too well, to believe that reserve or concealment of any circumstance or opinion, would be at all pleasing to me. The legallity of this Convention I do not mean to discuss, nor how problematical the issue of it may be. That powers are wanting, none can deny. Through what medium they are to be derived, will, like other matters, engage public attention. That which takes the shortest course to obtain them, will, in my opinion, under present circumstances, be found best. Otherwise, like a house on fire, whilst the most regular mode of extinguishing it is contended for, the building is reduced to ashes. My opinion of the energetic wants of the federal government are well known; publickly and privately I have declared it; and however constitutionally it may be for Congress to point out the defects of the fœderal System, I am strongly inclined to believe that it would not be found the most efficatious channel for the recommendation, more especially the alterations, to flow, for reasons too obvious to enumerate.

The System on which you seem disposed to build a National government is certainly more energetic, and I dare say, in every point of view more desirable than the present one; which, from experience, we find is not only slow, debilitated, and liable to be thwarted by every breath, but is defective in that secrecy, which for the accomplishment of many of the most important national purposes is indispensably necessary; and besides, having the Legislative, Executive and Judiciary departments con-centered, is exceptionable. But at the sametime I give this opinion, I believe that the political machine will yet be much tumbled and tossed, and possibly be wrecked altogether, before such a system as you have defined will be adopted. The darling Sovereignties of the States individually, The Governors elected and elect. The Legislators, with a long train of et cetera whose political consequence will be lessened, if not anihilated, would give their weight of opposition to such a revolution. But I may be speaking without book, for scarcely ever going off my own farms I see few people who do not call upon me; and am very little acquainted with the Sentiments of the great world; indeed, after what I have seen, or rather after what I have heard, I shall be surprized at nothing; for if three years since any person had told me that at this day, I should see such a formidable rebellion against the laws and constitutions of our own making as now appears I should have thought him a bedlamite, a fit subject for a mad house. Adieu, you know how much, and how sincerely I am etc.

Mrs. Washington joins me in every good wish for yourself, Mrs. Knox and the family.   [MS.H.S.]

To HENRY LEE

Mount Vernon, February 4, 1787.

My dear Sir: I thank you for asking my commands to Fredericksburg. It is not my wish to be your competitor in the purchase of any of Mr. Hunters tradesmen: especially as I am in a great degree principled against increasing my number of Slaves by purchase and suppose moreover that Negroes sold on credit will go high. yet if you are not disposed to buy the Bricklayer which is advertized for Sale, for your own use, find him in the vigour of life, from report a good workman and of tolerable character and his price does not exceed one hundred, or a few more pounds, I should be glad if you would buy him for me. I have much work in this way to do this Summer. If he has a family, with which he is to be sold; or from whom he would reluctantly part I decline the purchase, his feelings I would not be the means of hurting in the latter case, nor *at any* rate be incumbered with the former. I am, etc.[64]

To THOMAS PETERS

Mount Vernon, February 9, 1787.

Sir: As your last letter of the 3d. inst. places me on better ground with respect to seed Barley (than) your former one of the 18th of November did, and as (it) will be inconvenient and injurious to me to withhold some of my best ground from Oats till it may be too late to put this ground in to advantage from the uncertain expectation of Barley.

This letter is to pray that you will decline all further trouble in inquiring for the latter, on my account. as I have wrote to the same Gentlemen who procured me 50 Bushels (and could

[64] From the "Letter Book" copy in the *Washington Papers*.

then have got an 100) to add 50 more if now to be had. If your Barley from the Eastward should arrive in Season to be sown, is of the spring sort, and good in quality, and you can spare a few bushels to put me in Seed against another year I shall be obliged by it; a dozen bushels may suffice.

Clover Seed I have supplied myself with long ago. I hope you will have the goodness to excuse me for the trouble I have given you in making enquiries. I am, etc.[65]

To CLEMENT BIDDLE

Mount Vernon, February 11, 1787.

Dear Sir: As we are now on the verge of the middle of Feby: and the season is fast approaching when the ground should be in readiness to receive spring grain, permit me to remind you of the Barley you were so obliging as to procure for me, and beg (as I have been disappointed in another expectation) that the 50 bushels may be encreased to one hundred, if in your power to do it conveniently. At any rate write me decidedly, what I have to expect, that I may not, in expectation of Barley, with-hold my best grounds from oats till it is too late to sow them, to advantage. Ascertain the freight, in the Bill of Lading that I am to pay for the Barley and Clover Seed: without this is previously done, impositions are but too commonly met with.

Since writing to you I have met with, and obtained the quantity wanted, of Jerusalem Artichoke. What price would well cured Herrings sell for with you, by the barrel? Are they in demand? and what would be the freight from this River to Philadelphia? I have about 50 Barrels that I am told are good. With great esteem I am, etc.

[65] From the "Letter Book" copy in the Washington Papers.

P. S. If the Vessel by which you send the Barley and should not have sailed, pray send me two good and Strong linnen Wheels.

I would thank you for paying Messr. Sedden and Co. for the Columbian Magazines which they have sent me.[66]

To PRESIDENT BENJAMIN FRANKLIN

Mount Vernon, February 11, 1787.

Dear Sir: On the 3d. of Novr., I had the honr. of addressing your Excelly, a letter of which the enclosed is a copy. Having heard nothing from you since, I am led to apprehend a miscarriage of it, and therefore give you the trouble of a duplicate; not knowing what reply to make to Sir Edward Neweham, or what more to do in this business untill I am favoured with your answer. With the greatest respect and regard. I have the honor etc.[67]

To THOMAS NEWTON, JUNIOR

Mount Vernon, February 11, 1787.

It is now two or three months since I requested, in very explicit terms, that if my flour was not then sold, that it might be disposed of for whatever it would fetch, and the money remitted to me by Doctr. Stuart who was then attending the Assembly, or some other safe conveyance. As I have heard nothing from you since, it is probable the letter may have miscarried. I therefore beg that no further delay may arise in transmitting me the proceeds, as I want the money.

In the letter alluded to above, to the best of my recollection I asked if well cured Herrings commanded a ready sale at Norfolk and what pr. Barrel? I am, etc.[66]

---

[66] From the "Letter Book" copy in the *Washington Papers*.
[67] From a facsimile. The original was in the possession of a Col. Ellicott F. Shepard in 1889.

To CHARLES WASHINGTON

Mount Vernon, February 14, 1787.

Dear Charles: When the enclosed was written, I knew nothing of George's[68] intention of visiting Berkeley. The safe conveyance afforded by him, is very favorable, and [I] gladly embraced it.

Having seen Bushrod and Corbin Washington on their way from Berkeley, their information is the subject of this letter and is exceedingly distressing to me, inasmuch as I have not the means of affording immediate relief. By them I learn that the remaining negros of my deceased Brother Samuel's Estate are under an execution, and a momentary sale of them may be expected, and this too by the extraordinary conduct of Mr. White in applying moneys received towards the discharge of a Bond *not in Suit* when they ought to have given it in payment of Mr. Alexander's claim, on which judgment had been, or was on the point of being obtained. How in the name of Heaven came Mr. White to be vested with powers to dispose of the money he should recover unaccompanied with instructions respecting the disposal. will not Mr. Alexander when he sees every exertion making to pay him have mercy on the orphan? Can he as a Father and man of feeling see the Fatherless reduced from Competency to distress untouched? If there was an unwillingness to pay him, if property had not been sold for the express purpose of doing it, and if there was not a prospect of [its] being done in a very short time, it would be right in Mr. Alexander to push matters to extremity; but when (as I am informed) in the case every exertion is making to satisfy him, to cause perhaps three pounds worth of property to be sold to raise 20/ cash, this would be inconsistent with that

---

[68] George Augustine Washington.

benevolence which should be characteristic of every man and to which, from what I have heard of the Gentleman, he is justly entitled. I therefore think as Executor to the will and guardian to the boys, you should before the dye is cast apply by fair and candid representation to Mr. Alexander on this subject, not in the cold mode of letter, but personally, to see if this evil cannot be averted. Vain would it be for me to offer Mr. Alexander any assurances of the money at a short given day. I cannot get it from those who owe me without suit, and I hate to sue them. I have offered lands for sale at very moderate prices, but have not been able to sell them. Otherwise, or if I could raise the money by any other means, I would relieve my nephews without hesitation from the impending evil. Indeed, I would essay any thing to save the estate; for if the negros are sold for ready money, they will go for a song. To add aught to this is unnecessary. With the most affectionate regards.

My love, in which Mrs. Washington joins, to my sister and the family.[69]

To MARY WASHINGTON

Mount Vernon, February 15, 1787.

Hond. Madam: In consequence of your communication to George Washington,[70] of your want of money, I take the (first safe) conveyance by Mr. John Dandridge to send you 15 Guineas, which believe me is all I have, and which indeed ought to have been paid many days ago to another, agreeable to my own assurances. I have now demands upon me for more than 500 £, three hundred and forty odd of which is due for the tax of 1786; and I know not where or when, I shall receive one shilling with which to pay it. In the last two years I made

---

[69] From the "Letter Book" copy in the *Washington Papers*.
[70] George Augustine Washington.

no crops. In the first I was obliged to buy corn and this year have none to sell, and my wheat is so bad, I cannot either eat it myself nor sell it to others, and Tobacco I make none. Those who owe me money cannot or will not pay it without suits, and to sue is to do nothing; whilst my expences, not from any extravagance, or an inclination on my part to live splendidly, but for the absolute support of my family and the visitors who are constantly here, are exceedingly high; higher indeed than I can support without selling part of my estate, which I am disposed to do, rather than run in debt, or continue to be so; but this I cannot do, without taking much less than the lands I have offered for sale are worth. This is really and truely my situation. I do not however offer it as any excuse for not paying you what may really be due; for let this be little or much, I am willing, however unable, to pay to the utmost farthing; but it is really hard upon me when you have taken every thing you wanted from the Plantation by which money could be raised, when I have not received one farthing, directly nor indirectly from the place for more than twelve years, if ever, and when, in that time I have paid, as appears by Mr. Lund Washington's accounts against me (during my absence) Two hundred and sixty odd pounds, and by my own account Fifty odd pounds out of my own Pocket to you, besides (if I am rightly informed) every thing that has been raised by the Crops on the Plantation. Who to blame, or whether any body is to blame for these things I know not, but these are facts; and as the purposes for which I took the Estate are not answered, nor likely to be so, but dissatisfaction on all sides have taken place, I do not mean to have any thing more to say to your Plantation or negros since the first of January, except the fellow who is here, and who will not, as he has formed connections in this neighborhood, leave it. As experience has proved him, I will hire. Of this my intention,

I informed my brother John sometime ago, whose death I sincerely lament on many accounts, and on this painful event condole with you most sincerely. I do not mean by this declaration to withhold any aid or support I can give from you; for whilst I have a shilling left, you shall have part, if it is wanted, whatever my own distresses may be. What I shall then give, I shall have credit for; now I have not, for tho' I have received nothing from your Quarter, and am told that every farthing goes to you, and have moreover paid between 3 and 4 hundred pounds besides out of my own pocket, I am viewed as a delinquent, and considered perhaps by the world as [an] unjust and undutiful son. My advice to you, therefore, is to do one of two things with the Plantation. Either let your grandson Bushrod Washington, to whom the land is given by his Father, have the whole interest there, that is, lands and negros, at a reasonable rent; or, next year (for I presume it is too late this, as the overseer may be engaged) to let him have the land at a certain yearly rent during your life; and hire out the negros. This would ease you of all care and trouble, make your income certain, and your support ample. Further, my sincere and pressing advice to you is, to break up housekeeping, hire out all the rest of your servants except a man and a maid, and live with one of your children. This would relieve you entirely from the cares of this world, and leave your mind at ease to reflect undisturbedly on that which ought to come. On this subject I have been full with my Brother John, and it was determined he should endeavor to get you to live with him. He alas is no more, and three, only of us remain. My house is at your service, and [I] would press you most sincerely and most devoutly to accept it, but I am sure, and candor requires me to say, it will never answer your purposes in any shape whatsoever. For in truth it may be compared to a well resorted tavern, as scarcely any strangers who are going from north to south, or from south to north, do not spend a day or two at it. This would, were you to be an inhabitant of it, oblige you to do one of 3 things: 1st, to be always dressing to appear in company; 2d, to come into [the room] in a dishabille, or 3d, to be as it were a prisoner in your own chamber. The first you'ld not like; indeed, for a person at your time of life it would be too fatiguing. The 2d, I should not like, because those who resort here are, as I observed before, strangers and people of the first distinction. And the 3d, more than probably, would not be pleasing to either of us. Nor indeed could you be retired in any room in my house; for what with the sitting up of company, the noise and bustle of servants, and many other things, you would not be able to enjoy that calmness and serenity of mind, which in my opinion you ought now to prefer to every other consideration in life. If you incline to follow this advice, the House and lots on which you now live you may rent, and enjoy the benefit of the money arising therefrom as long as you live. This with the rent of the land at the little falls,[71] and the hire of your negros, would bring you in an income which would be much more than sufficient to answer all your wants and make ample amends to the child you live with; for myself I should desire nothing; if it did not, I would most cheerfully contribute more. A man, a maid, the phaeton and two horses, are all you would want. To lay in a sufficiency for the support of these would not require $\frac{1}{4}$ of your income, the rest would purchase every necessary you could possibly want, and place it in your power to be serviceable to those with whom you may live, which no doubt would be agreeable to all parties.

There are such powerful reasons in my mind for giving this advice that I cannot help urging it with a degree of earnestness which is uncommon for me to do. It is, I am convinced, the

---

[71] Of the Rappahannock.

only means by which you can be happy. The cares of a family, without any body to assist you; the charge of an estate the profits of which depend upon wind, weather, a good overseer, an honest man, and a thousand other circumstances, cannot be right or proper at your advanced age, and for me, who am absolutely prevented from attending to my own plantations, which are almost within call of me, to attempt the care of yours, would be folly in the extreme; but [by] the mode I have pointed out, you may reduce your income to a certainty, be eased of all trouble, and if you are so disposed, may be perfectly happy; for happiness depends more upon the internal frame of a person's own mind, than on the externals in the world. Of the last, if you will pursue the plan here recommended, I am sure you can want nothing that is essential. The other depends wholly upon yourself, for the riches of the Indies cannot purchase it.

Mrs. Washington, George and Fanny join me in every good wish for you, and I am, honored madame, your most dutiful and aff. son.[72]

To BATTAILE MUSE

Mount Vernon, February 15, 1787.

Sir: I have just received your letter of the 4th. inst. and the 50 pounds sent by Mr. A. Morton.

Mr. Wales accepted the order upon him and says he will endeavour to pay it when it becomes due, but as the time of payment has not yet arrived I cannot say anything decided upon it. It is not in my power to send a person to Leesburg agreeable to your request as the time which you mentioned to be there has already elapsed.

Tho' I am not in want of Horses at present, yet, as it may prevent my tenants from being distressed, and perhaps be the

---

[72] From the "Letter Book" copy in the *Washington Papers*.

only chance I may have to secure my rent, I will consent to take a few, at a reasonable price, provided they are young, strong and serviceable I should prefer good breeding mares, but old horses I will not receive at any rate. The cut money in the 50 pounds mentioned above fell short by weight 10/6 I do not regard the present difficiency, but only mention it, that in future, you may receive it by weight as that is the only way in which it will pass here. I am, etc.[73]

To CHARLES WILLSON PEALE

Mount Vernon, February 16, 1787.

Sir: You will receive by the Stage the body of my Gold Pheasant, packed up in wool agreeable to your directions. He made his Exit yesterday, which enables me to comply with your request much sooner than I wished to do. I am afraid the others will follow him but too soon, as they all appear to be drooping; whether it is owing to their being confined, or to the Climate, I am not able to say: I am very desirous of giving them Liberty, but the danger of their being taken by the Hawkes prevents me. I am etc.[74]

To THOMAS STONE[75]

Mount Vernon, February 16, 1787.

Dear Sir: Your favor of the 30th Ulto. came duly to hand. To give an opinion in a cause of so much importance as that which has warmly agitated two branches of your legislature, and which, from the appeal that is made, is likely to create great and perhaps dangerous divisions, is rather a delicate

---

[73] From the "Letter Book" copy in the *Washington Papers*.
[74] In the writing of Tobias Lear. From a photostat of the original in the possession of Miss Eleanor Bruno, of Ridley Park, Pa.
[75] Member of the Maryland Senate.

matter; but, as this diversity of opinion is on a subject which has, I believe, occupied the minds of most men, and as my sentiments thereon have been fully and decidedly expressed long before the Assembly either of Maryland or this State were convened, I do not scruple to declare that, if I had a voice in your Legislature, it would have been given decidedly against a paper emission upon the general principles of its utility as a representative, and the necessity of it as a medium. and as far as I have been able to understand its advocates (for the two papers you sent me were the same, and contained no reasons of the House of Delegates for the local want of it in your State, though I have seen and given them a cursory reading elsewhere) I should have been very little less opposed to it.[76]

To assign reasons for this opinion would be as unnecessary as tedious. The ground has been so often trod, that a place hardly remains untouched. But in a word, the necessity arising from a want of specie is represented as greater than it really is. I contend, that it is by the substance, not with the shadow of a thing, we are to be benefitted. The wisdom of man, in my humble opinion, cannot at this time devise a plan, by which the credit of paper money would be long supported; consequently depreciation keeps pace with the quantity of the emission, and articles, for which it is exchanged, rise in a greater ratio than the sinking value of the money. Wherein, then, is the farmer, the planter, the artisan benefitted? The debtor may be, because, as I have observed, he gives the shadow in lieu of the substance; and, in proportion to his gain, the creditor or the body politic suffer. Whether it be a legal tender or not, it will, as hath been observed very truly, leave no alternative. It must be that or nothing. An evil equally great is, the door it imme-

---

[76] The Maryland House of Delegates had passed an act to issue bills of credit for £350,000 for a loan, redeemable in 10 years at an interest rate of 6%. The Senate refused to agree to this.

diately opens for speculation, by which the least designing, and perhaps most valuable, part of the community are preyed upon by the more knowing and crafty speculators.

But, contrary to my intention and declaration, I am offering reasons in support of my opinion; reasons too, which of all others are least pleasing to the advocates for paper money. I shall therefore only observe generally, that so many people have suffered by former emissions, that, like a burnt child who dreads the fire, no person will touch it who can possibly avoid it. The natural consequence of which will be, that the specie, which remains unexported, will be instantly locked up. With great esteem and regard, I am, &c."

To DAVID HUMPHREYS

Mount Vernon, February 18, 1787.

My dear Humphreys: Colo. Wadsworth handed me your obliging and much esteemed favor of the 20th. ulto., for which I offer you my sincere thanks.

The tranquil State in which this Commonwealth is, affords me nothing to offer you in return for the interesting communications in your letter of the above date. The house of Delegates in Maryland, have, on the Contrary, broke up in high dudgeon because the Senate would not agree to a paper emission, on loan. Both houses, it is said, have appealed to their Constituents; which may, eventually, produce a Lilliputian rebellion in that State. Thus we go on.

As you are near the theatre of more important transactions, and have the Wheels of the Political machine much more in view than I have, I hope you will not find it incompatible with your military [duties?] to allot a few moments, now and then,

---

" From the "Letter Book" copy in the *Washington Papers*.

for the purpose of keeping me advised of their revolutions. My anxiety for the welfare of this Country increases with the attempts to destroy the peace of it. What is to be done is in every bodies mouth? Yet none can answer. Which is conviction to my mind that matters must get worse before they will be better.

You have the good wishes of every one in this family, and the warmest affection of your Sincere friend.[78]

To RICHARD HENRY LEE

Mount Vernon, February 20, 1787.

Dear Sir: Your favour of the 15th, with the seed of the honey locust came safe to hand, and claims my particular thanks. I have but one doubt of its forming the best hedge in the world; and that is, whether it can be sufficiently dwarfted. If this cannot be effected, the other purpose mentioned in your letter, and a valuable one too, of subserving stock, is alone sufficient to induce cultivation of the tree.

Mrs. Washington offers respectful compliments to Mrs. Lee, to whom, though I have not the honour of being known, I beg leave to tender mine; we both join in best wishes for you, and the young ladies, and with great esteem and respect, I have the honour etc.[79]

To MRS. JAMES KIRK [80]

Mount Vernon, February 20, 1787.

Madam: I must beg the favor of you to give the bearer (Mr Lear a young Gentleman who lives with me) a decided answer with respect to the money which is due to me from the Estate

---

[78] The text is from the *Washington-Humphreys* copies, in the American Antiquarian Society, Worcester, Mass., furnished through the kindness of R. W. G. Vail, librarian.
[79] The text is from the *Memoir of the Life of Richard Henry Lee and His Correspondence* (1825), vol. 2.
[80] Of Alexandria, Va.

of Mr. Kirk your late husband, I wish it may not be forgotten that the Flour for which this money is due ought to have been paid on the delivery of it notwithstanding I have been kept out of it so long.

I beg leave to add that it is from the real want of it I make such frequent, and pressing applications. I am, etc.[81]

To PRESIDENT EZRA STILES

Mount Vernon, February 23, 1787.

Sir: I have the pleasure to acknowledge the receipt of your letter of the 7th. instant[82] and likewise one of the 9th. of November handed to me by the Revd. Mr. Morse[83] together with your election Sermon for which I beg you will accept of my best thanks.

I am much obliged to you for the accounts which you gave me of the situation of affairs in Massachusetts, sincerely rejoice to find by that and other late advices, that the tumults in that State are likely to be soon suppressed that Government will again be established and peace and tranquility prevail. It must afford the greatest pleasure and satisfaction to every humane and feeling mind that there has been so little blood spilt in a contest which a few weeks ago threatened to drench the State of Massachusetts. I am, etc.[81]

To BENJAMIN LINCOLN, JUNIOR

Mount Vernon, February 24, 1787.

Sir: I have received your letter of the 24th. Ulto. and receipt for Messrs. Josiah Watson and Co. bill of Exchange which was

---

[81] From the "Letter Book" copy in the *Washington Papers*.
[82] In the *Washington Papers*. It has a roughly sketched map of the area of Shay's operations.
[83] Rev. Jedidiah Morse, then a tutor in Yale.

enclosed. I am much obliged to you for the account of the political situation of your State which you gave me, and am very happy to find by later advices that matters are likely soon to terminate entirely in favour of Government by the total suppression of the insurgents, and it adds much to the satisfaction which these accounts give that it may be effected with so little bloodshed, I hope some good will come out of so much evil, by giving energy and respectability to the Government.

General Lincoln's situation must have been very painful to be obliged to march against those men whom he had heretofore looked upon as his fellow Citizens and some of whom had perhaps been his companions in the field, but as they had by their repeated outrages forfeited all right to Citizenship, his duty and patriotism must have got the better of every other consideration and led him with alacrity to support the Government. I am, etc.[84]

To JACQUES CAMPION

Mount Vernon, February 24, 1787.

Sir: Your letter of the 26th. of Jany. came duly to hand. I am much obliged to you for your good wishes, and interest which you take in my welfare. The Asses are in very good order, but I am sorry to inform you that the Gold cock and the Silver hen pheasant are dead, the others appear to be drooping, and I am afraid that all the care and attention which is paid to them will not be able to preserve them. I am, etc.[84]

---

[84] From the "Letter Book" copy in the *Washington Papers*.

On February 24 Washington wrote also to James Maury, of Liverpool, England, stating that he had "wholly discontinued the cultivation of Tobacco," but if he should have occasion to transact any mercantile business with Liverpool "I shall take the liberty of applying to you." A copy of this letter is in the "Letter Book" in the *Washington Papers*.

*To HENRY KNOX

Mount Vernon, February 25, 1787.

Accept, my dear General Knox my affectionate thanks for your obliging favors of the 29th, 30th, and 31st. of Jany. and 1st. 8th. and 12th. of the present month. They were indeed, exceedingly satisfactory, and relieving to my mind which had been filled with great and anxious uneasiness for the issue of General Lincoln's operations, and the dignity of Government. On prospect of the happy termination of this insurrection I sincerely congratulate you; hoping that good may result from the cloud of evils which threatned, not only the hemisphere of Massachusetts but by spreading its baneful influence, the tranquillity of the Union. Surely Shays must be either a weak man, the dupe of some characters who are yet behind the curtain, or has been deceived by his followers. Or which may be more likely, he did not conceive that there was energy enough in the Government to bring matters to the crisis to which they have been pushed. It is to be hoped the General Court of that State concurred in the report of the Committee, that a rebellion did actually exist. This would be decisive, and the most likely means of putting the finishing stroke to the business.

We have nothing new in this quarter except the dissentions which prevailed in, and occasioned the adjournment of, the Assembly of Maryland; that an appeal might be made to the people for their sentiments on the conduct of their representatives in the Senate and Delegates respecting a paper omission; which was warmly advocated by the latter and opposed by the former, and which may be productive of great, and perhaps dangerous divisions. Our Affairs, generally, seem really, to be approaching to some awful crisis. God only knows what the result will be. It shall be my part to hope for the best; as to see this Country happy whilst I am gliding down the stream of life in tranquil retirement is so much the wish of my Soul, that nothing on this side Elysium can be placed in competition with it. I hope the postponement of your journey to this State does not amount to a relinguishment of it, and that it is unnecessary to assure you of the sincere pleasure I should have at seeing you under this roof. Mrs. Washington unites with me in every good wish for Mrs. Knox yourself and family. With sentiments of the warmest friendship etc.

PS. I had wrote this letter and was on the point of sending it with others to the Post Office when your favor of the 15th. instt. was handed to me. The spirit and decision of the Court[85] is very pleasing and I hope will be attended with happy consequences.   [MS. H. S.]

*To HENRY KNOX

Mount Vernon, March 8, 1787.

My dear Sir: Will you permit me to give you the trouble of making an indirect, but precise enquiry, into the alligations of the enclosed letters.[86] I flatter myself that from the vicinity of Elizabeth Town to New York, and the constant intercourse between the two, you will be able to do it without much trouble. It is but little in my power to afford the pecuniary aids required by the writer; but if the facts as set forth be true, I should feel very happy in offering my mite, and rendering any services in my power on the occasion. Be so good, when you write to me on this subject, to return the letters and translations.

---

[85] Legislature.
[86] From Chaunae, Comtesse d'Anterroches (or d'Anterroche). The comtesse wrote to Washington (September 18 and November 16). Both letters are in the *Washington Papers*, and in them she pleads for Washington to assist her son, formerly an ensign, 62d Foot, British Army. He had been taken prisoner at Saratoga, and when he learned of the French alliance, he joined the American cause. He was stated by Knox to be a relative of Lafayette.

The observations contained in your letter of the 22d. Ulto. (which came duly to hand) respecting the disfranchisement of a number of the Citizens of Massachusetts for their rebellious conduct may be just; and yet, without exemplary punishment, similar disorders may be excited by other ambitious and discontented characters. Punishments however ought to light on the principals.

I am glad to hear that Congress are about to remove some of the stumbling blocks which lay in the way of the proposed Convention; a Convention is an expedient I wish to see tried; after which, if the present government is not efficient, conviction of the propriety of a change of it, will dissiminate through every rank, and class of people and may be brought about in place; till which however necessary it may appear in the eyes of the more descerning, my opinion is, that it cannot be effected without great contention, and much confusion. It is among the evils, and perhaps is not the smallest, of democratical governments, that the people must *feel,* before they will *see.* When this happens, they are roused to action; hence it is that this form of governments is so slow. I am indirectly and delicately pressed to attend this convention.[87] Several reasons are opposed to it in my mind, and not the least my having declined attending the General Meeting of the Cincinnati, which is to be holden in Philadelphia, at the same time on account of the disrespect it might *seem* to offer to that Society, to be there on another occasion. A thought however has lately run through my mind, which is attended with embarrassment. It is, wheather my non-attendance in this Convention will not be considered as deriliction to republicanism, nay more, whether other motives may not (however injuriously) be ascribed to me for not exerting myself on this occasion in support of it.

[87] Knox's letters to Washington (Feb. 27 and Mar. 19, 1787) on the subject of Washington attending the convention are in the *Washington Papers.*

Under these circumstances let me pray you, my dear Sir, to inform me confidentially what the public expectation is on this head, that is, whether I will, or ought to be there? You are much in the way of obtaining this knowledge, and I can depend upon your friendship, candour, and judgment in the communication of it, as far as it shall appear to you. My final determination (if what I have already given to the Executive of this State is not considered in that light) cannot be delayed beyond the time necessary for your reply. With great truth etc.   [N.Y.P.L.]

To DAVID HUMPHREYS

Mount Vernon March 8, 1787.

My dear Humphreys: Colo. Wadsworth, as I informed you in my last, presented me your obliging favor of the 20th of January and the Post since has handed me the subsequent one of the 11th Ulto.

My sentiments, respecting the inexpediency of my attending the proposed Convention of the States in Philadelphia remain the same as when I wrote you last, tho' Congress I am informed are about to remove one of the objections by their recommendation of this Convention I am still indirectly and delicately pressed by many to attend this meeting; and a thought has run thro' my mind of late attended with more embarrassment than any former one. It is whether my not doing it will not be considered as an implied dereliction to Republicanism. nay more, whether (however injurious the imputation) it may not be ascribed to other motives. My wish is I confess to see this Convention tried; after which if the present form is not made efficient, conviction of the propriety of a change will pervade all ranks, and many [may] be effected by

---

[88] Knox's answer (April 9) stated: "It is the general wish that you should attend. It is conceived to be highly important to the success of the propositions of the convention." Knox's letter is in the *Washington Papers*.

peace. Till then, however necessary it may appear to the more discerning part of the community, my opinion is, that it cannot be accomplished without great contention and much confusion for reasons too obvious to enumerate. It is one of the evils, perhaps not the smallest, of democratical governments that the People must feel before they will see or act. Under this view of matters, and not doubting but you have heard the sentiments of many respectable characters since the date of your letter of the 20th of Jany. on this subject and perhaps since the business has been moved in Congress, of the propriety or impropriety of my attendance let me pray you, my dear Sir, to give me confidentially the public opinion and expectation as far as it has come to your knowledge of what it is supposed, I will or ought to do on this occasion. You will readily see the necessity of my receiving it soon, if it is to have an operation contrary to the former, because [if] my communications to the executive of this State are not considered as definitive, I must make these so shortly.

I congratulate you on the favourable Issue to the exertion of the Government of Massachusetts to quell the insurrection which at one period assumed an appearance of being formidable. you have the best wishes of everyone in this family; possess the sincere regard and Friendship of Dr. Sir yr. etc.[89]

To PRESIDENT JOSEPH WILLARD[90]

Mount Vernon, March 10, 1787.

Revd. Sir: Permit me to entreat, that my long delay in acknowledging the receipt of your polite letter of the 15th. of

---

[89] This letter has been so carelessly recorded in the "Letter Book" that it is almost impossible to be sure of the sense. It seems certain that several words, perhaps an entire line, has been omitted. Humphreys's letters to Washington (Mar. 24 and Apr. 9, 1787) on the subject of Washington attending the convention are in the *Washington Papers.*

[90] Of Harvard College.

May last, may be ascribed to any cause rather than the want of respect for your character, and gratitude for the favourable sentiments you have expressed of me. As the letter was intro-ductory of Mr. Lear, I found myself inclined, though desposed to give full credence to your acct. of the talents and good dis-position of this young Gentleman, to take time, and seek occa-sions, to form my own judgement of him; and it is with pleasure I now assure you that, his deportment since he came into this family has been such, as to obtain the esteem, confidence, and love of every individual in it. As (from the interest you have taken in his welfare) I persuade myself this testimony of my approbation of his conduct will not be displeasing to you, I could no longer with-hold it; especially as it affords an occasion of assuring you of my good wishes for the University over wch. you preside, and of the esteem and respect with which I have the honor etc.[91]

To THOMAS CUSHING

Mount Vernon, March 10, 1787.

Sir: By your letter and account of the 22d. of February 1786, there appears a balance in my favor of fifteen pounds thirteen shillings Lawful money, [for] which I take the liberty to draw a bill in favor of Mr. Thomas Porter of Alexandria payable ten days after sight.

I am happy to find by the last Accounts from the Northward that the disturbances in your State were almost totally sup-pressed, and hope before this, that peace and good order are again restored, Mrs. Washington joins me in my best wishes for Mrs. Cushing and yourself. I am, etc.[92]

[91] The text, from the *Yale Review* (spring of 1932), kindly furnished by Judge E. A. Armstrong, varies in minor verbal details from the "Letter Book" copy. Practically this same letter was also sent (March 10) to Rev. Samuel Haven and John Langdon. Copies of these letters are in the "Letter Book" in the *Washington Papers*.

[92] From the "Letter Book" copy in the *Washington Papers*.

To SIR EDWARD NEWENHAM

Mount Vernon, March 10, 1787.

Dear Sir: I shall not wonder if you should be surprized at my not acknowledging the receipts of your esteemed favor of the 12th. of last August at an earlier period. Immediately after it came to my hands, not knowing what you had written to Doct. Franklin or to Mr. Jay, or what steps might have been taken on the subject matter thereof by either or both of those Gentlemen I wrote to the former for information; giving assurances of my disposition to carry your wishes into full effect if there were not impediments in the way which could not, consistently, be surmounted. I waited from that period (early in November) till February in daily expectation of an answer; but receiving none, I addressed (supposing my first letter must have miscarried) a duplicate to the Doctrs. and receiving the answer which is enclosed.[93]

Though I had heard of the resolution alluded to in Mr. Jay's Letter to the Doctors previous to my writing to him yet I was willing to know the truth, and to see how far Congress would think it right to adhere to the policy of their resolution.

I beg leave to make a tender of my best wishes to Lady Newenham, in which Mrs. Washington joins, and assurances of the respect and esteem with which I have the honor, etc.[94]

To THE SECRETARY FOR FOREIGN AFFAIRS

Mount Vernon, March 10, 1787.

Dear Sir: I stand indebted to you for two letters. The first, introductory of Mr. Anstey, needed no apology, nor will any be necessary on future similar occasions. The other of the 7th of

---

[93] No copy is now found in the *Washington Papers*.
[94] From the "Letter Book" copy in the *Washington Papers*.

January is on a very interesting subject deserving very particular attention.

How far the revision of the federal system, and giving more adequate powers to Congress may be productive of an efficient government, I will not under my present view of the matter, presume to decide. That many inconveniences result from the present form, none can deny. Those enumerated in your letter are so obvious and sensibly felt that no logic can controvert, nor is it likely that any change of conduct will remove them, and that attempts to alter or amend it will be like the proppings of a house which is ready to fall, and which no shoars can support (as many seem to think) may also be true. But, is the public mind matured for such an important change as the one you have suggested? What would be the consequences of a premature attempt? My opinion is, that this Country must yet feel and see more, before it can be accomplished.

A thirst for power, and *the bantling, I had liked to have said monster,* for sovereignty, which have taken such fast hold of the States individually, will when joined by the many whose personal consequence in the control of State politics will in a manner be annihilated, form a strong phalanx against it; and when to these the few who can hold posts of honor or profit in the National Government are compared with the many who will see but little prospect of being noticed, and the discontent of others who may look for appointments, the opposition will be altogether irresistable till the mass, as well as the more discerning part of the Community shall see the necessity. Among men of reflection, few will be found I believe, who are not *beginning* to think that our system is more perfect in theory than in practice; and that notwithstanding the boasted virtue of America it is more than probable we shall exhibit the last melancholy proof, that mankind are not competent to their own Government without the means of coercion in the Sovereign.

Yet, I would fain try what the wisdom of the proposed Convention will suggest: and what can be effected by their Councils. It may be the last peaceable mode of essaying the practicability of the present form, without a greater lapse of time than the exigency of our affairs will allow. In strict propriety a Convention so holden may not be legal. Congress, however, may give it a colouring by recommendation, which would fit it more to the taste without proceeding to a definition of the powers. This however constitutionally it might be done would not, in my opinion, be expedient: for delicacy on the one hand, and Jealousy on the other, would produce a mere nihil.

My name is in the delegation to this Convention; but it was put there contrary to my desire, and remains contrary to my request. Several reasons at the time of this appointment and which yet exist, conspired to make an attendance inconvenient, perhaps improper, tho' a good deal urged to it. with sentiments of great regard &c.

P. S. Since writing this letter I have seen the resolution of Congress recommendatory of the Convention to be holden in Philadelphia the 2d Monday in May.[95]

To THE GOVERNOR OF THE BAHAMA ISLANDS

Mount Vernon, March 11, 1787.

Sir: With your Excellencys permission, though I have not the honor of being known to you, I will take the liberty of recommending the bearer Mr. Fendall, his Lady, and Miss Lee, to your Civilities. They are much respected and esteemed in this Country. The Ill health of Mrs. Fendall have induced her Physicians to recommend the air of the Sea to her, and the Bahama Islands seem to be the object of their Voyage. I am

---

[95] From the "Letter Book" copy in the *Washington Papers*.

persuaded these worthy people will do Justice to my recommendation that a philanthropic attention to them will be as pleasing to yourself as to them; and that it will be the best apology I can offer for this freedom. I have the honor, etc.[96]

To CHARLES WILLSON PEALE

Mount Vernon, March 13, 1787.

Sir: I have received your letter of the 27th Ulto. acknowledging the reception of the body of the Golden Pheasant.[97] I have sent by the Dolphin Captn. Steward the body of a French hen Pheasant which died this day. I chose this mode of conveying it rather than by the Stage, as the Packet calls here to receive some things for Philadelphia; and I think, all circumstances considered, that it will meet with as quick and safe a conveyance as if it went by land. I wish you great success in the Mezzotinto Prints which you have undertaken,[98] and have no doubt but your abilities in works of Genius will ensure it. I am etc.[99]

To CLEMENT BIDDLE

Mount Vernon, March 14, 1787.

Dear Sir: Your letters of the 20th. and 27th. Ulto. are both before me. The Barley and other thing by the Dolphin are ar-

---

[96] From the "Letter Book" copy in the *Washington Papers*.

On March 12 Washington wrote briefly to William Goddard, requesting the insertion of an advertisement in his paper (*The Maryland Journal*) for three weeks. This was a notice that Royal Gift and The Knight of Malta would cover at Mount Vernon during the spring of 1787, at five guineas for the season, and Magnolio would cover for £4; good pasturage would be furnished at one-half a dollar per week. John Fairfax signed the advertisement as overseer. A copy of this letter is in the Toner Transcripts in the Library of Congress.

[97] Peale stuffed the pheasants and exhibited them in his "Museum."

[98] A broadside advertisement of one of his mezzotints, an allegorical picture of William Pitt, is among the undated Pennsylvania broadsides in the Library of Congress.

[99] In the writing of Tobias Lear. From a photostat of the original through the kindness of Judge E. A. Armstrong, of Princeton, N. J.

rived, and by the return of this Vessel I consign you, as per bill enclosed, 45 Barrls. of Herrings, which you will be pleased to dispose of to the best advantage, and place the proceeds to my credit. It is hardly necessary to add that, the sooner these fish are disposed of the higher the Sale of them probably will be, as the season for the new is near at hand. They are very good I am told, having been lately examined.

As I believe the half yearly interest of my Certificate is nearly due, and a small balance was in my favor previous to the purchasing the Articles by the Dolphin, I will wait for the Sale of the Fish to know how the Accts. between us will then be. In the interim, please to send me one dozn. of the best corn Scythes of a proper length, and strength at the heel, and in the backs, and the same number of the best Grass Scythes, two strong bramble Scythes; and two flax spinning wheels. The Dolphin returns to this Port in the course of next month, and will afford a good Conveyance. What does the best Hyson Tea, and dble. refined Sugar sell at with you? And how are linnens now? particularly those of the finer sort. With great esteem I am etc.

PS. How does White and red Lead, ground in Oil sell? are not these things often bought cheap at the Public Vendues? [1]

[H. S. P.]

To JAMES MERCER

Mount Vernon, March 15, 1787.

Dear Sir: Your favor of the 10th. came duly to hand, and with very sincere concern I read the acct. of your ill health; but if your other complaints have left you, the Asthma, though troublesome and distressing, is not a dangerous one; I will hope therefore that the agreeable season which is fast approaching, will perfectly restore you good health.

---

[1] In the writing of Tobias Lear. The P. S. is in the writing of Washington.

Under cover with this, you will receive the original Deed for the Lands on four miles run; which you will please to return when your purposes are answered by the reference to it, for drawing the deed of confirmation: for your justice in offering which, and kindness in drawing it, I pray you to accept my warmest acknowledgments.

The mode suggested by you to obtain the bond which I passed to Messrs. McCoull & Blair, is, in my judgment, the *only* proper one; so far as it respects you, or the Representatives of your father (if the credit is to be applied to that acct.) it is precisely the same whether you acct. with me, or them, for the principal and interest of the sum which was to have been paid for the Land under the circumstances of your claim; because if the right is determined to be in you, so much will have been discounted from my demand on the Estate. If in them, it is only paying to them, as Attorneys of Lindo and Cozenove[2] what otherwise would have been demanded of me. The case with me would be widely different, for if I allow this sum with interest in a settlement and my bond remains unretired, I am open to a prosecution thereon; and may be greatly distressed by the actual payment after having allowed it in a discount, before I could have any redress, which would very illy accord with the present State of my finances. Should Mr. McCoull[3] refuse to accede to your proposal, it would imply strongly, his intention of resorting to me for payment.[4]

However desirous I am, and always shall be, to comply with any commands of my Country, I do not conceive that I can, with consistent conduct, attend the proposed Convention to be holden in Philadelphia in May next. For besides the declaration

---

[2] Elias Lindo and John H. Casanove.

[3] Neil McCoul.

[4] The chain of title of this Four Mile Run land and much valuable information respecting it will be found in Charles W. Stetson's privately printed volume, *Four Mile Run Grants* (Mimeoform Press: Washington, D. C., 1935).

which I made in a very solemn manner when I was about to
retire, of bidding adieu to all public employment; I had just
before the appointment of delegates to this Convention, written and dispatched circular letters to the several State Societies
of the Cincinnati informing them of my intention not to attend
the General Meeting which was to take place about the same
time and at the same City. and assigned reasons which apply
as forcibly in the one case as the other. Under these circumstances, to attend the Convention might be considered disrespectful to a worthy set of men for whose attachment and support on many trying occasions, I shall ever feel the highest
gratitude and affection.

It is unnecessary I hope to assure you of the pleasure I shall
always receive at seeing you here, whenever business or your
health will permit. The latter, possibly, might be benefitted by
the change of Air. With sincere esteem and Regd. etc.[5]

To GENERAL BENJAMIN LINCOLN[6]

Mount Vernon, March 23, 1787.

My Dear Sir: Ever since the disorders in your State began to
grow serious I have been peculiarly anxious to hear from that
quarter; General Knox has from time to time transmitted to
me the state of affairs as they came to his hands; but nothing
has given such full and satisfactory information as the particular detail of events which you have been so good as to favor
me with, and for which you will please to accept my warmest
and most grateful acknowledgments. Permit me also, my dear
Sir, to offer you my sincerest congratulations upon your success.
The suppression of those tumults and insurrections with so

---

[5] From a copy, kindly furnished by Francis A. Foster, of the original letter owned
by Maj. Gen. Preston Brown, United States Army, retired, of Vineyard Haven, Mass.
[6] In command of State troops for suppressing Shay's rebellion.

little bloodshed, is an event as happy as it was unexpected; it must have been peculiarly agreeable to you, being placed in so delicate and critical a situation. I am extremely happy to find that your sentiments upon the disfranchising act are such as they are; upon my first seeing it, I formed an opinion perfectly coincident with yours, vizt., that measures more generally lenient might have produced equally as good an effect without entirely alienating the affections of the people from the government; as it now stands, it affects a large body of men, some of them, perhaps, it deprives of the means of gaining a livelihood; the friends and connections of those people will feel themselves wounded in a degree, and I think it will rob the State of a number of its inhabitants, if it produces nothing worse.

It gives me great pleasure to hear that your Eastern settlements succeeds so well the sincere regard which I have for you will always make your prosperity a part of my happiness. I am etc.[7]

To GEORGE WEEDON

Mount Vernon, March 25, 1787.

I have received your favor of the 19th. and thank you for the trouble you have taken to procure for me the Jerusalem Artichoke, but as Captn. Grymes has been so obliging as to send me five Bushels of them which I expect are enough to plant an acre of ground (which will be sufficient to make the experiment I had in contemplation) as there is no way of getting them but by the Stage or sending on purpose for them and as it might

---

[7] From the "Letter Book" copy in the *Washington Papers*.

On March 23 Washington wrote to John Parke, of Delaware, thanking him for his poetical works and "The Honor which you have done me in dedicating your book to me. . . . I always wish to give every possible encouragement to those works of Genius which are the production of an American."

On this same day (March 23) Washington wrote also to Matthew McConnell, thanking him for his *Essay on the Domestic Debts of the United States*. Copies of both of these letters are in the "Letter Book" in the *Washington Papers*.

have been inconvenient to Mr. Page to have spared what he furnished you with for my use, I pray you to return them to him with my thanks for the kind intention.

I shall follow the directions contained in your letter unless upon further inquiry of him or others a better can be suggested, but I shall be glad to know whether in hills, or in drills, is the usual mode of planting, and at what distance. I am, etc.[8]

To MARQUIS DE LAFAYETTE

Mount Vernon, March 25, 1787.

My Dear Marquis: Since writing you a hasty letter in November last, by a vessel which was then passing my door, I have been honored with your kind and obliging favor of the 26th of October; for the affectionate sentiments with which it is replete I pray you to accept my warmest and most grateful acknowledgments and the strongest assurances of everlasting friendship.

I am writing to you my Dear Sir but where will the letter find you? In Crimea, Constantinople, or the Archipelago? or will it await your return to Paris? About this time you must according to your account be setting out for the first, to make the tour of the latter. If it should get to your hands, before or during the interview you will have with her imperial majesty[9] it will afford you an opportunity of informing her personally, that the request she made to you for obtaining an Indian Vocabulary is in a proper train for execution. I have the strongest assurances from both General Butler who is now superintendent of Indian affairs and residing on the Ohio, and Mr. Hutchins the Geographer who is also employed in that Country

---

[8] The text is from a printed copy in a sales catalogue, 1924.
[9] Empress Catherine the Great, of Russia.

that they will delay no time nor spare any pains to make it as perfect as they can. As soon as I receive, I will forward it to you.

I fear this long trip will be the means of postponing your visit to this Country to the very great regret of all your friends and particularly so to me who would wish to see you once more before I go in search of Elysium. You will long ere this have heard of the Insurrection in the State of Massachusetts; to trace the causes would be difficult, and to detail their progress would be unnecessary as the steps taken by that government and the proceedings generally are very minutely related in the public gazettes with which I am informed you are regularly supplied. I shall therefore proceed to the more pleasing part of the business and inform you that the tumults are at an end and the principals fled to Canada. It is apprehended however that an act of the Legislature disfranchising those who were aiding or abetting, is pregnant with as much evil as good, as the operation is too extensive.

These disorders are evident marks of a defective government; indeed the thinking part of the people of this Country are now so well satisfied of this fact that most of the Legislatures have appointed, and the rest it is said will appoint, delegates to meet at Philadelphia on the second Monday in May next in a general Convention of the States to revise and correct the defects of the federal System. Congress have also recognised, and recommended the measure. What may be the result of this meeting is hardly within the scan of human wisdom to predict. It is considered however as the last essay to support the present form.

Your endeavors my dear Marquis to serve this Country are unremitted, the letter from the Minister to Mr. Jefferson (who I am happy to find is so much respected and esteem'd at the Court of France), which you had the goodness to send me, is a recent instance of it. and I wish the conduct of the States may entitle them to a continuation of your good offices as I also do that the Protestants may be grateful for the reliefs you have afforded them.

The Dutch, though a phlegmatic people, have been too long quarrelling to come now to blows and if matters there can be settled without it the probability is that the tranquillity of Europe may be of some continuance unless the disagreement between the Russians and Turks should become more serious. It seems almost nugatory to dispute about the best mode of dealing with the Algerines, when we have neither money to buy their friendship nor the means of punishing them for their depredations upon our people and trade. If we could command the latter I should be clearly in sentiment with you and Mr. Jefferson, that chastisement would be more honorable, and much to be preferred to the purchased friendship of these Barbarians. By me, who perhaps do not understand the policy by which the Maritime powers are actuated it has ever been considered as reflecting the highest disgrace on them to become tributary to such banditti, who might for half the sum that is paid them be exterminated from the Earth.

This want must turn our faces from the Western Posts, even should it be found that we have not been the first infractors of the Treaty. To investigate this matter, as there have been crimination on both sides, the Secretary for Foreign affairs is now employed.

General Greenes death is an event which has given so much general concern and is so much regretted by his numerous friends that I can scarce persuade myself to touch upon it even so far as to say that in him you lost a man who affectionately regarded and was a sincere admirer of you. Tho' last mentioned, it is among my uppermost thoughts to thank you once more, my dear Marquis for the valuable animals you sent me under the care of Mr. Campion and to request my dear friend that you will let me know the cost of them that I may remit the amount for be assured I have had it in contemplation to give you more than the trouble of procuring them. I have lately lost a Brother (Colo. John Augt. Washington which I mention to account for the black Seal of this letter) the rest of my friends, and every individual in the Family are tolerably well and join most cordially in every vow that can contribute to the health and happiness of Madam La Fayette yourself and family. Esqr Tab[10] will soon be able to offer you his own homage as he begins to write very prettily. I have no expression that can convey to you the warmth of my friendship and affectionate attachment. Adieu.

P. S. Mr Campion observing that red birds were not among the feathered tribe of France, and the wood or summer duck were very rare there I send you two pair of the latter and several of the former which Capt. Atkinson who is bound for Havre de gras has promised his care of.[11]

* To GOVERNOR EDMUND RANDOLPH

Mount Vernon, March 28, 1787.

Dear Sir: Your favor of the 11th. did not come to my hand till the 24th; and since then, till now, I have been too much indisposed to acknowledge the receipt of it.

To what cause to ascribe the detention of the [letter] I know not, as I never omit sending once, and oftener twice a week to the Post Office in Alexandria. It was the decided intention of the letter I had the honor of writing to your Excellency the

---

[10] George Washington Parke Custis(?).
[11] From the "Letter Book" copy in the *Washington Papers*.

21st. of December last, to inform you, that it would not be convenient for me to attend the Convention proposed to be holden
in Philadelphia in May next; and I had entertained hopes that
another had been, or soon would be, appointed in my place;
inasmuch as it is not only inconvenient for me to leave home,
but because there will be, I apprehend, too much cause to
charge my conduct with inconsistency, in again appearing on
a public theatre after a public declaration to the contrary; and
because it will, I fear, have a tendency to sweep me back into
the tide of public affairs, when retirement and ease is so essen-
tially necessary for, and is so much desired by me.

However, as my friends, with a degree of sollicitude which
is unusual, seem to wish for my attendance on this occasion, I
have come to a resolution to go, if my health will permit, provided, from the lapse of time between the date of your Excellency's letter and this reply, the Executive may not, the reverse
of which wd. be highly pleasing to me, have turned its thoughts
to some other character; for independantly of all other considerations, I have, of late, been so much afflicted with a rheumatic complaint in my shoulder that at times I am hardly able
to raise my hand to my head, or turn myself in bed. This, consequently, might prevent my attendance, and eventually a representation of the State; which wd. afflict me more sensibly than
the disorder that occasioned it.

If after the expression of these sentiments, the Executive
should consider me as one of the Delegates, I would thank your
Excellency for the earliest advice of it; because, if I am able,
and should go to Philadelpa., I shall have some previous arrangements to make, and would set off for that place the first,
or second day of May, that I may be there in time to account,
personally, for my conduct to the General Meeting of the Cincinnati which is to convene on the first Monday of that month.

My feelings would be much hurt if that body should otherwise, ascribe my attendance on the one, and not on the other occasion, to a disrespectful inattention to the Society; when the fact is, that I shall ever retain the most lively and affectionate regard for the members of which it is composed, on acct. of their attachment to, and uniform support of me, upon many trying occasions; as well as on acct. of their public virtues, patriotism, and sufferings.

I hope your Excellency will be found among the *attending* delegates. I should be glad to be informed who the others are; and cannot conclude without once more, and in emphatical terms, praying that if there is not a *decided* representation in *prospect,* without me, that another, for the reason I have assigned, may be chosen in my room without ceremony and without delay; for it would be unfortunate indeed if the State which was the mover of this Convention, should be unrepresented in it. With great respect I have the honor etc.   [H.S.P.]

*To JAMES MADISON

Mount Vernon, March 31, 1787.

My Dear Sir: At the sametime that I acknowledge the receipt of your obliging favor of the 21st. ult. from New York I promise to avail myself of your indulgence of writing only when it is convenient to me. If this should not occasion a relaxation on your part, I shall become very much your debtor, and possibly

---

On March 30 Washington wrote out the following memorandum, or certificate, at Mount Vernon: "On Monday the 12th. day of Septr. 1785. A Mr. Caywood, or some person in his behalf, presented an Acct. of Taxes, or the claims of the public for some Land I have in Charles County Maryland, which was the first application ever made to me, for the same. Whether previously, or subsequent to, that period any demand was ever made of Mr. Lund Washington who had charge of my business till the close of that year for them is more than I can determine, but, no doubt, can be resolved by him." The original of this memorandum is in the *Washington Papers.*

like others in similar circumstances (when the debt is burthensome) may feel a disposition to apply the spunge, or, what is nearly a-kin to it, pay you off in depreciated paper, which being a legal tender, or what is tantamount, being *that* or *nothing,* you cannot refuse. You will receive the nominal value, and that you know quiets the conscience, and makes all things easy, with the debtor.

I am glad to find that Congress have recommended to the States to appear in the Convention proposed to be holden in Philadelphia in May. I think the reasons in favor, have the preponderancy of those against the measure. It is idle in my opinion to suppose that the Sovereign can be insensible of the inadequacy of the powers under which it acts, and that seeing, it should not recommend a revision of the Fœderal system when it is considered by many as the *only* Constitutional mode by which the defects can be remedied. Had Congress proceeded to a delineation of the Powers, it might have sounded an Alarm; but as the case is, I do not conceive that it will have that effect.[12]

From the acknowledged abilities of the Secretary for Foreign Affairs, I could have had no doubt of his having ably investigated the infractions of the Treaty on both sides. Much is it to be regretted however, that there should have been any on ours. We seem to have forgotten, or never to have learnt, the policy of placing ones enemy in the wrong. Had we observed good faith on our part, we might have told our tale to the world with a good grace; but complts. illy become those who are found to be the first agressors.

[12]   On Feb. 21, 1787, Congress had resolved that it was expedient that a convention of delegates from the several States be held at Philadelphia on the second Monday of May next "for the sole and express purpose of revising the Articles of Confederation and reporting to Congress and the several legislatures such alterations and provisions therein as shall . . . render the federal Constitution adequate to the exigencies of Government and the preservation of the Union."

I am fully of opinion that those who lean to a Monarchial governmt. have either not consulted the public mind, or that they live in a region where the levelling principles in which they were bred, being entirely irradicated, is much more productive of Monarchical ideas than are to be found in the Southern States, where, from the habitual distinctions which have always existed among the people, one would have expected the first generation, and the most rapid growth of them. I also am clear, that even admitting the utility; nay necessity of the form, yet that the period is not arrived for adopting the change without shaking the Peace of this Country to its foundation. That a thorough reform of the present system is indispensable, none who have capacities to judge will deny; and with hand (and heart) I hope the business will be essayed in a full Convention. After which, if more powers, and more decision is not found in the existing form. If it still wants energy and that secrecy and dispatch (either from the nonattendance, or the local views of its members) which is characteristick of good Government. And if it shall be found (the contrary of which however I have always been more afrd. of, than of the abuse of them) that Congress will upon all proper occasions exercise the powers with a firm and steady hand, instead of frittering them back to the Individual States where the members in place of viewing themselves in their National character, are too apt to be looking. I say after this essay is made if the system proves inefficient, conviction of the necessity of a change will be dissiminated among all classes of the People. Then, and not till then, in my opinion can it be attempted without involving all the evils of civil discord.

I confess however that my opinion of public virtue is so far changed that I have my doubts whether any system without the means of coercion in the Sovereign, will enforce Obedience to the Ordinances of a Genl. Government; without which, every thing else fails. Laws or Ordinances unobserved, or partially attended to, had better never have been made; because the first is a mere nihil, and the 2d. is productive of much jealousy and discontent. But the kind of coercion you may ask? This indeed will require thought; though the non-compliance of the States with the late requisition, is an evidence of the necessity. It is somewhat singular that a State (New York) which used to be foremost in all fœderal measures, should now turn her face against them in almost every instance.

I fear the State of Massachusetts have exceeded the bounds of good policy in its disfranchisements; punishment is certainly due to the disturbers of a government, but the operations of this Act is too extensive. It embraces too much, and probably may give birth to new instead of destroying the old leven. Some Acts passed at the last Session of our Assembly respecting the trade of this Country, has given great, and general discontent to the Merchants of it. An application from the whole body of those at Norfolk has been made, I am told, to convene the assembly.

I had written thus far, and was on the point of telling you how much I am your obliged Servant, when your favor of the 18th. calls upon me for additional acknowledgments. I thank you for the Indian Vocabulary which I dare say will be very acceptable in a general comparison. Having taken a copy, I return you the original with thanks.

It gives me great pleasure to hear that there is a probability of a full representation of the States in Convention; but if the delegates come to it under fetters, the salutary ends proposed will in my opinion be greatly embarrassed and retarded, if not altogether defeated. I am anxious to know how this matter really is, as my wish is, that the Convention may adopt no temporizing expedient, but probe the defects of the Constitution to the bottom, and provide radical cures; whether they are agreed to or not; a conduct like this, will stamp wisdom and dignity on the proceedings, and be looked to as a luminary, which sooner or later will shed its influence.

I should feel pleasure, I confess, in hearing that Vermont is received into the Union upon terms agreeable to all parties. I took the liberty years ago to tell some of the first characters in the State of New York, that sooner or later it would come to that. That the longer it was delayed the terms on their part, would, probably be more difficult; and that the general interest was suffering by the suspence in which the business was held; as the asylem wch. it afforded, was a constant drain from the Army in place of an aid which it offered to afford. and lastly, considering the proximity of it to Canada if they were not with us, they might become a sore thorn in our sides, wch. I verily believe would have been the case if the war had continued. The Western Settlements without good and wise management of them, may be equally troublesome.

With sentimts. of the sincerest friendship &c. Be so good as to forward the enclosed. Mrs. Washington intended to have sent it by Colo. Carrington, but he did not call here.

[N.Y.P.L.]

To JOHN FRANCIS MERCER

Mount Vernon, April 1, 1787.

Sir: Enclosed I return the letter which you forwarded to me the 10th. of Feby. For particular reasons and purposes, whatever Money you may incline to pay me consequent of your promises would come very opportunely before the 25th of this month. To this period, sufficient time is allowed to obtain the Certificates you have at Richmond, after which I shall hold myself discharged from any obligation to receive them.

The detention has already deprived me of every advantage I could have made of them in the payment of Taxes whilst I am sustaining the loss by their depreciation in the hands of others. My Compliments if you please to Mrs. Mercer. I am ,etc.[13]

*To RICHARD SPRIGG

Mount Vernon, April 1, 1787.

Dear Sir: It is, I believe, beyond a doubt that your Jenny is with foal by my Spaniard. As I have two imported female Asses (very fine) which will be put to my Jacks this Season, and from which I may expect the pure breed; you are very welcome to the produce of your own, and the sooner you send for her the better, and less risk will be run in removing her. At present she is in very fine order having been well fed and attended through the winter. With compliments to Mrs. Sprig I am etc.[14]

*To HENRY KNOX

Mount Vernon, April 2, 1787.

My dear Sir: The early attention which you were so obliging as to pay to my letter of the 8th ulto. is highly pleasing and flattering to me. Were you to continue to give me information on the same point, you would add to the favor; as I see, or think I see, reasons for and against my attendance in Convention so near an equilibrium, as will cause me to Determine upon either, with diffidence. One of the reasons against it, is, an apprehension that all the States will not appear; and that some of them, being unwillingly drawn into the measure, will send their Delegates so fettered as to embarrass, and perhaps render nugatory,

---

[13] From the "Letter Book" copy in the *Washington Papers.*
[14] From a photostat of the original kindly furnished by George A. Ball, of Muncie, Ind.

the whole proceedings. In either of these circumstances, that is, a partial representation, or cramped powers, I should not like to be a sharer in this business. If the Delegates come with such powers as will enable the Convention to probe the defects of the Constitution to the bottom, and point out radical cures, it would be an honorable employment; but otherwise it is desirable to avoid it, and these are matters you may possibly come at by means of your acquaintances among the Delegates in Congress, who, undoubtedly know what powers are given by their respective States. You also can inform me what is the prevailing opinion with respect to my attendance, or non-attendance, is; and I would sincerely thank you for the confidential communication of it.

If I should attend the Convention, I will be in Philadelphia previous to the meeting of the Cincinnati, where I shall hope, and expect to meet you and some others of my particular friends the day before; in order that I may have a free and unreserved conference with you on the subject of it; for I assure you this is in my estimation, a business of a delicate nature.

That the design of the Institution was pure, I have not a particle of doubt. That it may be so still, is perhaps equally unquestionable. But, quære, are not the subsidence of the Jealousies of it, to be ascribed to the modification which took place at the last Genl. Meeting? Are not these rejected in toto by some of the State Societies, and partially acceded to by others? Has any State so far overcome its prejudices as to grant a Charter? Will the modifications and alterations be insisted on, or given up, in the next Meeting? If the first, will it not occasion warmth and divisions? If the latter, and I should remain at the head of this order, in what light would my signature appear in contradictory recommendations? In what light would the versatility appear to the Foreign members, who perhaps are acting agreeably to the recommendations of the last General Meeting?

These, and other matters which may be agitated, will, I fear, place me in a disagreeable predicament if I should preside, and were among the causes which induced me to decline the honor of it, previously to the meeting. Indeed my health is become very precarious. A Rheumatic complaint which has followed me more than Six months is frequently so bad, that it is with difficulty I can, at times, raise my hand to my head, or turn myself in bed. This, however smooth and agreeable other matters might be, might almost in the moment of my departure, prevent my attendance on either occasion. I will not at present touch upon any other parts of your letter, but would wish you to ponder on all these matters, and write to me as soon as you can.

With the most sincere friendship etc. [MS.H.S.]

To JOHN RUMNEY

Mount Vernon, April 6, 1787.

Sir: However desirous I may be of accomodating the wishes of so deserving a Lady as you represent Mrs. Wilson to be, yet Mrs. Washington concurs in sentiment with me that my family already is, and soon will be too large to admit of an increase.

I can say little more at this time respecting the Estate of the deceased Colo. Thos. Colvill than what is contained in my account of it to Major Swan (recited in one of the letters which you put into my hands) except that I have used every means in my power lately to Collect materials (and very defective indeed they are) for a final settlement of the Administration.

What the surplus of the estate will be, when the debts and Legacies are all paid, is more than I can inform you, the Testator himself, as will appear by his will, had a doubt of their being *any,* and what will be done with *it,* if there should, must be a matter for future determination, when the Administration is closed, which it is my sincere wish to do so as fast as the nature of the case will admit, I shall for my own justification, and security, take Council with respect to the application of the surplus, if any, under the existing Laws of this Country. The author of the letters of Instruction to you is mistaken I conceive when he says the claim of one Clowson was admtted, unless by admission he means that it was received. If this was not his idea, it will give him no pleasure to be informed that near twenty others, I believe, have been admitted in the same way under the indefinite, and I might add, indigested clause of the will which has stirred up so many pretenders as to render it a matter of difficult investigation to determine rightly in the case. With great esteem and regard, I am, etc.[15]

To HENRY EMANUEL LUTTERLOH

Mount Vernon, April 8, 1787.

Sir: I have received your letter of the 3d. of Jany. containing a proposition of the delivery of several hundred German families to settle some of those large tracts of unimproved Land in this State.

I cannot, as an individual, do any thing, at present, towards promoting your design having no occasion for people of the description mentioned in your letter except a few Mechanics, which I should be glad to procure; upon advantageous terms but as a member of a Company owning a tract of land known by the name of the Great Dismal Swamp. I can inform you that I know it is their wish and desire to have it settled. It lies in the Neighbourhood of Norfolk, contains of that which is

---

[15] From the "Letter Book" copy in the *Washington Papers.*

patented besides Entries about 40,000 Acres, and is capable of being made as valuable a tract of Land as any in the Country, as well on account of its vicinity to Norfolk Portsmouth and Suffolk and the State of North Carolina as its lying in such a situation as to have the Canal, which it is in contemplation to open between Albemarle sound and Elizabeth R: run directly through it and which will greatly facilitate the drawing of it. But the Company are so dispersed and, in a manner, inattentive to the business, that I am pretty certain they would not be brought to advance any money or incur any expence in settling it further than to give such a proportion of the Land as shall be to the mutual satisfaction of the parties, what this proportion would be I am not able to say, tho I have no reason to doubt but that it would be highly advantageous to the Settlers. I should think however, if you incline to enter upon this business, it would be best for you to view the land, that you might form an opinion of the proportion which it would be proper to give, and make your proposals accordingly. I would in that case use every endeavor to convince the Company that an agreement might be entered into. I conceive a proper introduction of those industrious people would be highly beneficial to this Country, and shall be happy to give you any assistance in my power towards the effecting of your plan. With very great esteem etc.[16]

To GOVERNOR EDMUND RANDOLPH

Mount Vernon, April 9, 1787.

My dear Sir: In reply to your favor of the 2d. I have to request that you will not be at the trouble of forwarding any money to me from the treasury.

---

[16] From the "Letter Book" copy in the *Washington Papers.*

If I should attend the Service, it will suit me as well to receive it from you in Philadelphia as at this place. If I should not, I have no business with it at all.

It gives me pleasure to find by your letter that there will be so full a representation from this State. If the case had been otherwise I would in emphatical terms have urged again that, rather than depend upon my going, another might be chosen in my place; for as a friend, and in confidence, I declare to you that my assent is given contrary to my judgment, because the act will, I apprehend, be considered as inconsistent with my public declaration delivered in a solemn manner at an interesting æra of my life, never more to intermeddle in public matters. This declaration not only stands on the files of Congress, but is I believe registered in almost all the Gazettes and magazines that are published, and what adds to the embarrassment is, I had previous to my appointment, informed by circular letter the several State Societies of the Cincinnati of my intention to decline the Presidency of that order and excuse myself from attending the next General meeting at Philadelphia on the first Monday in May, assigning reasons for so doing which apply as well in the one case as the other. Add to these, I very much fear that all the States will not appear in Convention, and that some of them will come fettered so as to impede rather than accelerate the great object of their convening which, under the peculiar circumstances of my case, would place me in a more disagreeable Situation than any other Member would stand in. As I have yielded however to what appeared to be the earnest wishes of my friends, I will hope for the best; and can assure you of the sincere and Affect. regard with which I am, etc.[17]

---

[17] From the "Letter Book" copy in the *Washington Papers*.

To JOHN LAWSON

Mount Vernon, April 10, 1787.

Sir: On the 8th. Instant Neptune delivered me your letter of the 2d. Instant. Although he does not profess to be a workman, yet as he has some little knowledge of Bricklaying, seems willing to learn, and is with a man who understands the business, I will keep him, and this shall be my obligation to pay you the sum for which he sold, at the time and agreeably to the terms of Mr. Hunters Sale. I am, etc.

P. S. Since writing the above, and informing Neptune of my determination to buy him he seems a good deal disconcerted on acct. of a wife which he says he has at Mrs. Garrards from whom he is unwilling to be so far removed this also embarrasses me as I am unwilling to hurt the feelings of anyone. I shall therefore if agreeable to you keep him awhile to see if I can reconcile him to the separation (seeing her now and then) in which case I will purchase him, if not I will send him back, and pay what hire you shall think fit and is reasonable to charge for the time he is here.[18]

To REVEREND WILLIAM GORDON

Mount Vernon, April 10, 1787.

Dear Sir: I have received your favor of the 13th. of July and 28th of Septr.

I am pleased to hear of your safe arrival in London and of the happy meeting with your friends. I wish you success in the publication of your work and that your future establishment (which you say was not then fixed) may be agreeable to your wishes.

---

[18] From the "Letter Book" copy in the *Washington Papers*.

The bill which was sent to Rhode Island had the good fortune to come back protested. Mr. Watson the drawer immediately gave me another (including interest) upon a Gentleman in Salem for £43.3.8 this Currency, which was forwarded to your friend Mr. Mason of Boston and paid.

It is not in my power to give you such accurate information of our Settlements in the Western Country as might answer the purposes of a publication, my own knowledge of it being more general than particular, and information you know is not always to be relied upon. The idea however, of it being made up of the scum and refuse of the Continent, that the people are opposed to Congress, and attached to the British government is of a piece with other doctrines and consequent publications which have recoiled upon the authors, and which one would think was enough to discourage such unfounded and short sighted reports.

Mrs. Washington having of late been much less troubled with the billious cholick than formerly has made no use of the prescription you were so obliging as to transmit but is not less thankful on that account for your kind attention to her in this instance and joins me, as does the rest of the family in every good wish for yourself and Mrs. Gordon. With great esteem and respect I am, etc.[19]

CERTIFICATE TO CHRISTOPHER LUDOWICK [20]

Mount Vernon, April 12, 1787.

I have known Mr. Christn. Ludwick from an early period of the War; and have every reason to believe, as well from observation as information that he has been a true and faithful

---

[19] From the "Letter Book" copy in the *Washington Papers*.
[20] Formerly Baker General of the Continental Army.

Friend, and Servant to the public. That he has detected and exposed many impositions which were attempted to be practiced by others in the department over which he presided. That he has been the cause of much saving in many respects. And that his deportment in public life has afforded unquestionable proofs of his integrity and worth.

With respect to the particular losses of which he complains, I have no personal knowledge of them, but have often heard that he has suffered from his zeal in the cause of his Country.[21]

To JOHN RAWLINS[22]

Mount Vernon, April 13, 1787.

Sir: I have received the freizes for the doors and windows which I think are very pretty, together with your letter sent by Capt. Man, but I did not think proper to comply with the contents of it at this time. Altho' it is not my desire to enter into any dispute respecting the payment of the money, yet before I do it I wish you to view the work, that you may, yourself judge of the execution. My sole motive for employing Mr. Tharp to execute the common plaster work, and giving a higher price than what I could have had it done for by others, was the expectation, that, agreeable to promise, it would have been done in a masterly manner; but this is not the case, and you would think so yourself, was you to see it, the Stucco work in the Parlour is much cracked and Stained, the plain work in the New Room and in every other part of the House, is in fact but little better than the plaster which was pulled down. Mr. Tharp said something should be done to hide the Stains and blemishes, but that it was not proper to do it when he was here,

---

[21] From the "Letter Book" copy in the *Washington Papers*.
[22] Of Baltimore, Md.

this I expect will be performed. There is likewise wanting to compleat the New Room 6 doz large hollows, 3 doz dble F. O. G.[23] and 6 feet of fluting, some person was to have been sent by you to decorate the pilasters, which has not yet been done. When the work is compleated and your engagement properly fulfil you will find on my part no inclination to withhold the pay. I am, etc.[24]

To JOHN CANNON

Mount Vernon, April 13, 1787.

Sir: I have recd. your letter of 22d of Jany. and as I wish to dispose of my Land near you (as well as the tract in Fayette County) I will with pleasure mention my terms to you, that you may make them known and give assurances of the title upon their being complied with. The Land in Washington County I will sell at 30/ Pensylvania Currency pr. Acre (payable in Specie), one fourth down, and the other ¾ in Annual payments with interest from the date of the Bonds, perhaps a longer time may be granted for the ¾ if the interest is paid punctually. I had much rather sell the whole tract together than to have it divided into Lots, but if a division would facilitate the sale I have no objection, provided the Lots do not interfere with, nor injure the sale of each other and if they sell one with another so as to average the above price for the whole.

As it is my primary object to sell all my lands in that part of the Country, I should not wish to have them leased for any long time, least it should obstruct the sale of them.

I am much obliged to you for your goodness in offering to manage my Land for me in Fayette County; and as Majr. Freeman is about to leave that part of the Country I will accept of

---

[23] Ogees(?).
[24] From the "Letter Book" copy in the *Washington Papers*.

your kind offer. My terms for that tract are 40/ Pensa. Currency pr. Acre the payments to be made as above, I have lately had an application for this tract from a Gentleman in Jersey, and am in daily expectation of his final answer to my terms, this however need not prevent the application of others as I am under no obligation to give the preference to anyone, but shall close with the first that comes to my terms. I recd. a letter from Mr. Smith in Feby. mentioning that unless I came upon terms with the defendts. it would be best to have the Sheriff execute writs of possession to my Agent before Harvest, that those who had put seed in the Ground might consider it as an obligation confered upon them, to be permitted to take off their Crops, whereas, if writs of possession were not executed, they would take them off of course as their right, but, I suppose, as they have become tenants the immediate necessity of this measure is superceded. I know nothing of any promise which Colo. Crawford made of leaving out any part of the land when he surveyed it, the patent was taken out agreeable to his return and cannot now be altered. However, if the Land is sold I will consider Mr. Hillis as a preferable purchaser of that piece which runs along his line so as to include his improvements, provided it does not affect the sale of the rest. With great esteem etc.

P. S. Inclosed is the form of the writs of Possession as forwarded to me by Mr. Smith, if it should be necessary to execute them.[25]

To JAMES GIBBONS[26]

Mount Vernon, April 15, 1787.

Sir: I have recd. your letter of the 26th. Ulto. wherein you request my opinion with respect to your obtaining the benefit

---

[25] From the "Letter Book" copy in the *Washington Papers*.
[26] Formerly a lieutenant of the Pennsylvania line, and aide to General Irvine.

of the Commutation. I am sorry that I cannot, with propriety comply with your request; as I have never interfered with, nor had any knowledge of the settlement of those Accts. I can have no grounds whereon to form an opinion. Mr. Pierce,[27] to whom you say Congress has referred your Case, is undoubtedly better qualified from the documents which he has, to judge of the propriety or impropriety of it than I can possible be. With respect to extensive furloughs, I can only say that I never considered myself authorized to grant them to officers to go off the Continent, but when application was made for that purpose I referred them to Congress. I am, etc.[28]

To SIR EDWARD NEWENHAM

Mount Vernon, April 20, 1787.

Dear Sir: Not till within these few days have I been honoured with your favours of the 13th. and 25th. of November last I should if they had come to hand sooner been earlier in my acknowledgment of them.

I sincerely wish that this letter may find Miss Newenham in a perfectly recovered State of health, and Lady Newenham and yourself relieved from those anxious cares and sollicitudes which her indisposition must naturally have created. I hope also that neither this, nor anything else, will prevent you from fulfilling your long intended voyage to America. Should this event take place at so early a period as your last letters indicated, any information on the points you have referred to me will hardly arrive in season yet, as there is a possibility of it, the enclosed, which I have obtained from a well informed Gentleman in Alexandria, (more conversant in matters of this kind than

---

[27] John Pierce, Paymaster General, United States Army.
[28] From the "Letter Book" copy in the *Washington Papers*.

I am), will answer your queries with respect to the sorts of linnens which are most saleable in our Markets. The prices of
provisions is governed by the Seasons, and quality, generally.
Beef and Mutton from the month of January till June fluctu-
ates from 4d. to 6d., from June till January from 2–1/9d. to 4d.
Veal and Lamb are commonly sold by the Quarter the latter
from 2/6 to 4/ the other in proportion to the age and quality
of the Meat. These prices you will please to observe are in the
Currency of *this* State which by the *legal* exchange is 33–1/3
worse then Sterling. Bills however are negotiated at 40 pr. Ct.
and have been so for sometime, which will enable you to determine whether money, or letters of credit, will answer your
purposes best. the former would give least trouble, tho' there is
some risk. Bills on London are in more general demand, and
consequently command the best prices.

The manner in which you employ your time at Bell Champ
(in raising nurseries of fruit, forest trees, and Shrubs) must not
only contribute to your health and amusement, but it is certainly among the most rational avocations of life; for what can
be more pleasing, than to see the work of ones own hands, fostered by care and attention, rising to maturity in a beautiful
display of those advantages and ornaments which by the Com-
bination of Nature and taste of the projector in the disposal of
them is always regaling to the eye at the sametime in their seasons they are a grateful [*sic*] to the palate.

I should have much pleasure in admiring your skill in the
propogation and disposal of these things in a visit to Bell Champ.
but declining health and an anxious wish to spend the remainder of my days in retirement will fix me to Mount Vernon and
a small circle round it whilst I tread on this Theatre.

I will not give you the trouble of receiving a long letter from
me at this time because the probability, I think is, that you will

have left Ireland before it can get thither. I shall only add therefore that it was with pain I gave the information contained in my last respecting the application for the Consulship at Marsailles: the Inclosures which I transmitted would account for the disappointment and though to be regretted in the present case the principle deserves more to be applauded than condemned for, few things being in the gift of Congress, it was thought that such as could be disposed of ought to be given to those who had suffered in the service of their Country during the late contest and a resolution to that effect having taken place in that body, which for the sake of consistency was obliged to adhere to it. I beg to be presented in respectful terms to Lady Newenham, and have the honor to be with great esteem and regard Dr. Sir Yr. etc.[29]

AGREEMENT WITH PHILIP BATER

April 23, 1787.

Articles of Agreement made this twelveth day of April Anno Domini one thousand seven hundred and eighty seven, by and between George Washington Esqr. of the Parish of Truro, in the County of Fairfax, State of Virginia, on the one part, and Philip Bater, Gardner, on the other Witness, that the said Philip Bater, for and in consideration of the covenants herein, hereafter, mentioned, doth promise and agree to serve the sd. George Washington, for the term of one year, as a Gardner, and that he will, during said time, conduct himself soberly, diligently and honestly, that he will faithfully and industriously perform all, and every part of his duty as a Gardner, to the best of his knowledge and abilities, and that he will not, at

---

[29] From the "Letter Book" copy in the *Washington Papers.*

any time, suffer himself to be disguised with liquor, except on the times hereafter mentioned.

In Consideration of these things being well and truly performed on the part of the sd. Philip Bater, the said George Washington doth agree to allow him (the sd. Philip) the same kind and quantity of provisions as he has heretofore had; and likewise, annually, a decent suit of clothes befitting a man in his station; to consist of a Coat, Vest and breeches; a working Jacket and breeches, of homespun, besides; two white Shirts; three Check Do; two pair of yarn Stockings; two pair of Thread Do; two linnen Pocket handkerchiefs; two pair linnen overalls; as many pair of Shoes as are actually necessary for him; four Dollars at Christmas, with which he may be drunk 4 days and 4 nights; two Dollars at Easter to effect the same purpose; two Dollars also at Whitsontide, to be drunk two days; A Dram in the morning, and a drink of Grog at Dinner or at Noon.

For the true and faithful performance of all and each of these things the parties have hereunto set their hands this twenty third day of April Anno Domini 1787.[30]

To GEORGE TURNER

Mount Vernon, April 26, 1787.

Sir: Your letter of the 5th. inst, and the box containing the diplomas for the officers of the State of So. Carolina, came duly to hand. I have signed the diplomas and sent the box to Doctr. Craik in Alexandria to be forwarded by a safe conveyance and have directed it to the care of Colo. Grayson as you requested. The enclosed list I have returned agreeable to your desire. I am, etc.[31]

---

[30] In the writing of George Augustine Washington.
[31] From the "Letter Book" copy in the *Washington Papers*.

*To HENRY KNOX

Mount Vernon, April 27, 1787.

My dear Sir: Hurried as I am I cannot (not expecting to see you in Philadelpa) withhold the copy of a Paragraph in a letter which came to my hands yesterday from Mr. Jefferson, and a translation of the Article "Cincinnati" from the Encyclopedie Methodique, forwarded to me by the same Gentleman as they relate to the Society and serve to shew the light in wch. it is viewed in France. I do not know what the Article from the Encyclopedie Methodique contains as it is in French further than from the purport of Mr. Jeffersons letter, and being received but yesterday it could not be translated previous to my departure but I have desired a Gentleman who lives in my family to do it and have left this letter to be sent with it.

In my present state of mind I can hardly form an opinion whether it will be best to lay the matter before the Society as coming from Mr. Jefferson or as from a person of as good information as any in France I must therefore leave it wholly with you to do as you may think most proper. You know my sentiments from the proceedings of the last General meeting and from my Circular letter. In haste I am etc.   [MS.H.S.]

To HENRY KNOX

Mount Vernon, April 27, 1787.

My dear Sir: After every consideration my judgment was able to give the subject, I had determined to yield to the wishes of many of my friends who seemed anxious for my attending the Convention which is proposed to be holden in Philadelphia the 2d Monday of May, and though so much afflicted with a Rheumatick complaint (of which I have not been entirely free for six months) as to be under the necessity of carrying my arm in a sling for the last ten days, I had fixed on Monday next for my departure, and had made every necessary arrangement for the purpose when (within this hour) I am called by an express, who assures me not a moment is to be lost, to see a mother and *only* sister (who are supposed to be in the agonies of Death) expire;[32] and I am hastening to obey this melancholy call after having just buried a Brother[33] who was the intimate companion of my youth, and the friend of my ripened age. This journey of mine then, 100 miles in the disordered frame of my body, will, I am persuaded, unfit me for the intended trip to Philadelphia, and assuredly prevent my offering that tribute of respect to my compatriots in Arms which results from affection and gratitude for their attachment to, and support of me, upon so many trying occasions.

For this purpose it was, as I had (tho' with a good deal of Reluctance) consented, from a conviction that our affairs were verging fast to ruin, to depart from the resolution I had taken of never more stepping out of the walks of private life, that I determined to shew my respect to the General meeting of the Society by coming there the week before. As the latter is prevented, and the other, it is probable, will not take place, I send such papers as have occasionally come to my hands, and may require the inspection, and the consideration of the Cincinnati. An apology for the order in which they are sent is highly necessary, and my present situation is the best I can offer. To morrow I had set apart for the Inspection and arrangement of them, that such only as were fitting, might be laid before the

---

[32] In Washington's "Diary" it is stated that he received the call between 4 and 5 o'clock in the afternoon of the 26th and set out the next morning about sunrise. He reached Fredericksburg before 2 o'clock the same day, finding both his mother and sister better than had been reported. He returned from Fredericksburg (April 30), reaching Mount Vernon about 6 p. m.

[33] John Augustine Washington.

Society; for unless I had time to go over them again with a person who understands the French language, I am not even certain that all of what I send may relate to the affairs of the Cincinati, and certain I am that some are too personal, the sending of which will not, I hope, be ascribed to improper motives, when the *only* one I had (as I am in the moment of my departure from home and uncertain of returning to it) is that nothing which has been referred to me, may be with held.

In the jumbled order you will receive them, I send them by Doctr. Craik in Alexandria to be forwarded by a safe hand in the Stage to Philadelphia.

I make a tender of my affectionate regard to the members who may Constitute the General Meeting of the Society and with sentiments of the highest esteem etc.[84]

To ROBERT MORRIS

Mount Vernon, May 5, 1787.

Dear Sir: When your favor of the 23d. Ulto. was sent here from the Post Office, I was at Fredericksburg (to which place I had been called, suddenly, by Express) to bid, as I was prepared to expect, the last adieu to an honoured parent, and an affectionate Sister whose watchful attention to my Mother during her illness had brought to death's door. The latter I hope is now out of danger, but the former cannot long Survive the disorder which has reduced her to a Skeleton, tho' she is somewhat amended.

I do not know how, sufficiently, to express my thankfulness to Mrs. Morris and you for your kind invitation to lodge at your house, and though I could not be more happy anywhere, yet as there is great reason to apprehend that the business of the

---

[84] From the "Letter Book" copy in the *Washington Papers.*

Convention (from the tardiness of some States, and the discordant opinions of others) will not be brought to a speedy conclusion, I cannot prevail on myself to give so much trouble to a private family as such a length of time must do. I hope therefore that Mrs. Morris and you will not take it a miss that I decline the polite and obliging offer you have made me.[35]

Mrs. Washington is become too domestick, and too attentive to two little Grand Children to leave home, and I can assure you, Sir, that it was not until after a long struggle I could obtain my own consent to appear again in a public theatre. My first remaining wish being, to glide gently down the stream of life in tranquil retirement till I shall arrive at the world of Spirits.

Mrs. Morris, yourself and family, have every good wish that Mrs. Washington and I can offer, and with the sincerest esteem and regard, I am, etc.[36]

To DAVID STUART

Mount Vernon, May 5, 1787.

Dear Sir: I have received your favor of the 30th and thank you for the enumerations contained in it. They are all clear and self-evident and in some instances may be enlarged. Did you communicate the plan to Cols. Fitzgerald and Hoes? and how far did you give either, or both, reason to believe they would be recommended to Mr. Jefferson (to whom I shall write as soon as I get to Philadelphia). I wish to be fully informed of this that I may govern myself accordingly.

On Monday after an early dinner or on Tuesday morning, I shall (my rheumatic complaint having got better) commence my journey, and I believe by the way of Annapolis to Philadelphia. It would therefore suit me very well to receive the sum

[35] After reaching Philadelphia, Washington consented to lodge with Robert Morris.
[36] From the "Letter Book" copy in the *Washington Papers*.

mentioned when you were here last, at that place; and probably as you are going to Richmond, it may be so ordered. Alexander's bills or Mr. Morris' would answer well; doubtful bills or bills which would be accompanied with delay, would by no means suit me, because the money would be applied—1st, toward paying a debt there, and 2nd, with purchase of some goods for the family, if I can get them cheap there.

If I can render you, or Mrs. Stuart any services while there, I shall be happy in the execution of your commission. With compliments and good wishes for the family, I am etc.[37]

To LUND WASHINGTON

Mount Vernon, May 7, 1787.

Dear Lund: Company, and several other matters which pressed upon me yesterday, and which has obliged me to postpone my journey a day longer is the reason why I did not acknowledge the receipt of your letter by Ned.[38]

I need not tell you, because a moment's recurrence to your own accounts will evince the fact, that there is no source from which I derive more than a sufficiency for the daily calls of my family, except what flows from the collection of old debts, and scanty and precarious enough, God knows this is. My estate for the last 11 years has not been able to make both ends meet. I am encumbered now with the deficiency. I mention this for no other purpose than to shew that however willing, I am not able to pay debts unless I could sell land, which I have publicly advertised without finding bidders.

The enclosed Bond I have had the most pointed assurances would be paid by the first of June. and for that reason if it will

---

[37] From a copy kindly furnished by Dean Academy, Franklin, Mass., which owns the original.
[38] Not now found in the *Washington Papers*.

answer your purpose you may collect and apply the money to the use for which you want it. If this will not do, there is some flour and wheat (if there be water to grind it) in the Mill which you may dispose of for the same end. because I would not wish you to be disappointed. I am etc.[89]

*To ARTHUR LEE

Philada., May 20, 1787.

Dear Sir: I have been honored with your favor of the 13th., since my arrival at this place.

My Rheumatic complaint having very much abated (after I had the pleasure of seeing you at Mount Vernon) I have yielded to what appeared to be the wishes of many of my friends, and am now here as a delegate to the Convention.[40] Not more than four States were represented yesterday. If any are come in since it is unknown to me. These delays greatly impede public measures, and serve to sour the temper of the punctual members who do not like to idle away their time.

Mrs. Washington intended to have given you the trouble of the enclosed, had it been prepared in time. As the case is, I take the liberty of committing it to your care. I have the honor etc.[41]

*To GEORGE AUGUSTINE WASHINGTON

Philadelphia, May 27, 1787.

Dear George: In my last[42] I acknowledged the receipt of your first letter; and I have now to do that of the 20th. instt. And once for all I will desire that you will not let your anxiety to

---

[89] From the "Letter Book" copy in the *Washington Papers*.
[40] On May 9 Washington left Mount Vernon to attend the convention in Philadelphia. He reached the city Sunday, May 13.
[41] From a photostat of the original kindly furnished by George A. Ball, of Muncie, Ind.
[42] Not now found in the *Washington Papers*.

carry on my business well, or fatiegue in the accomplishment
of it, go too far. This would not serve me, and may injure yourself. By attempting too much you may get sick, and do nothing
effectual, for me or yourself.

It gave me concern to find from your last letter that you were
still in want of rain; the Country here abouts is deluged; and
the farmers are complaining of the extra: quantity. In truth
scarcely a day passes without some, on Friday last an immense
quantity fell and as it had the appearance of a settled rain, I hope
it extended to us. If not, patience is the best substitute, indeed
the only remedy.

Hearing that Leather is to be had on better terms at Boston
than in this City, and Mr. Ingraham[43] being on a journey thither
I requested him to buy as much as would make 50 or 60 pair of
Shoes; if this is not enough, the difficiency can be made up here,
or in Alexandria. I also requested him to enquire into the price
of Corn, but this need not prevent your buying if it is to be met
with, as the quantity I want is too small, of itself, to engage a
vessel; and I have neither money, or inclination to speculate in
a larger purchase.

If you tried both fresh, and Salt fish as a manure, the different effect of them should be attended to. I have no objection to
putting the ground at Frenchs in Buck wheat, if the Farmer
shall think it best. This Crop, Potatoes, Pease, and Turnips,
were, if I recollect rightly, what I had designed for the grd. The
quantities of each, or the omission of any, may be governed by
circumstances; and weather; for in this, any more than in other
things, and at other plantations, there is no contending against
the Seasons. Nor should the Crops which are in the ground be
neglected for those that may be put there; if therefore, that part
of Timberlanding field, intended for Buck Wheat, cannot be

---

[43] Nathaniel Ingraham.

plowed before harvest without letting what you call Robins field go unplowed, it must be postponed; for the working of that Corn before harvest is indispensably necessary. In a word, the good attendance of Corn in the early growth of it; and till it has tassled, and put forth Shoots, is, in my opinion, all in all, to the Crop. After this period, I do not believe it is *much* to be hurt, either by weeds or the ground becoming hard.

How does the grass Seeds which were Sown with the grain, and flax, seem to come on? How does those which were sown in my little garden advance? And how does the Crops which are planted in drills between the Corn, come up, and progress. Also those in my experimental squares at Muddy hole; particularly the Carrots and J: Artichoke, the Seeds of which I had most cause to distrust. Is there a prospect of a good deal of Orchard grass seed? let none be lost. Inform me particularly of the appearances of Barley and Oats. The latter, because it composes a principal part of my Crop, and the other because I am anxious for its success, that it may constitute a part of my course of Crops hereafter.

I send by this conveyance some Pecon nuts; which plant as soon as you can. With respect to the quantity of Shells [44] which are, or may be wanted, it is hardly possible for me to say, for which reason, buy always when you can get them good, and Cheap, 16/8 I was informed they might be had for, if not at this, get them on the best terms you can. When you go about the repositary for the compost, at the mouth of the drain by the Stable, if the bottom should not be of good clay, put clay there and ram it well before you pave it, to prevent the liquid manure from sinking, and thereby being lost, this should also be done on the New sides wch. are to be walled up. Cornelius when he knows for what purpose this is required will, I presume, know how to do it.

---

[44] Oyster shells.

I hope the stray doe will not be lost; does any of them appear to be with young? Has any Mares been sent to the Jacks, and to Magnolio, and how many to each? If the state of the Mill run, and other circumstances will admit of it the opening, and thoroughly repairing of the race, will be an important object, because it cannot be done but in warm weather, and not to advantage but when the Water is low.

Have you made no mistake in your acct. of the pease that were drilled at Muddy hole? In your report of this (May 15th) you note that 1 Bushel from Colo. Lee's, and two of the large yellow (made at home) were sowed; and that of the first there were 16 rows, and of the latter 15 only; I should hardly have thought that the same quantity of Lees Pease, would have seeded double the ground the others had done; and is the whole field, that is every 8th. row from one end to the other sown? the quantity seems small for this also, as it does indeed in all the cuts at the different places; for if 3 Bushels were sufficient to sow the whole field at Muddy hole you must have a surplusage of seed, which might have been tried in broadcast, whilst I was apprehensive of a scarcity for the drill cultivation of them between the Corn rows.

Desire Mathew to furnish me with a Memo. of the Hinges wanted for the New-room, and to which hand they are to rise, that I may endeavor to provide them whilst I am in this place. As I see no prospect of a Speedy return (for contrary to my wish, I am made, by a unanimous vote, President of the Convention) I will, in due time furnish you with a plan for conducting your harvest. In the meantime, send me my last diary, which, by mistake, I left behind me. It will be found, I presume, on my writing Table. put it under a good strong paper cover, sealed up as a letter. Speaking of a Diary, it would be better in your report of the occurances, and the work done at the Plantations, to allow a paragraph to each. That is, when you change from one plantation to another, to begin a new line; for sometimes, without this, and perhaps not properly attending, I do not in the moment perceive the change; nor when I want to recur to it, is it so easily come at, as if in the daily report, all that related to each plantation was in paragraphs, as above mentioned. Give my love to Fanny, and best wishes to Mr. Lear. With best affectn. I am etc.

PS. Is the Seeds of the honey locust come up? They shd. be kept clean, as everything else in drills ought to be. Colo. Rogers of Baltimore was to have sent by the Baltimore packet to Alexandria for me a quantity of the English (imported) white thorn. If they are at hand let the Farmer manage them as he thinks proper. If I did not mention it in my last, a Plow was to have been sent by Majr. Snowden[45] to Mr. Hartshorn for me. Endeavor to keep the Willow in the Serpentine Walks upright by means of the Stakes, and tow yarn or grass, or something else to tye them thereto that will not rub, or fret the bark, the small, as well as the large trees in these walks should be staked up to give them a proper elevation.   [H.L.]

*To THOMAS JEFFERSON

Philadelphia, May 30, 1787.

Dear Sir: It has so happened, that the letter which you did me the honor of writing to me the 14th. of November last, did not come to my hands till the first of the present month; and at a time when I was about to set off for the Convention of the States, appointed to be holden in this City the 14th. Instt. Consequently, it has not been in my power at an earlier period, to reply to the important matters wch. are the subjects thereof.

---

[45] Maj. Thomas Snowden, of Elk Ridge, Md.

This, possibly, may be to be regretted if the house of de Coulteaux should, in the meantime, have directed its enquiries to Philadelphia, Baltimore or New York without having had the advantages which are to be derived from the extension of the inland Navigations of the Rivers Potomack and James, deliniated to them. Silence on this head may be construed into inferiority, when the fact (in my judgment) is, that Alexandria or Richmond, provided the communication with the latter can be conducted by the Green brier and Great Kanhawa (as some aver and others doubt) has infinite advantages over either of the Towns just mentioned. With respect to James River, I am not able to speak with so much precision as of the former, with which (having had opportunities to be so) I am much better acquainted. To this therefore I shall chiefly confine my observations.

In investigating the advantages of Alexandria as the most proper place for a principal deposit in the Fur Trade, I have thought it necessary to leave as little room for partiality and prejudice to operate as possible, by concealing, as far as may be, the object of the investigation. Tho' the result has been favourable to Alexandria, I trust it will be found to have arisen from such weighty considerations, as must be felt by every mind; particularly that of the Merchant whose interests on this subject must alone determine the scale. With A very superficial knowledge of the relative Geography of the places (Alexanda. Baltimore, Philada. New York) in contemplation by Monsr. Coulteaux to establish a concern in the Fur Trade to the Country yielding this Article, a meer glance at the Map must decide Alexandria in point of distance to be the most convenient spot. Hence, a considerable saving would accrue in the articles of Land carriage; an object of so much importance in the communication between places seperated by immense wildernesses, and rugged roads, as to render any comment on it to a Merchant, superfluous. But the difficulty arising from this sourse (tho' already less) will soon, in a great measure, be obviated with respect to Alexandria, by the extension of the Navigation of Potomack. The progress already made in this great National work, Not only justifies this opinion, but the most sanguine expectations wch. have been formed of its success. Granting therefore that the advantage of a greater proximity to the Fur Country, was not on the side of Alexandria, still the immense superiority which a communication almost by water, would give it, must be obvious to all who consider the case, with which the distant produce of the different, and opposite parts of the earth are mutually exchanged, by means of this element. As neither of the other places can ever enjoy this singular benefit to so great a degree, Alexandria must, of course, be the place to which the Inhabitants of the Western Country must resort with all their Commodities (unless by the other channel mentioned, Richmond should be found equal to it); and from whence they will take back their returns in foreign products with the least expence. The Act for opening a road from the highest point to which the Navigation of Potomack can be extended, to the Cheat river, must also be considered as an important circumstance in favour of Alexandria; and in the same light the Act of the last Session for opening a road to the Mouth of the little Kanhawa, from the road last mentioned, must be considered. Besides these, leave has been obtained from Pensylvania by the States of Virginia and Maryld., to open another road from Wills' Creek to the Yohiogani, by the nearest and best rout. By these Acts, great part of the Trade which has been accustomed to flow through Pittsburgh to Philadelphia must be derived in rich streams to the Potomack: for I believe it to be as true in commerce as in every thing else, that nature, however she may be opposed for a while, will soon return her regular course, neither therefore the attractive power of wealth, nor the exertions of industry, will long, it is presumed, with hold from Alexandria the advantages which nature has bestowed on her.

If the great extent of territory adjacent to the Fur Country, which Virginia possesses, in comparison with the States to wch. the other Towns belong, be viewed; Alexandria must still be consindered [*sic*] as the most proper place. The Country about the Illinois and wabash (Rivers which nearly reach the Lakes in their Course) has been long considered as the most abundant in Furs; and the completion of the Navigation of James River must, without doubt, render Richmond the most convenient for *these* of any other; if, as I have once or twice before observed, the Navigation of the Kanhawa can be improved to any good account. By those however who are not acquainted with the nature of the western waters, and the short portages between them, it may be objected that the Rivers above mentioned are too far South to meet with good Furs; but it may not be amiss to observe here, that the Rivers of lake Erie &ca. communicate to nearly, and with such ease, with those of the Ohio, as to afford the shortest and best transportation from Detroit; by which all the Furs of the upper lakes must pass; whether they go to Canada, New York, Philadelphia, Baltimore, Alexandria or Richmond; and that the routs, from thence to the two latter are thro' the territory of the United States; whereas the one to New York passes along the line, and is besides, Subject to interruptions by Ice when these are entirely free from it. These objections, particularly the latter, apply in a degree both to Philadelphia and Baltimore; because if either can avail itself of water transportation, it must be by the more Northern streams of the Ohio, with the Waters of the Susquehanna, considerably above the Monongahela, and still more so above the Great Kanhawa, the first of which communicates with the River Potomack, and the latter with that of James.

The last advantage which occurs to me in favor of Alexandria, is, that the business would be carried on there without any competition: No one having yet engaged so deeply in it, as to hold out any encouragement. I have even been informed that Waggons loaded with Furs, have sometimes passed through Alexandria to Baltimore in search of a Market; and from Winchester it is their common practice to go there with this Commodity; tho' Alexandria is much more convenient to them. On the side of New York, the most eligable Posts for this trade are in the possession of the British; and whenever they are ceded it will, I expect, be found, that the Merchants of that Nation, from their Wealth, long establishment, and consequent knowledge of the Country, will be such formidable competitors, as to draw the greater part of the Furs into Canada.

I shall now proceed to mention a person in whose skill and integrity Monsr. Coulteaux may, I think, have the fullest confidence; and tho' I am precluded in some measure from so doing by being told that it is required that he should be an American born; I shall still venture to name a Gentleman who is a native of Ireland, Colo. John Fitzgerald. The active Services of this Gentleman during the War, his long residence in the Country, and intermarriage in it (with one of the most respectable families, Digges of Maryland) all entitle him to be considered as an American. The laws of this Country know no difference between him and a Native of America. He has besides been bred to trade, is esteemed a Man of property and is at present engaged in the former in Alexandria. Lest however this should be considered as an insuperable obstacle, I shall name a second, Robert Townshend Hooe Esqr., who has every desired requisite. I shall just observe, that if the business is carried on extensively, it would probably require the various acquaintance and combined activity of each of those Gentlemen.

I come now to the other part of your letter, which concerns the Cincinnati, and here indeed I scarcely know what to say. It is a delicate, it is a perplexing subject. Not having the extract from the Encyclopedia before me, I cannot now undertake to enter into the merits of the publication. It may therefore perhaps be as much as will be expected from me, to observe that the Author appears in general to have detailed very candidly and ingenuously the motives, and inducements wch. gave birth to the Society. Some of the subsequent facts, which I cannot, however, from memory pretend to discuss with precision are thought by Gentlemen who have seen the publication to be misstated; in so much that it is commonly said, truth and falsehood are so intimately blended, that it will be difficult to sever them.

For myself, I only recollect two or three circumstances, in the narration, of which palpable mistakes seem to have insinuated themselves. Majr. L'Enfant did not arrive and bring the Eagles during the Session of the General meeting, but sometime before that Convention. The Legislature of Rhode Island never passed any Act whatever on the subject (that ever came to my knowledge) notwithstanding what Mirabeau and others had previously advanced. Nothing can be more ridiculous than the supposition of the author that the Society was instituted partly because the Country could not then pay the Army, except the assertion that the United States have now made full and compleat provision for paying not only the arrearages due to the Officers, but the half pay or commutation, at their option. From whence the Author deduces an argument for its dissolution. Though I conceive, this never had any thing to do with the

Institution; yet, the Officers, in most of the States, who never have, nor I believe expect to receive one farthing of the principal or interest on their final settlement securities, would doubtless be much obliged to the Author to convince them how, and when they received a compensation for their Services. No foreigner, nor American who has been absent sometime, will easily comprehend how tender those concerned are on this point. I am sorry to say, a great many of the Officers consider me as having in a degree committed myself by inducing them to trust too much in the justice of their Country. They heartily wish no settlement had been made, because it has rendered them obnoxious to their fellow Citizens, without affording the least emolument.

For the reason I have mentioned, I cannot think it expedient for me to go into an investigation of the Writers deductions. I shall accordingly content myself with giving you some idea of the part I have acted, posterior to the first formation of the Association.

When I found that you, and many of the most respectable characters in the Country would entirely acquiesce with the Institution as altered and amended in the first General Meeting of 1784, and that the objections against the obnoxious parts were wholly done away, I was prevailed upon to accept the Presidency. Happy in finding (so far as I could learn by assiduous enquiries) that all the clamours and jealousies, which had been excited against the original association, had ceased; I judged it a proper time in the last Autumn, to withdraw myself from any farther Agency in the business, and to make my retirement compleate agreeably to my original plan. I wrote circular letters to all the State Societies, announcing my wishes, informing that I did not propose to be at the trienniel meeting, and requested not to be re-elected President. This was the last step of a public nature I expected ever to have taken. But having since been appointed by my Native State to attend the National Convention, and having been pressed to a compliance in a manner which it hardly becomes me to describe; I have, in a measure, been obliged to sacrifice my own Sentiments, and to be present in Philadelphia at the very time of the General Meeting of the Cincinnati; after which I was not at liberty to decline the Presidency without placing myself in an extremely disagreeable situation with relation to that brave and faithful class of men, whose persevering friendship I had experienced on so many trying occasions.

The business of this Convention is as yet too much in embryo to form any opinion of the result. Much is expected from it by some; but little by others; and nothing by a few. That something is necessary, all will agree; for the situation of the General Governmt. (if it can be called a governmt.) is shaken to its foundation, and liable to be overset by every blast. In a word, it is at an end, and unless a remedy is soon applied, anarchy and confusion will inevitably ensue. But having greatly exceeded the bounds of a letter already I will only add assurances of that esteem, regard, and respect.[46]

*To HENRY KNOX

Philadelphia, May 31, 1787.

My dear Sir: It gave me great pleasure to find by your letter of the 29th. that you were freed from all apprehension on acct. of Miss Lucys eye, and that we might flatter ourselves with the expectation of seeing Mrs. Knox and you at this place. It was not untill Friday last that Seven States Assembled in Convention.

---

[46] From the *Jefferson Papers* in the Library of Congress.

By these I was, much against my wish, unanimously placed in the Chair. Ten States are now represented, and Maryland probably will be so in the course of a few days. Should New Hampshire come forward, Rhode Island will then stand very *singularly* alone.

As it is not even certain that this letter will get to New York before you shall have left it I will only add Compliments to Mrs. Knox and assurances of the sincerest friendship of Yr. etc.[47]

*To MARQUIS DE BOUILLÉ[48]

Philadelphia, June 1, 1787.

Sir: Under this cover you will do me the honor to receive a letter directed to the President, or Senior Officer of the Society of the Cincinnati in France;[49] enclosing a resolve of the General Meeting of that Society in these United States, holden in this City, last Month.

If any thing, Sir, could add to the pleasure I feel in obeying the Orders of this Society, it is the favourable opportunity that is afforded me of expressing to you the Sentiments of admiration and respect with which your character has inspired me; and to assure you of the esteem and consideration with which I have the honor etc.[50]

---

[47] From a photostat of the original in the *Washington Papers*.

On May 31 Washington also wrote to Diego de Gardoqui: "As I look with much pleasure to the moment which promises me the honor of a personal acquaintance with your Excellency, and you have assured me that this is not far distant, I will not, now, take up your time in professions of that esteem, regard etc." A copy of this letter is in the "Letter Book" in the *Washington Papers*.

[48] François Claude Amour, Marquis de Bouillé.

[49] This letter was also dated June 1 and is in facsimile in Contenson's *La Société des Cincinnati de France*. It states: "Persuaded I am that, Your Excellency will derive as much pleasure from offering to, and Investing the Marquis de Bouillé with the Order of the Cincinnati, as it gives me to communicate for these purposes the Sentiments of the Society."

[50] From a facsimile in Contenson's *La Société des Cincinnati de France*.

*To GEORGE AUGUSTINE WASHINGTON

Philadelphia, June 3, 1787.

Dear George: I am sorry to find by your letter of the 28th. Ulto. that you have had a return of your old complaint, my last caution'd you against too great exertions, and I now repeat it; because there is no occasion for it. To direct the Overseers how to apply the labour to advantage, is all that can be expected. To see to the execution, except in a kind of rotine, is impracticable; moderate exercise will accomplish this and be of service to you, whilst by attempting too much you will do nothing, as you do not appear to have a constitution fitted for violent exertions.

It is painful to hear that the fine rains which are constantly watering this Country, and which has given a vigour and Verdure to the grain and grass about this City which is hardly to be described, should not have extended to you. The coolness of the weather is common to both, and the complaint of too much rain here, is now accompanied with apprehensions, and indeed reports of damage from frost.

As there is not the smallest prospect of my returning before harvest, and God knows how long it may be after it, I enclose you the observations I made at last harvest, to be practiced on the ensuing one; because I think it will be found better than the old, at any rate it may be tried. Inform me in your next how your Grain, particularly the Barley and Oats, stand on the ground, that is, the height of them, whether thick or thin, how branched, how headed, and what the farmer (who ought to be a judge) thinks of their yield, provided no accident happens. I wish also to be particularly informed of the various kinds of grass seeds which have been Sown, as well in the fields as the smaller spots, and what prospect their is of their coming to any thing.

All the grass that is fit for Hay should be cut, or my horses
&ca. will be in a bad box next winter, the apparent dificiency
of this article, is an argument of weight for cutting the grain
whilst there is nutriment in the Straw in the manner mentioned
in the enclosed observations; this also makes it necessary to give
particular attention to the Corn Crop, more especially if the
Oats are likely to be short.

I am really sorry to hear that the Carrots and Parsnips are so
thinly come up. Does this appear to be the effect of bad Seed,
unfavourable Seasons, improper ground, or want of proper
Culture? Where does this dificiency of Carrots appear greatest
for on this information I shall be able to tell whether it proceeds from the first cause or not, that is bad seed, because I
have an acct. with me, I think, of the places in which the different kind were sown. I could wish, as well for the sake of the
experiments I had in view, as for the profit to be derived that
these, the Potatoes, Pease, &ca. were up well and w'd [*sic*]
stand. The Farmer should endeavor (as it appears from your
Acct. that there will be Seed enough for it) to put the ground
which has been, and now is, plowing at French's in Pease and
Potatoes; without these, or Buck Wheat, the Crop there, especially if the spring grain fails may be very trifling indeed. I
have no choice that preponderates much in favour of any one
of these Crops; for which circumstances may govern in favor of
one more than the other, or of all equally. It would be a pity
not to put the Potatoes and Pease in the ground if it be practicable as the first were bought, and the other reserved, for this
purpose.

In making Bricks let the Mortar be well neaded, much I believe depends upon it. Desire Cornelius or Mathew, to give me
the exact dimensions of the Chimney in the New room that I

may get neat castings for the back and sides of the precise size; in doing this mention the height of it also that the castings may be proportioned thereto, for they do not go all the way up. direct Mathew also to give me the circumference of the upper piece of Wood of the Cupulo on the House through which the iron spire for fastening the finishing part goes that I may get it executed and sent round from this place. The dimensions, with some kind of draft of it I conceive must be necessary for the government of the workman here, perhaps Mr. Lear or yourself can give a better draught of it (on paper) than Mathew.

Did no letter from Mr. Young,[51] accompany the plows and Seeds? I do not know what Seeds, or what kind of Plows he sent, but wish to be informed. Mr. Poseys Acct. you have sent. Pay Mrs. French the Sum of £87 on acct. of my assumsit in favor of Robinson.

The enclosed letters for Mr. Lear came under cover to me. request him to translate and return to me, the French letters under this cover. I would have written to him myself but it is now 11 oclock at Night and I am tired, the Post goes off at 6 in the Morning. My love to Fanny and best regards for Mr. Lear. I am etc.

PS. As the proceedings of the Convention are not intended to be made known till the business is finished I can give you no information on this score except that the sentiments of the different members seem to accord more than I expected they would, as far as we have yet gone. There are now 11 States represented and not much hope of another as Rhode Island refused to send and New Hampshire seems unable by some means or another to come on.   [H.L.]

---

[51] Arthur Young.

To MARQUIS DE LAFAYETTE

Philadelphia, June 6, 1787.

My dear Marqs. Not till within this hour was I informed of the intention of Mr. Rutledge[52] (son to the Governor Rutledge of South Carolina whom I believe you know) to embark in the Packet for France, or that he was to set out in the morning for New York, to take shipping the day after. Tho' totally, unprepared (immersed as I am in the business of the Convention) I cannot let this Gentleman depart without a remembrance of my friendship for you. It was, when I came here, and still is, my intention, to write you a long letter from this place before I leave it, but the hour is not yet come when I can do it to my own Satisfaction or for your information. I therefore shall wait till the result of the present meeting is more matured, and till the members who constitute it are at liberty to communicate the proceedings more freely before I attempt it.

You will I dare say, be surprized my dear Marquis to receive a letter from me at this place, you will probably, be more so, when you hear that I am again brought, contrary to my public declaration, and intention, on a public threatre, such is the viscissitude of human affairs, and such the frailty of human nature that no man I conceive can well answer for the resolutions he enters into.

The pressure of the public voice was so loud, I could not resist the call to a convention of the States which is to determine whether we are to have a Government of respectability under which life, liberty, and property will be secured to us, or are to submit to one which may be the result of chance or the moment, springing perhaps from anarchy and Confusion, and

---

[52] John Rutledge, jr.

dictated perhaps by some aspiring demagogue who will not consult the interest of his Country so much as his own ambitious views. What may be the result of the present deliberation is more than I am able, at present, if I was at liberty, to inform you, and therefore I will make this letter short, with the assurance of being more particular when I can be more satisfactory, to this period also I refer more than to acknowledge the receipt of your obliging favours of the 7th. of February last.

Every good wish that can flow from a warm and sincere heart, much attached to you, and every one connected with you, is presented to Madam de la Fayette and your little flock; and with sentiments of encreasing friendship and love. I am, etc.[53]

*To GOVERNOR GEORGE CLINTON

Philadelphia, June 9, 1787.

My dear Sir: At length, I have obtained the means for discharging the balle. I am owing you. Mr. Morris will direct his corrispondent in New York to pay you the sum of Eight hundred and forty dollars, which will be about the amount of £325.6.0 (the balle. of your Acct. as rendered to Jany. last) with inst. thereon of Seven pr Ct. till the middle of this month.

As this is intended as a letter of advice only, I shall add nothing more at present, than my best and respectful Complimts. to Mrs. Clinton and the rest of your family, and that I am with sentiments of very great esteem and regard My dear Sir Yr. etc.[54]

---

[53] From the "Letter Book" copy in the *Washington Papers*.

On June 6 Washington wrote also brief notes to Comte de Rochambeau, Comte D'Estaing, and Marquis de Chastellux, introducing John Rutledge, jr. Copies of these notes are in the "Letter Book" in the *Washington Papers*.

[54] From a photostat of the original in the *Washington Papers*.

*To GEORGE AUGUSTINE WASHINGTON

Philadelpa., June 10, 1787.

Dear George: I am very sorry to find by the last letters from Mount Vernon that you continue indisposed. My wish is, that you would not, in order to facilitate my business, expose yourself to what you have not a Constitution to bear. If a person is not able to undergo the heat of the Sun, or the fatigue of exercise in warm weather, no good, but real evil, will result from the attempt; and therefore no more should be undertaken than you can execute with easy and safety. This too, is the most effectual mode of rendering me Service.

I have received a letter from Mr. Ingraham since his arrival at Boston, informing me that he had purchased, and was about to ship for Alexandria, for my use, the leather he had been requested to procure for me; consequently, you may soon expect it; with this aid you cannot be at a loss in procuring the deficency, whatever it may be. Nor can you have any doubt of the Corn, if it was purchased from Mr. Hunter.[55] Speaking of Corn, it leads me to caution you against turning the furrow from the drilled Corn, especially after it has got to any size. I think the drilled Corn at Morris's last year was injured thereby, and to this it was that I inclined so strongly to the harrows; as I expected they would both weed, and stir the ground without throwing it either from, or to the Corn; the latter, two furrows (one on each side) if necessary, could always effect. The Corn that is manured with Fish, though it does not appear to promise much at first, may nevertheless be fine. This should be attended to, and particularly noted. For, in my conception it is not only possible, but highly probable. Delay no more time

---

[55] William Hunter.

than necessity obliges, in *commencing* your turnip sowing, that the whole may be put in before the season is too far advanced, and the prospect of a Crop thereby diminished. It gives me concern to hear that the prospect of obtaining a Crop of Carrots and parsnips is so unpromising. To ascertain the value of these articles, and their product, was my grand object; in which I must be disappointed if they do not come up. Both of these, as well drilled as in broad cast, should be thinned as soon as they appear to be well established in the ground. If your Oats are heading at not more than 6 or 8 Inches high, I do not, any more than the Farmer does, see any mode by which they can be cut; consequently next best thing must be done with them, and this I suppose he can point out. Let your Summer plowing (or fallows) for wheat, be well performed, desire the Farmer to attend particularly to this; not only at French's but wheresoever this work is going on. I would have you avoid using Mr. Youngs Plows till I return, at least the one he has proved. the other may be tried by his directions, and if found superior to any other, have some more made by it, exactly agreeable to his plan, measurement, &ca. But quere, is his plow *all* Iron, or *part* Iron and *part* wood? from his letter I am in the dark on this head.

Be particularly carefull of all the Seed sent by him, and Mr. Pacey.[56] Sow some of each, to try whether their vegitative properties are good, or are destroyed; and be particularly careful that they do not get mixed. The Seeds especially those which will be to be sown soon, should not only be tried, but attention had where each sort (of the same species) is put; that no mistakes may happen, and the different kinds preserved pure and unmixed. This is very essential with respect to the Wheat. But as I observed before, the first thing necessary to be done is to

---

[56] William Peacey.

ascertain the goodness of them; otherwise I may incur an expence in preparing for the reception of them unnecessarily. If the Turnip Seed should on trial (as we did the Clover Seed) prove good, do not fail to sow it in due Season, as I had rather depend upon that than the adulterated kind we have. I know not at what Season the different kind of Cabbage seeds sent me should be sown, or I would direct about them.

The Books intended for the Philadelphia agricultural Society, I desire you will send to me, first taking out the volume (the 6th. I think) which is intended for me. At the sametime (possibly the same package may do) send me my Blew Coat with the Cremson collar and one of those made of the Cloth sent me by the Spanish Minister, to wit that without lapels, and lined with white Silk, as I see no end to my staying here. get the Stage Master at Alexandria to take charge of it, or Mr. Porter,[57] or some Gentleman of that place, to embrace the oppertunity of a passenger (on whom dependance can be placed) coming quite through, to bring it to me.

If I understand rightly the report of the ditchers, they made a miserable hand of Ditching in Easter week. It appears I think by the report that Lawson worked 3 days, Daniel 1, Boatswain 2, and Paschall, Robben, Bath and Charles 4 days each. In all 22 days, and in this time that they only dug 31 rods of a 4 feet ditch 21 Inches deep, and foot wide at bottom. If this statement be true, Lawson ought to be spoken to; because it is not by any means, (unless there is something in the way of which I am not apprized) what ought to have been done.

I did not know that Knowles professed, or in any degree understood Brick making, and if this is the case, he will spoil all the Bks. he attempts to Burn; and I shall, in consequence, be disappointed in my work. What work is Cornelius about?

---

[57] Of Porter & Ingraham.

Who is at work with him? let this be brought into the weekly report as it is necessary I should know how he advances that I may provide for him accordingly. if I can, at this distance. What progress is made on the Green House? Desire Matthew to give me the exact dimension of the windows (one will do) of the dining room; within the casement (in the room) that I may get a Venetion blind, such as draws up and closes, and expands made here, that others may be made by it, at home. the height from the bottom to top, and width is all that is necessary within the casement.

The Miller must continue, though I do not think he understands the Manufacture of wheat equal to Roberts. It is of great importance to widen, repair, and cleanse the Race of the mill; but whether you can do it before, or after harvest, or at all, must depend upon circumstances; for it is impossible for me, at this distance, to determine, nor shall I pretend to give any opinion thereon.

Let Mr. Lear know that I have Franked and forwarded his letter to Mr. Lincoln, and now send him two which came under cover to me. also that I will chearfully do the same with any others that may come to my hands from, or to him. As the Convention do not publish their proceedings I have nothing more to communicate than what you will find in the Papers, which I have ordered to be forwarded to Mount Vernon. Give my love to Fanny, and best wishes to Mr. Lear.

With sincere Affection, and between ten and 11 oclock at Night, the Post going off at 6 in the Morning I am etc.

*To GEORGE AUGUSTINE WASHINGTON

Philadelphia, June 15, 1787.

Dear George: The only design of this letter is to acknowledge the receipt of the letters from Mount Vernon of the 10th and 11th; and to let you or your Aunt know that the Buckles and knives mentioned in my last as having been sent, were not forwarded. I expected when I was writing those letters that Mr. Porter would have been the bearer of them, but he is yet in this City. By him I mean to send the Buckles and Knives if I should think of them; when I will also write again, more fully.

The letters which come from Alexandria on Tuesday Morning, do not arrive at this place till thursday evening, sometimes as late as 8 Oclock, and the Post goig. off again next morning by 7 oclock leaves so little time for writing that unless it is in cases which are pressing, I shall delay doing it till next Post day; which is on the Monday following; and which will be in Alexandria on the Wednesday after, which I mention that in case my Letters do not reach you by the Post on Monday, they will probably be in Alexandria on the Wednesday.

When you send the two Coats wrote for in my last, accompany them with my Umbrella, I have a new one in my Study. Remember me Affectionately to all at home I am etc.   [H.L.]

*To CLEMENT BIDDLE

Friday Morng., June 28, 1787.

Dear Sir: By the Post of Yesterday I received the enclosed Memo. If you can comply with them in time, for the Alexandria Packet it wd. oblige me.

If the Hatt is already got for Washington,[58] it will be unnecessary to exchange it; If not, he prefers a black one, with such ornaments as would suit a boy of his age, and the colour of the hat.

I beg leave to remind you of the Linnen, two pieces, from Mr. Hazlehursts; and of the two pieces of finer than those you have purchased at 4/6. For the purposes they are wanted indeed, they should be a good deal finer. I am etc.   [H.S.P.]

---

[58] George Washington Parke Custis.

To ANNIS BOUDINOT STOCKTON

Philadelphia, June 30, 1787.

Madam: At the sametime that I pray you to accept my sincere thanks for the obliging letter with which you honored me on the 26th. Ulto (accompanied by a poetical performance for which I am more indebted to your partiality than to any merits I possess, by which your Muse could have been inspired. I have to entreat that you will ascribe my silence to any cause rather than to a want of respect or friendship for you; the truth really is that what with my attendance in Convention, morning business, receiving, and returning visits, and Dining late with the numberless[59] &ca., which are not to be avoided in so large a City as Philadelphia, I have Scarcely a moment in which I can enjoy the pleasures which result from the recognition on the many instances of your attention to me or to express a due sense of them. I feel more however than I can easily communicate for the last testimony of your flattering recollection of me. The friendship you are so good as to assure me you feel for me, claims all my gratitude and sensibility, and meets the most cordial return. with compliments to your good family I have the honor, etc.[60]

To MARQUIS DE LAFAYETTE

Philadelphia, June 30, 1787.

My dear Marqs. The Gentleman who will do the honor of presenting this letter to you is Mr. Shippen, Son of your old acquaintance Doctr. Shippen[61] of this City who having been at the Temple proposes to visit Paris, and of course to offer homage

---

[59] Omission of the "Letter Book" copyist. The word may have been "personages."
[60] From the "Letter Book" copy in the *Washington Papers*, which is addressed to Mrs. Richard Stockton.
[61] He died in 1798.

to you. He is a very sensible young man and as far as opportunities are afforded me to Judge, possess a well cultivated
mind which induces me without hesitation or apology to introduce him to your countenance and Civilities. To repeat to you
the assurances of that Friendship with which I am warmed
would not add ought to your conviction of it because you are
already persuaded of the sincere regard and affection etc.[62]

To DAVID STUART

Philadelphia, July 1, 1787.

Dear Sir: I have been favored with your letter of the 17th
ultimo.

In May, Mr. Alexr. Donald made me a remittance in Bills on
Robert Morris Esqr. of this City to the amount of 1094 35/90
Dollrs., and a few days since I received another draught on the
same Gentleman for 306 65/90 Dollars making together
1401 60/90 Dollrs. or Four hundred and twenty pounds ten
Shillings Virginia Currency, which I have placed to the Credit
of Mr. Custis's Estate.

Rhode Island, from our last accts. still preseveres in that im-
politic, unjust, and one might add without much impropriety
scandalous conduct, which seems to have marked all her public Councils of late. Consequently, no Representation is yet
here from thence. New Hampshire, tho' Delegates have been
appointed, is also unrepresented. Various causes have been assigned, whether well, or ill-founded I shall not take upon me

---

[62]From the "Letter Book" copy in the *Washington Papers*.
On June 30 Washington wrote to Comte de Rochambeau, introducing Young
Shippen. A copy of this letter is in the "Letter Book" in the *Washington Papers*.
Entered in the "Letter Book" under September 26 is a brief note to Thomas Jefferson,
also introducing Mr. Shippen.
On this same day (June 30) Washington wrote also to the president of the Agricultural Society of Philadelphia, forwarding Arthur Young's *Annals of Agriculture*
which Young had sent to Washington to be presented to the Philadelphia society. A
copy of this letter is in the "Letter Book" in the *Washington Papers*.

to decide. The fact, however, is that they are not here. Political contests, and want of money, are amidst the reasons assigned for the non-attendance of the members.

As the rules of the convention prevent me from relating any of the proceedings of it, and the gazettes contain, more fully than I could detail, other occurrences of a public nature, I have little to communicate to you on the article of news. Happy indeed would it be, if the convention shall be able to recommend such a firm and permanent government for this Union, that all who live under it may be secure in their lives, liberty, and property; and thrice happy would it be, if such a recommendation should obtain. Every body wishes, every body expects something from the convention; but what will be the final result of its deliberation, the book of fate must disclose. Persuaded I am, that the primary cause of all our disorders lies in the different State governments, and in the tenacity of that power, which pervades the whole of their systems. Whilst independent sovereignty is so ardently contended for, whilst the local views of each State, and separate interests, by which they are too much governed, will not yield to a more enlarged scale of politics, incompatibility in the laws of different States, and disrespect to those of the general government, must render the situation of this great country weak, inefficient, and disgraceful. It has already done so, almost to the final dissolution of it. Weak at home and disregarded abroad is our present condition, and contemptible enough it is.

Entirely unnecessary was it to offer any apology for the sentiments you were so obliging as to offer me. I have had no wish more ardent, through the whole progress of this business, than that of knowing what kind of government is best calculated for us to live under. No doubt there will be a diversity of sentiments on this important subject; and to inform the judgment, it is necessary to hear all arguments that can be advanced. To please all is impossible, and to attempt it would be vain. The only way, therefore, is, under all the views in which it can be placed, and with a due consideration to circumstances, habits, &c., &c., to form such a government as will bear the scrutinizing eye of criticism, and trust it to the good sense and patriotism of the people to carry it into effect. Demagogues, men who are unwilling to lose any of their State consequence, and interested characters in each, will oppose any general government. But let these be regarded rightly, and justice, it is to be hoped, will at length prevail. My best wishes attend Mrs. Stuart, yourself, and the girls. If I can render [you] any service whilst I remain here, I shall be happy in doing it. I am, &c.[63]

*To GEORGE AUGUSTINE WASHINGTON

Philadelphia, July 1, 1787.

Dear George: Your letter of the 24th, with the report, is before me; and such observations as occur, shall be handed to you.

In plowing the drilled Corn, it is to be remembered, that throwing the furrow always to the plant, will leave the land in high ridges; and make it more liable to wash, and run into Gullies; to avoid wch. was one of my principal motives for introducing the Hoe and common Iron toothed Harrows; because, had these succeeded, the grain would have been wed,[64] and the Earth pulverized, at the sametime that the land would have been left smooth and even. As these (owing to the uncommonly dry season) cannot be used to any good purpose, the other evil should, as far as it is practicable, without injury to the Corn, be avoided.

---

[63] From the "Letter Book" copy in the *Washington Papers*.
[64] Weeded.

I am glad to find that your prospect for Carrots at Dogue run and Muddy hole is not quite so gloomy as it at first appeared. If all these things are equally unproductive with the Spring grain, I shall have a melancholy prospect before me. As the first Potatoes at Market will probably sell high, examine now and then your forwardest; and when they are of sufficient size, dispose of them (if the price is more than equivalent to the loss which will probably be sustained by digging them prematurely) to those who may incline to purchase, in Alexandria, keeping an acct. of the quantity, that I may form some estimate of the yield, and portionate value of them to other Crops.

If the ground designed for fallowing, for wheat in the Autumn, is more than can be prepared *well,* the quantity should be reduced; as it is a folly to do things by halves; but before it is given up, oxen and everything should be attempted in the *Plow,* to accomplish it; as my whole System will be deranged, and my next years Crop become nothing, with out I again return back to Indian Corn, which I am aiming to get rid off. If however it is unavoidable, and the quantity *must* be reduced, let that field at Dogue run adjoining the upper meadow (and divided by the row of Stakes) be the first prepared, because it can be most conveniently inclosed; and will leave the rest in one common pasture. In fixing Youngs plow, go exactly by the directions he gives.

I am very glad to hear that all the imported Seeds have come up (except the rib grass, which in my opinion is the least valuable of any) The Season for Sowing the Cabbage Seed for this years Crop, is no doubt over, and it must be preserved for the next.

You may inform Thos. Greene that if Drunkness, or idleness constitutes any part of his conduct, that I have directed you to discharge him. practises of this sort are violations of the agreement, and I will keep no person in my Service who is addicted to them. Should he go, Mahony may be employed. In every place where I have been there are *many* workmen, and *little* work, which will bring these people to their Senses again.

I dare say the distribution of the Cradlers is good; if otherwise, you can easily alter it when harvest is fairly entered upon, and the defect at one place, or surplusage at another, is discovered.

If the Jacks do not perform what is expected from them, the Mares, unquestionably, must be sent to Magnolio, rather than let them go over.

Gerard Alexander, as an additional Security, I should think would be good, but I question much whether he will enter himself as such, for Bob;[65] and should this be the case, it will exhibit a fresh proof of the necessity of bringing matters to a close with the latter, before it is too late.

Endeavor, not only for the sake of the Corn, but for cleansing the ground, to till the New ground in front of the House well; as I wish very much to destroy all the Succours, sprouts, roots, &ca. in it most effectually, that I may lay it down in grass as soon as this can be accomplished perfectly.

The Jerusalem Artichokes ought not to be any more ploughed; or the roots will be all turned out of the ground. The only directions I have for their management was, I believe, left with you.

As you cannot do without a Fan for your grain, I ordered one of the best kind to be made; and expect you will receive it by a Vessel which has some things on board for me, and which, it is said, will Sail from this on Tuesday; tho' it will probably be later, as it was to have gone last friday, and then to day, &ca.

By the letter you sent me from Mr. Polk, he seems to understand the art of charging for his Plank, perfectly well; the payment however may be delayed till I return, and can enquire a little into matters.

---

[65] Robert Alexander.

I understand by Mrs. Washington's letter, that there is some part of the mouldings, or decorations with the plaister of Paris, that Mathew cannot put up; and says Mr. Rawlins was to send a hand to do it. If this is the case it would be well to write to Rawlins about it. I do not recollect that circumstance myself but do perfectly remember that the Stains, and other blemishes in the Stucco, was to be removed; when, as he said, the Walls were sufficiently seasoned: when he left the work, he added, it was not, at that time, in a proper State for these attempts. I have desired Colo. Biddle to send glass for the New room and suppose it will go (cut to the proper size) with the other things. I have directed 48 instead of 36 lights. The Wood part of the New room may be painted of any tolerably fashionable colour; so as to serve present purposes; and this might be a buff. Tis more than probable it will receive a *finishing* colour hereafter. The buff should be of the lightest kind, inclining to white.

Give my love to Fanny, and best wishes to Mr. Lear. I am etc.

[H.L.]

*To GEORGE AUGUSTINE WASHINGTON

Philadelphia, July 8, 1787.

Dear George: I have your letter of the first before me. In a late one, you have said, that application had been made to Dow, without effect, for the amount of his Bond; and therefore, Flour was sold for the use of Mr. L: Washington. Does the latter mean to receive the proceeds of the flour and keep the Bond (for it was put into his hands) too? If he does not, and the Bond is returned to you; I wish Mr. Lear or yourself, would make a pointed demand of the payment, and if not received, to place it without delay in the hands of Colo. Simms, there is no other way of dealing with such Men. I shall be perfectly satisfied, if he does not pay immediately, that his only object has been that of procrastination. The Security, Major Little, might as well be spoken to first.

I did not mean that you should make any offers to Branagan, such as I mentioned, unless application first came from him. I did not expect that it was such terms as he would embrace as long at least as his money lasted; for with this I conceive he will be constantly drunk; if he possessed prudence therefore he should leave this as deposit in your hands, even if he goes elsewhere in pursuit of work; for sure I am if he takes it into keeping he will not work whilst it lasts; or if he works *at all,* it will be under such circumstances as to bring discredit on himself.

I did not mean to express an idea that my instructions, by not being fully complied with, proceeded from any inattention or neglect. I well know that unfavourable Seasons will disconcert any plan, however wisely laid, or judiciously calculated on; all that can be done in such cases is to come as near as possible to the original intention. what made me anxious about the Summer fallows was, that it was intended to introduce rotation which will be defeated if I fail in the accomplishment, and for this reason it was that I recommended in my last that all the force of Oxen &ca. should be given to the Plows, as well to establish this System, as to aid me in my next years Crop; with out which, I must again return to Indian Corn, or some kind of Spring Crop neither of which would answer my purpose. Is there any prospect of your doing anything to the Mill race whilst the drought continues? This you know cannot be touched to advantage under any other circumstances.

How does your Pompkin Vines look? and what figure does the pease, Potatoes, Carrots and Parsnips make? Does your Turnips come up well, and do they escape the Fly?[66] How

---

[66] Cabbage fly.

does the Clover, and the other grass seeds which were sown this Spring look? Did you perceive any difference in the lay Wheat at Morris's? if so which had the preference? How was it, compared with the other wheat when they were ripe, and cut? How is the cape wheat likely to yield, and how did the latter sowed Wheat at Morris's (that was harrowed) come on? Did the Rye adjoining, which was so very thin when I left home, come to any thing, and how has the Spelts and flax turned out? I should suppose that all the Potatoes planted in the Pen (according to Grymes's directions) must be rotton except the upper layer, but attend to it notwithstanding. What was the general heights of your Barley and Oats particularly the former? and what is the Farmers opinion of them especially the first?

I am sorry to hear that the honey locust Seeds come up badly, pray keep them, and all these kind of things clean, and I had rather you should delay sowing the Turnip Seed than put it in grd. that is not well prepared, without this my labour is lost, and I shall in vain expect a Crop.

I would not have you buy shell faster than to secure lime for Cornelius work, they will rather fall than rise, it is a natural consequence of decrease of building. What quantity of Orchard grass Seed are you likely to save, and what are your prospects of Timothy seed? Give my love to Fanny and best wishes to Mr. Lear. I am etc.

PS. Keep the Shrubberies clean. What have you done to the Gravel Walks, or rather what remains to be done to them.

[H.L.]

On July 8 Washington also wrote a brief note of acknowledgment to Marquis de Chartier de Lotbinière, who was in New York City and had been introduced by a letter from Marquis de Lafayette. A copy of this note is in the "Letter Book" in the *Washington Papers.*

To HECTOR ST. JOHN DE CRÈVECŒUR

Philadelphia, July 9, 1787.

Sir: The letter you did me the honor of writing to me by Commodore Paul Jones came safe; as did the volumes of the *Farmer's Letters*.[67] For both, particularly for the compliment of the letter, I pray you to accept my best thanks. Let me express my gratitude to you, at the same time, Sir, for the obliging offer of transmitting any communications I may have occasion to make, to my good and much esteemed friend the Marquis de Lafayette, whose zeal and services in the cause of this country merit as much applause from his fellow citizens, as they meet admiration from the rest of mankind. I congratulate you on your safe arrival in this country, and with sentiments of great esteem &c.[68]

*To ALEXANDER HAMILTON

Philadelphia, July 10, 1787.

Dear Sir: I thank you for your Communication of the 3d. When I refer you to the state of the Councils which prevailed at the period you left this City, and add, that they are now, if possible, in a worse train than ever; you will find but little ground on which the hope of a good establishment can be formed. In a word, I *almost* despair of seeing a favourable issue to the proceedings of our Convention, and do therefore repent having had any agency in the business.

The Men who oppose a strong and energetic government are, in my opinion, narrow minded politicians, or are under

---

[67] Crèvecœur's *Letters from an American Farmer* (1782), which were, later (1784–87), republished in France in the French language.
[68] From the "Letter Book" copy in the *Washington Papers*.

the influence of local views. The apprehension expressed by them that the *people* will not accede to the form proposed is the *ostensible,* not the *real* cause of the opposition; but admitting that the *present* sentiment is as they prognosticate, the question ought nevertheless to be, is it, or is it not, the best form?[69] If the former, recommended it, and it will assuredly obtain mauger opposition. I am sorry you went away. I wish you were back.[70] The crisis is equally important and alarming, and no opposition under such circumstances should discourage exertions till the signature is fixed. I will not, at this time trouble you with more than my best wishes and sincere regards. I am &c.[71]

To GOVERNOR GEORGE CLINTON

Philadelphia, July 11, 1787.

Dear Sir: The bearer Mr. Timothy Tuttle has been with me to obtain on some terms (I did not enquire what) part of the Land we have a Joint interest in, up the Mohawk River. The answer I have given him is, that whatever you shall do concerning them I will abide by. With great esteem and Regd. I am, etc.[72]

* To GEORGE AUGUSTINE WASHINGTON

Philadelphia, July 15, 1787.

Dear George: Your letter and report came to hand in the ordinary course of the Post. I do not recollect how I expressed myself with respect to the painting of the New room, that is whether, when speaking of this business, you would under-

---

[69] The "Letter Book" has, at this point, "that such a Country as this can adopt?"
[70] Hamilton was present in the convention June 29, but left Philadelphia on that day. He apparently was not in the convention again until August 13.
[71] From the *Hamilton Papers.* The text varies slightly from that found in the "Letter Book" in the *Washington Papers.*
[72] From the "Letter Book" copy in the *Washington Papers.*

stand, that it was to be done by a proper, and good painter. This was my meaning; and therefore having no high opinion of the skill, though a favourable one of the Industry, of the one who was there last; I advise you to try Peales Nephew, or some one more knowing, both in the mixtures, and laying on of Paint, than Morrison (I think his name was). It will require small brushes, and considerable attention to paint the carved mouldings, to prevent their filling too much with the paint. None but the wood work, and the Ornaments annexed to them, are to be painted. I mean by this that the Stucco walls are not to be touched.

I am getting a Venetian blind made[73] to send round; that others may be made at home, by it. Tell Mathew to have poplar sawed for this purpose, as thin as it can be, that it may Season against the Pattern arrives. When dressed the pieces will be about the length that the Window is wide; not more than the ⅛ of an Inch thick, and about 5 Inches wide each piece.

I only mentioned plowing with Oxen to shew my anxiety to get the ground, which was intended for Wheat, broke up for it; that I might, if possible, pursue my course; but if Carting, and other things are opposed to it, as I believe they are; the disappointment must be submitted to.

I would have you, as soon as possible, begin to Sow Wheat in Corn ground. I do not think that Corn receives any benefit from working after it begins to Tassle and Shoot, but sure I am, that nine years out of ten, early sown Wheat will be best. It was not my intention (could I have pursued my newly adopted course of cropping) to have sown wheat among the drilled Corn except at the Ferry and in the Neck; therefore, as necessity only will drive me to do it, I would let it be the *last*

---

[73] On July 12 Washington wrote a brief note to Clement Biddle, requesting that the upholsterer Davis be sent to him to make "one of the Venetian blinds." This note is in the Historical Society of Pennsylvania.

sown at the other place. At the Ferry, there will be the Stoney field, besides the drilled and other Corn, for Wheat; as also the ground that was intended to be fallowed: but it is to be remembered that Rye must be sown in the poorest parts of these grounds. The like in the poorest part of the fallowed grd. at French's. The like also at Dogue run, (if you should be able to get it in order) and the like at Muddy hole. In the Neck *all* the ground now in Corn will be laid down in Wheat and Rye. Robins field wholly in the first. The other (now in drilled Corn on the River) partly in both. The Rye going into the weakest, and sandiest land. It was also intended, if it could be effected, to put the Orchard Inclosure (now in Oats) into Wheat. Having mentioned these matters, circumstances must govern in the ordering of them. I must again repeat however, that the sooner your Seeding commences in Corn land, the better it will be for the Wheat; and none the worse I conceive for the Corn; as I do not believe the latter is benefitted by working after it Shoots and Tassels. The cleaner however the ground is, when the grain is sown, the better.

The mode you propose to adopt, of following the Plows in the drilled Corn with the Harrows, to prevent high ridges, is very proper, and will be essential for the Wheat. If time would permit, I am of opinion, if the harrows were to follow the plows, the sowing follow the harrows, and then the harrows to cover the Seed, that it would be best. But experience has fully proved the efficacy of early sowing of Wheat. to get it into the ground therefore soon, is of all others the most interesting consideration, next to it; is that of preparing the ground *well* for its reception.

What does the Farmer *guess,* the Barley and Oats will yield to the Acre? to come at it with exactness, is not to be expected; but now it is cut, a man acquainted with these matters can form a tolerable conjecture, at least of the fields he particularly attends to. Do not suffer the different kinds of Oats to get mixed. especially those of Spotswoods with any other. Sprinkling Brine with your Cut Oats, is very proper; but as soon as you can chop the Rye at the Mill your work horses should be fed with it, and cut Straw; the cut Oats to be used for the Saddle Horses.

The ground on which the Flax grew, is as good as any to rot it on. I cannot find out by the Ditchers report, where they are at work. Branagans staying, even on the terms I have proposed, is perfectly indifferent to me, on his, totally inadmissible. Mr. Lear's letter is franked and sent on. My love to Fanny, and good wishes to him. I am etc.

PS. Have you thinned the Carrots which were too thick?

[H.L.]

To RICHARD HENRY LEE

Philadelphia, July 19, 1787.

Dear Sir: I have had the honor to receive your favor of the 15th instant, and thank you for the ordinance which was enclosed in it. My sentiments, with respect to the navigation of the Mississippi, have been long fixed, and are not dissimilar to those which are expressed in your letter. I have ever been of opinion that the true policy of the Atlantic States would be instead of contending prematurely for the free navigation of that river (which eventually, and perhaps as soon as it shall be our true interest to obtain it) must happen, to open and improve the natural communications with the western country, through which the produce of it might be transported with convenience and ease to our markets. Till you get low down the Ohio, I conceive, that it would, (considering the length of the voyage to New Orleans, the difficulty of the current, and the time necessary to perform it in) be the interest of the inhabitants to bring their produce to our ports; and sure I am, there is no other tie by which they will long form a link in the chain of federal union. I believe, however, from the temper in which those people appear to be, and from the ambitious and turbulent spirit of some of their demagogues, that it has become a moot point to determine (when every circumstance which attends this business is brought into view) what is best to be done. The State of Virginia having taken the matter up with so high a hand, is not among the least embarrassing or disagreeable parts of the difficulty.

Will you permit me to put the enclosed under cover to you; from the Gentleman to whom it is addressed, I have lately received a letter to which this is an acknowledgment. with very great esteem and regard. I have the honor etc.[74]

*To JOSEPH RAKESTRAW

July 20, 1787.

Sir: Perceiving a Vessell advertized for Alexandria, you would oblige me much in hastening the Work you have undertaken for me, that I may send it by her.

I should like to have a bird (in place of the Vain)[75] with an olive branch in its Mouth. The bird need not be large (for I do not expect that it will traverse with the wind and therefore may receive the real shape of a bird, with spread wings), the point of the spire not to appear above the bird. If this, that is the bird thus described, is in the execution, likely to meet any difficulty, or to be attended with much expence, I should wish to be informed thereof previous to the undertaking of it. I am etc.[76]

---

[74] From the "Letter Book" copy in the *Washington Papers.*
[75] For the top of the cupola at Mount Vernon.
[76] From a photostat of the original through the kindness of Dr. A. S. W. Rosenbach, of New York City.
On July 21 Washington wrote briefly to Lafayette, introducing Mr. Rucker, partner in Constable, Rucker & Co. of New York, and agent for Robert Morris. A copy of this letter is in the "Letter Book" in the *Washington Papers.*

*To CHEVALIER JOHN PAUL JONES

Philadelphia, July 22, 1787.

Sir: I avail myself of the liberty you have been so obliging as to give me, to trouble you with the care of the enclosed packet. It was my intention to have added to this trouble by encreasing the number of my letters, but business has prevented; let me pray therefore that you will do me the honor to present me, in affectionate terms to the Marqs. de la Fayette, and assure him, that though hurried, I should not have slipped so favourable an opportunity of writing to him, if the business of the Convention (for I have nothing else new, to offer him) could have been communicated in the present unfinished state of it. To the Count de Rochambeau, Marqs. de Chartellux and others, with whom I have the honor of a particular acquaintance, I tender my best regards. I wish you a pleast. Voyage; and the attainment of the objects of it. and have the honor etc.[77]

*To GEORGE AUGUSTINE WASHINGTON

Philadelphia, July 24, 1787.

Dear George: For the benefit of exercise, I left the City at 5 Oclock on Sunday Morning, and did not return in time to write by the Post on Monday.[78] I now acknowledge the receipt of your letter and report of the 15th. and shall observe upon such parts of them as may require it.

I would not wish you to ask Mr. Lund Washington for Dows Bond; but when you see him you may tell him that I

---

[77] From a facsimile of the original in a sales catalogue, 1931.

[78] From Washington's "Diary," Sunday, July 22, is the following: "Left Town by 5 oclock, A. M. Breakfasted at General Mifflin's. Rode up with him and others to the Spring Mills and returned to Genl. Mifflin's to Dinner, after which proceeded to the City." (Spring Mill was a short distance below Conshohocken, the Matsons Ford of the Revolution.)

had directed you (if it was returned) to put it *without delay* in suit; this, no doubt will bring on an explanation of his intentions respecting it.

Notwithstanding the idea which I gave to you in my last, respecting fallowing, my wish now is, that the ground, be it little or much that is got into Wheat, may be *well prepared* (the Farmer no doubt can judge of this) and sowed in *good time.* I am now determined to sow no more Wheat in the Fallow ground than what can be put in in this manner, hoping that a smaller quantity sown in time, in well dressed Land, will yield as much as a larger qty. put in late, and in a slovenly manner whilst the residue of the ground intended for fallow may be preparing (after the Winter grain is in) for Barley and Oats in the Spring.

I am in hopes you are mistaken with respect to the injury the Wheat has sustained by rust if it only siezed it a few days previous to harvest. The grain never can be damaged by this malady if it has got hard before it appears. If the case, in the present instance is otherwise, mine is peculiarly a hard one; not only to have a very thin crop, but that injured also when our accts. from all parts of Virginia are, that a better Crop both as to quantity and quality has not been in that State for many years. If however the Rye, next adjoining the latter sowed Wheat at Morris's has turned out well, it will make *some* amends; for in truth I did not expect, when I saw it last, that a Scythe would ever be put into that part which bordered on the lay Wheat.

If the Farmer disapproves of the Barley he grew last year, and will describe a better sort, I will make enquiry for, and if to be obtained, procure and send some home, but quæry, has not Mr. Young sent the right sort? Three pecks is, from the best information I can Procure, the quantity of Buckwheat usually sown to an Acre; and may regulate your conduct in future.

Be careful to thresh the Oats wch. grew in the experimental grounds by themselves, and in the manner directed, that the result may be precisely known. What kind (I mean as to their quality) of Oats, grew in front of the house, and what prospect is there of that ground being covered with clover and orchard grass?

How is the Corn in the new ground fronting the house likely to turn out? and what are your present prospects for that grain? I will enquire into the price of Timothy seed in this City; but the sooner you can, conveniently, ascertain the quantity you have, or will be able to save yourself, the better; that on advice thereof, I may know what quantity to provide.

Such parts of the Mill race (if the whole cannot be done) as is attempted, *do well,* agreeably to the directions I left. I beg that the Shrubberries on both sides of the Serpentine walks, between them and the Walls, may be spaded up and the ground made not only clean but light. In doing this care must be taken not to injure any of the young plants.

It is indispensably necessary to lay Cills, and good heavy ones, well morticed together, on the brick work of the Stercorary; without it, the walls will soon be down. You do very right in cutting every thing that will make Hay. The Pea vines I expect will yield a good deal of food, especially for Sheep. for this reason; I conceive they ought to be cut in that State, when the Pease appear to be *generally* ripe, and before those which first ripen begin to open, or shatter with a stroke of the Scythe.

After finishing the part of No. 6 at the Ferry, in which the Plows were when you wrote, they may proceed next to the Part of it which was in Wheat. And then, if I should not return home before, to the part that was in Rye, provided the latter does not appear to be well taken with Timothy; in which case I would not break it up; but bestow more culture on the other parts of that field, No. 6. What kind of Oats did the new meadow at that place produce, and how does the ground appear to be taken with Timothy?

Remember me affectionately to Fanny, and offer my best wishes to Mr. Lear. I am etc.   [H.L.]

To PHILIP MARSTELLER

Philadelphia, July 25, 1787.

Sir: You would oblige me by letting me know whether there is a prospect of your purchasing, on the terms specified in my letter of Instructions, any of the Articles mentioned in the list handed to you therewith particularly Blankets as the Season in which these will be wanted is now fast approaching and against which they must be provided for the accomodation of my Negros. If there is a moral certainty of obtaining them through your means, I will depend thereon, if not, I must look out in time, and therefore give you the trouble of this Enquiry. I am, etc.[79]

*To GEORGE AUGUSTINE WASHINGTON

Philadelphia, July 29, 1787.

Dear George: Your letter of the 22d. is before me. If the outer doors of the new room are adapted to receive Mortice locks, it will make the room more uniform; and I can get them here of good quality from Seven Inches downwards. I shall decline sending any kind 'till I hear from you again thinking it best that the whole should be of this kind if any are.

---

[79] From the "Letter Book" copy in the *Washington Papers*.

Perceiving you have little chance of sowing much Wheat in Fallow land this Fall (as the plowing of it at some of the Plantations is not yet begun) and little prospect of Plowing *any* ground well; it is indispensably necessary (in order that I may have something to depend upon next year) that *all* the Corn ground at *all* the Plantations, should be laid down in either Wheat or Rye, as shall be best suited to the land; and I request it may be done accordingly; and with as little delay as possible. The Season for it is now come, and putting it in, gives the last stirring to the Corn.   A Bushel, or what my Seedsmen usually bestows to the Acre, of Wheat, is, I conceive sufficient; but where there is an exact similarity of Soil, it may not, for the sake of experiment, be amiss to try different quantities from two, to eight pecks, to the acre. and of Rye from two to Six pecks. If the Barley should turn out 16 Bushels to the Acre, I shall be very well satisfied; and according to your Acct. of the drought, it is more than could be expected. Should the Oats turn out in that proportion, my case will not be quite so disperate as I expected.

I am glad you settled with Rawlins as I do not like to be in debt to workmen, and could you, if there is means, pay Elizabeth Alton part of her demand, it would also be pleasing; as her frequent applications are disagreeable.

Priming the roof of the Green house may be delayed till I return, or till you here from me again, on the subject. in the mean while inform me what the Alexandria prices of white and red lead ground in oil, and yellow Oaker unground, are. I desire that the honey suckles against the Houses and brick walls, may be nailed up; and made to spread regularly over them. Should those near the Pillars of the Colonades, or covered ways, be dead, their plants should be supplied with others; as I want them to run up, and Spread over the parts which are painted green.

I am glad to hear that Mr. Youngs Plow answers in practice, and approved of by the Farmer; who should take care to keep it in order. Is *all* that field at French's, the fallowing of which was begun before I left home (I mean the one which you enter after crossing the ford, between Manley's houses and the South side of the Swamp) sowed, or Planted? and with what?

How does the grain which you have got out, yield, in quantity and quality? What has Morris been doing to his carts to require a new one to be made, and another repaired? I am certain he had a New one this spring or rather last Winter and the old one repaired, his wants of these so soon again, is inconceivable upon fair ground.

If Hezh. Fairfax is going to leave the Ferry, and John Fairfax is desirous of going there on the same terms his brother now is; I have no objection to it. but I shall not employ him at that place on standing Wages; neither shall I encrease his present lay at the Home House; nor exempt him, if he lives with me, from looking after the Fishery, provided I keep it in my own hands, which is uncertain, as a good rent would induce me to let it, that I might have no trouble or perplexity about it. As to giving a Man standing wages who looks after a Plantation, and has the hands to himself, and engaged in cropping, I have no idea of it. About a home house where there is no settled work from the profit of which an Overlooker can derive a proportionate benefit, there is a necessity for it. And whatever John Fairfax may think, he or I is a good deal mistaken, if there is any business he can fall into, which he can (Clothes excepted) clear £40 a yr.; when it is next to impossible to get money on any terms. Like others however he is never to be satisfied; and strange it is to me, that so soon as a man, by doing his duty, becomes useful; and without it, would be turned away disgracefully; and perhaps have his wages stopped. that he immediately thinks his Services can never be sufficiently rewarded; and without considering what others *really* make, when all expences are paid, or what he himself could raise under like circumstances, is forever demanding what, from the nature of the thing, cannot be given. I like John Fairfax very well, and have no inclination to change but shall make no alteration in his lay; and had rather he should remain about the house than go to the Ferry, as he has a better knowledge than a new hand would have, of what is required of such a character.

As to Cornelius's brother it is scarcely possible to decide any thing. In the first place he may not come. In the next place, his appearance may be very much against him; and he may have no testimonials that can be relied on: he may be too young, or he may not possess those qualities which Cornelius's partially has bestowed on him. and lastly, I can hardly believe that a raw Irishman can be well qualified to manage Negros. If I could employ him to any advantage, I should have no objection to it, but I must see the man, and have something to judge by, before this can happen or some body on my behalf must do it for me. Give my love to Fanny, and good wishes to Mr. Lear. Let him know that Mr. Langden is here, and very well, as is Mr. Gilman (who used to be in the Adjutant Generals department) as Deligates from New Hampshire. request Mr. Lear to translate the enclosed Letters. With great esteem etc.

[H.L.]

*To CLEMENT BIDDLE

August 7, 1787.

Dear Sir: In addition to the articles contained in the Memo. given to you some time since, I pray you to procure, and send by Captn. Steward the following.

A Wimble bit—compleat. Pickled Walnuts and India Mangoes none were sent before. Thompsons Seasons, and Guthries Geography and the art of Speaking.[80] Some Pamphlets which have been sent to me since I came to Town; and Books purchased for my amusement whilst in it, I now send to be packed up, and sent round.

The Top of the Cupulo (from Mr. Rakestraw).[81] The Venetian blind from Mr. Davis. A hogshead of Plaister of Paris, and a coob with two or three fowls, from Mr Barge; and the Chair.[82] I mean shall take the opportunity afforded by the Dolphin of going to Mount Vernon, and I pray you to recommend them to the particular care of the Captn. I have bought one and mean to buy another, piece of fine linnen which I shall send to you. I am etc.   [H.S.P.]

To MARQUIS DE LAFAYETTE

Philadelphia, August 15, 1787.

My dear Marqs: Altho' the business of the Fœderal Convention is not yet clos'd, nor I, thereby, enabled to give you an account of its proceedings; yet the opportunity afforded by Commodore Paul Jones' Return to France is too favourable for me to omit informing you, that the present expectation of the members is, that it will end about the first of next month; when, or as soon after as it shall be in my power, I will communicate the result of our long deliberation to you.

---

[80] Thompson's *Seasons* cost 11 shillings; Guthries *Geography*, 18s. 9d., and the *Art of Speaking*, 4 shillings.

[81] The cupola top from Joseph Rakestraw cost £24:7:1.

[82] In Washington's memoranda of expenses while at the Constitutional Convention is an entry under August 8: "By a fan Chair £ 1.12.6."

On August 18 Washington dined at Thomas McKean's; and framed in the entrance hall of "Collingwood," which was Tobias Lear's home on the "River Farm" of Mount Vernon, is the following note: "Genl. Washington presents his compliments to the Hon: Chief Justice McKean and will do himself the honor of dining with him on Saturday next, agreeably to invitation."

News paper accts. inform us that the Session of the Assembly of Notables is ended. and you have had the goodness (in your letter of the 5th. of May) to communicate some of the proceedings to me. among which is that of the interesting motion made by yourself respecting the expenditure of public money by Monsr. de Callonne, and the consequence thereof.

The patriotism, by which this motion was dictated throws a lustre on the action, which cannot fail to dignify the Author, and I sincerely hope with you, that much good will result from the deliberations of so respectable a Council, I am not less ardent in my wish that you may succeed in your plan of toleration in religious matters. Being no bigot myself to any mode of worship, I am disposed to indulge the professors of Christianity in the church, that road to Heaven, which to them shall seem the most direct plainest easiest and least liable to exception. Had not the account of your recovery accompanied that of your indisposition I should have felt many anxious and painful moments from the recital of the former. but let the first admonish you, my dear Marquis, against application too intense. This may disqualify you for the laudable pursuits to which zeal for the good of your Country and the honor of human nature may prompt you, and which may prove injurious both to yourself and it.

The politicians of this Country hardly know what to make of the present situation of European affairs. If serious consequences do not follow the blood which has been shed in the United Netherlands these people will certainly have acted differently from the rest of Mankind; and in another quarter one would think there could hardly be so much Smoke without some fire between the Russian and Turk. Should these disputes kindle the flame of war it is not easy to prescribe bounds to its extension or effect. The disturbances in Massachusetts have subsided; but there are seeds of discontent in every part of this Union; ready to produce other disorders if the wisdom of the present Convention should not be able to devise, and the good sense of the people be found ready to adopt a more vigorous and energetic government, than the one under which we now live; for the present, from experience, has been found too feeble and inadequate to give that security, which our liberties and property render absolutely essential, and which the fulfilment of public faith loudly requires.

Vain is it to look for respect from abroad, or tranquillity at home; vain is it to murmur at the detention of our Western Posts, or complain of the restriction of our commerce; vain are all the attempts to remedy the evils complained of by Mr Dumas to discharge the interest due on foreign loans, or satisfy the claims of foreign Officers, the neglect of doing which is a high impeachment of our National character, and is hurtful to the feelings of every well wisher to this Country in and out of it; vain is it to talk of chastising the Algerines, or doing ourselves Justice in any other respect, till the wisdom and force of the Union can be more concentrated and better applied. In what accountable terms, My dear Marquis, shall I express or convey to you, my thanks for the Maltese Asses. Believe me, however, when I assure you, that your friendship in this respect has embarrassed me not a little for with much truth I can declare that nothing was further from my thoughts than to make you more than the medium of application or to saddle you with more than the first advance in obtaining them thro' you alone, I was enabled to accomplish this matter, and the desire of introducing animals of so much use into this Country prompted me to accept of your influence with Admiral de Suffran, to whom, if I am under obligation, you would do me a singular favour to make my acknowledgments acceptable. With sentiments of the highest respect, and most perfect regard for Madam de la

Fayette and the rest of your family and with the most Affecte. attachment to you, I am ever yours, &c.[83]

*To HENRY KNOX

Philadelphia, August 19, 1787.

My dear Sir: By slow, I wish I could add and sure, movements, the business of the Convention progresses; but to say when it will end, or what will be the result, is more than I can venture to do; and therefore I shall hazard no opinion thereon. If however, *some* good does not proceed from the Session, the defects cannot, with propriety, be charged to the hurry with which the business has been conducted: Yet, many things may be forgot, some of them not well digested, and others become a mere nullity. Notwithstanding which I wish a disposition may be found in Congress, the several States Legislatures, and the community at large to adopt the Government which may be agreed on in Convention; because I am fully persuaded it is the best that can be obtained at the present moment, under such diversity of ideas as prevail.

I should have had great pleasure in a visit to New York during the adjournment of the Convention; but not foreseeing the precise period at which it would take place, or the length of it; I had, previously thereto, put my carriage into the hands of a workman to repair, and had not the means of going. I condole very sincerely with Mrs. Knox and yourself on your late misfortune; but am sure, however severe the trial, each of you have fortitude enough to meet it. Nature, no doubt, must feel severely before *calm* resignation will over come it.

I offer my best respects to Mrs. Knox, and every good wish for the family, with great regard and unfeigned Affectn. Iam etc.

[MS.H.S.]

---

[83] From the "Letter Book" copy in the *Washington Papers.*

*To CLEMENT BIDDLE

August 22, 1787.

Dear Sir: Since I came to this City, if I recollect rightly, you asked me if I now had, or could put up, a quantity of Herrings next season, for Sale.

Having revolved the matter in my mind, I wish in turn to be informed, if there is any responsible character who would enter into a contract for a number, to be delivered next Season? What number of Barrls. he would contract for? and at what price; to be paid on delivery, or on a credit to be agreed on? Answers to these questions would enable me to determine with respect to the propriety of entering into such a Contract, and in case of it, to prepare accordingly.

Be so good as to inform me whether you have engaged the gudgeens for my Mill, or not, and when they will be ready? also with respect to the price of Window glass 9 by 11. I shall want near 300 lights or Squares. I am etc.   [H.S.P.]

To ALEXANDER SPOTSWOOD

Philadelphia, August 26, 1787.

Dear Sir: Having heard nothing from you, in reply to a letter I wrote you in answer to yours of the 25th. of June, respecting your wishes to enter your Son on [*sic*] board the French Navy, I am led to apprehend a miscarriage, or that the letter to or from you may be lying in some of the Post Offices (a thing not very unusual) I therefore address you again on the subject.

The purport of my former letter was to ask, whether you had been encouraged to hope, or to expect much (from any Gentleman competent to advise you) from such a project, if not, whether it would not be better to delay your decisions on this point till enquiry could be first made, and that, under the impression of the propriety of it, I would detain your letter for France till I could hear further from you on this subject among others for the Following reasons.

1. Because I think your Sons going into the French Navy would be attended with greater expence than you apprehend.

2. That the highest rank he could expect to meet at entrance would be that of Midshipman.

3. That for want of an interest always at hand his prospect of rising would be very unpromising

4. That from a difference of Country, language, religeon and manners, the Service would soon become irksome and disagreeable to him and in the last place. Because I do not think that they are such good Seamen as the British or Americans.

Friendship and regard for you and your Son, induced me to make these observations before I parted with your letters (supposing a small delay could make no great difference in your plan) but if you have been well advised in the matter and will write me again I will immediately forward your letters with one of my own to the Marqs. de la Fayette, as the delay of your answer has far exceeded anything that could have been expected, I shall be concerned if any inconvenience should have resulted from it having every disposition to comply with your wishes in this, or any other respect wherein I can do it consistently. My love to Mrs. Spotswood. I am, etc.[84]

To GEORGE AUGUSTINE WASHINGTON

Philadelphia, August 26, 1787.

Dear George: Not having received any letter from you last Week (by the Post which arrives here on Thursdays) I have of

---

[84] From the "Letter Book" copy in the *Washington Papers*.

course, nothing to reply to; but request to be informed of the depth of the well (by the Kitchen door) from the level of the brick pavement, which surround it, to the surface of the water within; and the depth of the water. To be clear, if I am not so already, I want the whole depth from the surface and level of the pavement to the bottom of the well; with the depth of water therein. I have some intention of placing a pump in it, instead of drawing the water up in a Bucket as at present, and for this purpose the enquiry is made. I also request that you wd. send me the dimensions (in the same way you did the former one) of the chimneys in the parlour, common dining room, and your aunts bed chamber; and let me know if the present back and Sides of the one in the dining room can be fitted to any other chimney that has no plates and which is in common use. The Mill Irons will go by the next vessel and I would send glass for the green house also but it appears to me that the price here is equally high with that in Alexandria; here it is 100/ by the box wch is equal to 80/. with you; and the freight, duty and Comn. would be to be added. I go on the presumption that Each box contains 12 doz. 144 panes; of this, inform me how the case is in Alexandria or how many square feet a box is said to contain there. If the top for the Cupulo, and the directions which accompanied it, are well understood, I would (supposing every thing is on the spot necessary for it) have it put up immediately whilst the weather is mild, still and warm.

I have promised Mr. Morris an exact pattern, made of wood, of Mr. Young's Iron Plow. When I speak of wood, I mean such parts of it as *Nat* cannot make *true* and *perfect* such as the beam &c. You will readily perceive that as this is intended for a model to make them by, that the whole of it ought to be as exact as it can be made, for this reason and knowing that Nat is a clumsey fellow, and supposing that Mathew wd. do it in wood more correctly, that I have mentioned wood; but as you know the intention, it may either be of Wood, or Iron, or partly of both as shall be judged best on consulting Mathew and Nat. All I want is, that the model may be a perfect representation in all its parts, and the putting of them together likewise of the original. The directions for fixing or setting you have in Mr. Youngs letter.

You may make enquiry for a fit person to supply the place of Fairfax at the Ferry, but do not engage any before I return or you shall hear from me, because I do not know but I may find it convenient to put both that and Frenchs under the care of the Farmer, or some one Man.

I had written thus far when your letter of the 20th (which came by the Post yesterday Evening) was delivered to me. I am happy to find by it that you have at length, had a good rain. The young Corn, Buckwheat, grain newly sown, and vegetables of every kind will undoubtedly be benefitted by it and may undergo a considerable change if the weather should continue to be favorable.

If I am to form an opinion of the last harvest of Wheat and rye from the produce of the Wheat and Rye at Muddy hole it must be miserable indeed, the first containing 10 acres, yielding only 32½ Bush; and the other containing 13 acres, but 47½ of Rye. In neither case 4 bushels to the acre. If all turns out like these my prospect is indeed poor, not a moment therefore should be lost if the Fly is among the wheat to get it ground up before the little that is made be injured by this destructive insect. I beg therefore that this matter may be closely attended to. If merchantable flour cannot be made of the old Wheat, it had undoubtedly better be given to the Negroes, and if necessity obliges you to resort to the Potatoes and Pease for their support

I desire that the quantity used by them may be (of both) measured that I may not only know what they use, but what I make, without which my experiments will be inconclusive.

I am very well satisfied with the disposition of the Stock agreably to the list inclosed to me, but it would be very well to compare this list with the one taken some time ago (in the Winter, I believe it was or fall) and make the Overseer if there is a difference acct. for it; unless this is done no reliable end is attained by taking such lists; and they may sell, kill, or otherwise dispose of any part thereof with impunity.

How does your grass seed come on? particularly the clover; What sort of Clover is that in the back of the last years sowing? how does it look at all the places, old as well as new?

Your aunt informs me that there is a probability Mr. B. Bassett will be married soon; and that should it take place before I return, you do not incline to carry Fanny down; thinking it may be improper to leave home while I am absent; but should the event happen I desire that this may be no bar to your accompanying her, as I see no inconvenience that can happen by so doing. Give my love to Fanny, and best wishes to Mr. Lear. I am, etc.[85]

To WILLIAM HARTSHORNE

Philadelphia, August 30, 1787.

Sir: The Gentleman who will present this letter to you is Major Baylies[86] of Massachusetts, Son in law to Genl. Lincoln. He is on business to Virginia, and at his request, I give you the trouble of receiving it as introductory of him, believing him to be a man of character and worth.

---

[85] The text is from a copy kindly furnished by Mrs. C. Grattan Crawford, of Kernstown, Va.
[86] Hodijah(?) Baylies.

I understand, that the subscribers to the Potomack Navigation has been called upon for another advance, my proportion of which shall be paid so soon as I return, which cannot, now, be at a distant period. With great esteem, I am, etc.[87]

*To GEORGE AUGUSTINE WASHINGTON

Philadelphia, September 2, 1787.

Dear George: Your last letter of the 27th Ulto. came in due of Post, and gave me the pleasure to hear that you had had a continuance of rain. Seasonable weather may bring on young Corn, and help that which was not too far gone. At any rate the Buck Wheat, and vegitables of every kind, must receive benefit.

When I expressed a wish to have the race widened from the Mill upwards, it was on a Supposition that the water had not been turned into it; had I believed this was the case I should not have requested it; tho' I shall not be at all dissatisfied at the delay occasioned by it, provided the work is well done; for to accomplish this was all I had in view

The Acct. you have given of the present State of the different species of Crops, is very satisfactory; a similar one, weekly, would give me a precise idea of them; but I trust I shall not remain here more than a fortnight longer to receive these accts., or any thing else.

By your Aunts letter to me, I find that Mr. Hanson[88] has applied to, and received payment from Mr Porter[89] for the board of George and Lawrence Washington.[90] I beg you will

---

[87] From the "Letter Book" copy in the *Washington Papers.*
[88] Samuel "of Sams" Hanson.
[89] —— Porter, an Alexandria merchant.
[90] George Steptoe Washington and Lawrence Augustine Washington, sons of the General's brother, Samuel.

request (Mr Hanson) never to do the like again. Mr. Porter must conceive very strangely of this; I am sure I do; and cannot acct. for the application. And I further beg that you will, in my name, let your father[91] know, in explicit terms, that if he will not keep me furnished with the means to defray the expences of these boys that he must take the whole of their affairs on himself. The demands upon me for money are too numerous and heavy to answer the calls I have on their acct. He seems not to consider that the calls on me for their schooling, board, cloathing &ca. encrease with time, but on the contrary when a sum is once paid, that the matter is done with. Another quarter I suppose must be due, or nearly so, by this time, besides the Schooling, the Cloathing from Mr. Porter &ca. &ca. all of which I shall, I expect to be saluted by, as soon as I return. He ought to put the produce of their Estates (if they have any, and if they have not, I know what to depend upon) as fast as it is raised into my hands. This certainly would be as proper as to be keeping me constantly in advance, and exposed to Duns on their acct. when I know not which way to turn, to obtain money to pay the pressing calls for Cash I owe on my own Acct.

I am sorry to find that the Green paint which was got to give the dining room another Coat should have turned out so bad; such impositions (besides the disappointment) are really shameful. I did not know that any part of the Boston leather was black, consequently could have no particular design in view at the time it was sent; but as it is so, and good, it may be appropriated for Shoes for the House Servants, Overseers &ca.

In my last I wrote to you for an exact model of Youngs Plough, to be made of Wood or Iron, or partly of both as Mathew and Nat might agree for Mr. Robt. Morris; what I

---

[91] Charles Washington.

meant by a model was that it should be exactly of the size in all its parts, and as truely put together as Mr. Young's is; that the representation may be perfect for others to be made, and fixed by. Send it by the first Vessel after it is ready. And send with it also, a peck of what you conceive to be Youngs Spring Wheat; which, unquestionably, is the most indifferent looking of the two red kinds. accompany the Plow and Wheat with a line to Mr. Morris.

I am well satisfied from the account given of the New ground, in your last letter, (in front of the House) that the Succours and Sprts. together with the Huckleberry shrubs &ca, are not sufficiently destroyed to sow grain in; and therefore if you have not begun to do it desire that it may be delayed untill I return home.

Fairfax's[92] Terms, I suppose must be agreed to, though he seems disposed to make hay (or in other words Cloaths) whilst the Sun shines. Hardly any weekly report comes to hand by which it does not appear that Thos. Greene is absent one or more days. I desire you will tell him that this custom is a bad one, contrary to any ideas I entertained when he was bargained with, and that it must be broke.

I desire you will send me the number of New blankets your Aunt has in her Store room. They are not to be had here but in high terms, and yet this is the year that *all* my people are entitled to receive them, except the Women who have had Children and been supplied on that occasion. do you know the Alexandria price for the large striped dutch blanketing? (15 I believe are in a piece). If you do not, pray enquire and let me know when you next write. Also the price of Bills of Exchange drawn on London at 30 days sight? that I may know whether it is best to sell here, or there.

---

[92] John Fairfax.

Miss Allan's letter has been given to Mr. Rutlidge who has promised to forward, or carry it safe to Major Read. My love to Fanny, and best wishes to Mr. Lear. With sentiments of great regard I am etc.[93]

*To THE SECRETARY FOR FOREIGN AFFAIRS

Philadelphia, September 2, 1787.

Dear Sir: I avail myself of the polite assurance of your last, to trouble you with the enclosed. If the Commodore should have left New York, you would oblige me by forwarding it. I regretted exceedingly, not having had it in my power to visit New York during the adjournment of the Convention, last Month. Not foreseeing with any precision the period at which it was likely to take place, nor the length of it, I had put my Carriage in the hands of a Workman to be repaired, and had not the means of moving during the recess but with, or on the curtesy of, others.

I thank you for the hints contained in your letter, and with best wishes for Mrs. Jay, and great Affection for yourself I am, etc.[94]

To CHEVALIER JOHN PAUL JONES

Philadelphia, September 2, 1787.

Sir: Should this letter reach you in time, the purport of it is, to beg your care of the enclosed to the Marqs. de la Fayette; and to inform you that all the letters, Memorials, and Papers of every kind which had been transmitted to me as President General of the Society of the Cincinnati, were forwarded (not

---

[93] From a photostat of the original kindly furnished by the secretary of the Sulgrave Manor Board, London.

[94] From a facsimile in a sales catalogue, 1925.

expecting to attend it myself) to the last General meeting holden in this City but how they were acted upon is not in my power to inform you, not being at it.

I have received, and have forwarded to my house the Bust[95] you did me the honor to present me with, and shall place it with my own. Wishing you every possible felicity I have the honor, ect.[96]

To CHARLES PETTIT

Philadelphia, September 7, 1787.

Sir: Having received the dimensions of three more of my Chimneys for which I want castings, I have to request them as follows.

3. 6½ high in front
1. 6½ deep   } First
3. 3. Wide at the back

3. 2½ high in front
1. 6½ Deep   } Second
3. 5. Wide at the back

3. 1. high in front
1. 10 Deep   } Third
3. 5. Wide at the back

The above being the exact size of the Chimneys (already built and in use) it is not to be forgotten that the thickness of the *back* plate is to be deducted from the width of those on the sides or vica versa as shall be adjudged best.

The mould already made, may subserve for the above Casting reducing it first to the largest of the above Chimneys, then

---

[95] The bust of Jones was a replica of the original by Houdon and is listed in the "Inventory of the Contents of Mount Vernon" as "1 Bust in Plaster of Paul Jones" and appraised at $20.

[96] From the "Letter Book" copy in the *Washington Papers*.

to the second size, and lastly to the smallest. the crest and Cypher to each.

I should be glad to receive them as soon as possible and the money shall be immediately paid for them. I am, etc.[97]

*To CLEMENT BIDDLE

Monday, September 10, 1787.

Dear Sir: I have received both your Notes of this morning, and thank you for Notice of the Vessel's Sailing. The Books, I perceive, are only small treatises upon education, referred to by Doctr. Rush, which I can get, and carry in my Trunk. Remember the Clothes baskets. I send a small box containing a Lamp,[98] it is a present, but could not have cost 20/. If the hounds presented to me by Captn. Morris are not provided for, will it not be necessary to lay something in for them? I think of nothing else at this time; therefore, if you will let me know how the Acct. stands between us I would wish to square it.   [H.S.P.]

*To CLEMENT BIDDLE

Saturday Morng., September 15, 1787.

Genl. Washington prests. his Compliments to Colo. Biddle and would be glad to know if the Vessel for Alexandria is gone. The lowest price the best dutch (Striped) Blankets sell at, by the piece. And how his Acct. stands since the late purchases made by him as he has expectations that the business of the Convention will be brought to a close, or nearly so this day.

[H.S.P.]

---

[97] From the "Letter Book" copy in the *Washington Papers*.
[98] A reflecting lamp for the hall from Mrs. Eliza Powel.
Under date of Sept. 12, 1787, is a printed copy of the report of the Committee of Style and Arrangement of that date, of the Constitutional Convention, with manuscript marginalia of Washington and William Jackson, bringing it into conformity with the Constitution as completed by the Convention.

To THOMAS SMITH

Philadelphia, September 16, 1787.

Sir: You will be puzzled to acct. for my long silence, the truth is, before I came to this City I resolved to postpone writing till I should have arrived at and should have met a direct conveyance from it, and afterwards. The variety of matters which have occurred and pressed upon me, have, in some measure, put it out of my power to do it at an earlier period than now.

I wish, sincerely, that you had been so obliging as to have designated the sum with which you would have been satisfied for conducting my Ejectments, I still wish that you would do this, and receive it out of the money which (by Major Freemans report to me) you must be on the point of recovering, and permit me to add moreover that I wish, yet more ardently I had it in my power to pay you in a more agreeable manner, but the fact is my expences in this City have been so much greater than I expected that it has deprived me of the means. Freemans letter to me, contains this Paragraph.

At March term I delivered Mr. Smith sundry obligations and took his rect. for them, which with the one in his hands befor, amounted to £533.19.0. I make no doubt he will soon recover the money and transmit it to you.

He adds, I have lodged with Mr. Richard Noble near Redstone old Fort £38.1.3. this sum I have requested Mr. Noble to pay you, if it has not been forwarded to me, thro' some other channel, and I hope measures has been, or will be taken to obtain from my opponants the legal fees and other costs which they burthened me with, by means of the ejectments. Mr. Smiley handed me a letter some time after my arrival at this City, accompanied by £12.10. recovered from one Cunningham.

For the anxiety you express to have undergone during the prosecution of this Suit, I feel myself exceedingly obliged and pray you to accept my thanks for this proof of your attachment as well as for the care with which the business was conducted. I am, etc.[99]

To JOHN CANNON

Philadelphia, September 16, 1787.

Sir: I was surprized to find by your letter of the 8th. of May, dated in this City (received after I came to it) that you had not got the letter I wrote to you sometime before under cover to Colo Bayard of Pittsburg especially as the Colonel has acknowledged the receipt of it, and promised that it should be carefully forwarded to your house.

In that letter, to the best of my recollection, I requested that you would take charge of all my concerns, as well as those in Fayette, as Washington Counties and act for me as you would do for yourself. To this, if my memory serves me, your powers already extend, if not, I now give them to you by this letter.

I cannot consent to take two dollars a acre for the Land in Washington County. If the Government of this Country gets well toned, and property perfectly secured, I have no doubt of obtaining the price I have fixed on the land, and that in a short time, in the meanwhile, I had rather rent it from year to year than give leases for a term of years as the latter will certainly impede the Sale.

For the Land in Fayette County, I have been offered the price I had fixed on it, viz Forty Shillings pr. Acre, by a number of New Jersey people but we have differed with respect to the mode of payment and perhaps shall never agree. I would not therefore have you Slip an opportunity of disposing of that

---

[99] From the "Letter Book" copy in the *Washington Papers*.

Tract, if that price and the payment thereof is well secured. I would, as I think you have already been informed; be content with one fourth of the money paid down, the remainder in four annual payments with interest.

I willing to take usual allowance of the Crops which were in the ground and hope you have taken your measures accordingly less than this, the Tenants cannot I should conceive think of giving, as the whole of them might have been demanded. I am, etc.[1]

To RICHARD NOBLE

Philadelphia, September 16, 1787.

Sir: By a letter which I have received from Major Thomas Freeman since I came to the City I am informed that he has lodged some money of mine in your hands, as also a receipt from Thomas Smith Esqr. for £533.19.0 with sundry other papers. I shall be obliged by your forwarding the money to me by the First good conveyance; the papers I beg you to place in the hands of Colo. Cannon of Washington County to whose care I had committed my business in that County long before I had any knowledge or information from Major Freeman of his having committed these matters to you. If no sure and safe conveyance should offer for sending the money immediately to me I request in that case that you would be so obliging as to deliver it to Thomas Smith Esqr. Attorney at Law who will apply it to the uses, and agreeable to the advice I have given. I am, etc.[1]

---

[1] From the "Letter Book" copy in the *Washington Papers*.

On September 16 Washington wrote short notes to Comte de Rochambeau, Marquis de Lafayette, and Marquis de Chastellux, introducing Charles Pinckney, of South Carolina. Copies of these notes are in the "Letter Book" in the *Washington Papers*.

On September 17 Washington wrote briefly to Col. William Washington, inclosing the business card of the Philadelphia coach-maker who had repaired his carriage, recommending him. A copy of this letter is in the "Letter Book" in the *Washington Papers*.

To THOMAS JEFFERSON

Philadelphia, September 18, 1787.

Dear Sir: Yesterday put an end to the business of the Fœderal Convention. Inclosed is a copy of the Constitution by it agreed to, not doubting but that you have participated in the general anxiety which has agitated the minds of your Countrymen on this interesting occasion, I shall be excused I am certain for this endeavor to relieve you from it; especially when I assure you of the sincere regard and esteem with which I have the honor, etc.[2]

*To MRS. JOHN PENN[3]

Tuesday, September 18, 1787.

Genl. Washington takes the liberty of offering his respectful compliments to Mrs. Penn, and the Vision of Columbus. It is one of several Copies for which he subscribed some years ago and received since he came to this City. To the merit, or demerit of the performance, the General can say nothing, not having had time to read it.[4]

To MARQUIS DE LAFAYETTE

Philadelphia, September 18, 1787.

My dear Marqs: In the midst of hurry, and in the moment of my departure from this City, I address this letter to you. The principal, indeed the only design of it, is to fulfil the promise I made, that I would send to you the proceedings of the Fœderal

---

[2] From the "Letter Book" copy in the *Washington Papers*.
[3] Mrs. Penn was Ann Allen, daughter of Chief Justice William Allen, of Pennsylvania.
[4] From a photostat of the original kindly furnished by E. F. Bonaventure, of New York City.

convention, as soon as the business was closed. More than this, circumstanced as I am at present, it is not in my power to do. nor am I inclined to attempt it, as the enclosure,[5] must speak for itself, and will occupy your thoughts for some time.

It is the production of four months deliberation. It is now a Child of fortune, to be fostered by some and buffeted by others. what will be the General opinion on, or the reception of it, is not for me to decide, nor shall I say any thing for or against it: if it be good I suppose it will work its way good; if bad, it will recoil on the Framers. My best wishes attend you, and yours; and with the sincerest friendship and most Affectionate regard etc.[6]

*To CLEMENT BIDDLE

Head of Elk, September 19, 1787.

Dear Sir: Yesterday before I left the City, I wrote to Captn. Morris[7] requesting the favor of him to furnish me with a description of the hounds he was so good as to give me, that I might know how to *apply* the names contained in the list you sent me; for without, though I had eight names, I might not apply one right; Whether Captn. Morris sent the discription, or not, I will not say, but it did not come to my hands, and without it, I shall find myself at a loss. I asked some other questions also; answers to which would be satisfactory, and I would thank you for obtaining, and forwarding them to me by the first Post after this letter shall have reached you; my letter to him, will remind him of them, on your application. I am etc.

[H. S. P.]

---

[5] The Constitutional Convention had Dunlap & Claypoole print 500 copies of the Constitution after it had been engrossed on parchment and signed. The inclosure above was, doubtless, one of these.

[6] From the "Letter Book" copy in the *Washington Papers.*

Washington left Philadelphia in the afternoon of September 18 for Mount Vernon, which he reached about sunset on Saturday the 22d.

[7] The letter to Morris is not now found in the *Washington Papers.*

To PATRICK HENRY

Mount Vernon, September 24, 1787.

Dear Sir: In the first moment after my return I take the liberty of sending you a copy of the Constitution which the Fœderal Convention has submitted to the People of these States. I accompany it with no observations; your own Judgment will at once discover the good, and the exceptionable parts of it. and your experience of the difficulties, which have ever arisen when attempts have been made to reconcile such variety of interests and local prejudices as pervade the several States will render explanation unnecessary. I wish the Constitution which is offered had been made more perfect, but I sincerely believe it is the best that could be obtained at this time; and, as a constitutional door is opened for amendment hereafter, the adoption of it under the present circumstances of the Union, is in my opinion desirable.

From a variety of concurring accounts it appears to me that the political concerns of this Country are, in a manner, suspended by a thread. That the Convention has been looked up to by the reflecting part of the community with a solicitude which is hardly to be conceived, and that if nothing had been agreed on by that body, anarchy would soon have ensued, the seeds being richly [*sic*] sown in every soil. I am &c.[8]

---

[8] From the "Letter Book" copy in the *Washington Papers*.

This same letter was also sent to Benjamin Harrison and Thomas Nelson.

Henry answered (October 19): "I have to lament that I cannot bring my Mind to accord with the proposed Constitution. The Concern I feel on this Account, is really greater than I am able to express. Perhaps mature Reflection may furnish me Reasons to change my present Sentiments into a Conformity with the Opinions of those personages for whom I have the highest Reverence."

On October 4 Harrison replied: "I feel myself deeply interested in every thing that you have had a hand in, or that comes from you, and am so well assured of the solidity of your judgment, and the rectitude of your intentions, that I shall never stick at trifles to conform myself to your opinion; in the present instance, I am so totally uninform'd as to the general situation of America, that I can form no judgment of the necessity the convention was under to give us such a constitution as it has

To JOHNZEE SELLMAN

Mount Vernon, September 25, 1787.

Sir: As I observe by the Baltimore advertiser that you are Administrator of the later Mr. John Rawlins, I take the liberty to mention to you an error which happened in the payment of an order drawn by Rawlins upon me during my late absence from home, and which was not discovered till I pointed it out since my return from Philadelphia.

Sometime last fall I agreed with Mr. Rawlins to furnish me with a number of friezes and mouldings, for which I was to pay forty three pounds twelve Shillings Virginia Currency, but in consequence of some defect in the work, he afterwards wrote (which letter I have now by me) to me informing me that he should charge but forty five pounds Maryland currency, he furnished them accordingly; and in July last sent one Thomas Hammond to wash some stucco work, which was done by himself and Mr. Thorp,[9] and gave him an order for the above forty five pounds, but did not mention in the order, whether it was Maryland or Virginia Currency. The person who paid the money (not recuring to Mr. Rawlins's agreement which was in the house) paid it in Virginia currency and took Mr. Hammonds receipt for the same, specifying virginia currency in the receipt.

---

done; If our condition is not very desperate, I have my fears that the remedy will prove worse than the disease. Age makes men often over cautious; I am willing to attribute my fears to that cause, but from whatever source they spring, I cannot divest myself of an opinion, that the seeds of civil discord are plentifully sown in very many of the powers given both to the president and congress, and that if the constitution is carried into effect, the States south of the potowmac, will be little more than appendages to those to the northward of it. . . . I shall only say, that my objections chiefly lay agst. the unlimited powers of taxation and the regulations of trade, and the jurisdictions that are to be established in every State altogether independent of their laws. The sword, and such powers will; nay in the nature of things they must sooner or later, establish a tyranny, not inferior to the triumvirate or centum viri of Rome." Both these letters are in the *Washington Papers.*

[9] Tharp.

I must therefore request Sir, that you will investigate the matter and have the difference of exchange in the above sum (which will be thirty dollars) returned. I am, etc.[10]

To SAMUEL HANSON

Mount Vernon, September 27, 1787.

Sir: By your letter of the 23d., with which I have been favoured since my return home, I perceive there has been a misconception on my part of the transaction between you and Mr. Porter respecting payment for the board of my Nephews. it thus arose: in the enumeration of monies which remained for me to pay according to the account transmitted. I found the sum of £17.10 due to Mr. Porter on your account, this, and the recollection (I believe I am not mistaken therein) finding the like sum paid by that Gentleman before any application had been made to me for it, led me to suppose (as I had requested you to apply to that Gentleman for such articles of Clothing as the boys really wanted) that application had been made to him for their board also which as no deposit was made in his hands to answer such demands, would had the case really been so have given him cause to think, strangely of me, this idea of mine was the cause of the letter you recd. from my nephew.

A draught in favor of Mr. Porter, or in behalf of any other Gentleman, is, unquestionably as proper as any other mode of application and will be equally agreeable to me.

For any particular care or attention which you have shewn, or may shew my Nephews I shall always think myself obliged and thinking as I certainly have done, that the board was high I receive with pleasure the information of your intention of

---

[10] From the "Letter Book" copy in the *Washington Papers*.

reducing it, for without intending a compliment I repeat the satisfaction I feel from the consideration of their being under the eye of a Gentleman so capable as you are of advising and exacting a proper conduct from them. I am, etc.[11]

*To RICHARD SPRIGG[12]

Mount Vernon, September 28, 1787.

Dear Sir: I have this moment been favoured with your letter without date from Prince George County, and have ordered the Jennies to be delivered to Mr. Dove, hoping both will prove with foal. Royal Gift never fails, the other is a young hand, but I hope will be equally sure.

I am glad to hear that the Jenny you sent to R. G. last year has produced a Jack, and that you have been so successful in your importation of Deer. My Country Does have brought Fawns, and I have a buck and doe of those given me by Mr. Ogle; yet, if you shd. be successful, I would thank you for a pair (male and female) of yours.

My best respects if you please to Mrs. Sprigg; and thanks for your kind congratulations on my safe return home, after a long absence from it. I am etc.[13]

To CHARLES PETTIT

Mount Vernon, October 2, 1787.

Sir: By the charming Polly Capt. Ellwood[14] I send you patterns for the hearths of Chimneys which I beg may be cast and

---

[11] From the "Letter Book" copy in the *Washington Papers*.
[12] Of Annapolis, Md.
[13] From a photostat of the original in the *Washington Papers*.
[14] Capt. John Ellwood, jr.

sent to me by the first conveyance to Alexandria; the cost you will please to annex to the other plates, bespoke before I left the City,[15] and the amount shall be paid when it is made known to, Sir, Yr. etc.[16]

To ROBERT MORRIS

Mount Vernon, October 2, 1787.

Dear Sir: By the charming Polly Capt. Ellwood I forward you a perfect model of the plough which was sent to me by Mr. Young with the direction of that Gentleman for setting it for use; from the character I have received of it, its performance surpasses any that has ever been tried before, on my Farms. I also send you a part of the summer wheat with which Mr. Young has furnished me as springing from seed sent by the Empress of Russia to his Britanic Majesty for the advantage it may have over other wheat I shall not vouch, to vary the seed time of this grain must, I conceive be its best recommendation, you will likewise receive part of the Sainfoin Seed I had come in, sufficient I think to sow a quarter of an acre in broad cast if good; and much more in drills. It is held in high estimation in England. the grass delights in dry soil. if it be stoney so much the better; Sow it without delay with wheat or Rye, or very early in the spring with Barley or Oats.

My mind will ever retain warm, impressions of, and feel very sensibly the polite and friendly attentions I received from Mrs. Morris and yourself whilst I was in Philadelphia; to have opportunities of proving the sincerity of this declaration would give me much pleasure but in no place to the same degree as under this roof.

---

[15] The "cast iron backs and jambs" were shipped from Philadelphia, November 6, at a total cost of £18:5:1. The invoice is in the *Washington Papers*.

[16] From the "Letter Book" copy in the *Washington Papers*.

Mrs. Washington begs that you and Mrs. Morris will accept her respectful compliments and best wishes; mine in a particular and affectionate manner are added not only to you both but to all the young folks of the Family and to Govr. Morris[17] Esqr. I am, etc.

P. S. Will you be so obliging as to give me your process for preparing the Duck wheat straw for fodder. The effects of the drought with me has exceeded anything I could have conceived and has driven me to even substitute for Hay. It is possible I may avail myself of your kind offer of sending for India Paper for my new Room but presuming there is no opportunity to do it soon; I shall not, at this time give you the demensions of it.[18]

To CHARLES PETTIT

Mount Vernon, October 4, 1787.

Sir: The enclosed ought to have accompanied the letter and the box by Capt. Ellwood. That it did not was an omission.

In addition to the Plates there written for, let me request two others; three feet nine each square, I want them for a Green house and would have quite plain and full as thick as they are *usually* cast for Chimney backs. I am, etc.[18]

To GOVERNOR WILLIAM SMALLWOOD

Mount Vernon, October 6, 1787.

Dear Sir: When I had the honor of being at your house last Fall, you gave me some reason to believe that you would become the purchaser of my land adjoining yours, in Charles County, and, if I recollect rightly, was to have written to me on that Subject from Annapolis.

---

[17] Gouverneur Morris.
[18] From the "Letter Book" copy in the *Washington Papers*.

I am still disposed to part with this land; and I should be glad if you could make it convenient to be the purchaser thereof. I told you in the convention we had on this subject that I would endeavour to make the payments as easy as my own circumstances would admit, this I repeat. and if you have corn to dispose of, at a moderate price, I would take at least 500 Barrells in payment and wheat (if good, clean, and free from the Fly) delivered at my Mill, to which Boats can come, at the Cash price in Alexandria, your answer by the bearer would much oblige Dr. Sir, Yr. etc.[19]

To GEORGE MASON

Mount Vernon, October 7, 1787.

Dear Sir: Doctr. Stuart whom I have seen since his return from Gunston informs me (of what indeed you had done before) that your Crop of Corn is very short, and that you had it in contemplation to draw a supply from No. Carolina where it might be had cheap.

My crop is much below what I had conceived, even from the destressing accounts which were handed to me, I much doubt whether the aid of 300 Barrels will be more than sufficient to carry me thro' the year. If therefore you have matured any plan by which my adding 500 barrels would be the means of facilating, I should be glad to be informed of it. In that case, if I can see my way to obtain the money (necessary for the payment) I would gladly join you.

I am sorry to hear you met with an accident on your return. I hope you experience no ill effect from it. The family join me in compliments and good wishes to you, Mrs. Mason and Family. I am, etc.[19]

---

[19] From the "Letter Book" copy in the *Washington Papers*.

To JAMES MADISON

Mount Vernon, October 10, 1787.

My dear Sir: I thank you for your letter of the 30th ulto. It came by the last Post. I am better pleased that the proceedings of the Convention are submitted from Congress by a unanimous vote (feeble as it is) than if they had appeared under strong marks of approbation without it. This apparent unanimity will have its effect. Not every one has opportunities to peep behind the curtain; and as the multitude are often deceived by externals, the appearance of unanimity in that body on this occasion will be of great importance. The political tenets of Colo. M.[20] and Colo. R. H. L.[21] are always in unison. It may be asked which of them gives the tone. Without hesitation I answer, the latter; because I believe the latter will receive it from no one. He has I am informed rendered himself obnoxious in Philadelphia by the pains he took to disseminate his objections amongst some of the leaders of the seceding members of the Legislature of that State. His conduct is not less reprobated in this Country. How it will be relished generally is yet to be learnt, by me.

As far as accounts have been received from the Sn. and Wt.[22] Counties the sentiment with respect to the proceedings of the Convention is favourable. Whether the knowledge of this, or conviction of the impropriety of withholding the Constitution from State conventions has worked most in the breast of Colo. M. I will not decide, but the fact is, he has declared unequivocally (in a letter to me) for its going to the People. Had his sentiments however been opposed to the measure, his instructions

---

[20] Col. George Mason.
[21] Col. Richard Henry Lee.
[22] Southern and western.

(for the delegates of this Country are so instructed) would have compelled him to vote for it. yet I have no doubt but that his assent will be accompanied by the most tremendous apprehensions which the highest coloring can give to his objections. To alarm the people seems to be the groundwork of his plan. The want of a qualified Navigation act is already declared to be a mean by which the price of produce in the Southern States will be reduced to nothing, and will become monopoly of the Eastern and northern States. To enumerate the whole of his objections[23] is unnecessary, because they are detailed in the address of the seceding members of the Assembly of Pennsylvania, which no doubt you have seen.

I scarcely think any powerful opposition will be made to the Constitutions being submitted to a Convention of this State. if it is given, it will be there at which I hope you will make it convt. to be present. explanations will be wanting, and none can give them with more accuracy and propriety than yourself. The sentiments of Mr. Henry with respect to the Constitution are not known, in these parts. Mr. Jos. Jones (who it seems was in Alexandria before the Convention broke up) was of opinion, that they would not be inimical to the proceedings of it; others think as the advocate of a paper emission he cannot be friendly to them.

From circumstances, which have been related, it is conjectured that the Governor[24] wishes he had been among the subscribing members, but Time will disclose more than we know at present with respect to the whole of the business, and when I hear more, I will write to you again. In the mean while I pray you to be assured of the sincere regard and affection with which &c.

---

[23] These objections were published in the *Pennsylvania Packet* Oct. 4, 1787.
[24] Edmund Randolph.

P. S. Having received, (in a letter) from Colo Mason, a detail in writing of his objections to the proposed Constitution,[25] I enclose you a copy of them.[26]

To DAVID HUMPHREYS

Mount Vernon, October 10, 1787.

My dear Humphreys: Your favor of the 28th. Ulto. came duly to hand, as did the former of June. With great pleasure I received the intimation of your spending the winter under this Roof. The invitation was not less sincere, than the reception will be cordial. The only stipulations I shall contend for are, that in all things you shall do as you please: I will do the same; and that no ceremony may be used or any restraint be imposed on any one.

The Constitution that is submitted is not free from imperfections. but there are as few radical defects in it as could well be expected considering the heterogenious mass of which the Convention was composed and the diversity of interests that are to be attended to. As a Constitutional door is opened for future amendments and alterations, I think it would be wise in the People to accept what is offered to them and I wish it may be by as great a majority of them as it was by that of the Convention; but this is hardly to be expected because the importance and sinister views of too many characters, will be affected by the change. Much will depend however upon literary abilities, and the recommendation of it by good pens should be *openly,* I mean, publickly afforded in the Gazettes. Go matters however as they may, I shall have the consolation to reflect that no objects but the public good, and that peace and harmony which

---

[25] Mason's letter of October 7 and his abstract of objections to the Constitution are in the *Washington Papers.*

[26] From the "Letter Book" copy in the *Washington Papers.*

I wished to see prevail in the Convention, obtruded even for a moment in my bosom during the whole Session long as it was. what reception this State will give to the proceedings in all its extent of territory, is more than I can inform you of; in these parts it is advocated beyond my expectation; the great opposition (if great there should be) will come from the Southern and Western Counties from whence I have not as yet, received any accts. that are to be depended on.

I condole with you on the loss of your Parents; but as they lived to a good old age you could not be unprepared for the shock, tho' it is painful to bid an everlasting adieu to those we love, or revere. Reason, Religion and Philosophy may soften the anguish of it, but time alone can eradicate it.

As I am beginning to look for you, I shall add no more in this letter but the wishes of the Family and the affectionate regards &c.[27]

To HENRY KNOX

Mount Vernon, October 15, 1787.

My Dear Sir: Your favor of the 3d. came duly to hand. The fourth day after leaving Philadelphia I reached home[28] and found Mrs. Washington and the Family tolerably well, but the fruits of the Earth almost entirely destroyed by one of the severest droughts (in this neighborhood) that has ever been experienced. The Crops, pretty generally, have been injured in this State below the Mountains, but not to the degree that mine, and some others in a small circle around me, have suffered.

The Constitution is now before the Judgment Seat. It has, as was expected, its adversaries and supporters. Which will

---

[27] From the "Letter Book" copy in the *Washington Papers*.
[28] See footnote 7 to letter to Clement Biddle, Sept. 19, 1787, *ante*.

preponderate is yet to be decided: the former, more than probably will be most active, as the major part of them will, it is to be feared, be governed by sinister and self important motives, to which every thing in their breasts must yield. The opposition from another class of them may perhaps, (if they should be men of reflection, candour, and information) subside in the solution of the following simple questions. 1. Is the Constitution which is submitted by the Convention preferable to the Government (if it can be called one) under which we now live? 2. Is it probable that more confidence would at the time be placed in another Convention, provided the experiment should be tried, than was placed in the last one, and is it likely that a better agreement would take place therein? 3. What would be the consequences if these should not happen, or even from the delay, which must inevitably follow such an experiment? Is there not a Constitutional door open for alterations or amendments? and is it not likely that real defects will be as readily discovered after as before trial; and will not our successors be as ready to apply the remedy as ourselves if occasion should require it? To think otherwise will, in my Judgment, be ascribing more of the amor patria, more wisdom and more virtue, to ourselves, than I think we deserve.

It is highly probable that the refusal of our Govr. and Colo. Mason to subscribe to the proceedings of the Convention will have a bad effect in this State; for, as you well observe, they *must* not only assign reasons for the Justification of their own conduct, but it is highly probable that these reasons will be clothed in most terrific array for the purpose of alarming; some things are already addressed to the fears of the people and will no doubt have their effect. As far however as the sense of *this* part of the Country has been taken, it is strongly in favor of the proposed Constitution; Further I cannot speak with precision. If a powerful opposition is given to it, the weight thereof will, I apprehend, come from the South side of James River and from the Western Counties. I am, &c.[29]

*To DAVID STUART

Mount Vernon, October 17, 1787.

Dear Sir: As the enclosed Advertiser contains a speech of Mr. Wilson's (as able, candid, and honest a Member as any in Convention) which will place the most of Col. Mason's objections in their true point of light, I send it to you. The re-publications (if you can get it done) will be of service at this juncture. His ipso facto objection does not, I believe, require an answer; every mind must recoil at the idea. And with respect to the Navigation Act, I am mistaken if any three men, bodies of men, or Countries, will enter into any compact or treaty if *one* of the three is to have a negative controul over the other two. There must be reciprocity or no Union, which is preferable will not become a question in the Mind of any true patriot. But granting it to be an evil, it will infallibly work its own cure, and an ultimate advantage to the Southern States. Sincerely and Affectly, I am etc.[30]

*To ALEXANDER HAMILTON

Mount Vernon, October 18, 1787.

Dear Sir: Your favor without date came to my hand by the last Post. It is with unfeigned concern I perceive that a political dispute has arisen between Governor Clinton and yourself. For both of you I have the highest esteem and regard. But as

---

[29] From the "Letter Book" copy in the *Washington Papers.*
[30] From a photostat of the original in the *Washington Papers.*

you say it is insinuated by some of your political adversaries, and may obtain credit, "that you *palmed* yourself upon me, and was *dismissed* from my family;" and call upon me to do you justice by a recital of the facts. I do therefore, explicitly declare, that both charges are entirely unfounded. With respect to the first, I have no cause to believe that you took a single step to accomplish, or had the most distant idea of receiving, an appointment in my family 'till you were envited thereto. And, with respect to the second, that your quitting it was altogether the effect of your own choice.

When the situation of this Country calls loudly for unanimity and vigor, it is to be lamented that Gentlemen of talents and character should disagree in their sentiments for promoting the public weal; but unfortunately, this ever has been, and most probably ever will be the case, in the affairs of man.

Having scarcely been from home since my return from Philadelphia, I can give but little information with respect to the *general* reception of the New Constitution in *this* State. In Alexandria however, and some of the adjacent Counties, it has been embraced with an enthusiastic warmth of which I had no conception. I expect notwithstanding, violent opposition will be given to it by *some* characters of weight and influence, in the State. Mrs. Washington unites with me in best wishes for Mrs. Hamilton and yourself. I am &c.[31]

*To JAMES MADISON

Mount Vernon, October 22, 1787.

My dear Sir: When I wrote to you, I was uninformed of the Sentiments of this State beyond the circle of Alexandria, with respect to the New Constitution. Since, a letter which I

---

[31] From the original in the *Hamilton Papers* in the Library of Congress.

received by the last Post, dated the 16th, from a member of the assembly, contains the following paragraphs.

I believe such an instance has not happened before, since the revolution, that there should be a house on the first day of the Session, and business immediately taken up. This was not only the case on Monday, but there was a full house; when Mr. Prentice [32] was called up to the Chair, as Speaker, there being no opposition. Thus, the Session has commenced peaceably.

It gives me much pleasure to inform you that the sentiments of the members are infinitely more favourable to the Constitution than the most zealous advocates for it could have expected. I have not met with one in all my enquiries (and I have made them with great diligence) opposed to it, except Mr. Henry, who I have heard is so, but could only conjecture it, from a conversation with him on the subject. Other members who have also been active in their enquiries tell me, that they have met with *none* opposed to it. It is said however that old Mr. Cabell of Amherst disapproves of it. Mr. Nicholas has declared himself a warm friend to it. The transmissory note of Congress was before us to day, when Mr. Henry declared that it transcended our powers to decide on the Constitution; that it must go before a Convention. As it was insinuated he would aim at preventing this, much pleasure was discovered at the declaration.

Thursday next (the 25th.) is fixed upon for taking up the question of calling the Convention, and fixing the time of its meeting: In the meantime, five thousand copies are ordered to be printed, to be dispersed by the members in their respective Counties for the information of the People. I cannot forbear mentioning that the Chancellor, Pendleton, espouses the Constitution so warmly as to declare he will give it his aid in the Convention, if his health will permit. As there are few better judges of such subjects, this must be deemed a fortunate circumstance. [33]

As the above quotations is the sum of my information, I shall add nothing more on the subject of the proposed government, at this time.

---

[32] Joseph Prentis (Prentice).
[33] This letter is from Benjamin Harrison, and is in the *Washington Papers*.

Mr. C. Pinkney is unwilling (I perceive by the enclosures contained in your letter of the 13th.) to loose any fame that can be acquired by the publication of his sentiments. If the discussion of the navigation of the Mississippi *could* have remained as silent, and glided as gently down the Stream of time for a few years, as the waters do, that are contained within the banks of that river, it would, I confess, have comported more with my ideas of sound policy than any decision the case can obtain at this juncture. With sentiments the most Affecte. and friendly &c.

To FRANCIS MENTGES

Mount Vernon, October 27, 1787.

Sir: In answer to your favor of the 12th. I shall inform you that without unpacking my public Papers (which would be very troublesome to me as they are voluminous and in a variety of [places] I cannot ascertain with *precision* the commencement of your superintendance of the Hospital in Williamsburg; and if these were to be unpacked I might not come at the date of your recall from this duty. I should suppose you acted under written orders in both cases, these therefore will go fully to the points you want to establish.

That you must have taken charge of the Hospital in Williamsburg at the time you say, viz, the 5th. of November 1781, can I believe, admit of no doubt as all the distributions were then making and as far as the recollection of circumstances will aid me, I think you must have remained on that duty till the latter part of the spring following. If this testimony of the matter, and a thorough persuasion of your having discharged the trust reposed in you with intelligence and fidelity can avail your case this certificate may be adduced from. I am, etc.[34]

---

[34] From the "Letter Book" copy in the *Washington Papers*.

To MATHEW CAREY

Mount Vernon, October 29, 1787.

Sir: The last post brought me your letter of the 22d. your application to me for the loan of £100 is an evidence of your unacquaintedness with my inability to lend money. To be candid, my expenditures are never behind my income, and this year (occasioned by the severest drouth that ever was known in this neighborhood) instead of selling grain which heretofore has been my principal source of revenue it is not £500 that will purchase enough for the support of my family. after this disclosure of my situation you will be readily persuaded that inclination to serve without the means of accomplishing it, is of little avail. This however is the fact so far as it respects the point in question.

As you seem anxious that the contents of your letter should not be known I put it in your own power to destroy it by returning it under the same cover with this.

I wish success to your Museum and am &c.[35]

To JAMES WOOD

Mount Vernon, October 29, 1787.

Dr. Sir: I beg you to accept my thanks for the friendly information contained in your letter of the 20th. Instt. but from an entire unacquaintedness with business of the land office, since the alterations which have taken place consequent of the Revolution, I really know not how to avail myself of it. The case you allude to is, on the 2d. of April 1752. I surveyed for one Thomas Mullen (under authority of the Proprs. Office) a tract of waste land in Frederick County, lying on the timber ridge

---

[35] From the "Letter Book" copy in the *Washington Papers.*

near great Cacapon head of Smiths run, 400 acres Extending
So. W 320 to 3 hicys. in a hollow near a drain, No. Wt. 200
poles to 3 black Oaks on a ridge No. Et. 320 poles to a black
Oak and 2 White Oaks on a ridge, So. Et. 200 poles to the beginning, containing as above 400 Acres; for making this Survey I received no compensation. indeed at *that* time it was
done, the Land was (by others) thougt. inadequate to the Fee,
and that Mullen was a madman. soon after this Mullen, who
was a single man, and I believe without connections, ran away
and finding no prospect of getting paid by him I caveated the
Land intending if no near or better claimant should appear to
obtain a patent in my own name. In this situation I *presume* it
lay till I was called from home in the year 1775 afterwards, and
till you had the goodness to remind me of the transaction never
once occurred to my recollection. If under this statement which
I believe is candid and accurate, it shall be thought that my right
to the land is preferable or equal to that of any other, I should
be glad to Obtn. it; if not I shall rest contented; your advice and
assistance (if proper) would be esteemed a further mark of your
Friendship. With great regard etc.[36]

To ARCHIBALD JOHNSTON

Mount Vernon, October 30, 1787.

Sir: My fixed determination is, that no person whatever shall
hunt upon my grounds or waters. To grant leave to one, and
refuse another, would not only be drawing a line of discrimina-
tion which would be offensive, but would subject one to great
inconvenience; for my strict, and positive orders to all my people are, if they hear a gun fired upon my Land to go immediately in pursuit of it. Permission therefore to any one would
keep them either always in pursuit, or make them inattentive

---

[36] From the "Letter Book" copy in the *Washington Papers*.

to my orders under the supposition of its belonging to a licensed person by which means I should be obtruded upon by others who to my cost I find had other objects in view. Besides, as I have not lost my relish for this sport when I can find time to indulge myself in it, and Gentlemen who come to the House are pleased with it, it is my wish not to have the game within my jurisdiction disturbed. For these reasons I beg you will not take my refusal amiss, because I would give the same to my brother if he lived off my land. I am, &c.[37]

*To ARTHUR YOUNG

Mount Vernon, November 1, 1787.

Sir: Your favor of the 1st. of Feby. came to hand about the middle of May last. An absence of more than four months from home, will be the best apology I can make for my silence 'till this time. The Grain, Grass-seeds, Ploughs &ca. arrived at the same time agreeable to the list; but some of the former were injured (as will always be the case) by being put into the hold of the Vessel; however, upon the whole they were in much better order than those things are generally found to be, when brought across the Atlantic.

I am at a loss, Sir, how to express the sense which I have of your particular attention to my commissions; and the very obliging manner in which you offer me your services in any matters relating to Agriculture, that I may have to transact in England. If my warmest thanks will in any measure compensate for these favors, I must beg you to accept of them. I shall always be exceedingly happy to hear from you, and shall very readily and chearfully give you any information relative to the state of Agriculture in this Country, that I am able.

---

[37] From the "Letter Book" copy in the *Washington Papers*.

I did myself the honor to hand the set of Annals to the Agriculture Society in Philadelphia, which you sent to that body, through me. The President wrote a letter to you expressive of the sense they entertained of the favor which you did them; and mentioned therein the effects of some experiments which had been made with Plaster of Paris, as a manure; I intended to have given you an acct. of it myself, as I find the subject is touched upon in your Annals, but this letter has precluded the necessity of it. The 5th. volume of the Annals wch. was committed to the care of Mr. Athawes for me, did not come to hand till sometime after I had received the 6th.

The quantity of Sainfoin which you sent me was fully sufficient to answer my purpose; I have sown part of it, but find that it comes up very thin, which is likewise the case with the Winter Wheat, and some other Seeds which I have sown.

I have a high opinion of Beans as a preparation for wheat, and shall enter as largely upon the cultivation of them next year, as the quantity of seed I can procure, will admit.

I am very glad that you did not engage a ploughman for me at the high wages which you mention, for I agree with you, that that single circumstance, exclusive of the others which you enumerated, is sufficiently objectionable.

I have tried the Ploughs which you sent me and find that they answer the description which you gave me of them; this is contrary to the opinion of almost every one who saw them before they were used, for it was thought their great weight would be an insuperable objection to their being drawn by two Horses.

I am now preparing materials to build a Barn precisely agreeable to your plan, which I think an excellent one.

Before I undertake to give the information you request respecting the arrangements of farms in this neighborhood &ca.

I must observe that there is, perhaps, scarcely any part of America where farming has been less attended to than in this State. The cultivation of Tobacco has been almost the sole object with men of landed property, and consequently a regular course of crops have never been in view. The general custom has been, first to raise a Crop of Indian Corn (maize), which, according to the mode of cultivation, is a good preparation for wheat; then a crop of wheat, after which the ground is respited (except from weeds, and every trash that can contribute to its foulness) for about eighteen months; and so on, alternately, without any dressing; till the land is exhausted; when it is turned out without being sown with grass seeds, or any method taken to restore it; and another piece is ruined in the same manner. No more cattle is raised than can be supported by lowland meadows, swamps, &ca.; and the tops and blades of Indian Corn; as very few persons have attended to sowing grasses, and connecting cattle with their Crops. The Indian corn is the chief support of the labourers and horses. Our lands, as I mentioned in my first letter to you, were originally very good; but use, and abuse, have made them quite otherwise.

The above is the mode of cultivation wch. has been generally pursued here, but the System of husbandry which has been found so beneficial in England, and which must be greatly promoted by your valuable Annals, is now gaining ground; There are several (among which I may class myself), who are endeavouring to get into your regular and systematic course of cropping as fast as the nature of the business will admit; so that I hope in the course of a few years, we shall make a more respectable figure as farmers than we have hitherto done.

I will, agreeable to your desire, give you the prices of our products as nearly as I am able, but you will readily conceive from the foregoing acct., that they cannot be given with any precision. Wheat for the four last years will average about 4/. sterlg pr Bushl. of 8 Gallns. Rye abt. 2/4. Oats 1/6. Beans, Pease &ca., have not been sold in any quantities. Barley is not made here, from a prevailing opinion that the climate is not adapted to it, I, however, in opposition to prejudice, sowed about 50 Bushl. last Spring and found that it yielded a proportionate quantity with any other kind of grain which I sowed; I might add more. Cows may be bought at abt. £3 Sterlg per head. Cattle for the slaughter vary from 2¼ to 4½ sterlg pr. lb; the former being the currt. price in summer, the latter in the winter or Spring. Sheep at 12/. sterlg. pr. head, and wool at abt. 1/. Sterlg pr. lb. I am not able to give you the price of labour as the land is cultivated here wholly by Slaves, and the price of labour in the Towns is fluctuating, and governed altogether by circumstances.

Give me leave to repeat my thanks for your attention to me, and your polite offer to execute any business relating to husbandry, which I may have in England; and to assure you that I shall not fail to apply to you for whatever I may have occasion for in that line. I am etc.

PS. I observe in the 6th. Volume of your Annals, there is a plate and description of Mr. Winlaws Mill for seperating the grain from the heads of Corn.[38] Its utility or inutility has, undoubtedly, been reduced to a certainty before this time; if it possesses all the properties and advantages mentioned in the description, and you can, from your own knowledge, or such information as you *entirely* rely on, recommend it as a useful machine, where labourers are scarce, I should be much obliged to you to procure one for me (to be paid for, and forwarded by Mr. Welch, provided it is so simple in its construction as to be

---

[38] Among the undated manuscripts at the end of the *Washington Papers* is a plan and description of a rolling mill signed by Lawrence Taliaferro.

worked by ignorant persons without danger of being spoiled (for such only will manage it here) and the price of it, does not exceed £15 as mentioned in the Annals, or thereabouts.[39]

*To GEORGE MASON AND DAVID STUART

Mount Vernon, November 4, 1787.

Gentn: In consequence of a resolution which passed at the last meeting of the Potomk. Company, and in behalf of the Directors, I transmit the enclosed petition to you, for the consideration of your Honble. House. The Petition is short. We therefore rely on you, if the sentiment shall meet your approbation, for argument in support of it; begging at the sametime (as the *sole* end is to obtain a more summary mode of recovering the dividends) that you would make such alterations (keeping the object in view) as will entitle it to a favourable reception.

It is, I believe, almost needless to add, that unless some relief is afforded by the Assembly in this instance, that the work will soon stop. The delinquences are great, and the legal process to enforce payment so low, that it seems *almost* endless and unavailing to attempt it by the mode prescribed by the act of incorporation. Under these circumstances the *willing* members are discouraged; and too good a pretext is afforded to a third class, who are neither punctual in their payments, nor yet *very great* delinquents, to with-hold the dividends which have already been required, and to oppose fresh calls, till the old arrearages are paied up. The consequences of all this is easily to be foreseen, if no redress can be had from the quarter it is sollicited.

---

[39] From a photostat of the original through the kindness of Dr. A. S. W. Rosenbach, of New York City.

Whatever may be the fate of the Petition, I do, in behalf of the board pray, that you would give me the earliest advice of it; because a similar application must be made (but at present it is suspended) to the Assembly of Maryland, when I shall have heard from you on this subject, that the Acts may be in unison. With very great esteem etc.   [H. S. P.]

To NOAH WEBSTER

Mount Vernon, November 4, 1787.

Sir: I have received your letter of the 17th. Ulto., together with your remarks on the proposed Constitution;[40] for which you will please to accept my best acknowledgments, and the assurance of being Sir etc.   [N. Y. H. S.]

To JOHN FRANCIS MERCER

Mount Vernon, November 5, 1787.

Sir: Presuming that it may have been from the want of your knowing of a safe conveyance that I am not furnished with the sum promised me by you at Philadelphia, I shall be glad to know by return of the Post when I may send for it.

Had you been so good as have favoured me with it by Genl. Pickney or Mr. Houston who stopped at annapolis and took this in their way to the Southward, or by any of the many opportunities to Alexa. it would have saved me the expence of a special messenger, the cost of which will, it is probable, sink the Interest of the sum which shall be received if not larger than was promised, but this the exigency of my calls will oblige me to submit to. I am, etc.[41]

---

[40] Webster's *Leading Principles of the Federal Constitution* was published in October, 1787.
[41] From the "Letter Book" copy in the *Washington Papers*.

*To DAVID STUART

Mount Vernon, November 5, 1787.

Dear Sir: I thank you for the communications in your letters of the 16th and 26th ult., both of which came safe. It gives me pleasure to hear that the Assembly has sent the Constitution to a Convention by an unanimous vote, unstamped with marks of disapprobation. If Mr. Charles Lee however, has been able to form a just opinion of the sentiments of the Country with respect to it, it is, that the Major voice is opposed to it, particularly in the Southern and Western parts of the State. Is this your opinion, from what you have seen, heard and understood?

Maryland, tho' the Assembly has not yet met (from which source anything can have been drawn) is, we are told, exceedingly well disposed to the adoption of it. Nay further, that Mr. Chase[42] is become a convert to it. The accts. from the States, Northward and Eastward speak the same language, though the papers team with declamation against it, by a few. A paper in favor of it, written, as I am informed by, or under the auspices of Mr. Wilson,[43] in numbers, I herewith send you.

With respect to the payment of British debts, I would fain hope (let the eloquense or abilities of any man, or set of men, in opposition be what they may) that the good sense of this Country will never suffer a violation of a public treaty, nor pass acts of injustice to Individuals. Honesty in States, as well as Individuals will ever be found the soundest policy.

We have nothing new in this quarter. The Constitution which is submitted, seems to have absorbed all lesser matters. Mrs. Stuart (who had got very well) and your two little girls went from this on Tuesday last, for Chotank, under the escort

---

[42] Samuel Chase.
[43] James Wilson.

of your brother; and the wind being high kept the Potomack on their left to ensure their journey.

I must engage *absolutely,* Six hundred barrels of Corn. Less, I am sure will not carry me through the year. Had I the money or was I certain of getting it in time (but this is not to be depended upon) I might, as I am informed through different channels, engage my quantity on very moderate terms on the Eastern shore of Maryland. But as I dare leave nothing to chance, I must take it from Mr. Henly. The price, as it is ready money to me, will I expect, be proportioned thereto. It will not be safe to remove the Corn until after January, as it does not get sufficiently dry to lye in bulk sooner. The last I had from Yorktown got damaged in spite of every exertion in my power to save it. And I must entreat as I shall give Mr. Henly timely notice of my sending that it may be beat out on plank floors, and in a dry house; otherwise it will contract dampness, which will render its preservation precarious even at that Season.

I beg also that he may be clear and decided with respect to his furnishing me with the quantity I want, viz. Six hundred Barrels; for I must meet with no disappointment of what is engaged.

Herewith is a letter jointly to Col. Mason and yourself on the business of the Potk. Company. With great esteem and sincere regards etc.[44]

*To JAMES MADISON

Mount Vernon, November 5, 1787.

My dear Sir: Your favor of the 18th. Ulto. came duly to hand. As no subject is more interesting, and seems so much to engross the attention of every one as the proposed Constitution, I shall, (tho' it is probable your communications from

---

[44] From a photostat of the original in the "Washington Photostats."

Richmond are regular and full with respect to this, and other matters, which employ the consideration of the Assembly) give you the extract of a letter from Doctr. Stuart, which follows—

Yesterday (the 26th. of Octr.) according to appointment, the calling of a Convention of the people was discussed. Though no one doubted a pretty general unanimity on this question ultimately, yet, it was feared from the avowed opposition of Mr. Henry and Mr. Harrison, that an attempt would be made, to do it in a manner that would convey to the people an unfavourable impression of the opinion of the House, with respect to the Constitution: And this was accordingly attempted. It was however soon baffled. The motion was to this effect; that a Convention should be called to adopt, reject, or amend, the proposed Constitution.

As this conveyed an idea that the House conceived an amendment necessary, it was rejected as improper. It now stands recommended to them, on (I think) unexceptionable ground, for "their full and free consideration." My collegue arrived here on the evening before this question was taken up: I am apt to think that the opponants to the Constitution were much disappointed in their expectations of support from him, as he not only declared himself in the fullest manner for a Convention, but also, that notwithstanding his objections, so federal was he, that he would adopt it, if nothing better could be obtained. The time at which the Convention is to meet, is fixed to the first of June next. The variety of sentiments on this subject was almost infinite; neither friends or foes agreeing in any one period. There is to be no exclusion of persons on acct. of their Offices.

Notwithstanding this decision the accounts of the prevailing sentiments without, especially on James River and Westwardly, are various; nothing decisive, I believe, can be drawn. As far as I can form an opinion however, from different persons, it should seem as if Men judged of others, by their own affection, or disaffection to the proposed government. In the Northern Neck the sentiment I believe, is very generally for it. I think it will be found such thro the State.

The Doctor further adds:

The subject of British debts was taken up the other day when Mr. Henry, reflected in a very warm declamatory manner, on the circular letter of Congress, on that subject. It is a great and important matter and I hope will be determined as it should be notwithstanding his opposition.

So far as the sentiments of Maryland, with respect to the proposed Constitution, have come to my knowledge, they are strongly in favor of it; but as this is the day on which the Assembly of that State *ought* to meet, I will say nothing in anticipation of the opinion of it. Mr. Carroll of Carrolton, and Mr. Thos. Johnson, are declared friends to it.

With sincere regard and Affecte.   [N.Y.P.L.]

To BATTAILE MUSE

Mount Vernon, November 8, 1787.

Sir: Your letter of yesterday was handed me by your Servant. I shall agreeable to your advice, Send to Mr. Waless on Friday evening for the thirty pounds.

I do not wish to have Lemert and Shover so far distressed as to break them up, but I should think they might find some method of paying a part, at least, of what they owe, or of securing the debt to me.

If the Tenants do not comply with Covenants of their Leases, they cannot expect that I shall sit quietly under it, for the sole motive of leasing the land at the low rents which they give, was in expectation of having such improvements made thereon as are mentioned in the leases, if that is not done a great end for which they were leased are defeated.

I send, agreeable to your desire, six leases signed, I hope you will be cautious in filling them up.

I am sorry to find that there is any difficulty on procuring tenants for any of my Lots. Mr Bushrod Washington, informed me that he had leased out his land at £17 per hundred and could have disposed of a million of acres at that rate if he had them. I am etc.[45]

---

[45] From a copy in the Toner Transcripts in the Library of Congress.

*To WARNER WASHINGTON

Mount Vernon, November 9, 1787.

Dear Sir: Having received an Official acct. (from Mr. Athawes) of the death of Colo. Geo: Wm. Fairfax, together with the enclosed letter, I take the safe conveyance afforded by Mr. Muse, of forwarding them to you.

On this occasion I sincerely condole with Mrs. Washington and yourself. Colo. Fairfax has appointed me an Executor of his Will, in this Country; but the multiplicity, and perplexed state of my own affairs, and of those with which I have been concerned, (occasioned by a long absence from home, and continual interruptions since my return) render my acceptance of the trust altogether inadmissible, however well disposed I otherwise should have been to pay this last tribute of respect to his Memory. The Letter which is enclosed does, I presume, give information of the bequest to your lady, but in case it shd. not the following is the only mention which is made of either of you, in the Will: "I give devise and bequeath unto my Sister in law Hannah Washington (wife of Warner Washington Esqr.) the sum of five hundred pounds currt. money of the said State of Virga. besides the lands I gave her Husband."

The Will being very long I have sent it to the other Executors in this Country, viz. Wilson Cary, and George Nicholas Esqrs. without taking a copy of it. The principal part of his Estate (at the decease of Mrs. Fairfax) is given to his Nephew, Ferdinand, Son of Mr. Bryan Fairfax, as appears by some extracts I have taken from the Will.

Mrs. Washington joins me in best wishes for your Lady and family, and I am etc.   [N.Y.H.S.]

To CHARLES THOMSON

Mount Vernon, November 10, 1787.

Sir: In compliance with the resolve of Congress contained in your letter of the 27 Ulto. I have the honor of sending you a copy of the paper enclosed in Mr. President Laurens letter to me of the 19th. of February 1778; endorsed " Committees report."[46]

It would, I confess, give me a great pleasure to hear that the important Services of the Baron de Steuben had met with a reward adequate to his merits and sacrafices. what may have been his verbal or other engagements with Congress is not for me to say further than is contained in the paper herewith enclosed but certain it is he hazarded his life and fortune at a critical period of our affairs without those obligations on his part which impelled Americans to do it and from that moment to the close of the war, rendered essential Services to the cause in which we were engaged.

I embrace this, as I shall do every occasion of expressing to you the esteem and regard with which I am, etc.[47]

To BARON STEUBEN

Mount Vernon, November 10, 1787.

Sir: The letter with which you were pleased to honor me, dated the 26th. Ulto. came duly to hand, by the same Post I received a letter from Mr. Secretary Thompson, requesting, by order of Congress, a Copy of the Report of a Committee which was transmitted to me by Mr. President Laurens in Feby. 1778.

---

[46] "Committee of conference with Baron Steuben." (See *Journals of the Continental Congress*, Oct. 25, 1787, and Jan. 22, 1788.)
[47] From the "Letter Book" copy in the *Washington Papers*.

This is accordingly sent and is the counterpart of the Paper I herewith enclose for your own information.

As I do not recollect ever to have had any further information of the contract you speak of than what is therein contained, it is not in my power to speak more fully to the point; but in my letter to the Secretary I have expressed in unequivocal terms a wish that your merits and Sacrafices may be rewarded to your entire satisfaction. If they should not and it proves a means of your withdrawing from the United States, I shall be among the number of those who will regret the event, as it would give me pleasure that you should continue in a Country the liberties of which owe much to your Services. I have the honor, etc.[48]

*To ALEXANDER HAMILTON

Mount Vernon, November 10, 1787.

Dear Sir: I thank you for the Pamphlet and for the Gazette contained in your letter of the 30th Ult. For the remaining numbers of Publius, I shall acknowledge myself obliged, as I am persuaded the subject will be well handled by the Author.[49]

The new Constitution has, as the public prints will have informed you, been handed to the people of this state by a unanimous vote of the Assembly; but it is not to be inferred from hence that its opponants are silenced; on the contrary, there are many, and some powerful ones. Some of whom, it is said by overshooting the mark, have lessened their weight: be this as it may, their assiduity stands unrivalled, whilst the friends to the Constitution content themselves with barely avowing their

[48] From the "Letter Book" copy in the *Washington Papers*.
[49] Hamilton was "Publius." These essays by him, John Jay, and James Madison, who also used the same pseudonym, have come to be known as "The Federalist."

approbation of it. Thus stands the matter with us, at present; yet, my opinion is, that the Major voice is favourable.

Application has been made to me by Mr. Secretary Thompson (by order of Congress) for a copy of the report, of a Committee, which was appointed to confer with the Baron de Steuben on his first arrival in this Country; forwarded to me by Mr. President Laurens. This I have accordingly sent. It throws no other light on the subject than such as are to be derived from the disinterested conduct of the Baron. No terms are made by him " nor will he accept of any thing but with general approbation." I have however, in my letter enclosing this report to the Secretary, taken occasion to express an unequivocal wish, that Congress would reward the Baron for his Services, sacrafices and merits, to his entire satisfaction. It is the only way in which I could bring my Sentiments before that honble. body, as it has been an established principle with me, to ask nothing from it. With very great esteem and regard etc.[50]

To BUSHROD WASHINGTON

Mount Vernon, November 10, 1787.

Dear Bushrod: In due course of Post, your letters of the 19th. and 26th. Ult. came to hand and I thank you for the communications therein; for a continuation in matters of importance, I shall be obliged to you. That the Assembly would afford the People an opportunity of deciding on the proposed Constitution I had scarcely a doubt, the only question with me was, whether it would go forth under favourable auspices, or receive the stamp of disapprobation. The opponents I expected, (for it ever has been that the adversaries to a measure are more

---

[50] From the original in the *Hamilton Papers* in the Library of Congress.

active than its Friends) would endeavor to stamp it with unfavourable impressions, in order to bias the Judgment that is ultimately to decide on it, this is evidently the case with the writers in opposition, whose objections are better calculated to alarm the fears, than to convince the Judgment, of their readers. They build their objections upon principles that do not exist, which the Constitution does not support them in, and the existence of which has been, by an appeal to the Constitution itself flatly denied; and then, as if they were unanswerable, draw all the dreadful consequences that are necessary to alarm the apprehensions of the ignorant or unthinking. It is not the interest of the major part of those characters to be convinced; nor will their local views yield to arguments, which do not accord with their present, or future prospects.

A Candid solution of a single question to which the plainest understanding is competent does, in my opinion, decide the dispute: namely is it best for the States to unite, or not to unite? If there are men who prefer the latter, then unquestionably the Constitution which is offered must, in their estimation, be wrong from the words, we the People to the signature inclusively; but those who think differently and yet object to parts of it, would do well to consider that it does not lye with any *one* State, or the *minority* of the States to superstruct a Constitution for the whole. The separate interests, as far as it is practicable, must be consolidated; and local views must be attended to, as far as the nature of the case will admit. Hence it is that every State has some objection to the present form and these objections are directed to different points. that which is most pleasing to one is obnoxious to another, and so vice versa. If then the Union of the whole is a desirable object, the component parts must yield a little in order to accomplish it. Without the latter, the former is unattainable, for again I repeat it, that not a single State nor the minority of the States can force a Constitution on the Majority; but admitting the power it will surely be granted that it cannot be done without involving scenes of civil commotion of a very serious nature let the opponents of the proposed Constitution in this State be asked, and it is a question they certainly ought to have asked themselves, what line of conduct they would advise it to adopt, if nine other States, of which I think there is little doubt, should accede to the Constitution? would they recommend that it should stand single? Will they connect it with Rhode Island? or even with two others checkerwise and remain with them as outcasts from the Society, to shift for themselves? or will they return to their dependence on Great Britain? or lastly, have the mortification to come in when they will be allowed no credit for doing so?

The warmest friends and the best supporters the Constitution has, do not contend that it is free from imperfections; but they found them unavoidable and are sensible, if evil is likely to arise there from, the remedy must come hereafter; for in the present moment, it is not to be obtained; and, as there is a Constitutional door open for it, I think the People (for it is with them to Judge) can as they will have the advantage of experience on their Side, decide with as much propriety on the alterations and amendments which are necessary [as] ourselves. I do not think we are more inspired, have more wisdom, or possess more virtue, than those who will come after us.

The power under the Constitution will always be in the People. It is entrusted for certain defined purposes, and for a certain limited period, to representatives of their own chusing; and whenever it is executed contrary to their Interest, or not agreeable to their wishes, their Servants can, and undoubtedly will be, recalled. It is agreed on all hands that no government can be well administered without powers; yet the instant these

are delegated, altho' those who are entrusted with the administration are no more than the creatures of the people, act as
it were but for a day, and are amenable for every false step they
take, they are, from the moment they receive it, set down as
tyrants; their natures, one would conceive from this, immediately changed, and that they could have no other disposition
but to oppress. Of these things, in a government constituted
and guarded as *ours* is, I have no idea; and do firmly believe
that whilst many *ostensible* reasons are assigned to prevent the
adoption of it, the real ones are concealed behind the Curtain,
because they are not of a nature to appear in open day. I believe further, supposing them pure, that as great evils result
from too great Jealousy as from the want of it. We need look
I think no further for proof of this, than to the Constitution, of
some if not all of these States. No man is a warmer advocate
for proper restraints and wholesome checks in every department of government than I am; but I have never yet been able
to discover the propriety of placing it absolutely out of the
power of men to render essential Services, because a possibility
remains of their doing ill.

If Mr. Ronald can place the Finances of this Country upon
so respectable a footing as he has intimated, he will deserve
much of its thanks. In the attempt, my best wishes, I have nothing more to offer, will accompany him. I hope there remains
virtue enough in the Assembly of this State to preserve invio-
late public treaties and private Contracts; if these are infringed,
farewell to respectability and safety in the Government.

I have possessed a doubt, but if any had existed in my breast,
reiterated proofs would have convinced me of the impolicy of
all commutable Taxes. If we cannot learn wisdom from experience, it is hard to say where it is to be found. But why talk
of learning it; these things are *mere* Jobs by which few are

enriched at the public expense; for whether premeditation, or ignorance, is the cause of this destructive scheme, it ends in oppression.

You have I find broke the Ice; the only advice I will offer to you on the occasion (if you have a mind to command the attention of the House) is to speak seldom, but to important Subjects, except such as particularly relate to your Constituents, and, in the former case make yourself *perfectly* master of the Subject. Never exceed a *decent* warmth, and submit your sentiments with diffidence. A dictatorial Stile, though it may carry conviction, is always accompanied with disgust. I am, &c.[51]

To SAMUEL VAUGHAN

Mount Vernon, November 12, 1787.

Dear Sir: The letter without date, with which you were pleased to honor me, accompanied by a plan of this Seat, came to my hands by the last Post. For both I pray you to accept my sincere and hearty thanks. The plan describes with accuracy the houses, walks, and shrubberies etc. except in the front of the Lawn, west of the Ct. yard. There the plan differs from the original; in the former you have closed the prospect with trees along the walk to the gate; whereas in the latter the trees terminate with two mounds of earth on each side of which grow Weeping Willows leaving an open and full view of the distant woods. The mounds are at sixty yards apart. I mention this, because it is the only departure from the origl.

Altho' I can have little doubt of the pleasure you must feel at the prospect of being soon reunited to your lady and family in England, I do not scruple to confess that I shall be among those, who will view your departure from this Country with regret;

---

[51] From the "Letter Book" copy in the *Washington Papers*.

at the same time I beg leave to add that I shall reflect with pleasure on the friendship with which you have honored me. The testimonies you have left of this, could my mind be so ungrateful as to forget it, would be constant remembrancers. For your kind offer of Services in England I shall feel myself ever obliged and should occasion require it I shall avail myself of your kindness.

I am sorry it was not in my power to take you by the hand the day I left Philadelphia. I called once and as you were not within I did not leave my name intending to have called again but circumstance preventing it I requested Mr. Gouvr. Morris to offer you my apology and best wishes. should your Son who is lately arrived from England, be prompted by business or inclination to travel into this State it would give me much pleasure to shew him every civility in my power; the same to any branch of your family, or any of your friends. In wishing you (whenever it shall be undertaken) a pleasant and prosperous voyage, and a happy meeting with Mrs. Vaughan and the other parts of your family and friends in England, I am with great cordiality and sincerity, joined by Mrs. Washington the Major and Fanny, and with sentiments of the most perfect esteem and regard, &c.[52]

To WILSON MILES CARY AND GEORGE NICHOLAS

Mount Vernon, November 15, 1787.

Gentn: A few days ago, the letter herewith sent from Mr. Athawes, accompanying the Will of our much esteemed and greatly to be lamented friend, the Honble. George Wm. Fairfax Esqr. came to my hands, on which melancholy occasion I sincerely condole with you.

---

[52] From the "Letter Book" copy in the *Washington Papers*.

The small package containing the watch (which is mentioned in the Will) and the two letters spoken of in Mr. Athawes letter (one for Thomas Fairfax Esqr. and the other for Colo. Warner Washington) I have (presuming it would be your wish) forwarded to their respective addresses by safe conveyances.

However desirous I may be of giving unequivocal proofs of my respect for the deceased, and of my regard for, and attachment to the amiable lady he has left behind; yet, such is the peculiar situation of my own concerns so much are they deranged, and so much more attention is due to them occasioned by nine years absence and bad management than in my power to give them that it would be folly in the extreme in me, to undertake a fresh trust which I am Confident is not in my power to discharge agreeable either to the intention of the testator, or to the dictator of my own Judgment. In a word, from a variety of causes with the enumeration of which I shall not trouble you, I have not leizure to recover my own affairs (and some others which are involved with them) from that disordered state into which they have fallen. But if there are any friendly Offices in this part of the Country and within my reach in the discharge of which I can be useful, I shall have great pleasure in rendering them.

Having said thus much, it is unnecessary for me to add that the legacy bequeathed me by the Will becomes a nullity.

Permit me to remind Mr. Nicholas that there is an escruitore with many Papers belonging to the deceased in my possession many of them of great Value. They might be packed in a Trunk and sent by the Stage to Richmond but a careful and responsible person ought to take charge of them. With the greatest esteem, etc.[53]

---

[53] From the "Letter Book" copy in the *Washington Papers*.

To CATHERINE MACAULAY GRAHAM

Mount Vernon, November 16, 1787.

Madam: Your favor of the 10th. of October, 1786 came duly to hand and should have had a much earlier acknowledgment had not the business of the public (in which I have been, in a manner, compelled to engage again) engrossed the whole of my time for several months past, and my own private affairs required my unremitted attention since my return home. I do not know to what cause I shall impute your not receiving my letter of the 10th. of Jany. 1786 till the last of June, it went by the common rout, and was subject to the common incidents.

Mr. Pine's Historical painting does not appear to go on very rapidly, he informed me, when I was in Philadelphia, that he had been collecting materials to enable him to proceed with it, but that it must be a work of time to accomplish it.

You will undoubtedly, before you receive this, have an opportunity of seeing the Plan of Government proposed by the Convention for the United States. You will very readily conceive, Madam, the difficulties which the Convention had to struggle against. The various and opposite interests which were to be conciliated; the local prejudices whch were to be subdued, the diversity of opinions and sentiments which were to be reconciled; and in fine, the sacrifices which were necessary to be made on all sides for the General welfare, combined to make it a work of so intricate and difficult a nature, that I think it is much to be wondered at, that any thing could have been produced with such unanimity as the Constitution proposed. It is now submitted to the consideration of the People, and waits their decision. The legislatures of the States which have been convened since the Constitution was offered have readily agreed to the calling a convention in their respective

States; some by a unanimous vote and others by a large majority, but whether it will be adopted by the People or not, remains yet to be determined. Mrs. Washington and the rest of the family join me in Compts. I have the Honor etc.[54]

To HENRY BANKS

Mount Vernon, November 22, 1787.

Sir: For the letter you did me the favor to write to me on the 21st. Ulto. I offer you my thanks. No application has ever been made to *me* or to any person on *my* account that has ever come to my knowledge, for the taxes of my land in Greenbrier, and totally ignorant am I of the amount of them. If you can inform me, I would thank you.

I have no objection to the settlement of my Lands on the Great Kanhawa, or on the Ohio above it, provided it would be done to the reciprocal benefit Landlord and tenant. Every advantage of situation and Soil is possessed by these lands in a superlative degree, full conviction of this fact, a firm belief that I can obtain no rent *now* which will be adequate a few years hence to the value of the land, by which to be induced to lease it. and having thoughts of selling some, if not the whole, If I can get what I conceive to be the worth, have been the means of its lying in a dormant State till this time,[55] but if it is likely to be pressed with taxes, something must be done with it and soon, it not being convenient for me to pay these without some return; preparative therefore to this I should have no objection in the first instance to let as many families as may incline, live on it three years Rent free, on condition of their making certain Improvements which may be stipulated; but what agree-

---

[54] From the "Letter Book" copy in the *Washington Papers*
[55] That is, the reason of its lying in a dormant state.

ment (under the circumstances I have mentioned) to make with them afterwards is a difficulty which weights powerfully in my mind. If leases are given for money Rents, they must either commence high or rise proportionately to the increasing value of the land, otherwise I shall not receive a compensation. To let the land for 1/3 of the produce may do well for the Landlord whose eye is always on the tenant; but would not I conceive, be very productive to him who lives 3 or 400 Miles distant from them unless he should happen to hit upon a faithful and attentive agent. Something however as I observed before must be done, and 3 years Rent free, any families may be upon a certainty of holding it and a preference given to them at the end thereof *on* the *terms* which may be offered by others. I have none of my printed advertisements left, or I would trouble you with one of them. They offered the Land to the best of my recollection, in three ways, first for 21 years at five pd. p. Hundred Acres; 2d. for ever at an annual Rent of £10; and 3d. for 999 years the rent to commence at £5. and encrease in a certain Ratio every two years. In each case an exemption from Rent was allowed for the 3 first years and in all of them certain buildings and other improvements were required.

Your having mentioned that you hold land at the mouth of Coal River, I would beg leave to observe that I have one tract of 2000 Acres in the point of fork between that River and the Kanhawa running up the 1st. about 2 Miles (from the point) and up the latter more than 4, and on the opposite 2 Miles above the fork another of my tracts for 3000 Acres begins, and runs upwards 6 Miles bordering on the River for quantity; as these tracts are in the vicinity of yours it is possible you may have been on them in which case I would thank you for your opinion of them. From the mouth of Pokitellico on the East side the River for 13 Miles down the Kanhawa I hold the land;

and on the other side, from within 2 or 3 Miles of the mouth I have a tract which runs near 20 Miles along the River equal to any and I have ever seen all of which may be Seated as hath been mentioned, together with that on the Ohio above. I am, etc.[56]

To THOMAS JOHNSON

Mount Vernon, November 22, 1787.

Sir: The letter with which you have been pleased to honor me, dated the 16th. inst came to my hand the day before yesterday. By to morrow's Post this answer will be forwarded to you.

Mr. Rumsey has given you an uncandid account of his explanation to me, of the principle on which his Boat was to be propelled against [the] stream. At the time he exhibited his model, and obtained [my] certificate I had no reason to believe that the use of steam was contemplated by him, sure I am it was not mentioned; and equally certain I am, that it would not apply to the project he then had in view; the first communication of which was to me made in September 1784 (at the springs in Berkley); the Novr. following, being in Richmond, I met Mr. Rumsey there who was at that time applying to the Assembly for an exclusive Act. He then spoke of the effect of Steam and the conviction he was under of the usefulness of its application for the purpose of inland Navigation; but I did not conceive, nor have I done so at any moment since, that it was suggested as part of his original plan, but rather as the ebullition of his genius. It is proper however for me to add, that some time *after this* Mr. Fitch[57] called upon me on his way to Richmond and explaining his scheme, wanted a letter from

[56] This is another one of the letters which is copied in an exceptionally careless and ignorant manner in the "Letter Book" in the *Washington Papers.*
[57] John Fitch.

me, introductory of it to the Assembly of this State the giving of which I declined; and went so [far] as to inform him that tho' I was bound not to disclose the principles of Mr. Rumsey's discovery I would venture to assure him, that the thought of applying steam for the purpose he mentioned was not original but had been mentioned to me by Mr. Rumsey; this I thought myself obliged to say that, whichever (if either) of them, was the discoverer might derive the benefit of the invention.

To the best of my recollection of what has passed between Mr. Rumsey and me, the foregoing is an impartial recital.

Permit me to ask you, my good Sir, if a letter which I wrote to you during the sitting of your last Assembly, enclosing one from Mr. Wm. Wilson to me, concerning the confiscated property of (I think) Messrs. Dunlap & Co. of Glasgow ever reached your hands? and if it did, whether anything was, or can be done in that business? As an Executor of the Will of Colo. Thomas Colvill it behoves me to know precisely what is to be expected from that quarter as a large sum is due from that Company to his Estate. I am the more anxious to do it immediately, as Mr. Wilson who is concerned in the House of Dunlap & Co. is about to leave the Country. With great esteem etc.[58]

To SAMUEL HANSON

Mount Vernon, November 24, 1787.

Sir: I am sorry it is not convenient for you to board my Nephews any longer, Mr. Lear is desired to see what can be done with them. For the advice you have given them I feel myself obliged and wish they had sense and prudence enough to be governed by it. I am, etc.[59]

---

[58] From the "Letter Book" copy in the *Washington Papers*. The words in brackets have been supplied, they are not in the "Letter Book" copy.
[59] From the "Letter Book" copy in the *Washington Papers*.

* To GOVERNOR THOMAS PINCKNEY

Mount Vernon, November 25, 1787.

Sir: Genl. Lawson[60] who will do me the honor of presenting this letter to your Excellency, and whom I take the liberty of introducing to your civilities, is called by business to Charleston and Georgia. He is a Gentleman of character and merit in this State; having been a Colonel in the Continental Army and is now a Member of our Assembly. I have the honor etc.   [H.L.]

To DIEGO DE GARDOQUI

Mount Vernon, November 28, 1787.

Dear Sir: I have received your letters of the 29th. of October[61] and 9th. of Novr. The latter was handed to me by Colo. H. Lee, together with 4 Vols. of Don Quixote which you did me the honor to send to me. I consider them as a mark of your esteem which is highly pleasing to me, and which merits my warmest acknowledgment, I must therefore beg, my dear Sir, that you will accept of my best thanks for them.

Your wish to establish a permanent and sincere amity between these States and the Court of Spain is highly meritorious; and if, as you observe, no two nations apply more exactly to each other, a connexion between them upon the basis of reciprocal interest must be a very desirable event.

Altho no man could feel more pleasure and satisfaction than myself in seeing this Country form such connexions as would render it happy and flourishing, yet my being totally detached from all matters of government, entirely prevents my interfering,

---

[60] Robert Lawson.
On November 25 Washington inclosed this letter in a brief note to Lawson. The letter is in the Huntington Library.
[61] Gardoqui's letter is in the *Washington Papers.*

with any degree of propriety, in an affair of this nature, I am far removed from, and have as little to do in the publick transactions of this State as any citizen in it; and in matters which come under the cognizance of the United States I have been careful not to have any concern, unless when called upon for information respecting any subject which was connected with my publick employment during the war.

I shall be exceedingly sorry to see you obliged to abandon an object which has in view the interest and advantage of both our countries, and I cannot yet despair of their being connected in such a manner as to ensure a mutual benefit. With Sentiments of the Most perfect consideration and respect, etc.[62]

To SAMUEL POWEL

Mount Vernon, November 30, 1787.

Dear Sir: With much pleasure we received the acct. of the safe arrival of Mrs. Powell and yourself in Philadelphia; and that your journey was attended with fewer accidents and less delay than might have been expected.

The Mr. Morris's gave us the pleasure of their companies two days and Nights as they journeyed to Richmond, and did not leave us without hopes of their taking this rout as they return.

By this evenings Post (for the Newspapers brot. by it, I am now sending to Alexandria) we expect to receive the decision of your State on the Fœderal Government. In this, matters remain I believe in Statu quo.

I would with great pleasure have sent you more of the Spanish Chestnuts, but the few which I saved for my own use were planted before your letter came to hand, next year, if the trees bear I will save as many as you or your friends may have occasion

---

[62]From the "Letter Book" copy in the *Washington Papers*.

for and lest I should forget it I beg you to remind me, about the first of October.

Mrs. Washington and the Family join me in affecte. regards to Mrs. Powell and yourself, and both of us beg you to accept our grateful thanks for the kind offers you have respectively made us. With great esteem etc.[63]

*To DAVID STUART

Mount Vernon, November 30, 1787.

Dear Sir: Your favor of the 14th. came duly to hand. I am sorry to find by it that the opposition is gaining strength. At this however I do not wonder. The adversaries to a measure are generally, if not always, more active and violent than the advocates; and frequently employ means which the others do not, to accomplish their ends.

I have seen no publication yet, that ought, in my judgment, to shake the proposed Government in the mind of an impartial public. In a word, I have hardly seen any that is not addressed to the passions of the people; and obviously calculated to rouse their fears. Every attempt to amend the Constitution at this time, is, in my opinion, idly vain. If there are characters who prefer disunion, or seperate Confederacies to the general Government which is offered to them, their opposition may, for ought I know, proceed from principle; but as nothing in my conception is more to be depricated than a disunion, or these seperate Confederacies, my voice, as far as it will extend, shall be offered in favor of the latter. That there are some writers (and others perhaps who may not have written) who wish to see these States divided into several confederacies is pretty evident. As an antidote to these opinions, and in order to investigate the ground of objections to the Constitution which

---

[63] From the "Letter Book" copy in the *Washington Papers*.

is submitted to the People, the Fœderalist, under the signature of Publius, is written. The numbers which have been published I send you. If there is a Printer in Richmond who is really well disposed to support the New Constitution he would do well to give them a place in his Paper. They are (I think I may venture to say) written by able men; and before they are finished, will, if I am mistaken not, place matters in a true point of light. Altho' I am acquainted with some of the writers who are concerned in this work, I am not at liberty to disclose their names, nor would I have it known that they are sent by *me* to *you* for promulgation.

You will recollect that the business of the Potomack Company is withheld from the Assembly of Maryland until it is acted upon in this State. That the sitting of that Assembly is expected to be short. And that our operations may be suspended if no other recourse is to be had than to common law processes to obtain the dividends, which are called for by the Directors, and not paid by the Subscribers.

Certificate, and Commutation taxes I hope will be done away by this Assembly. And that it will not interfere either with public treaties, or private contracts. Bad indeed must the situation of that Country be, when this is the case. With great pleasure I received the information respecting the commencement of my Nephews political course. I hope he will not be so buoyed up by the favourable impression it has made as to become a babbler. If the Convention *was* such a tumultuous, and disorderly body as a certain Gentleman has represented it to be, it may be ascribed, in a great degree to some dissatisfied characters who would not submit to the decisions of a majority thereof. I shall depend upon the Corn from Mr. Henley. All here are well and join me in good wishes for you. I am etc.[64]

---

[64] From a photostat of the original through the kindness of Judge E. A. Armstrong, of Princeton, N. J.

To EMBREE & SHOTWELL

Mount Vernon, December 3, 1787.

Gentn: Colo. Henry Lee (who called upon me as he returned home from New York) informed me that you dealt
largely in grass seeds (saved in this Country), that you sold
none but what was good, and those on the most moderate
terms.

Under this information I beg leave to ask the price of the
following, and whether an opportunity could be depended upon for sending them by water to Alexandria before the month
of March next. Red Clover Seed. Timothy Do. Orchard
grass Do.

He told me that he had bought some of the first from you
and he thinks at 4 dollars pr. Bushl. but not having the Bill at
hand could not be positive. Imported Seeds or the Seeds of this
Country if not of the last years growth I would not purchase.
the first, unless brot. in the Cabbin is always injured and the
latter is not to be depended upon.

Your answer to this letter by the Post will oblige Gentn.
Yr. etc.[65]

To CLEMENT BIDDLE

Mount Vernon, December 3, 1787.

Dear Sir: Your letters of the 23d. of Septr. and 15th. of Novr.
came duly to hand. You may inform Mr. Haines that my Barley, this year, shared the same fate with my other crops. The
drought during the summer was so excessive that I cannot
form any just opinion of what it might produce in a seasonable
year; it yielded about 14 bushls. to the Acre which was a proportionate crop to any other kind of Grain which I sowed; and

---

[65]From the "Letter Book" copy in the *Washington Papers.*

if I judge of its success from this circumstance it must be favourable. This information I would have given you sooner had I been able to have ascertained the quantity of Barley that was made.

I have requested Thomas Smith Esqr. of Carlyle, who, I expect, has, or will recover some money which is due to me in the Western Country, to put it into your hands, unless he has an opportunity of forwarding it directly to Alexandria; if you should receive it I will thank you to deposit it in the bank for me, and send me the notes that I may negotiate them here as I have occasion for the Money. I enclose to you a letter to Mr. Smith which I will thank you to forward in as safe and expeditious a manner as you can. As I imagine you have, by this time, recd. the interest due upon my warrant in your hands, or if you have not, Mr. Smith will, upon receiving the enclosed letter, forward some money to you, I must request you to pay Mr. Charles Pettit's bill for 4 Backs and 8 Jambs[66] sent to me, which amounts to £18.5.1.

I will thank you to inform me the lowest prices for which good fresh Clover, Timothy and Orchard Grass seed can be purchased with you. I am etc.

P. S. The Leopard skin sent by Captn. Steward arrived safe.[67]

[H.S.P.]

To THOMAS SMITH

Mount Vernon, December 3, 1787.

Sir: I have received your letter of the 26th. Octr. and am much surprised to find that my letters to the Western Country so often miscarry. I inclose a duplicate of a letter which I wrote to you from Philadelphia, and committed to the care of a Capt.

---

[66] For the fireplaces.
[67] In the writing of Tobias Lear.

Bradley who informed me that he lived at the Court House in Washington County, should pass thro Carlisle, and promised to deliver it himself.

I have written to Mr. Smith[68] of Baltimore requesting him to forward to me the money which you informed me you had lodged in his hands for me.

The money which you recover on my account may be put into the hands of Clement Biddle Esqr. of Philadelphia, who will be so good as to give me information thereof. but if a safe opportunity should offer to Alexandria I would prefer having it lodged there in the Hands of Mr. Wm. Hunter Junr.

Permit me Sir to repeat my thanks to you for your attention to my business, and one more to request that you and Mr. Ross will mention the sum with which you will be satisfied for conducting my Ejectments and receive it out of the money which you may recover on my acct. I am, etc.[69]

To JOHN LANGDON

Mount Vernon, December 3, 1787.

Sir: I have received your letter of the 6th. Ulto. and am much obliged to you for the information contained in it. I am happy to find that dispositions in your part of the Continent are so favourable to the proposed plan of Government: if the true interest of the United States was consulted I think there could be but little opposition to it in any part of the country.

The Publick papers have undoubtedly announced to you, before this, the proceedings of the legislature of this State upon the business; they have appointed the convention to meet on the first monday in June; whether putting it off to so late a

[68] Nathaniel Smith.
[69] From the "Letter Book" copy in the *Washington Papers*.

period will be favourable or otherwise, must be determined by circumstances, for if those States whose conventions are to meet sooner, should adopt the plan I think there is no doubt but they will be followed by this, and if some of them should reject it, it is very probable that the opposers of it here will exert themselves to add this State to the number. I am, etc.[70]

To GEORGE WEEDON

Mount Vernon, December 3, 1787.

Dear Sir: I have received your letter of the 25th. Ulto. enclosing the proceedings of the Cincinnati of this State, which I am much obliged to you for forwarding to me.

I will, agreeable to your request, send some cuttings of the Golden willow to Alexandria to be forwarded to you, but I imagine this is an improper season to put them out, for as they are to be propagated from the slip the spring seems to be the most suitable time for setting them; should these fail I will send you more in the spring if you will remind me of it. I am, etc.[70]

To BUSHROD WASHINGTON

Mount Vernon, December 3, 1787.

Dear Sir: A Mr. H. Banks, of your Assembly is disposed to be kind to me or has some view of being so to himself. Charity leads to the first, suspicion to the latter opinion. He has informed me that the Sherif of Greenbrier has a considerable demand upon me for the taxes of my land on the Great Kanhawa, in that Country; but has forborne (through *his* means) from proceeding to extremities till *he* could advise me thereof. This is the first intimation directly or indirectly I have had of

---

[70] From the "Letter Book" copy in the *Washington Papers*.

these taxes. He thinks I might settle these lands immediately, if an exemption from Rent was allowed for a term; moderate Rents agreed for hereafter, and these to be in specific Articles proportionate to the Crop. After naming one Hines, or Stines as his Agent in that Country, and a Capt. William L. Lovely, whose continuance there he says is doubtful he offers any services in his power to facilitate any plan I may adopt for seating. He also wants to buy some of the Land but is not able. Under this Statement let me ask, *confidentially,* the Character and circumstances of this Banks; and I would thank you for obtaining the most satisfactory answers, from the Representatives of Greenbrier, Montgomery, Bottetourt or other Counties in that quarter to the following questions.

1st. The distance from Stanton to Green Court House?

2d. From thence to the Mouth of Coal River, a branch of the Great Kanhawa?

3d. Whether there is a direct Road from G. K. Court Ho. to the last mentioned place, or whether this road crosses or comes to the Kanhawa above, or below the Mouth of Coal River?

4th. What sort of a road it is, to wit, Mountainous, or tolerably level, and what kind of a Country does it pass thro', and how Settled?

5th. Whether there is any road leading, from the mouth of Coal River, or that part of the Kanhawa to which the Greenbrier road strikes into the mouth.

6th. The distance and what kind of a road, if any?

7th. Whether Colo. Lewis (the Son of Genl. Andw. Lewis) lives at the mouth of the Kanhawa?

8th. And what Settlement there is at that place whether by the Roads above enumerated in his rout, or is the most direct road from Staunton to the mouth of the Great Kanhawa, and whether the distances from place to place a description thereof:

9th. What are the *rich* bottom lands on the Kanhawa supposed to be worth? and for what would they Sell, credit being given.

10th. For what would they Rent?

11th. The most advantageous and practicable mode of doing this?

12th. Is there any person of character living on the Kanhawa from the mouth of local River to the confluence of it with the Ohio, in whom confidence could be placed to Rent my lands there? and transact business for me?

13th. How are the Counties of Greenbrier, Botetourt and Montgomery divided? or in what County is the lands on the East of the Kanhawa from the mouth of Coal to the Ohio. and in what County or Counties are the lands *on* the Ohio between the mouths of the two Kanhawas?

14th. Supposing a person was to undertake a Journey from Alexandria to the Great Kanhawa which would be his best rout and what the distance from place to place exclusive of the way by Fort Pitt?

Necessity will compel me to do something, and soon, with these lands. It will not do to pay taxes and receive nothing in return for them. Knowing that the quality and Situation of them is exceeded by none in the western Counties, I may have held them in [too?] high estimation to obtain Tenants on the terms which have been advertised by me and it is difficult to fix rents on land encreasing every day in value that will be an equivolent some years hence. unless on the terms suggested by Mr. Banks that is to receive 1/3 of the Crops to this however elegable it may be to a landlord on the spot, many reasons may be opposed by one at a distance viz. Idleness and want of honesty in the tenant. Want of Care, attention and integrity in the agent. and want of a market if the other two could be obviated.

Yet something must be done, and by getting them seated, and in some degree improved it would enable me to rent them more advantageously hereafter.

I wish you would let me know (if you can come at the means of doing it) what taxes these lands of mine are subject to. Tho' I requested, in answer to Mr. Banks's letter to me, (to which I have received a reply) to be informed of this, he has passed it over in silence.

Write to me on all the points here submitted, as soon as you can obtain information, as I shall postpone a second letter to Mr. Banks till I hear from you. My land on the Ohio lyes between the Mouths of the two Kanhawas, and on the great Kanhawa in 4 tracts from within two Miles of the mouth to and above the Mouth of Coal River. I am, etc.[71]

To JAMES MADISON

Mount Vernon, December 7, 1787.

My dear Sir: Since my last to you, I have been favored with your letters of the 28th. of October and 18th. of November. With the last came 7 numbers of the Fœderalist, under the signature of Publius, for which I thank you. They are forwarded to a Gentleman in Richmond for republication; the doing of which in this State will I am persuaded, have a good effect as there are certainly characters in it who are no friends to a general government; perhaps I should not go too far was I to add, who have no great objection to the introduction of anarchy and confusion.

The Sollicitude to discover what the several State Legislatures would do with the Constitution is now transferred to the several Conventions. the decisions of which being more

---

[71] From the "Letter Book" copy in the *Washington Papers*.

interesting and conclusive is, consequently, more anxiously expected than the other. What Pennsylvania and Delaware have done, or will do must soon be known.[72] Other Conventions to the Northward and Eastward of them are treading closely on their heels; but what the three Southern States have done, or in what light the new Constitution is viewed by them, I have not been able to learn. North Carolina it has been said (by some accts. from Richmond) will be governed in a great measure by the conduct of Virginia. The pride of South Carolina will not I conceive suffer this influence to work in her councils; and the disturbances in Georgia will or I am mistaken show the people of it the propriety of being United, and the necessity there is for a general Government. If these with the States Eastward and Northward of us, should accede to the Fœderal Government, I think the citizens of this State will have no cause to bless the opposers of it here if they should carry their point. A paragraph in the Baltimore Paper has announced a change in the Sentiments of Mr. Jay on this subject; and adds that, from being an admirer of the new form, he has become a bitter enemy to it. This relation (without knowing Mr. Jay's opinion) I disbelieve, from a Conviction that he would consider the matter well before he would pass any Judgment. It is very unlikely therefore that a man of his knowledge and foresight should turn on both sides of a question in so short a space. I am anxious however to know the foundation (if any) for this.

It would have given me great pleasure to have complied with your request in behalf of your foreign acquaintance. At present I am unable to do it. The survey of the Country between the Eastern and Western Waters is not yet reported by the Commissioners tho' promised to me very shortly, (the Survey

---

[72] Delaware ratified the Constitution Dec. 7, 1787, and Pennsylvania, the second State to ratify, on December 12.

being compleated) by one of them. no draught that can convey a proper idea of the work on this River has yet been taken. much of the labor except at the great fall has been bestowed in the bed of the River in a removal of the rocks and deepening the Water. At the Great falls the labour has indeed been great; the water there is taken into a canal about 200 yards above the Cataract and conveyed by a level cut (thro' a solid rock in some places and very Stoney ground in others) more than a mile to the lock seats; [five] in number, by means of which the Craft when these locks are compleated will be let into the River below the fall (which in all is 76 feet). At the Seneca falls six miles above the great fall a channel which has been formed by the river in freshes is under improvement for the navigation; the same at Shannondoah in part. At the lower fall (where nothing has yet been done) a level cut and locks are proposed. These constitute the principal part of the work to compleat the navigation; the parts of the river between requiring loose stones only to be removed in order to deepen the water where it is too shallow in dry seasons.

P. S. Since writing the foregoing, I have received a letter from a member (of the Assembly) in Richmond dated the 4th. Inst. giving the following information.

I am sorry to inform you, that the Constitution has lost ground so considerably that it is doubted whether it has any longer a majority in its favor. From a vote which took place the other day, this would appear certain, tho' I cannot think it so decisive as the enemies to it consider it. It marks however the inconsistency of some of its opponents. At the time the resolutions calling a Convention were entered into Colo M———— sided with the friends to the Constitution, and opposed any hint being given, expressive of the Sentiments of the House as to amendments. But as it was unfortunately omitted at that time to make provision for the subsistence of the Convention, it became necessary to pass some resolution providing for any expence whh. may attend an attempt to make amendments. As M————— had on the former occasion declared, that it would be improper to make any discovery of the Sentiments of the House on the subject, and that we had no right to suggest any thing to a body paramt. to us, his advocating such a resolution was matter of astonishment. It is true, he declared it was not declaratory of our opinion; but the contrary must be very obvious. As I have heard many declare themselves friends to the Constitution since the vote, I do not consider it as altogether decisive of the opinion of the House with respect to it.

I am informed, both by Genl. Wilkinson (who is just arrived here from New Orleans by way of No. Carolina) and Mr. Ross, that North Carolina is almost unanimous for adopting it. The latter received a letter from a member of that Assembly now sitting.

In a debating Society here, which meets once a week, this subject has been canvassed at two successive meetings, and is to be finally decided on tomorrow evening; as the whole Assembly, almost has attended on these occasions, their opinion will then be pretty well ascertained; and as the opinion on this occasion will have much influence, some of Colo. Innis's friends have obtained a promise from him to enter the list.

The bill respecting British debts has passed our house but with such a clause as I think makes it worse than a rejection.

The letter, of which I enclose you a printed copy, from Colo. R H Lee to the Govr. has been circulated with great industry in manuscript, four weeks before it went to press, and said to have had a bad influence. The enemies to the Constitution leave no stone unturned to encrease the opposition to it. I am, &c.[73]

To THOMAS JOHNSON AND THOMAS SIM LEE

Mount Vernon, December 9, 1787.

Sir: Presuming that Colo. Fitzgerald according to his promise has communicated to you the vote of the Potomack Co. passed at the last general Meeting, held at George Town, and the measures consequent of it, taken by the directors, I shall

[73]From the "Letter Book" copy in the *Washington Papers*.

trouble you with no more than the result which you will find in the enclosed authenticated Act of the Assembly of this State.

It is scarcely necessary to observe to you, Gentlemen, that unless a similar one is obtained from your Assembly, during its present Session that the work of navigation will soon be at a stand. You know what steps have been taken, and how ineffectually, to collect the dividends from the tardy members. The others think it hard to be further called on and some indeed have announced they will advance no more until the arrearages are paid up. To recover these will be a work of immense time under the existing law.

You know best under what form to bring this matter before your Assembly. If by way of Petition you will please to have one drawn, and if it is necessary the name of the President should be affixed thereto, I hereby authorize you to give it my signature with great esteem I am, etc.[74]

*To DAVID STUART

Mount Vernon, December 11, 1787.

Dear Sir: Not recollecting till this moment, the Winter regulation of the Post; and being desirous of getting the Loan Office certificates (herewith enclosed) to you, before you shall have left Richmond; I have scarcely time to acknowledge the receipt of your favor dated the 4th. Instt., much less to write more fully on the subject of my Back Lands. I now pray, if it is in your power to obtain the Interest on my Certificates that you would do it, for I can truly say that at no period of my life have I ever felt the want of money so sensibly as now; among other demands upon me, I have no means of paying my Taxes, the Certificate for the Executed Negro ought to be discharged, I

---

[74] From the "Letter Book" copy in the *Washington Papers*.

should think; this I also send. And let me beg of you to enquire in what manner, and by what certain channel, I could
open a corrispondence with Mr. Lewis (his Chn. name I know
not)[75] on the Kanhawa; and whether it is likely he would act as
an Agent for me in the Renting of my Lands on the Kanhawa,
and Ohio above it. I have not time to add more; hardly expecting this letter will get to the Post Office in time. Yrs. Sincerely.

[H.S.P.]

To CHARLES CARTER

Mount Vernon, December 14, 1787.

Dear Sir: Your favor of the 21st. of Octr. would not have
remained so long unacknowledged could I with any degree of
precision have answered your quæries sooner. I wish it was in
my power to do it satisfactorily now. The drought of last Summer in *this* neighbourhood was so unconscionably severe, that
the experiments I contemplated were by no means conclusive, the result such as it is, I will give you.[76]

In level ground, as equal in quality as I could obtain it, I
laid of 10 squares, each square containing by exact measurement, half an acre. half of each of these I manured at the rate
of 200 bushel of well rotted farm yard dung to the Acre to ascertain the difference between slight manuring such as we
might have it in our power to give the land, and no Manure.
The whole of this ground received the first plowing in the winter; and each square previous to sowing, or planting was worked
exactly alike afterwards. Two of these were sown with Oats
(of different sorts) on the   [77] of   . Two with Barley (of
different sorts) on the   of   . One with Buck wheat

---

[75] Thomas.
[76] See Washington's "Diary" for Oct. 25, 1787.
[77] This and the following blanks are left so in the "Letter Book" in the *Washington Papers*.

on the   day of   ; another with Jerusalem Artichokes on
the   day of   ; another with Irish Potatoes on the day
of   ; another with sweet (or Country) Ditto on the
day of   ; another that is to say 1/3 with the *common* sort
of homony bean; 1/3 with the bunch homony bean and the
other one third with very small, and round black eyed Pease
called the Gentlemans Pea. The two squares was sown half
in Carrots, and half in Turnips both in Broad Cast.

Yield as Follow.	Acres of Land.	Dung	Undung	Total
The 2 squares of oates makg. together	1	14½	11	25½
2 of Barley not worth dividg. for the same reason	1	2	1⅝	3⅝
1 Do Jerm. Artichoke	½	29½	29	58½
1 Do Buck Wheat	½	2¼	1⅓	4
1 Do Irish Potatoes	½	19¼	9¼	29¾
I Do Sweet Do	½	6½ la 5 la / 5½ Seed 5½ rd.		22½
I Do ½ Carrots	½	12	12	24
½ Turnips	¼			
1 Square a ⅓ in Comn. homony beans	⅙			
⅓ in Bunch Do Do	⅙			
⅓ in sml. 2d. bla. eyed Pease	⅙			

I have already observed, that the drought was too intense to
authorize any just conclusion from these experiments; for besides occasioning many of the seeds and plants to come up
badly, the growth of all was so much retarded as to leave little
hope at one time that anything would be produced from some
of them.

The Barley was exceedingly *thin;* in some parts of the ground
hardly any. of the Buck Wheat ¼ of the square (undunged
parts) had not a plant. Of the Jerusalem Artichoke out of 442
hills 417 were Missing; both kinds of Potatoes were a good deal

missing; and the Irish sort had not roots as big as a Pea the first of Septr. when in a commonly seasonally year they would at that time have been fit for use. The Carrots and Turnips were thin, as were the Pease and Beans.

Adjoining to these squares I laid of exactly 10 Acres in an oblong form and drilled them with Corn in rows 10 feet a part, and 18 Inches asunder in the rows, between these rows Irish Potatoes, Carrots, Turnips, and the common blackeyed Pease were alternately planted and sown (that no advantage of soil or situation should be more in favor of one than the other). By this mode you will perceive that *half* the Rows were in Corn, an ⅛ in Potatoes, an ⅛ in Turnips (for I ought rather to have said were intended for them but they could not be got to grow).

The Corn yielded only . . . 4   43 Bushels of sound
      Potatoes 47¾
      Carrots 22

Pease these by mistake got mixed with others and the quantity could not be ascertained but did not yield much.

The Potatoes were missing. The Carrots much more so. from this experiment which is not more conclusive than the other, it appears that the Potatoe rows, though but a fourth of the Corn Rows, yielded nearly as many bushels; and that the Carrots also but a fourth of the Corn rows amounted to nearly half. Had the Potatoes stood as well as the Corn, the numbers of bushels would have been more than that of Corn, and had the Carrots stood as well as the Potatoes, the quantity of bushels it is supposed would not have fallen short of the Potatoes. From the quantity of Corn (but a barrell to the Acre which in a moderately seasonable year would have yielded 2 or 2 and an half to the Acre) you may form some conception of the severity of the drought, as the ground was well tilled and especially when I add that all my grass seeds were destroyed by it. The Potatoes, ultimately, grew to a good size, and the Carrots were

remarkably large, few smaller than the wrist, and numbers
larger than the small of the leg. Inconclusive as these trials have
been I am nevertheless clearly of opinion that Corn in Drills 3
feet apart and the plants 18 Inches asunder in the rows, with
Carrots or Potatoes or both (for the Seasons to put them in the
ground and taking them up differing, the farmer is less hurried) in his operations will be found a most profitable husbandry. I have no doubt that an Acre of Corn planted in this
manner will yield as much as an Acre of the same quality in
the usual mode of planting. If this be true (and I have very
little doubt of it) the Potatoes and Carrots are nearly clear profit
as very little more labour is required in this mode of cultivating of them than the Corn would need, and receive if nothing
was between it. The only consideration then is, whether the
production is too much for the Land? The books say *generally,*
that neither Carrots nor Potatoes are exhausters. But as the cultivation of them, with me, is new, I shall decide nothing on
this point but shall practice the mode untill I meet with dis-
couragements.

I do not know that the Agricultural Society of Philadelphia
have adopted any regular mode of communicating the information they receive to the Public, good would certainly result
from such communications and I presume after it has got a
little better established this will be the case. That I have not
received any answer to my letter respecting the Wolf dogs is
matter of surprize to me, when I do, the result shall be communicated to you.

I thank you for your Congratulations on my return from the
Convention and with what you add respecting the Constitution. My decided opinion of the matter is that there is no alternative between the adoption of it and anarchy. If one State
however important it may conceive itself to be should suppose,

or a minority of the States, that they can dictate a Constitution to the Majority unless they have the power of administering to good effect, administering the Ultema ratio they will find themselves deceived. All the opposition to it, that I have yet seen, is I must confess addressed more to the passions than to the reason, and clear I am if another Fœderal Convention is attempted the sentiments of the members will be more discordent or less Conciliatory than the last, in fine, that they will agree upon no genl. plan. General Government is now suspended by a thread I might go farther and say it is really at an end, and what will be the consequence of a fruitless attempt to amend the one which is offered, before it is tried, or of the delay from the attempt, does not in my Judgment need the gift of prophecy to predict. I am not a blind admirer (for I saw the imperfections) of the Constitution to which I have assisted to give birth, but I am fully persuaded it is the best that can be obtained at *this* day and that it or disunion is before us; if the first is our choice when the defects of it are experienced Constitutional door is open for amendments and may be adopted in a peaceable manner without tumult or disorder. I am, etc.[78]

*To GEORGE WEEDON

Mount Vernon, December 17, 1787.

Dear Sir: This letter is accompanied by a bundle (containing 50 cuttings) of the yellow, or golden Willow. As I observed to you in my last, I do not conceive the season so favourable as the Spring, yet there can be little doubt of their succeeding. Should they do it however you can at any time get more as I have an abundance of them. I am etc.[79]

---

[78] From the "Letter Book" copy in the *Washington Papers.*
[79] From a photostat of the original in the possession of the Mount Vernon Ladies' Association of the Union.

*To DAVID STUART

Mount Vernon, December 22, 1787.

Dear Sir: To the best of my recollection I have sent you Seven numbers of the Fœderalist, under the Signature of Publius. The subsequent numbers that have come to my hands, I herewith enclose.

Have you received a letter from me, enclosing one for my Nephew Bushrod Washington; containing queries respecting my lands in the Western Country? It is sometime since it was dispatched from this, and having received no acknowledgment of it, I apprehend a miscarriage.

From your acct. this letter will hardly find you in Richmond, from that of others the Assembly will set till Feby. Under this uncertainty I only add the Compliments and good wishes of this family to you, and the assurance of the regard with which I am etc.

PS. A Number of Certificates were sent to you a few days ago, have these been received by you from me?   [H. S. P.]

To THOMAS LEWIS

Mount Vernon, December 25, 1787.

Sir: It is my desire, and I am told that it is the wish of many and sure I am policy requires it, that the uncultivated tracts of land on the Great Kanhawa and Ohio belonging to the Military should be settled. The difficulty with me respecting mine has been, how to draw the line of mutual advantage for Landlord and Tenant, with respect to the terms; and where to find a confidential person on or near the spot who would act for me as Agent.

Two reasons, hitherto, have restrained me from making application to you, on this head, first, the uncertainty I was under of your having become an actual resident in those parts, and second a doubt whether it might be agreeable to you to accept this trust on account of the trouble, and little profit that would derive from the agency, at least for some time.

The first cause being removed, (having understood by means of some members in Assembly that you live at Point Pleasant) I shall take the liberty of trying you on the second; under a hope, that more from the desire of seeing the country settled the neighborhood strengthened and property thereby secured; and the value of it encreased; than from any pecuniary considerations at the present moment, you may be induced to aid me in seating my lands on the great Kanhawa and on the Ohio between the mouths of the two Rivers bearing that name.

If you accept the trust this letter shall be your authority, fully, and amply given and binding upon me and my heirs for the following purposes.

First. To place as many Tenants on the several tracts of Lands (Plats of which with my signature annexed to them shall accompany this Power) as you can obtain consistently with your Judgment, and suggestions hereafter mentioned.

Second. That an exemption from the payment of Rents for the term of three years shall be allowed them provided certain reasonable improvements such as you shall stipulate for, and which I think (but leave the matter to you) ought to be comfortable houses, Acres of Arable and Acres of Meadow Land, and a certain number of frute Trees planted.

Third. That for the fourth year, rents shall become due, and shall consist (as I am told the custom of the Country is) of a third of whatever is raised on the premises, which rents shall be annually paid thereafter to you, or my agent for the time being in that Country.

Fourth. That under this tenure they may be assured of the places (if they incline to remain, and will go on to improve them) for the term of — years; were these not to exceed ten, it would be more pleasing to me than any extension beyond that number; but if this limitation will not be acceded to on the part of the Tenant, I must leave it to your discretion to augment them, making the term definite, and not for lives, which is not only uncertain, but often introductory of disputes to ascertain the termination of them. Instances of which have happened to me. All mines and minerals will be reserved for the landlord, and where there are valuable streams for water works, the Rents must bear some proportion to the advantages which are likely to result from them.

Fifth. Whether custom authorizes, or justice requires that the tenant should pay the land tax of what he agrees to hold before the rent becomes due; or afterwards, in whole, or part, must be governed by the practice which prevails and consequently is left to your decision.

Sixth. I do not conceive it necessary, nor should I incline to go into much, or indeed any expence in laying the Land off into Lots till it begins to be thick settled and productive. The first comers will of course have the first choice; but they and all others are to be informed that their lotts (be the quantity little or much) will be bounded by water courses, or (where this is not the case) by convenient and regular forms. And as most of my Tracts (as you will see by the plats) have extensive boundaries on the rivers running but a little ways back it is my wish indeed, it naturally follows, that back part of the land should be considered as the support of that which will be first settled and cleared on the margins of the Rivers and a sufficiency of it reserved for that purpose.

Seventh. For your trouble in negotiating this business, I am very willing to allow the usual Commission for collecting, converting into Cash and transmitting to me, the rents after they shall commence and whatever you may think proper to charge me (in reason) for your trouble till this shall happen, I will cheerfully agree to pay.

Whether you accept this trust or not, you will do me a favor in the communication of your sentiments on the subject; there are two ways by which letters will come safe. Viz thrown into the Post Office at Philadelphia or into that at Richmond. Colo. Bayard an acquaintance of mine, or any acquaintance you may have at Fort Pitt, will forward them to the first place, and the means of doing it to the latter you must be a better Judge of than myself. If the letters once get into the Post Office I shall be sure of them. On private conveyances there is no reliance; they are tossed about and neglected so as rarely to reach their intended destination when sent in this manner.

If you should incline to act under this power your own good sense and Judgment will at once dictate the propriety, indeed necessity of promulgating it as extensively as you can by Advertisements to those parts from whence settlers are most likely to be drawn over and above the opportunities which your situation gives you of communicating the matter to travellers by water on the Ohio.

On the other hand if you do not incline to act I would thank you for returning me the papers herewith enclosed as it will save me the trouble of making other copies.

Whether the improvements which I had made on the Lands (of which you have herewith the draughts) in the years 1774 and 5 will be of use to Settlers at this day, or not, you [who] are on the spot can best determine; they cost me, or were valued to between £ 1500 and 2000. if they are useful the exemption from rent should be shorter. I thought it necessary to bring the matter into view tho' my expectations from it are small. I am, &c—

P. S. I have a small tract called the round bottom containing abt. 600 Acres, which I would also let. It lyes on the Ohio, opposite to pipe Creek, and a little above Capteening.[80]

To SIR EDWARD NEWENHAM

Mount Vernon, December 25, 1787.

Dear Sir: I have recd. your letters of the 9th of Decr. 1786; 27th of Feby. and 2d of March 1787. They should have had an earlier and more regular acknowledgment had not the public business in which I was, in a manner, compelled to engage the last summer, joined to the unremitting attention which my own private affairs require rendered it almost impossible to observe that punctuality with my correspondents that I could wish. I thank you, my dear Sir, for the information which you gave me in your several letters, relative to the state of publick affairs in your Country. I hope the exertions of good men, and a concurrence of circumstances, will finally produce that tranquillity, concord and happiness among you which you so earnestly wish for.

The public attention here is at present wholly employed in considering and animadverting upon the form of Government, proposed by the late convention for these States. The inefficacy of our present general system is acknowledged on all hands, and the proposed one has its opponents but they bear so small a proportion to its friends that there is little or no doubt of its

---

[80] From the "Letter Book" copy in the *Washington Papers*.

taking place. Three States have already decided in its favor; two unanimously, and the other by a majority of two to one; these are the only States whose conventions have as yet determined upon the subject, but from every information, the others will be found pretty fully in sentiment with them. The establishment of an energetic general Government will disappoint the hopes and expectations of those who are unfriendly to this Country, give us a national respectability, and enable us to improve those commercial and political advantages which Nature and situation have placed within our reach.

I wrote to you some time since and enclosed a letter from Doctor Franklin to me in answer to one which I had written respecting your Sons being appointed Consul at Marseilles; he applied to Mr. Jay, Minister of foreign Affairs, (whose answer to him I likewise forwarded to you); the result of the application was, that it could not be granted because there existed a resolution of Congress declaring that none but an American citizen should be appointed to that Office. Mrs. Washington joins me in the Compliments of the season to Lady Newenham and yourself, and in wishing you many happy returns of it. I am &c.[81]

To REVEREND WILLIAM McWHIR

Mount Vernon, December 25, 1787.

Sir: I have recd. your letter of yesterday and in answer to it must observe that however desireous I may be to comply with your request and gratifying your wishes I do not consider myself at liberty to give an opinion on the subject, for altho' I was appointed a visitor or Trustee yet having never acted in that capacity or taken any part in the management of the Academy

[81] From the "Letter Book" copy in the *Washington Papers*.

I should not wish to interfere on this occasion, but will readily and cheerfully agree to whatever may be done by the Trustees on the subject.

I am very glad to find that you have agreed to take my Nephews to board with you. I shall feel myself under less apprehension of any irregular and improper conduct on their parts while they are under your immediate inspection, than if they were to be placed with a person to whose advice or direction they would not consider themselves obliged to pay any attention. I am, etc.[82]

To EMBREE & SHOTWELL

Mount Vernon, December 30, 1787.

Gentn: Your letter of the 14th. came duly to hand. Colo. Lee either did not comprehend the price of your Seeds or I have misunderstood him for they are higher than I was led to conceive. However as I want seeds on which I can depend, I will, provided they can be got to me by the end of March *at farthest* and as much sooner as you please, take ten Bushels of red clover seed, and 8 Bushels of Timothy seed; both of the last years growth, clean and good.

If in consideration of the quantity, and the prospect of my dealing with you every year for a large supply of these articles (if I find my interest in it) you should be disposed to lower the retail prices mentioned in your letter to me, it may prove mutually advantageous to you, (if the Seed is sent) to whom, or in what manner the cost of them shall be remitted.

Be so good, upon the receipt of this letter as to inform me if there be a moral certainty of a supply from you in the above mentioned time for should I depend thereon and be disappointed

---

[82] From the "Letter Book" copy in the *Washington Papers.*

it will be very injurious to me as the whole is for my own sowing, and the ground will be prepared for it. I am, etc.[83]

*TO THOMAS JEFFERSON

Mount Vernon, January 1, 1788.

Dear Sir: I have received your favor of the 15th. of August, and am sorry that it is not in my power to give any further information relative to the practicability of opening a communication between Lake Erie and the Ohio, than you are already possessed of. I have made frequent enquiries since the time of your writing to me on that subject while Congress were sitting at Annapolis, but could never collect anything that was decided or satisfactory. I have again renewed them, and flatter myself with better prospects of success.

The accts. generally agree as to its being a flat country between the waters of Lake Erie and Big-Beaver; but differ very much with respect to the distance between their sources, their navigation, and the inconveniences which would attend the cutting a canal between them. From the best information I have been able to obtain of that Country, the sources of the Muskingham and Cayohoga approach nearer to each other than any water of Lake Erie does to Big-Beaver. But a communication through this River would be more circuitous and difficult; having the Ohio in a greater extent, to ascend; unless the latter could be avoided by opening a communication between James River and the Great Kanhawa, or between the little Kanhawa and the West branch of Monongahela, which is said to be very practicable by a short portage. As testimony thereof, the States of Virginia and Maryland have opened (for I believe it is compleated) a road from the No. branch of Potomack,

---

[83] From the "Letter Book" copy in the *Washington Papers*.

commencing at, or near, the mouth of Savage River, to the Cheat River, from whence the former are continuing it to the Navigable Water of the little Kanhawa.

The distance between Lake Erie and the Ohio, through the Big-Beaver, is, however, so much less than the rout through the Muskingham, that it would, in my opinion, operate very strongly in favor of opening a canal between the sources of the nearest water of the Lake and Big-Beaver, altho the distance between them should be much greater and the operation more difficult than to the Muskingham. I shall omit no opportunity of gaining every information relative to this important subject; and will, with pleasure, communicate to you whatever may be worthy of your attention.

I did myself the honor to forward to you the plan of Government formed by the Convention, the day after that body rose; but was not a little disappointed, and mortified indeed (as I wished to make the first offering of it to you) to find by a letter from Commode. Jones, dated in New York the 9th. of Novr. that it was, at that time, in his possession. You have, undoubtedly recd. it, or some other 'ere now, and formed an opinion upon it. The public attention is, at present, wholly engrossed by this important subject. The Legislatures of those States (Rhode Island excepted) which have met since the Constitution has been formed, have readily assented to its being submitted to a Convention chosen by the People. Pensylvania, New Jersey, and Delaware are the only States whose Conventions have as yet decided upon it. In the former it was adopted by 46 to 23 and in the two latter unanimously.

Connecticut and Massachusetts are to hold their Conventions on the 1st. and 2d. tuesdays of this month; Maryland in April, Virginia in June, and upon the whole, it appears, so far as I have had an opportunity of learning the opinions of the people in the several States, that it will be received. There will, undoubtedly, be more or less opposition to its being adopted in most of the States; and in none a more formidable one than in this; as many influential characters here have taken a decided part against it, among whom are Mr. Henry, Colo. Mason, Govr. Randolph and Colo R. H. Lee; but from every information which I have been able to obtain, I think there will be a majority in its favor notwithstanding their dissention. In New York a considerable opposition will also be given.

I am much obliged to you, my dear Sir, for the Acct. which you gave me of the general state of Affairs in Europe. I am glad to hear that the Assemblée des Notables has been productive of good in France. The abuse of the finances being disclosed to the King, and the Nation, must open their eyes, and lead to the adoption of such measures as will prove beneficial to them in future. From the public papers it appears that the Parliaments of the several Provinces, and particularly that of Paris, have acted with great spirit and resolution. Indeed the rights of Mankind, the priviledges of the people, and the true principles of liberty, seem to have been more generally discussed and better understood throughout Europe since the American revolution than they were at any former period.

Altho' the finances of France and England were such as led you to suppose, at the time you wrote to me, would prevent a rupture between those two powers, yet, if we credit the concurrent accts. from every quarter, there is little doubt but that they have commenced hostilities before this. Russia and the Porte have formally began the contest, and from appearances (as given to us) it is not improbable but that a pretty general war will be kindled in Europe. should this be the case, we shall feel more than ever the want of an efficient general Government to regulate our Commercial concerns, to give us a national respectability, and to connect the political views and interests of the several States under one head in such a manner as will effectually prevent them from forming seperate, improper, or indeed any connection, with the European powers which can involve them in their political disputes. For our situation is such as makes it not only unnecessary, but extremely imprudent for us to take a part in their quarrels; and whenever a contest happens among them, if we wisely and properly improve the advantages which nature has given us, we may be benifitted by their folly, provided we conduct ourselves with circumspection and under proper restrictions, for I perfectly agree with you, that an extensive speculation, a spirit of gambling, or the introduction of any thing which will divert our attention from Agriculture, must be extremely prejudicial, if not ruinous to us. but I conceive under an energetic general Government such regulations might be made, and such measures taken, as would render this Country the asylum of pacific and industrious characters from all parts of Europe, would encourage the cultivation of the Earth by the high price which its products would command, and would draw the wealth, and wealthy men of other Nations, into our bosom, by giving security to property, and liberty to its holders. I have the honor &c.[84]

To REVEREND WILLIAM GORDON

Mount Vernon, January 1, 1788.

Revd. Sir: I have recd. your letter of the 6th. of Septr. with flower-seeds accompanying it, for which I beg you will accept my best thanks. I am glad to find by your letter, that you have begun printing your history of the revolution; you have my best wishes for its success.

---

[84] From the original in the *Jefferson Papers* in the Library of Congress.

Our information from Europe is so various and contradictory as to render it still doubtful whether a rupture will take place between England and France; some accounts have even gone so far as to declare that hostilities have already commenced others, that vigorous preparations are making on both sides and a war is inevitable; and others again mention pacific dispositions of the Courts. But let their political views and interests be what they may I hope we shall have wisdom enough not to take a part in their quarrels.

I would have forwarded to you a copy of the Constitution proposed by the late Convention for the United States, but as you must undoubtedly have seen it before this, through the medium of the newspapers, or some other publication, the necessity of my doing it is superseded. I have the pleasure, however, to inform you, that there is the greatest prospect of its being adopted by the people. It has its opponents, as any system formed by the wisdom of man would undoubtedly have; but they bear but a small proportion to its friends, and differ among themselves in their objections. Pennsylvania, Delaware, and New Jersey have already decided in its favor, the first by a majority of two to one, and the two last unanimously. The dispositions in the other States, so far as I have been able to learn, are equally favorable, at least with Pennsylvania, and it is expected that their conventions will give a similar decision. New York, and possibly this State, may prove exceptions. I am &c.[85]

*To ————

Mount Vernon, January 5, 1788.

Dear Sir: As you have not yet sent for your Jenny, the presumption is that the many letters which have been written to

---

[85] From the "Letter Book" copy in the *Washington Papers*.

you requiring of it, have all miscarried; and therefore, you have the trouble of this. She is now in good order, and with foal, which may be lost (as several of my own have been) from the number that are together, struggling for what little I have it in my power from the scantiness of my last years Crop to give them.

I do not mean to charge you for the use of my Jack; nor for the time, or expence your Jenny has incurred, but wish she was now taken away; for I again repeat it, that I think she runs a considerable risk by remaining here. I have already lost several Mule Colts, and the Night before last a Jack Colt, from one of my imported Jenny's, for which I would not have taken a large sum of money had he come to maturity. I am etc.

[MS.H.S.]

To PETERSON & TAYLOR

Mount Vernon, January 5, 1788.

Gentlemen: When I wrote to you last upon the subject of furnishing me with scantling, Plank &c. agreeable to the enclosed bill we could not come to any determination with respect to the matter, because the price of herrings, in which I proposed to make payment, could not be fixed. I now make the following proposal, viz, I will allow you 6/ per Hundred for the scantling, reduced measure, 6/ per Hundred for the inch plank and 7/6 ped [*sic*] do for inch and quarter Do. As I understand you will want a large quantity of herrings in the fishing season, you shall give a preference to my landing for a supply provided a price can, at that time, be agreed upon between us; if it cannot, I will pay you for the scantling &c. in Cash after the fishing season is over as I have allotted the fish, or the money arising from the sale of them to supply me with the enclosed bill of scantling. The scantling must be furnished and delivered at my Landing by or before the first of March as I must have the frame &c. prepared before the season for cutting grass comes on when my Carpenters will then be obliged to go into the field.

If you acceed to the above proposal and will supply the scantling at the time mentioned you will write me a line by the bearer that will put the matter upon a certainty. I am, etc.

P. S. If you cannot furnish the scantling so soon as mentioned above you will be so good as to let me know the earliest period in which you can supply it.[86]

A BILL OF SCANTLING AND PLANK
TO BE PROVIDED BY PETERSON & TAYLOR

		feet		Inches	
170	Sleepers	14	long	10 by 4	This scantling can-
125	Joists	16	do	8 by 4	not be furnished too
6	Plates	30	do	9 by 6	soon; at any rate it
6	do	15	do	9 by 6	will be wanted in the
2	do	30	do	8 by 6	months of March.
8	do	24	do	8 by 6	Feby. would be pre-

160 Rafters 6 inches at bottom

ferred, infinitely

and 4½ at top by 3 inches 20 do

40 Rafters 12½ ft. long

6 and 4½ by 3

40	Window beams	16	do	4 by 3
20	do	11	do	4 by 3
31	Studs	10	do	6 by 4
16	do	11	do	4 by 3
8	Rails	15	do	6 by 4

Note: The whole of the above must be surved, and good of its kind, Pine, or it will not answer my purpose. 10,000 feet of Inch plank (as much of it as possible to be seasoned), and

---

[86] From the "Letter Book" copy in the *Washington Papers*.

wide as it can conveniently be obtained. 2,000 feet of Inch and quarter Do seasoned, if to be had and wide also.[87]

To PETERSON & TAYLOR

Mount Vernon, January 7, 1788.

Gentn: I have recd. your letter of the 5th. inst. wherein you mention your compliance with the terms proposed so far as to furnish the Scantling, but leave the time for the delivery of it undetermined; this will wholly set aside the object which I had in view in wishing to contract with you to supply me with the bill sent you on Saturday, for I have not the smallest doubt of being able to furnish myself with Scantling upon lower terms than I have proposed to you provided the time which I have allotted to have it framed would permit me to take the chance of procuring it from the Vessels which pass from the Eastern Shore up to Alexandria (or if I could convey a letter seasonably to a Mr. Joseph De Shields[88] of Maryland) who as I have been informed by Gentlemen of veracity that it has been and can generally be bought for 12/ per hundred measured side and edge which makes a difference of near 25 per Cent less than what I have engaged to give you. You therefore see, Sir. that my object in contracting with you is that I may depend upon its being delivered at a particular time and not subject myself to the hazard of not procuring it in time for my people to frame it before the season for cutting grass and Harvest come on. I am very willing to make any reasonable allowance for delays occasioned by weather or the River being blocked

---

[87] From the "Letter Book" copy in the *Washington Papers*.

On Jan. 5, 1788, Charles Hagan entered into an agreement with Washington to serve as a brickmaker at £4:10 per month of 26 working days. This agreement, signed by Washington and Hagan, is in the *Washington Papers*. On it is the note that Hagan commenced work on Apr. 16, 1788.

[88] Joseph Dashield, of Salisbury, Md.

up, but still I cannot consent to leave the time of delivering it wholly unfixed, and would thank you to let me know. I am, etc.[89]

To WILLIAM PEACEY

Mount Vernon, January 7, 1788.[90]

Sir: I have received your letter of the 2d of Feby. 1787. I am much obliged for your attention in sending me the seeds, which arrived agreeable to the bill. Mrs. Bloxham received of Wakelin Welch Esqr. of London £10.1.10, which sum, she informed him, was what she paid you for the seeds on my account. I am not sorry that Caleb Hall did not come out, for I proposed his coming more to please Bloxham, who was very desirous of having him here, than from a want of his services myself. I thank you, Sir, for your obliging offer to furnish me with Black-smiths and a Mill-wright; I have two of the former occupation, who, tho' not very neat workmen, answer all my purposes in making farming utensils etc. in a plain way; the latter I shall have no occasion for as I have not work enough to employ him in his own line; and indeed I doubt whether they would find [it to] their advantage in coming over at present, because I hardly think they will meet with constant employ: for altho' I should be extremely glad to see the honest and industrious mechanic come into this Country from any and every part of the Globe, yet I would not wish to encourage them unless they could be benefitted by it.

Whenever we have a regular and firm government established, the prospect for these people will be much more pleasing than it is at present. Bloxham and his family are in good health, and appear to be contented with the country. I am etc.[91]

---

[89] From the "Letter Book" copy in the *Washington Papers*.

[90] The "Letter Book" dates this letter 1787.

[91] In the writing of Tobias Lear. From a photostat of the original in the possession (1932) of Forest G. Sweet, of Battle Creek, Mich.

To GOVERNOR EDMUND RANDOLPH

Mount Vernon, January 8, 1788.

Dear Sir: The letter, which you did me the honor of writing to me on the 27th Ulto. with the enclosure,[92] came duly to hand. I receive them as a fresh instance of your friendship and attention. For both I thank you.

The diversity of Sentiments upon the important matter which has been submitted to the People, was as much expected as it is regretted, by me. The various passions and motives, by which men are influenced are concomitants of fallibility, engrafted into our nature for the purposes of [the] unerring wisdom; but had I entertained a latent hope (at the time you moved to have the Constitution submitted to a second Convention) that a more perfect form would be agreed to, in a word that any Constitution would be adopted under the impressions and instructions of the members, the publications, which have taken place since would have eradicated every form of it. How do the sentiments of the influential characters in *this* State who are opposed to the Constitution, and have favoured the public with their opinions, quadrate with each other? Are they not at variance on some of the most important points? If the opponents in the *same* State cannot agree in *their* principles what prospect is there of a coalescence with the advocates of the measure when the different views, and jarring interests of so wide and extended an Empire are to be brought forward and combated?

To my Judgment, it is more clear than ever, that an attempt to amend the Constitution which is submitted, would be productive of more heat and greater confusion than can well be

---

[92] Randolph's letter is in the *Washington Papers* but the pamphlet, *A Letter . . . on the Federal Constitution* (1787), is not found therein.

conceived. There are some things in the new form, I will readily acknowledge, wch. never did, and I am persuaded never
will, obtain my *cordial* approbation; but I then did conceive,
and do now most firmly believe, that, in the aggregate, it is the
best Constitution that can be obtained at this Epocha, and that
this, or a dissolution of the Union awaits our choice, and are
the only alternatives before us. Thus believing, I had not, nor
have I now any hesitation in deciding on which to lean.

I pray your forgiveness for the expression of these sentiments.
In acknowledging the receipt of your Letter on this subject,
it was hardly to be avoided, although I am well disposed to let
the matter rest entirely on its own merits, and mens minds to
their own workings. With very great esteem &c.[93]

To PIERRE ROUSILLES[94]

January 8, 1788.

Sir: I have received your letter and memorial of the 12 of
Augt. and in answer to them can only say, that however just
and reasonable your demands may be, and however desireous
I am to assist the injured in obtaining Justice, it is not in my
power to do anything more than appears, by your memorial,
to have been already done, that is, to refer you to the boards and
officers which take cognizance of matters of that nature. As I
have, long since, lain aside all publick business and live 300
miles from New York where the Congress sits and the publick
Offices are established, I cannot, with any degree of propriety,
interfere in your case. I am, etc.

P. S. I return your original documents which you may have
occasion for.[93]

---

[93] From the "Letter Book" copy in the *Washington Papers*.
[94] Of Bordeaux, France.

To COMTE DE ROCHAMBEAU

Mount Vernon, January 8, 1788.

My dear Sir: I have received your letters of the 28th of June, 1786 and 12th of May, 1787. In the former you mention your having just returned from Holland and were so obliging as to give me an account of the state of political affairs in that Country. Since the time of your writing their intestine disputes have been brought to a crisis and appear to have terminated rather against the Patriots. What changes may be made in their Government; what revolutions in their political œconomy, and how far their connections with the several powers in Europe may be affected by the termination is yet unknown to us.

I am very glad to hear that the Assemblée des Notables has been productive of good in France; the State of your finances was really alarming and required a strict investigation and the sanative hand of the nation to restore them to their proper tone.

I now begin to hope that the period is not very distant, when this country will make a more respectable figure in the eyes of Europe than it has hitherto done. The constitution formed by the late Convention appears, as far as my information extends, to be highly acceptable to the people of these States. Jersey, Delaware and Pensylvania have already decided in its favor, the two former unanimously and the latter by a majority of two to one; the Conventions in the other States have not yet determined upon it but their dispositions are very favourable. Whenever this Government is established we shall regain thus [*sic*] confidence and credit among the European powers which a want of energy in the present confederation has deprived us of; and shall likewise feel the benefit of those commercial and political advantages which our situation holds out to us. This event must be extremely pleasing to every friend of humanity and peculiarly so to you and others, who must feel interested in the happiness and welfare of this country, from the part which you took in establishing her liberty and independence.

I lament with you, my dear Sir, that the distance between us is so great, as to deprive us of the pleasure and satisfaction of a frequent and regular communication by letter, for it often happens either through the inattention of the person to whom letters are committed, or from some other cause, that they do not come to hand till months after their date. You will please to accept the compliments of the season with my sincere wishes for many happy returns of it to you, and believe me to be &c.[95]

To SAMUEL ATHAWES

Mount Vernon, January 8, 1788.

Sir: I have received your letter of the 26th. of July last, informing me of the death of our much esteemed and worthy friend George William Fairfax Esqr. I sincerely condole with you and his other friends in England upon this occasion. Altho' the precarious state of his health for several years past, must have prepared his friends, in some measure, for his death, yet the event could not take place without being sincerely lamented by all who know him.

The appointment of Executors and Trustees in each country for his Estates and affairs in each, seperately and without any dependance on each other was in my opinion, a very judicious and necessary step; for the delays and inconveniences which the distance would unavoidably produce, would have been an insuperable objection to their being joined, not to mention the difficulties, which must have arisen from the difference of the laws upon this point, in the two countries.

---

[95] From the "Letter Book" copy in the *Washington Papers*.

The small case, which you directed to the care of Colo. Burwell was forwarded by him and came safe to hand. I have sent the watch to Mr. Fairfax, and the letters to their respective addresses. Notwithstanding the long and uninterrupted friendship which subsisted between Colo. Fairfax and myself, and however desirous I may be to give every proof of my affection for him and his amiable relict yet I must decline acting as an Executor for his Estate here. The deranged situation of my own private affairs, occasioned by my long absence from home during the late war, and the continual applications which are made to me for information, advice or assistance, in consequence of a publick office which I sustained, require my constant and unremitting attention, and would prevent a faithful discharge of the trust on my part, if I should accept it. I am &c.[96]

To WAKELIN WELCH & SON

[January 8, 1788.]

Gentn: I have recd. your letter of the 7th. of March and 14th. of July, the former enclosing my acct. current, in which my drafts upon you &c. are justly and properly Stated.

The seeds, Ploughs &c. sent by the Mary, Capt. Andrews, arrived safe, but some of the former were injured by being put into the hold of the Vessel; they were in casks, and the Capt. said he did not know the contents of them or they should have been deposited in a more suitable place; however, upon the whole, they arrived in much better order than those things generally do.

I thank you for your attention to Mr. Youngs two drafts for £11.2 and £9.12.6 should I have occasion to apply to that Gentn. for anything more I shall advise you thereof, and your further attention to his bills will be very obliging.

---

[96] From the "Letter Book" copy in the *Washington Papers*.

Mrs. Bloxham's receiving £10.1.10 of you, which she had paid to Mr. Peacey for seeds on my acct. was perfectly agreeable to me; while I was in Philadelphia last summer I drew upon you for £100 in favor of Robert Morris Esqr. and advised you regularly thereof. I am, etc.[97]

To NICOLAS SIMON AND LUCRETIA WILHEMINA VAN WINTER[98]

Mount Vernon, January 8, 1788.

I have received your letter of the 26th. Feby., accompanied by the Poem entitled "Germanicus" I consider your sending the latter to me as a mark of polite attention which merits my warmest acknowledgments, I beg you to accept my thanks for that, as well as for the many obliging expressions in your letter.

The muses have always been revered in every age, and in all Countries where letters and civilization have made any progress. As they tend to alleviate the misfortunes and soften the sorrows of life they will ever be respected by the humane and virtuous. I am, etc.[99]

To THE COUNTESS D'ESSARTS[1]

Mount Vernon, January 8, 1788.

Madam: I have received your letter of the first of May and the books accompanying it which you did me the honor to send me.

The works of those men who have dedicated their time and fortunes to the purposes of humanity will always be read with

---

[97] From the "Letter Book" copy in the *Washington Papers.*

[98] Mrs. Van Winter's maiden name was Van Merken.

[99] From the "Letter Book" copy in the *Washington Papers.* The original of this letter is said to be in Amsterdam.

[1] Daughter of C. H. P. de Chamousset, whose *Works,* in two volumes, were published in 1787.

pleasure by the good and virtuous citizens of every country, as they contain the pure sentiments of a noble mind divested of local prejudices and particular attachments. I must therefore beg, Madam, that you will accept my warmest acknowledgments for the favor you have conferred by sending me the works of M. de Chamousset. I have the honor, etc.[2]

To MONSIEUR BOURDON[3]

Mount Vernon, January 8, 1788.

Sir: I have recd. your letter of the 6th. of Decr. 1786,[4] wherein you request me to represent your situation to Congress, and apply to that body, in your behalf, for a grant of land in some part of the United States where you may form a settlement.

Altho' no incident in life could afford me more pleasure than to see all those who have exerted themselves in the cause of this country amply recompensed for their meritorious services, and however desirous I may be to contribute all in my power towards there obtaining a compensation, yet I cannot, consistent with the declaration which I made when I quitted my publick employment, bring forward applications of this nature to Congress. I hope, Sir, you will not think that act a singular part, with respect to you by not complying with your request, when I assure you I have ever declined the repeated applications of this kind which have been made to me.

I think it is not improbable but that the Court of France, upon a reconsideration of the services of the Count de Grass, may be induced to recompence the merits of him and his friends in the manner which they deserve. I am, etc.[2]

---

[2] From the "Letter Book" copy in the *Washington Papers*.
[3] There are five different Bourdons listed in the French Navy in *Combattants Français de la Guerre Americaine* (Washington, Government Printing Office: 1905).
[4] Not now found in the *Washington Papers*.

To ROBERT FENNING[5]

Mount Vernon, January 8, 1788.

Sir: I have received your letters of the 5th. of Septr. In answer to which I can only say, that I am not at present in want of a person of your description, but if you are desireous of settling in this country, and will let me know precisely what your terms and expectations are, I think it is very probable I shall hear of some Gentleman who would be willing to engage you for the purpose of superintending their farms, provided your knowledge and experience in husbandry &c. is such as you have mentioned and you can bring authentic testimonials thereof and your terms are not extravagant. I am, etc.[6]

To WILLIAM McINTOSH

Mount Vernon, January 8, 1788.

Sir: I have received your letter of the 28 of August[7] enclosing your plan of Government[8] suggested for the United States of America. As a Citizen of these States, I return you my best thanks for the interest you take in their happiness and prosperity; and as an individual, you will please to accept of my acknowledgments for your polite attention in sending to me your sentiments upon so important a subject.

The want of an efficient General Government in this country is universally felt and acknowledged. The convention, which met at Philadelphia in May last for the purpose of forming a Constitution for the United States have handed to the

---

[5] Of London.
[6] From the "Letter Book" copy in the *Washington Papers.*
[7] August 20.
[8] McIntosh's letter and scheme of government, dated from Avignon, France, is in the *Washington Papers.*

People one (of which I now enclose you a copy) for their consideration and acceptance; it is to be submitted to conventions chosen by the people in the several States and by them approved or rejected. Two[9] States only have as yet decided upon it, two of which accepted it unanimously and the other by a majority of 2 to 1. Similar dispositions seem to prevail in the other States and there is no doubt but that they will give it a determination equally favorable.

When a Government is established in America that can give energy to its laws and security to property, it is not to be doubted, that many persons of respectability and interest from the old world will make a valuable addition to the citizens of the new. I am &c.[10]

To MAUDUIT DU PLESSIS

Mount Vernon, January 8, 1788.

Sir: I have to acknowledge the reception of your three letters, viz of the 12th. of Feby. the 26th. of March and the 20th. July. I was exceedingly sorry to hear of the disasters which you met with after you left this place, before you reached Georgia, and was very unhappy to find, when you arrived there, that your expectations, with respect to your property were so much disappointed, and that your misfortunes were aggravated by the death of your family.[11] I sincerely regret the causes which induced you to Return to Europe, not only on account of the loss which America will sustain of a person who would have been a most valuable citizen, but that a worthy man should leave the country with unfavourable impressions and wounded feelings.

---

[9] Three.
[10] From the "Letter Book" copy in the *Washington Papers*.
[11] His surgeon and domestics. Du Plessis's wife and children were in France.

I congratulate you upon your safe arrival in France and hope you will receive that degree of happiness and satisfaction in your return to your family and friends which will compensate for the misfortunes you sustained here.

Mrs. Washington has recd. the fans which you were so polite to send to her from Charleston and begs you would accept her best thanks for them. I have likewise received the Ribbon which you did me the honor to send to me and request you to accept my warmest acknowledgements for that as well as for your obliging offer to execute anything which I might have occasion to do in France, and the very polite expressions with which your letters abounded.

It would give me a particular pleasure to comply with your request by sending you an engraved copy of my portrait similar to the one which you saw in my dining Room; but as that was a present to me from the Engraver, Mr. Brown of London,[12] and the only one of the kind that I ever saw, it is not in my power to gratify your wish.

When I was in Philadelphia last summer I signed a number of Diplomas for the foreign officers, members of the Cincinnati, which were sent by the Secretary General to the Counts De Estaing and Rochambeau this, I presume, will supercede the necessity of my sending one to you as you desired. I have the honor, etc.[13]

To PETERSON & TAYLOR

Mount Vernon, January 9, 1788.

Gentn: Your letter of the 7th. inst. came duly to hand. I accede to the proposal therein made, for you to have the Scantling

---

[12] This engraving was, apparently, made by Valentine Green, of London, from a portrait painted by Joseph Brown, after Charles Willson Peale. The engraving was published in 1785, and is in Charles Henry Hart's *Catalogue of Engraved Portraits of Washington*, (New York: 1904), p. 12.

[13] From the "Letter Book" copy in the *Washington Papers*.

and plank delivered at my landing, agreeable to the bill sent you, in all the month of March, as you say it will be for your interest to deliver it sooner if possible, it will be infinitely more pleasing to me to have it done. You will please to have it delivered at my fishing landing near the ferry, as it will be more convenient for me there than at any other place. I expect the scantling will be of a good quality agreeable to promise, and if any of the plank can be had seasoned, particularly the Inch and quarter, it will be very desirable. I am, etc.[14]

To JOHN FITZGERALD

Mount Vernon, January 9, 1788.

Dear Sir: In a card I sent you the other day, at the sametime that I enquired if your express brought any answer from Govrs. Johnson and Lee I requested to be informed at what precise spot the meeting of the directors[15] was appointed to be held, I should be glad now to know.

I had made my arrangements for setting off on Saturday to proceed on this side of the River; and will do so if I am able but having taken a very severe cold this day Senight in a night ride from Alexandria I have been confined almost ever since getting little rest from a continual cough (which has greatly disordered my breast) and by slow fevers which has constantly attended it.

As I am very desirous that this should be a full meeting, I will make it a point to attend, if the State of my health on Saturday will in any degree enable me to encounter the ride, cold houses and Bad Beds. If it should not I will thank you for assigning the reason (when you get up) for my non attendance.

---

[14] From the "Letter Book" copy in the *Washington Papers*.
[15] Of the Potomac Company.

Every paper which we may have occasion for, I hope will be carried. Colo. Humphreys proposed to accompany me. Colo. Gilpin (with Mr. Smith)[16] I am informed propose doing some work in their way on the other side of the river. How far it will be convenient to you, to Join our party (if I should be able to go) you are best able to decide, of the pleasure we should have in your Company you can have no doubt. I am, etc.[17]

To MICHAEL RYAN[18]

Mount Vernon, January 9, 1788.

Sir: I have received your letter of the 23d. of December[19] wherein you express a wish that I would become a Joint proprietor with yourself and some other Gentlemen in a large tract of Land which you have upon the Western waters of Virginia. I am much obliged to you, Sir, for your politeness in making the proposal to me and submitting the plan of settling the land &c. to my consideration. But I must decline taking any part in it, however advantageous the terms may be, and however desireous I am to promote any laudable plan for the settlement of the Country; for the lands which I already possess in those parts are untenanted, and I am at present endeavouring to have them seated, this will engage me as extensively in business of this nature as I wish to be, and operates as one strong reason against my embarking any further in it, another, still more weighty, is the constant and unremitting attention which the arrangement and cultivation of my estate here requires. I am, etc.[17]

---

[16] Clement Smith, one of the directors of the Potomac Company.
[17] From the "Letter Book" copy in the *Washington Papers*.
[18] Formerly Inspector General of Pennsylvania.
[19] Ryan's letter was written from Fredericksburg, Va.

To RICHARD BUTLER

Mount Vernon, January 10, 1788.

Dear Sir: I have received your letter of the 30th. of November accompanied by the Indian Vocabulary[20] which you have been so obliging as to forward to me. I am so far from thinking any apology necessary on your part for not having furnished me with the Vocabulary at an earlier period, that I assure you it is a matter of surprise to me to find that you have been able to compleat a work of such difficulty and magnitude, as this appears to be, in so short a time, under the pain which you must have suffered, and the delays occasioned by your misfortune in breaking your leg.

The pleasing satisfaction which you must enjoy from a reflection that you have exerted yourself to throw light upon the original history of this Country, to gratify the curiosity of the Philosopher, and to forward researches into the probable connection and communication between the northern parts of America and those of Asia must make you a more ample compensation for the laborious task which you have executed than my warmest acknowledgments, which, however I must beg you to accept.

The observations contained in your letter, respecting the different tribes of Indians inhabiting the Western Country, The traditions which prevail among them, and the reasoning deduced therefrom, are very valuable and may lead to some useful discoveries. Those works which are found upon the Ohio[21] and other traces of the country's having been once inhabited

---

[20] A copy of the Vocabulary (separately bound) is in the *Washington Papers,* and contains an extract of Butler's letter to Washington, Nov. 30, 1787, which letter is not now found in the *Washington Papers.*

[21] The mound builders.

by a race of people more ingenious, at least, if not more civil-
ized, than those who at present dwell there, have excited the
attention and inquiries of the curious to learn from whence
they came, whither they are gone, and something of their history; any clue, therefore, which can lead to a knowledge of
these must be gratefully received.

As you have had opportunities of gaining extensive knowledge and information respecting the western territory, its
situation, rivers, and the face of the Country, [I must beg the
favor of you, my dear Sir, to resolve the following quæries,
either from your own knowledge, or certain information (as
well to gratify my own curiosity, as to enable me to satisfy
several Gentlemen of distinction in other Countries who have
applied to me for information upon the subject.)

1st. What is the face of the Country between the sources or
Canoe navigation of the Cayahoga (which empties itself into
Lake Erie) and the Big-Beaver and between the Cayahoga and
the Muskingum?

2d. The distance between the waters of the Cayahoga and
each of the two rivers abovementioned?

3d. Would it be practicable (and not very expensive) to cut
a canal between the Cayahoga and either of the above rivers so
as to open a communication between the waters of lake Erie
and the Ohio?

4th. Whether there is any more direct; practicable, and easy
communication between the waters of lake Erie and those of
the Ohio (by which the Fur and Peltry of the Upper Country
can be transported) than these?

Any information you can give me relative to the above quæries,
from your own knowledge, will be most agreeable; but if that
is not sufficiently accurate for you to decide upon, the best and

most authentic accounts of others will be very acceptable.]
Your letter to the Marquis de la Fayette shall be particularly
attended to, and forwarded with mine. I am etc.[22]

To FREDERICK WEISSENFELS

Mount Vernon, January 10, 1788.

Sir: I have received your letter of the 10th. of December[23] in
answer to that, as well as those which you wrote to me in June
last, I am sorry to inform you that I cannot, with any propriety, make application to Congress had[24] the offices to bestow
or any other publick body in your behalf for an appointment;
because it would be acting directly contrary to a resolution
which I made, when I quitted the publick service, not to make
application for, or interfere with appointments of any kind.

It is a matter of regret as well as surprize that you should
apply to me in an affair of this nature in preferrence to those
persons among whom you live and have been more immediately employ'd and who must, from their long acquaintance
with you, have a much better knowledge of your merits and
sufferings than I can be supposed to have. If you expect relief
from the Cincinnati, it is to the State Society you must look
for it, or apply to the General-meeting, when convened, for I
cannot, as an individual, transact any business of this kind relating to the Society. I am, etc.[22]

---

[22] From the "Letter Book" copy in the *Washington Papers.*
On January 11 Washington wrote to William Irvine a letter which was practically
identical with that portion of this letter which is inclosed in brackets. He added:
"As a determination of the points referred to, may tend to promote the commerce,
population and welfare of the Country, I know it will, to you my dear Sir, be a Sufficient apology for any trouble which this letter may give." A copy of this letter is in
the "Letter Book" in the *Washington Papers.*
[23] Not now found in the *Washington Papers.*
[24] Careless copying. The meaning evidently was: "which has the office to bestow."

To JAMES MADISON

Mount Vernon, January 10, 1788.

My dear Sir: I stand indebted to you for your favors of the 20th. and 26th. Ulto. and I believe for that of the 14th. also, and their enclosures. It does not appear to me, that there is any *certain* criterion in this State, by which a decided judgment can be formed, as to the opinion which is entertained by the mass of its citizens with respect to the new Constitution. My belief on this occasion is, that whenever the matter is brought to a final decision, that not only a majority, but a large one, will be found in its favor. That the opposition should have gained strength, among the members of the Assembly at Richmond, admitting the fact, is not to be wondered at when it is considered that the powerful adversaries to the Constitution are all assembled at that place, acting conjunctly, with the promulgated sentiments of Col. R— H— L— as auxiliary. It is said however, and I believe it may be depended upon, that the latter, (tho' he may retain his sentiments) has withdrawn, or means to withdraw his opposition; because as he has expressed himself, or as others have done it for him, he finds himself in bad company; such as with M—Sm—th[25] &c, &c. His brother, Francis L. Lee on whose judgment the family place much reliance, is decidedly in favor of the new form, under a conviction that it is the best that can be obtained, and because it promises energy, stability, and that security which is, or ought to be, the wish of every good Citizen of the Union.

How far the determination of the question before the debating club (of which I made mention in a former letter) may be considered as auspicious of the final decision of the Convention, I shall not prognosticate; but in this club, the question it

---

[25] Meriwether Smith.

seems, was determined by a very large majority in favor of the Constitution; but of all arguments which may be used at this time, none will be so forcible, I expect, as that nine States have acceded to it. and if the unanimity, or majorities in those which are to follow, are as great as in those which have acted, the power of those arguments will be irrisistable. The Governor has given his reasons to the Publick for with holding his Signature to the Constitution A copy of them I send you.

Our Assembly has been long in Session, employed chiefly (according to my information) in rectifying the mistakes of the last, and committing others for emendations at the next. Yet " who so wise as we are " We are held in painful suspence with respect to European Intelligence. Peace or War, by the last accts. are equally balanced a grain added to either scale will give it the preponderancy. I have no regular corrispondt. in Massachusetts; otherwise, as the occasional subject of a letter I should have had no objection to the communication of my sentiments on the proposed Government as they are unequivocal and decided. With the greatest esteem etc.

P. S. I have this momt. been informed, that the Assembly of No Carolina have postponed the meeting of the Convention of that State until July; this seems evidently calculated to take the Tone from Virginia.[26]

To MARQUIS DE LAFAYETTE

Mount Vernon, January 10, 1788.

My dear Marqs: I fear my dear Marqs., you will believe me to have been remiss in attentions to you. My last letters I find,

---

[26] From the text printed in the sales catalogue of the *Washington-Madison Papers* (McGuire Collection, 1892). The copy in the "Letter Book" shows unmistakable evidence of careless, not to say ignorant, transcribing, and the texts printed by Ford and Sparks vary from this and each other in unexpected and unjustifiable details.

have been unaccountably concentred in the same hands, and unreasonably delayed; entirely contrary to my expectation. When you have received them by the Chevalier Paul Jones, you will acquit me of any intended or real neglect. One of these letters, containing the form of Government which has been submitted by the fœderal Convention to the People of these States I wished to have got to your hands by the first conveyance, as it was my intention that you should be among the first to be informed of the proceedings of that body.

It is with great pleasure I transmit to you, by this conveyance, a Vocabulary of the Shawanese and Delaware languages. Your perfect acquaintance with Genl. Richard Butler, the same worthy officer who served under your orders, and who has taken the trouble to compile them, supersedes the necessity of my saying any thing in support of their veracity [and] correctness. I likewise send a shorter specimen of the language of the southern Indians. It was procured by that ingenious gentleman, the Hble. Mr. Hawkins,[27] a member of Congress from North Carolina, and lately a Commissioner from the United States to the Indians of the South. I heartily wish the attempt of that singular great character, the Empress of Russia, to form a universal Dictionary, may be attended with the merited success.

To know the affinity of tongues seems to be one step towards promoting the affinity of nations. Would to god, the harmony of nations was an object that lay nearest to the hearts of Sovereigns; and that the incentives to peace (of which commerce and facility of understanding each other are not the most inconsiderable) might be daily encreased! Should the present or any other efforts of mine to procure information respecting the different dialects of the Aborigines in America, serve to reflect

---

[27] Benjamin Hawkins.

a ray of light on the obscure subject of language in general, I shall be highly gratified. For I love to indulge the contemplation of human nature in a progressive state of improvement and melioration; and if the idea would not be considered visionary and chimerical, I could fondly hope, that the present plan of the great Potentate of the North might, in some measure, lay the foundation for that assimilation of language, which, producing assimilation of manners and interests, which, should one day remove many of the causes of hostility from amongst mankind.

At this moment, however, it appears by the current of intelligence from your side of the Atlantic, that but too many motives and occasions exist for interrupting the public transquillity. A war between the Russians and Turks, we learn, has broken out. How far, or in what manner, this may involve other nations seems to us, at this distance, uncertain. Extraordinary speculations and expectations arise from the conduct of the King of Prussia [28] in the Dutch, and the Emperor of Germany [29] in the Austrian Netherlands. Nothing as yet, has come to our knowledge, which indicates with certainty, whether hostilities will take place between France and England, or, in that event, how extensively the flames of war will spread. We are apprehensive that we have but too much reason to bewail the fate of the Dutch Patriots.

To guard against the similar calamities of domestic discord or foreign interposition, and effectually to secure our liberties with all the benefits of an efficient Government, is now the important subject that engrosses the attention of all our part of America. You will doubtless have seen, in the public papers, in what manner the new Constitution has been attacked and

[28] Frederick William II.
[29] Joseph II.

defended. There have been some compositions published in its defence, which I think will, at least, do credit to American genius. I dare say its principles and tendencies have, also, before this time been amply discussed in Europe. Here, that is in United America, it is strongly advocated by a very great and decided majority. The Conventions, in the States of New Jersey and Delaware, have *unanimously* adopted it: and that of Pennsylvania by a majority of two to one. No other State has yet had an opportunity of deciding. New England (with the exception of Rhode Island, which seems itself, politically speaking, to be an exception from all that is good) it is believed will chearfully and fully accept it: and there is little doubt but that the Southern States will do the same. In Virginia and New York its fate is somewhat more questionable: though, in my private opinion, I have no hesitation to believe there will be a Clear majority in its favor, in the former: of the latter I can say nothing from my own knowledge, its advocates, there, generally conclude that they shall carry it. Upon this summary view, you will perceive, my dear Marquis, the highest probability exists that the proposed Constitution will be adopted by more than nine States, at some period early in the coming summer.

To morrow I shall set out on a journey to view the progress which has been made in clearing the upper falls of the Potomack. This business, in general, has been attended with as much success as could possibly have been expected. I have nothing more to add, but that Mrs. Washington and those under this roof desire to be affectionately presented to yourself and those under yours. For myself, my dear Marquis, I am etc.

P. S. Under cover with this letter, is one from Genl. Butler which I forward to you at his request. as this Gentleman's knowledge of the Indian languages is more extensive and accurate in the Shawane than it is in the Delaware and the vocabulary less copious in the latter than in the former, I send you the Delaware Indian and English spelling Book by Mr. Zeisberger,[30] as it may throw light on the subject.[31]

*To HENRY KNOX

Mount Vernon, January 10, 1788.

My dear Sir: I beg you to accept of my thanks for your obliging favor of the 11th. Ult; which, owing to the dullness of the season, and want of matter to amuse you, has lain unacknowledged till this time.

Three States, to wit. Pensylvania New Jersey, and Delaware having adopted the New Constitution in so decisive a manner and those of New Hampshire, Massachusetts and Connecticut having discovered such favourable sentiments of it, places the final Success of it, in my judgment, upon unequivocal ground. Maryland, most unquestionably, will adopt it; from No. Carolina (so far as accts. have been received in this quarter) the disposition of the People towards it is favourable; from the States South of it I have no direct intelligence; but in the situation Georgia is, nothing but insanity, or a desire of becoming the Allies of the Spaniards or Savages, can disincline them to a Governmt. which holds out the prospect of relief from its present distresses. The opposition in this State, tho' headed by very influencial characters; is not, in my opinion (tho' I may be an incompetent judge, never going from home, and seeing no body except those who call upon me) much to be apprehended. My opinion of the matter is, that the New form on the final decision in our Convention, will be acceded to by a large majority. The determination of New York, of all others, seems most problematical; and yet, I can hardly

---

[30] Rev. David Zeisberger, Moravian missionary.
[31] From the "Letter Book" copy in the *Washington Papers*.

entertain an idea that She will be disposed to stand alone, or with one or two others, if the States bordering on her should Confederate.

Whether War or Peace will be the issue of the dispute between France and England, seems as yet undecided. If the former, we shall certainly get involved, unless there is energy enough in Government to restrain our People within proper bounds; and that the power of the present Government is inadequate to accomplish this, I believe none will deny.

Mrs. Washington joins me in offering compliments of congratulations to Mrs. Knox and yourself on the increase of yr. family by the birth of a son, and I pray you to accept the acknowledgment of my sense of the honor you have conferred on me by giving him my name. I hope he will live to enjoy it long after I have taken my departure for the world of spirits and that he may prove a blessing and comfort to you both in your declining years. With sentiments of the greatest esteem I am etc.

PS. Colo. Humphreys has lost no flesh since he came to Virginia. He undertakes a journey tomorrow with me to the upper falls of this River whither I am called on business of the Potomack Company. How far this ride, The cold weather &ca. may effect a change can best be determined after our return in about ten days.   [MS.H.S.]

To JOHN FRANCIS MERCER

Mount Vernon, January 11, 1788.

Sir: The People on board Mr. Spriggs Vessel have been already supplied with Provisions, and shall receive every other aid they may require, and I can give. The conduct either of the Skipper, or your Overseer, has been egregiously wrong. The Vessel, it seems, came up in the night of thursday; but not till near dusk on friday had I any information of it, and then by [way] of enquiry from your People after their Overseer, whom they said was put on shore at my point, opposite to Mr. Digges and had not at that time Joined them. In strong terms I then urged them to go immediately on board and get the Vessel as near as possible to my warf *that night* as there was every appearance of a severe frost. Instead of doing this the Vessel kept her position (more than a mile of) and, as I expected, was frozen up next morning and unable to deliver a grain of the Corn until the afternoon of Saturday Then but 16 Barrels whereas had they stopped on thursday the whole might have been landed before friday evening and the Vessel discharged, as I had a large Boat of my own and had collected my Plantation Carts (as soon as I was advised of the Vessels being here) to expedite the work.

Mr. Whites letter is returned to you and I should be glad to know precisely whether I am to expect any and what part of the £200 of which you assured me in Philadelphia I might absolutely rely and the half of which you informed me in November, should be sent to me by your Servant in ten days if you could not get the residue? I have put the Sheriff of this County off 3 times, if he comes again, I must if I have no further expectn. from you suffer him to make distress, as I raised nothing last year for sale, and allotted this money for the payment of my taxes.

Mrs. Washington and myself would have been glad to have seen you and Mrs. Mercer here. This she would do still. In the morning I shall leave home for a meeting of the Directors of the Potomack Co. at the Falls of the Shanandoah from whence I do not expect to be returned in less than ten days. I am, etc.[32]

---

[32] From the "Letter Book" copy in the *Washington Papers*.

To CHARLES CARTER

Mount Vernon, January 12, 1788.

Dear Sir: I find that an extract from my letter to you,[33] is running through all the newspapers; and published in that of Baltimore with the addition of my name. Altho' I have no disinclination to the promulgation of my Sentiments on the proposed Constitution (not having concealed them on any occasion) yet I must nevertheless confess, that it gives me pain to see the hasty and indigested production of a private letter, handed to the public, to be animadverted upon by the adversaries of the new Government.

Could I have supposed, that the contents of a private letter (marked with evident haste) would have composed a newspaper paragraph, I certainly should have taken some pains to dress the Sentiments (to whom known is indifferent to me) in less exceptionable language, and would have assigned some reasons in support of my opinion, and the charges against others. I am persuaded your intentions were good, but I am not less persuaded, that you have provided food for strictures and criticisms. be this however as it may, it shall pass off unnoticed by me, as I have no inclination and still less abilities for scribbling. With very great esteem and regard, I am &c.[34]

To WILLIAM THOMPSON[35]

Mount Vernon, January 12, 1788.

Sir: I have recd. your letter of the 7th. inst. When I requested my nephew to apply to you for a craft, I expected that he would have engaged your largest, which he had last winter, upon the

---

[33] See Washington's letter to Charles Carter, Dec. 14, 1787, *ante.*
[34] From the "Letter Book" copy in the *Washington Papers.*
[35] Of Colchester, Va.

same terms that he then employed her viz: at £20 for the trip and allow her to be detained below for four days on his account if she exceeded that time by his desire, he was to give 20/ per day for every day she might be so detained over the four Stipulated.

My corn will be received about the place where your Vessel was last year. I shall have enough to employ your largest, two trips, which I had rather do than engage two Crafts. If you are willing to let me have the same Vessel which Majr. Washington had last winter, and upon the same terms above mentioned, I would thank you to drop me a line by the post. I am going from home to day and shall not return in less than 10 days. I should wish, if you agree to let me have the Vessel, that she might be ready to go down as soon as the frost and weather will permit. I am, etc.[36]

To DAVID STUART

Mount Vernon, January 15, 1788.

Dear Sir: In answer to your enquiries in behalf of Mr. Custis and which you requested I would commit to writing, you will please to receive and convey, the following information.

Namely. That the lands which I have to dispose of beyond the Alligany mountains, are contained in the following tracts.

2314. Acres in Bottetourt County on the Ohio, beginning about 4 miles below the mouth of the little Kanhawa and bounded by the Ohio 1720 poles; being the first large bottom on the East side of that River, below the mouth of the little Kanhawa.

2448. Acres in the same rout and on the said river about 16 miles below the above tract being the 4th. large bottom on the east side, below the little Kanhawa; this tract is bounded by the Ohio 1012 poles, has a fine Creek running through it on which (as I am informed) are Mill seats.

---

[36] From the "Letter Book" copy in the *Washington Papers*.

4395. Acres, in the same County and on the Ohio also about 3 Miles below the last mentioned tract and on the same, that is the East side and above the great bend which is about 25 Miles from the mouth of the Great Kanhawa bounded by the River 1670 poles.

In all, 9,157 Acres, on the Ohio, betwn. the great and little Kanhawa.

10,990 Acres, on the Great Kanhawa, West side of it in Montgomery County. Beginning about 2 or 3 Miles from its Conflux with the Ohio. Bounded by the former, that is the Kanhaw, 5491 poles, or 17 Miles and 51 poles. Having many valuable streams passing through it.

7276 Acres, about 2 Miles above the latter on the other or East side of the said river in Green brier County and bounded thereby 3947 poles or 12½ Miles.

2000 Acres about 6 Miles above the last mentioned tract on the west side of River laying in the fork of the Kanhawa and Coal River; bounded on the first 1400 and on the latter 588 poles.

2950. Acres on the east side of the Kanhawa in Green brier County part whereof its opposite to the last mentioned tract. this is bounded by the River 1939 poles.

In all 23,216 Acres on the Great Kanhawa. and
    <u>9,157</u> on the Ohio
Total 32,373 on both Rivers.

That these several tracts, *some* from my own observation, and *all* from good information, are of the richest low grounds; being the first choice of the Country, by a competent Judge and are well watered, and superabounding in fine meadow.

That the whole are to be let, on the Conditions hereafter mentioned.

That the two first mentioned on the Ohio, and the two last named on the Kanhawa may be purchased, as indeed all of them may if any one person for himself or in behalf of a number, will strike for the whole. without this and not because they are of inferior quality, but because what remains will be more concentered I incline to sell those that are farthest apart first.

That if I sell these, I shall expect (considering the quality of the Soil there situations on navigable waters; and the advantages they possess on account of Fish, wild fowl &c.) Twenty Shillings pr. Acre. part of the monies to be paid down, and such credit as can be agreed upon, given for the residue, I have been in treaty with some foreigners (thro' their agent Mr. Charson) who have large tracts of land back of or in the vicinity of some of these Lands of mine and who know them perfectly well, for the *whole* of them at the price of 30,000 guineas, but as they are not yet returned from Europe and the time is elapsed in which they were to have given me a definitive answer, I do not consider myself bound any longer to them, tho' it has been the cause (in a great measure) of the lands remaining unsold.

That the enclosed Gazette will explain my ideas of what I conceive the Rents *ought* to be. but this, it seems, is not the mode which is practiced by, and most agreeable to, the people in that Country, possibly from the scarcity of money, or want [*sic*] hitherto must conform to the custom of it and of established markets. I have accordingly within the course of the last month authorized Colo. Thomas Lewis who lives at Point Pleasant (a town at the mouth of the Great Kanhawa in which I am told 30 or 40 families are settled) and which is in the center, between my several tracts to let them on the following terms. that is to say.

First. With an exemption from the payment of rent 3 years. provided in that time a reasonable quantity of land is cleared and cultivated; a comfortable House, or houses for the accomodation of a family is built and a reasonable number of fruit trees planted. And provided also (if it be customary) that the Land tax of whatever the tenant may be inclined to hold is paid by them.

Second. That after the expiration of the third year Rents shall commence and, as the custom of the Country, is to be received in the specific articles that are raised on the tenement and in the proportion of one third, by my Collector, or agent living near the premises.

Third. That under this tenure the tenant may have a certainty of holding their places (if they incline to remain and will continue to improve them) for a certain number of years (but not for lives) which may be agreed on.

Fourth. That all mines and minerals; with free egress and regress, shall be reserved. and an extra allowance made for Mill Seats, or a reservation of them if there is not.

Altho', in the hands of Industrious tenants, and a good and faithful Collector, Rents paid in this manner and proportion, would far exceed what I have required in my printed proposals, yet I must confess that it is not a pleasing thing to me to let them on these terms because there is no certainty in the revenue which will arise from it. Idle tenants will pay little, dishonest ones will cheat me, and an indolent, or speculating Collector, will make poor returns. Otherwise as I have already observed no money rents that can be fixed would be so productive, for Instance: Suppose a farm of 100 acres (which of such land is enough for any man who has only a wife and their children to assist him) and ten only of these for the land is most easily cleared, is in cultivation, Corn we will say at the expiration of the 3d. year; this it is agreed *on all hands,* will yeild from 60 to 100 Bushels to the acre, but call it 50 only, it makes 500 Bushels the 1/3 of which is 166 bushels, the demand for which in a Country whose population is encreasing every year by thousands of emigrants will hardly ever let this article be under a Shilling; but was it more than *half,* which is scarcely within the bounds of possibility, it would amount to £4.3 pr. Hundred Acres.

If Mr. Custis, or his neighbours of whom you made mention to me has any inclination to buy or rent any of my Lands here described, It would not be improper to suggest to them that the sooner something is resolved on the better; for as well formerly as lately, it has been told me, that I may soon fill my lands, with tenants agreeably to the terms on which Colo. Lewis has been empowered to grant them; and on which if nothing more pleasing to *both* parties can be agreed, Mr. Custis's neighbours may have them.

Should these circumstances, and conditions on which I have offered to sell part or Rent the whole of these lands induce Mr. Custis to take a trip by water, or land, to this place, I will shew him the plats of the several tracts, the manner in which the land lays, give him a more ample description of the advantages which attends it and if any terms can be agreed upon between us will endeavour in time to prevent the seating of them by Colo. Lewis, by whose agreements I must be bound, if he makes any, as I have given him full powers to let the Land. I am, etc.[37]

To SAMUEL POWEL

Mount Vernon, January 18, 1788.

Dear Sir: Having nothing either interesting or entertaining in this quarter to communicate, our faces being turned to the

---

[37] From the "Letter Book" copy in the *Washington Papers.*

Eastward for news I felt no inclination to give you the trouble of perusing a dull scrawl merely to acknowledge the rect. of your obliging favor of the 12th. Ulto and to thank you for the information it conveyed. hoping that in a little time something might occur more worthy of your attention but herein I am disappointed.

It is with pleasure I find that the States of Pennsylvania, New Jersey and Delaware have adopted the proposed Constitution for a fœderal Government: the two latter unanimously and the former by so large a majority. Connecticut, Massachusetts and New Hampshire come next, in the order they are mentioned and will I hope with a decision equal to those which have preceeded them give their voices in favor of it. Of Maryland there can be little doubt and tho the Constitution in this State has powerful adversaries little doubt of its adoption has a place in my mind, but in this I may be mistaken. for as I never go from home and see few besides travellers, my conjectures may be founded in error. North Carolina has, it seems, postponed the meeting of its Convention to a later period than that of Virginia which it indicates I conceive of a disposition to take the tone from hence from the States South of it, I have no information that can be relied on, except that Georgia in appointing a Convention, have accompanied the act with powers to alter or amend the Fœderal Constitution; but if a weak State with the Indians on its back and the Spaniards on its flank does not see the necessity of a General Government there must I think be wickedness or insanity in the way.

The unanimity, and generosity, with which the County of Philadelphia has been offered for the Seat of the Fœderal government by the landholders thereof, gives much weight and merit to the invitation and will probably be an inducement to others to follow the example.

I offer my best wishes and affectionate Compliments to Mrs. Powell and assurance to you of the esteem etc.[38]

*To DAVID STUART

Mount Vernon, January 18, 1788.

Dear Sir: As the enclosed will be transmitted to Mr. Custis, I will blend nothing else with it; but beg, for the reason therein assigned, that you would contrive it by the first safe conveyance.

The Certificates which I thought had been sent to you, are found. I suppose, after the list was taken, it was found unnecessary to send them, and they were, consequently, withheld.

When Mrs. Stuart was here, I informed her that Peters year, according to his own acct., which is all the acct. I have; was up at Christmas, and she would direct what was to be done with him. She answered, he might stay here till you returned, when this happened, the hurry we were both in occasioned my forgetting to mention it to you, he now awaits your orders.

Patcy[39] has been a little unwell but better. All join in love and best wishes to Mrs. Stuart and the family with Dear Sir Yr. etc.[40]

To CHARLES CARTER

Mount Vernon, January 20, 1788.

Dear Sir: Your favor of the 21st. of last month, came to my hands last night *only;* where it has been resting, or through whose hands it has passed, I know not. I wish it had reached me in time for the prevention of the hasty and indigested

---

[38] From the "Letter Book" copy in the *Washington Papers.*
[39] Martha Custis.
[40] From a photostat of the original in the possession of W. S. Johns and Cornelia Johns Grice, of Norfolk, Va.

sentiments of my former letter, going to the press. not, as I observed in my last, because I had the least repugnance to the communication of them in a proper dress accompanied with reasons for their support if any person whatever was desireous of knowing them.

You give me some reason to hope for the result of your *thoughts,* or *experiments,* on a more eligable system of agriculture. To receive it would afford me pleasure. That the one which is now in general practice (if it can be called a system) is beyond description ruinous to our lands, need no other proof of the fact than the gullied, and exhausted state of them, which is every where to be met with; but what chance is most likely to restore the land with such means as is in our power to apply which will at the sametime be productive to the Proprietor, is the question, and an important one. a question too which admits of no other satisfactory solution than such as is derived from a *course* of experiments by intelligent and observant farmers, who will combine things and circumstances together. Theoretical opinions should have no share in the determination and what is good, and profitable husbandry in one Country, may not be so in another. Articles which are very saleable in Europe might find no market in America and if produced abundantly would answer no other end than to encumber our Barns, or Graneries. Consequently two things must be engrafted into our plan: 1st. Crops which are useful on our farms, or saleable in our markets, and 2d. the intermixing these crops by such relations and with such dressings as will improve, instead of exhausting of our lands. To effect these is the great desiderata of Farming, and ought to be the pursuit of every farmer. on this ground every experiment is a treasure, and the authors of them valuable members of Society. Hence also the Societies which are formed for the encouragement, and promulgation, of these experiments in other Country's have rendered such essential services to the improved and improving States of agriculture in the old world and are so worthy of imitation in the new.

My best respects, in which Mrs. Washington joins, is offered to Mrs. Carter and your family I am, etc.[41]

To THE SECRETARY FOR FOREIGN AFFAIRS

Mount Vernon, January 20, 1788.

Dear Sir: Your goodness upon a former occasion accompanied with assurances of forwarding any despatches I might have for Europe in future is the cause of my troubling you with the letters herewith enclosed. The one for the Marquis de la Fayette contains vocabularies of the Delaware and Shawanese languages for the Empress of Russia. I beg leave, therefore, to recommend it to your particular care. To send it by Post from Havre, I am informed, would be expensive. To trust it to chance might be still worse. I leave it to your judgment, therefore, to convey it in such a manner as you shall think best.

We are locked fast in frost; expecting as soon as the weather breaks to hear what the Conventions of Connecticut and Massachusetts have resolved on, with respect to the Government which is submitted to them. The determinations of your State on this important subject seem more problematical than any other; yet, little doubt remains in my mind of the adoption of it in Virginia. I may be mistaken, for going seldom from home and seeing few besides travellers, my information may be defective. North Carolina we are told has fixed a late period for the meeting of its Convention; hence (it is not unfair to infer) they mean to take the tone from this State.

---

[41] From the "Letter Book" copy in the *Washington Papers.*

I have heard with much concern that both Mrs Jay and yourself have been indisposed. I hope you are now perfectly restored, the best wishes and most affecte. regards of Mrs. Washington and myself are presented, and I am &c.[42]

To CHARLES CARTER

Mount Vernon, January 22, 1788.

Dear Sir: I return the letters which you were so obliging as to forward to me under cover of the 17th. I am satisfied you had not agency in publishing the extract of my letter to you which is now to be traced through all the news Papers, and am sorry that I signifyed any concern on this occasion, as it has given you so much trouble.

With very great esteem and regard I am, etc.[42]

To DAVID STUART

Mount Vernon, January 22, 1788.

Dear Sir: As you have no immediate occasion for Peter in the *only* line in which he will be useful to you, I shall be very glad to keep him, as well on acct. of my Jacks, Stud Horses, Mares, etc as because he seems unwilling to part with his wife and Children.

When you are in this way (and if it is not more profitable to you, than it is to me, you had better keep out of it) he may be serviceable, but hardly in any other, as he will do nothing but peddle about the stables, and conceives it to be a kind of degredation to bestow his attention on horses of plebean birth.

With great esteem and regard I am etc.[43]

---

[42] From the "Letter Book" copy in the *Washington Papers.*
[43] The text is from the *Historical Magazine,* vol. III, p. 243.

To JAMES KEITH

Mount Vernon, January 24, 1788.

Sir: The friends of Miss Anderson;[44] and the residuary lega-
tees named, or described in the will of the deceased Colo.
Thomas Colvill are frequently applying to me; the first for
the legacy which is bequeathed to that Lady, the others (but
more particularly one who claims under the name of Shott)
to know what the residue of that Estate is.

No man can be more anxious to have all these matters finally
settled upon equitable and legal ground than I am, and so far
as my agency in the Administration of that Estate has gone
there can be no difficulty in closing the Accts., and at any moment to satisfy the claims of every one, if there is no interference by the laws which passed during the Revolution and may be
in force. In a word to do everything which I can do with safety.

Let me entreat therefore, Sir, that you would inform me.

1st. What progress you have made in the statement of these
Accts.

2d. Whether any more papers for the better illustration of
them have been handed to you by Mr. Thomas West (Son
of Mr Jno. West)? By the Revd. Mr. William West: or by any
others who have been applied to by me for this purpose?

3d. Whether you have yourself obtained any lights with respect to the Bills of Exchange which are unaccounted for, and
which I have reason to believe were applied by Mr John West
in discharge of a protested bill due to Mr Thomas Kirkpatrick?

4th. What, if any, are the impediments which oppose a final
settlement with the Court?

5th. Whether there is any prospect of overcoming them *satisfactorily?*

---

[44] Miss Harriet Rebecca Anderson.

6th. What steps, if there is no further expectation of aid from the papers of Mr. John West, ought to be taken to close them? and

7th. What measure necessary for me to adopt for my safety and Justification under such circumstances?

It will never, I fear, be more in my power to make Mr. West's Estate answerable for neglects, or misapplications (if any there be) in his administration than at present; this then is among other important reasons which makes me extremely anxious to bring this business to a close. I therefore pray that you will favor me with answers, as soon as it is convenient, to the foregoing questions, and if there is no further hope (which I am fully persuaded is the case) of aid from the heirs and Executors of Mr. John West that the Accts. maybe made up in the clearest and best manner the nature of the case will admit, and that you will be so good as to accompany them with your advice in writing in what manner I shall proceed.

1st. I submitting to the Court.

2d. In case it should appear, as has already been mentioned, that the transactions of Mr. West cannot be satisfactorily accounted for, and a consequent delinquency, what in that case is incumbent on me to do?

3d. Whether the legacy due to Miss Anderson may safely be paid? whether it ought to bear interest? and in that case, from what period?

4th. In case a surplus should be found after all the debts and legacies are paid, what mode will be best for me to adopt, and safest, in the disposal of it; so as not to defeat the Testators intentions, nor to draw myself into a scrape from the variety of claims which have been presented; some of which are now in the hands of Mr. Remney [45] of Alexandria.

---

[45] John Rumney.

And lastly I wish to know what debts, by the papers in your hands, appear to be due *to* and *from* the Estate, and what measures I had best take to obtain the former, especially in the case of the Bond from Mr. Montgomerie[46] and others. In the close investigation of this business, other matters, not herein enumerated, may occur on which your advice may be equally necessary and for which I shall be not less obliged. I am, etc.[47]

To CLEMENT BIDDLE

Mount Vernon, January 24, 1788.

Dear Sir: I wrote to you on the 3d. Ulto. and as I have not received any answer to my letter of that date, I am led to suspect that it never reached your hands; I therefore enclose you a duplicate of it.

My reason for requesting you to pay Mr Pettit £18.5.1 (as mentioned in the enclosed duplicate) when I was not certain of your having money of mine in your hands to that amount, was in consequence of his informing me, in his letter, that you had offered to discharge it at the time the Backs and Jambs were shipped, but he then declined accepting it, not knowing how far it might comport with my arrangements to do; and I likewise expected that a sum of money would, very shortly after my writing to you, have been lodged in your hands, on my account, by Thomas Smith Esqr. If you have not paid the money to Mr. Pettit and should find the smallest inconvenience in so doing I wish you to inform me of it that I may convey it to him through some other channel.

I will thank you to forward the enclosed letter to General Butler by the first safe and direct conveyance, and am etc.[48]

[H.S.P.]

---

[46] Robert Montgomerie.
[47] From the "Letter Book" copy in the *Washington Papers*.
[48] In the writing of Tobias Lear.

To JOHN RUMNEY

Mount Vernon, January 24, 1788.

Sir: In answer to your letter of the 22d. I can only, in addition to what I have formerly written to you on the subject of the claims on the surplus (if any) of the estate of the deceased Colo. Thomas Covill, say, that *I*, who in fact had very little to do in the administration of that Estate *previous* to the despute with Great Britain, and nothing during the continuation of it for the nine or ten years that I was absent, have done every thing in my power, since my return home, to bring the accts. to a close in some manner or another. To this end I have called upon the Son and Heir of Mr. John West (deceased) who was the principal acting Executor of Colo. Colvill, upon the Revd. Mr. West and Colo. George West his Brothers, the former of whom is, and the latter was (before his death) the Executors of John West. and upon Major Little, the Agent of Lord Tankerville, for all the papers and information that can throw lights on these accts. and such as I have been able to obtain; imperfect indeed they are! are placed in the hands of a Gentleman of the Law, well acquainted with this kind of business to make a proper digest and arrangement of them, which, when accomplished, will be exhibited to the Court. and then, as I mentioned in a former letter, whatever is right and proper for me to do under the will agreeable to Law, I shall do with out delay, or hesitation.

It must seem strange to persons not acquainted with the Circumstances, that a matter of this sort should lye in an unfinished state so long. The truth of the case is, that Colo. Thomas Colvill's affairs were so blended with his brother John Colvill (to whom he was sole Executor and a Legatee), and these again so entangled with debts, to the Tankerville family, also with an important sale of land made by Thomas Colvill, as Executor of John Colvill, to John Semple which involved disputes, references &c. and moreover with Law-suits in other cases, all of which together, with more exertion than I believe fell to the lott of Mr. West, could not have brought matters to a close before hostilities commenced; and the Courts of Justice were shut; after this, the death of Mr. West, and my absence (Mrs. Colvill the Executrix of the will being also dead) put an entire stop to this business; and since, the disordered state in which that Gentleman has left his papers, or rather no papers, has occasioned more trouble and vexation to me engrossed as my time is with a multitude of other matters than any private circumstance of my life has ever done to renew and bring this business if possible to a satisfactory issue. However, I am determined that the accounts and disputes shall be liquidated, and the best, or worst known without much more delay, for this purpose I have this day written to the Gentleman who is vested with all the Papers to have them adjusted upon the best ground he can take for the accomplishment of this work. I am, etc.[49]

To BENJAMIN LINCOLN

Mount Vernon, January 31, 1788.

Dear Sir: Your favor of the 9th. Inst. came to hand last evening. As you know whatever concerns your happiness and welfare cannot be indifferent to me, you will very readily believe me when I assure you that I take a feeling part in your anxiety and distress on account of your son, and most sincerely wish for his recovery.

I thank you, my dear Sir, for your observations upon the advantages, which might accrue from a settlement of the eastern

---

[49] From the "Letter Book" copy in the *Washington Papers*.

parts of your State.[50] I am very sorry to find there is likely to be so powerful an opposition to the adoption of the proposed plan of Government with you; and I am entirely of your opinion that the business of the Convention should be conducted with moderation, candor and fairness which are not incompatible with firmness; for altho', as you justly observe, the friends of the new System may bear down the opposition, yet they would never be able, by precipitate or violent measures, to soothe and reconcile their minds to the exercise of the Government, which is a matter that ought as much as possible to be kept in view, and temper their proceedings.

What will be the fate of the Constitution in this State is impossible to tell, at a period so far distant from the meeting of the Convention; my private opinion of the matter however is, that it will certainly be adopted; there is however, no doubt but the decision of other States will have great influence here particularly of one so respectable as Massachusetts. You have undoubtedly seen my sentiments upon the Constitution in an extract of a letter written by me to a Gentleman in Fredericksburg, which I find has circulated pretty generally through the papers; I had not the most distant idea of its ever appearing before the publick, for altho' I have not the least wish or desire to conceal my Sentiments upon the subject from any person living, yet, as the letter containing the paragraph alluded to was written upon several other matters quite foreign to this and intended only for that Gentleman's own inspection, I did not attend to the manner of expressing my ideas, or dress them in the language I should have done, if I had the smallest suspicion of there ever coming to the publick eye through that channel.

---

[50] Now the State of Maine.

I feel myself much obliged by your promise to inform me of whatever transpires in your convention worthy of attention and assure you that it will be gratefully received. With the sincerest regard and the most ardent desire that your distress may be removed by the recovery of your Son, I am &c.[51]

To ANDREW LEWIS

Mount Vernon, February 1, 1788.

Sir: The white Doe with which you have been pleased to present me, and which is indeed, a very great curiosity, came safe to hand, this day, for which and so obliging a mark of your attention and politeness I beg you to accept my best acknowledgments and thanks.

Doctr. Stuart informed me by letter from Richmond, that you had it in contemplation of offering me a Buffaloe calf, of which you were possessed; and desired to know if it would be acceptable. In answer, I assured him it would be very much so, as I had been endeavouring for sometime to get a pair (male and female with a view of propagating the breed for the draught)[52] and requested him to inform you thereof; but it seems you had left Richmond before my letter which was enclosed in it for your Brother Colo. Thomas Lewis who I requested, and had accordingly empowered, to rent my Lands on the G. Kanhawa, and Ohio above it. This last was, I believe, sent by a Mr. Clendenia,[53] and I should be glad to know whether it got safe to hand, and whether the Colo. will act as my agent in that Country or not; with the letter was enclosed draughts of all these Lands.

---

[51] From the "Letter Book" copy in the *Washington Papers*.
[52] Draft.
[53] George Clendinen, of Philadelphia, Pa.

Is it with you, or your Brother I hold the Burning spring and a small quantity of surrounding Land, in Partnership? What is, or can be done with it? Mr. Porter tells me you are expected at Alexa. this spring: should you fulfil your intention of coming thither I can, without a compliment assure you that I shall have great pleasure in seeing you at this place for though I have not the honor of an intimate acquaintance with you I had such with your deceased Father for whom I had a very sincere friendship and regard. I am, etc.[54]

To JOHN FOWLER

Mount Vernon, February 2, 1788.

Sir: I have received your letter of today, and in answer to it must inform you that I have no inclination to purchase the Negro fellow which you mention as I have already as many Slaves as I wish, and I cannot engage to give another, or others in exchange for him, because I do not think, it would be agreeable to their inclinations to leave their Connexions here, and it is inconsistent with my feelings to compel them. I did agree to take him from Mr. Robt. Alexander but it was in part payment of a debt which he owed me and upon any other consideration I would not receive him. I am, etc.[54]

To BURWELL BASSETT

Mount Vernon, February 3, 1788.

Dear Sir: Mr. Dandridge for reasons which he can better explain to you than I, has requested that the enclosed Bonds may be put in Suit. I beg it may be done accordingly.

---

[54]From the "Letter Book" copy in the *Washington Papers*.

Upon so great a change as has lately taken place in your career of life I ought, possibly to have begun this letter with compliments of congratulation but as they are not less sincere on account of there being made the second Paragraph of the epistle you will please to accept and present them to your lady in the manner which will be most pleasing to you both. In doing which include your Aunts.

It is unnecessary, I hope, for me to add that whenever, and at all times, that you and Mrs. Bassett can find inclination and leizure to visit your friends at Mount Vernon we shall be happy to see you at it. I am, etc.

P. S. Inform me by the first Post after this letter is received of its safe arrival that I may be relieved from any apprehension of its miscarriage.[55]

To JONATHAN TRUMBULL

Mount Vernon, February 5, 1788.

My dear Sir: I thank you for your obliging favor of the 9th. Ulto. which came duly to hand, and congratulate with you on the adoption of the new Constitution in your State by so decided a Majority and so many respectable Characters. I wish for the same good tidings from Massachusetts but the accts. from thence are not so favourable. The decision, it is even said, is problematical; arising, as I believe 9/10ths of the opposition does, from local circumstance and sinister views. The result of the deliberations in that State will have considerable influence on those which are to follow, especially in that of New York where I fancy the opposition to the form will be greatest.

Altho' an inhabitant of this State, I cannot speak with decision on the publick sentiment of it with respect to the proposed

---

[55] From the "Letter Book" copy in the *Washington Papers*.

Constitution; my private opinion however of the matter is, that it will certainly be received but in this opinion I may be mistaken. I have not been ten miles from home since my return to it from Philadelphia; I see few who do not live within that circle, except Travellers and strangers and these form opinions upon too slight ground to be relied on. The opponents of the Constitution are indefatigable in fabricating and circulating papers, reports, &c. to its prejudice; whilst the friends *generally* content themselves with the goodness of the cause and the necessity for its adoption, supposing it wants no other support.

Mrs. Washington, and others of this family with whom you are acquainted (among which is Colo. Humphries) join me in every good wish for you, Mrs. Trumbull and family and with sentiments of the sincerest regard &c.[56]

*To HENRY KNOX

Mount Vernon, February 5, 1788.

My dear Sir: Soon after my last was dispatched to you, I was favoured with the receipt of your letter of the 14th. Ult; by which, and other accts. of more recent date, I am sorry to find that the important question under deliberation in Massachusetts, stands on such precarious ground. The decision of that State will, unquestionably, have considerable influence on those which are to follow; especially on the one in which you now are; at the sametime that an unfavourable issue, will strengthen the cords of dissention in others, which have already decided.

What may be the final determination on this Subject in Virginia, is more, I believe, than any man can say with precision. Every one, with whom you converse, delivers his own sentiment as the sentiments of the State; whilst there is *no* just

---

[56] From the "Letter Book" copy in the *Washington Papers*.

criterian that *I* know of, to form a decided judgment. My own opinion of the matter is, as I observed to you in my last, that it will certainly be received; but, for the reasons then assigned, I may be mistaken; not having been from home ten miles (my journey up the river being prevented by bad weather and a slight indisposition) since I returned from Philadelphia, and from not having seen many beyond that circle, except travellers and strangers, whose means of information is too often defective to be relied on.

The poor Patriots of Holland, must either have been greatly decieved, or they have acted from weakness and precipitency. The first, I conceive to be the case, and the peculiar situation of the affairs of France, perhaps too, divisions among themselves, will acct. for it. Be this as it may, their case is pitiable.

The Navigation of this river has been stopped for near five weeks. At this moment we are locked fast by Ice, and the air of this day is amongst the keenest I ever recollect to have felt. Mrs. Washington joins me in every good wish for you and Mrs. Knox, and I am etc.

PS. Pray, if it is not a secret, who is the author, or authors of Publius?   [MS. H. S.]

To CHARLES CARTER

Mount Vernon, February 5, 1788.

Dear Sir: At length I have got *some* answer to my application for wolf dogs. I wish it were more satisfactory, but such as it is I give it, as suspence, of all situations, is the most disagreeable. The information comes from Sir Edward Newenham, a gentleman of family and fortune in Ireland, and is in these words:

I have just received a letter from your noble and virtuous friend, the Marquis de la Fayette, in which he communicates your wish to obtain a breed of the true Irish wolf dog, and desires me to procure it. I have been these several years endeavoring to get that breed without success; it is nearly annihilated. I have heard of a bitch in the north of Ireland, but not of a couple anywhere. I am also told that the Earl of Altamont has a breed that is *nearly* genuine; if he has I will procure two from him. The Marquis also wants some at his domain, where he is troubled by the wolves. If mastiffs would be of any service I could send you some large ones, which are our guard dogs; you will honor me with your commands about them. They are very fierce, faithful, and long-lived.

If, upon this information, you think I can be further useful, I shall be happy to render any service in my power. Mastiffs, I conceive, will not answer the purposes for which the wolf dog is wanted. They will guard a pen, which pen may be secured by its situation, by our dogs, and various other ways; but your object, if I have a right conception of it, is to hunt and destroy wolves by pursuit, for which the mastiff is altogether unfit. If the proper kind can be had I have no doubt of their being sent by Sir Edward, who has sought all occasions to be obliging to me. I am etc.[57]

To JAMES MADISON

Mount Vernon, February 5, 1788.

My dear Sir: I am indebted to you for several of your favors, and thank you for their enclosures. The rumours of War between France and England have subsided; and the poor Patriots of Holland, it seems, are left to fight their own Battles or negotiate, in neither case with any great prospect of advantage. They must have been deceived, or their conduct has been divided, precipitate, and weak. the former, with some blunders, have, I conceive, been the causes of their misfortunes.

I am sorry to find by yours, and other accts. from Massachusetts, that the decision of its Convention (at the time of their

[57] From a copy in the Toner Transcripts in the Library of Congress.

dates) remains problematical.[58] A rejection of the New form by that State will invigorate the opposition, not only in New York, but in all those which are to follow; at the same time that it will afford materials for the Minority in such as have adopted it, to blow the Trumpet of discord more loudly. The acceptance by a *bare* majority, tho' preferable to a rejection, is also to be deprecated. It is scarcely possible to form any decided opinion of the general sentiment of the people of this State, on this important subject. Many have asked me with anxious solicitude, if you did not mean to get into the Convention; conceiving it of indispensable necessity. Colo Mason, who returned only yesterday, has offered himself, I am told for the County of Stafford; and his friends add, he can be elected not only there, but for Prince William and Fauquier also. The truth of this I know not. I rarely go from home, and my visitors, who, for the most part are travellers and strangers, have not the best information.

At the time you suggested for my consideration, the expediency of a communication of my sentiments on the proposed Constitution, to any correspondent I might have in Massachusetts, it did not occur to me that Genl Lincoln and myself frequently interchanged letters; much less did I expect, that a hasty, and indigested extract of one which I had written, intermixed with a variety of other matter to Colo Chas Carter, in

---

[58] Madison had written (January 22): "The intelligence from Massachusetts begins to be very ominous to the Constitution. The antifederal party is reinforced by the insurgents, and by the province of Mayne, which apprehends greater obstacles to her scheme of a separate Government, from the new system than may be otherwise experienced. And according to the prospect at the date of the latest letters, there was very great reason to fear, that the voice of that State would be in the negative. The operation of such an event on this State may easily be foreseen. . . . The decision of Massachusetts either way will involve the result in this State. The minority in Penna. is very restless under their defeat. If they can get an Assembly to their wish they will endeavor to undermine what has been done there. If backed by Massts. they will probably be emboldened to make some more rash experiment. The information from Georgia continues to be favorable. The little we get from S. Carolina is of the same complexion." Madison's letter is in the *Washington Papers*.

answer to a letter I had received from him respecting Wolf dogs, Wolves, Sheep, experiments in Farming &c &c &c.[59] was then in the press, and would bring these sentiments to public view by means of the extensive circulation I find that extract has had. Altho' I never have concealed, and am perfectly regardless who becomes acquainted with my sentiments on the proposed Constitution, yet nevertheless, as no care had been taken to dress the ideas, or any reasons assigned in support of my opinion, I feel myself hurt by the publication; and informed my friend the Colonel of it. In answer, he has fully exculpated himself of the *intention,* but his zeal in the cause prompted him to distribute copies, under a prohibition (which was disregarded) that they should not go to the press. As you have seen the rude, or crude extract (as you may please to term it) I will add no more on the subject.

Perceiving that the Fœderalist, under the signature of Publius, is about to be republished, I would thank you for forwarding to me three or four Copies, one of which to be neatly bound, and inform me of the cost. Altho' we have not had many, or deep Snows yet we have since the commencement of them, had a very severe Winter; and if the cold of this day is proportionately keen with you a warm room, and a good fire will be found no bad, or uncomfortable antidote to it. With sentiments of perfect esteem etc.[60]

To CHEVALIER DE LA LUZERNE

Mount Vernon, February 7, 1788.

Sir: The Compte de Moustier your successor in office hath forwarded from New York, the letter in which you did me the

---

[59] The "Letter Book" reads at this point: "Wolves wolf-dogs Sheep, and the lord knows what else.

[60] The text is from that printed in the sales catalogue of the *Washington-Madison Papers* (McGuire Collection, 1892).

honour to bring me acquainted with the merits of that Nobleman. Since it is the misfortune of America not to be favored any longer with your residence, it was necessary, to diminish our regrets, that so worthy and respectable a character should be appointed your successor. I shall certainly be happy in cultivating his acquaintance and friendship. The citizens, from gratitude as well as from personal considerations, will, I am persuaded, treat him with the greatest respect. Congress, I doubt not, will by every means in their power desire to make his sojourn in the United States as agreeable as it possibly can be.

But, Sir, you may rest assured your abilities and dispositions to serve this Country were so well understood, and your services so properly appreciated, that the residence of no public Minister will ever be longer remembered or his absence more sincerely regretted. It will not be forgotten that you were a witness to the dangers, the sufferings, the exertions and the successes of the United States from the most perilous crises to the hour of triumph. The influence of your agency on the Cabinet to produce a co-operation and the prowess of your Countrymen co-operating with ours in the field to secure the liberties of America have made such an indelible impression on the public mind as will never be effaced. Wherever you may be, our best wishes will follow you. And such is our confidence in your disinterested friendship, that we are certain you will wish to be useful to us, in whatever Mission you may be honored by your King: it has been surmised, on I know not what authority, that there was a probability of your being employed in the Diplomatic Corps at the Court of London; should this be the case, your zeal may still find occasions of being servicable to America, and profitable to your own Country at the same time; for I conceive the commercial interests of the two nations are in many instances blended, and in opposition to those of great Britain.

By intelligence of a more recent date than that brought by the Compte de Moustier, we learn that the political clouds which threatened to burst in a storm on France and England are blown over. The poor Dutch Patriots, however, seem to have had the objects for which   [61] off (if I may use the same metaphor) by a corner of the hurricane. The Dutch Patriots, I fear have been disunited, imprudent, impetuous: and that the King of Prussia has not acted worthily or wisely; should his measures drive the Courts of Versailles and Vienna into an union of plans; should the embers of war be but imperfectly quenched, he may yet repent the timerity of intermeddling with the internal affairs of a foreign Power. In the meantime the new scene that is opened in the north, by the rupture between the Russians and Turks must call men's attention to that quarter, as it can hardly avoid producing events, which will be attended with serious, extensive, and desirable consequences.

I feel, Sir, not only for myself, but in behalf of my Country, under great obligations for the affectionate wishes you have the goodness to make with respect to the tranquillity and happiness of America. Separated as we are by a world of water from other Nations, if we are wise we shall surely avoid being drawn into the labyrinth of their politics and involved in their destructive wars.

You will doubtless have seen long before this time, the Constitution which was proposed by the Fœderal Convention for the United States. Only four States as yet (to my knowledge) have had an opportunity of acting upon it. The Pensylvania State Convention adopted it by a Majority of two to one, those of Jersey and Delaware Unanimously, and that of Connecticut by more than three to one. In Massachusetts the Convention is

---

[61] Left blank in the "Letter Book" in the *Washington Papers.*

now in session. The Merits of this Constitution have been discussed in a great variety of news paper and other Publications. A periodical Essay in the New York Gazettes, under Title of the Federalist, has advocated it with great ability. In short it seems (so far as I have been able to learn) to be a prevalent opinion, that it will have been accepted by nine States or more early in the ensuing summer. With sentiments of great respect and consideration, I have the honor &c.[62]

To ELÉONOR FRANÇOIS ÉLIE, COMTE DE MOUSTIER [63]

Mount Vernon, February 7, 1788.

Sir: I have received the letter which your Excellency did me the honor to address to me on the 24th of January, and take the earliest occasion of expressing my warmest acknowledgments for your favourable opinion as well as offering my sincerest congratulations on your safe arrival in this country. I am at the same time to return you my thanks for the trouble you had the goodness to take in conveying to me the letters of my noble friends the Marquis de la Fayette and the Chevr. de la Luzerne, indeed nothing was wanting to the pleasure afforded by their communications, but that of having received them at your hands and thereby having had an opportunity of demonstrating the promptitude of my attention to their recommendations. In the mean time I have taken the liberty (which I beg your Excellency to excuse) of remitting my answers for them to your care.

The fidelity, honour and bravery of the troops of your nation, to which I have been a witness; the enlightened sentiments

---

[62] From the "Letter Book" copy in the *Washington Papers.*
[63] Minister from France to the United States.

of patriotism and the delicate feelings of friendship which have
actuated great numbers of your compatriots, with whom I
may boast the happiness of being intimately connected; and
above all that lively interest which your illustrious Monarch
and his faithful subjects took in the success of the American
Arms and the confirmation of our Independence have en-
deared the National Character to me, and formed attachments
and left impressions which no distance in time or contingency
in event can possibly remove. Though but a private citizen
myself and in a measure secluded from the world, I am conscious the assertion will be [well] founded, while I venture to
affirm that such are the feelings and such the affections of the
American People.

Deprived of the felicity of having been able to form a personal acquaintance with your Excellency, by your arrival at a
distance: it is mine peculiarly to regret that misfortune and
earnestly to wish some favorable circumstance may hasten the
moment so desirable to me. And I pray you will be persuaded
that I should be truly happy to receive you, in the plain un-
ceremonious American style, on the banks of the Potomack.
The partial knowledge of your merits which had preceded
your advent and the very honorable testimonials of our friends
in France, added to the advantage you possess in being the
Representative of a Sovereign, (the earliest, most faithful and
most powerful Ally of these infant States) cannot fail to make
your presence extremely agreeable to Congress and the American People. Permit me to add the assurance, Sir, that your
Mission cannot be more acceptable, to, or your friendship more
flattering to any American, than to him who has the honour
to subscribe himself, Sir Yr. Excellency's &c.[64]

---

[64] From the "Letter Book" copy in the *Washington Papers*.

To MARQUIS DE LAFAYETTE

Mount Vernon, February 7, 1788.

My dear Marqs: You know it always gives me the sincerest pleasure to hear from you, and therefore I need only say that your two kind letters of the 9th and 15th of Octr. so replete with personal affection and confidential intelligence, afforded me inexpressible satisfaction. I shall myself be happy in forming an acquaintance and cultivating a friendship with the new Minister Plenipotentiary of France, whom you have commended as a "sensible and honest man;" these are qualities too rare and too precious not to merit one's particular esteem. You may be persuaded, that he will be well received by the Congress of the United States, because they will not only be influenced in their conduct by his individual merits, but also by their affection for the nation of whose Sovereign he is the Representative. For it is an undoubted fact, that the People of America entertain a grateful remembrance of past services as well as a favourable disposition for commercial and friendly connections with your Nation.

You appear to be, as might be expected from a real friend to this Country, anxiously concerned about its present political situation. So far as I am able I shall be happy in gratifying that friendly solicitude. As to my sentiments with respect to the merits of the new Constitution, I will disclose them without reserve, (although by passing through the Post offices they should become known to all the world) for, in truth, I have nothing to conceal on that subject. It appears to me, then, little short of a miracle, that the Delegates from so many different States (which States you know are also different from each other in their manners, circumstances and prejudices) should unite in forming a system of national Government, so little liable to well founded objections. Nor am I yet such an enthusiastic, partial or undiscriminating admirer of it, as not to perceive it is tinctured with some real (though not radical) defects. The limits of a letter would not suffer me to go fully into an examination of them; nor would the discussion be entertaining or profitable, I therefore forbear to touch upon it. With regard to the two great points (the pivots upon which the whole machine must move,) my Creed is simply,

1st. That the general Government is not invested with more Powers than are indispensably necessary to perform the functions of a good Government; and, consequently, that no objection ought to be made against the quantity of Power delegated to it.

2ly. That these Powers (as the appointment of all Rulers will for ever arise from, and, at short stated intervals, recur to the free suffrage of the People) are so distributed among the Legislative, Executive, and Judicial Branches, into which the general Government is arranged, that it can never be in danger of degenerating into a monarchy, an Oligarchy, an Aristocracy, or any other despotic or oppressive form, so long as there shall remain any virtue in the body of the People.

I would not be understood my dear Marquis to speak of consequences which may be produced, in the revolution of ages, by corruption of morals, profligacy of manners, and listlessness for the preservation of the natural and unalienable rights of mankind; nor of the successful usurpations that may be established at such an unpropitious juncture, upon the ruins of liberty, however providently guarded and secured, as these are contingencies against which no human prudence can effectually provide. It will at least be a recommendation to the proposed Constitution that it is provided with more checks and barriers against the introduction of Tyranny, and those of a nature less liable to be surmounted, than any Government hitherto instituted among mortals, hath possessed. We are not to expect perfection in this world; but mankind, in modern times, have apparently made some progress in the science of government. Should that which is now offered to the People of America, be found on experiment less perfect than it can be made, a Constitutional door is left open for its amelioration.

Some respectable characters have wished, that the States, after having pointed out whatever alterations and amendments may be judged necessary, would appoint another federal Convention to modify it upon those documents. For myself I have wondered that sensible men should not see the impracticability of the scheme. The members would go fortified with such Instructions that nothing but discordant ideas could prevail. Had I but slightly suspected (at the time when the late Convention was in session) that another convention would not be likely to agree upon a better form of Government, I should now be confirmed in the fixed belief that they would not be able to agree upon any System whatever. So many, I may add, such contradictory, and, in my opinion unfounded objections have been urged against the System in contemplation; many of which would operate equally against every efficient Government that might be proposed. I will only add, as a further opinion founded on the maturest deliberation, that there is no alternative, no hope of alteration, no intermediate resting place, between the adoption of this, and a recurrence to an unqualified state of Anarchy, with all its deplorable consequences.

Since I had the pleasure of writing to you last, no material alteration in the political state of affairs has taken place to change the prospect of the Constitution's being adopted by nine States or more, Pennsylvania, Delaware, New Jersey and Connecticut have already done it. It is also said Georgia has acceded. Massachusetts, which is perhaps thought to be rather more doubtful than when I last addressed you, is now in convention.

A spirit of emigration to the western Country is very predominant. Congress have sold, in the year past, a pretty large quantity of lands on the Ohio, for public Securities, and thereby diminished the domestic debt considerably. Many of your military acquaintances such as the Generals Parsons, Varnum, and Putnam, the Colos. Tupper, Sprout and Sherman, with many more, propose settling there. From such beginnings much may be expected.

The storm of war between England and your Nation, it seems, is dissipated. I hope and trust the political affairs in France are taking a favorable turn. If the Ottomans wod. suffer themselves to be precipitated into a war, they must abide the consequences. Some Politicians speculate on a triple Alliance between the two Imperial Courts and Versailles. I think it was rather fortunate, than otherwise, that the incaution of Ambassador and the rascality of a Rhinegrave prevented you from attempting to prop a falling fabric.

It gives me great pleasure to learn that the present ministry of France are friendly to America; and that Mr. Jefferson and yourself have a prospect of accomplishing measures which will mutually benefit and improve the commercial intercourse between the two Nations. Every good wish attend you and yrs. I am, &c.[65]

To BENJAMIN LINCOLN

Mount Vernon, February 11, 1788.

My dear Sir: As you must be convinced that whatever affects your happiness or welfare cannot be indifferent to me I need not tell you, that I was most sensibly affected by your letter of the 20th of January. Yes, my dear Sir, I sincerely condole with you the loss of a worthy, amiable, and valuable Son! Altho' I

---

[65] From the "Letter Book" copy in the *Washington Papers*.

had not the happiness of a personal acquaintance with him, yet the character which he sustained, and his near connexion with you, are, to me, sufficient reasons, to lament his death. It is unnecessary for me to offer any consolation on the present occasion; for to à mind like yours it can only be drawn from that source which never fails to give a bountiful supply to those who reflect justly. Time *alone* can blunt the keen edge of afflictions; Philosophy and our Religion holds out to us such hopes as will, upon proper reflection, enable us to bear with fortitude the most calamitous incidents of life and these are all that can be expected from the feelings of humanity; is all which they will yield.

I thank you my dear Sir, for the information which you forwarded me of the proceedings of your Convention. It is unhappy that a matter of such high importance cannot be discussed with that candour and moderation which would throw light on the subject and place its merits in a proper point of view; but in an assembly so large as your Convention must be and composed of such various and opposite characters, it is almost impossible but that some things will occur which would rouse the passions of the most moderate man on earth. It is however, to be hoped that your final decision will be agreeable to the wishes of good men and favourable to the Constitution. Mrs. Washington thanks you for your kind remembrance of her and joins me in the sincerest condolence for your loss. With sentiments of the highest esteem &c.[66]

To ALEXANDER SPOTSWOOD

Mount Vernon, February 13, 1788.

Dear Sir: Your favor of the 20th. Ult, accompanied by a bag of Seeds, did not get to my hands untill the middle of last week

---

[66] From the "Letter Book" copy in the *Washington Papers*.

or it should have received an earlier acknowledgment; as you now do my thanks for the latter.

I feel myself obliged by the measures you have pursued to stock me with Turnip seed; but if I am *tolerably* lucky, I shall raise a sufficiency from seed sent me by Arthur Young Esqr.; many hundreds of the Turnips being set out for that purpose: injudiciously tho' I fear, as they will be exposed to Poultry, especially Turkies, a circumstance that did not occur to me when I made choice of the spot (in other respects favourable) for the transplantation of them. I am not less obliged to you for the offer of spring Wheat; but a little of this also I got from England, from the same Gentleman, Mr. Young, together with winter Vetch, Sainfoin and other seeds. But from neglect too common among Master's of Vessels (of stowing them in the hold) I fear vegitation in most of them is injured, if not entirely destroyed. This was the case *nearly* with a little wheat, the Sainfoin and some other seeds which were imported and sown last Autumn. With care and attention however I may, possibly raise a little from each in which case I shall be very ready to oblige you in my turn. Exchanges, and Services of this kind, are what Farmers owe to one another; and in the practice of which I should feel much pleasure.

I think with you that the life of a Husbandman of all others is the most delectable. It is honorable. It is amusing, and, with judicious management, it is profitable. To see plants rise from the Earth and flourish by the superior skill, and bounty of the laborer fills a contemplative mind with ideas which are more easy to be conceived than expressed.

I am glad to find that your first essay to raise Indian Corn in drills has succeeded as much to your satisfaction; but I am inclined to think, unless restoratives were more abundant than they are to be found on Common farms, that 6 feet by 2 will be too oppressive to your land. Experience has proved that every soil will sink under the growth of this plant; whether from the luxuriancy and exhausting quality of it, or the manner of tillage or from both, is not *very* certain, because instead of 2420 plants which stand on an Acre at six feet square, with two stalks in a hill (as is usual in land of middling quality,) you have 3630 at 6 feet by 2, single stalks. How far the exposing of land to the rays of the Sun in Summer is injurious, is a question yet more difficult to solve than the other. My own opinion of the matter is, that it does; but this controverts the practice of Summer fallows, which (especially in heavy land) some of the best practical Farmers in England contend for as indispensably necessary notwithstanding the doctrine of Mr. Young, and many others who are opposed to them.

The reason, however, which induced me to give my Corn rows the wide distance of ten feet, was not because I thought it essential to the growth of that *plant,* but because I introduced other plants between them. And this practice, from the experience of two years, one the wettest, and the other the driest that ever was felt on my Estate, I am resolved to continue untill the inutility of it, or something more advantageous, shall point out the expediency of a change; but I mean to practise it with variations, fixing on 8 by 2 feet as the medium, or standing distance which will give more plants by 300 to the acre, than six feet each way with two stalks in a hill will do.

As all my Corn will be thus drilled, so between all, I mean to put in, drills also, Potatoes, Carrots (as far as my seed will go) and Turnips alternately; that not one sort, more than another, may have the advantage of Soil; thereby to ascertain the comparative quantity, and value of each of these plants as food for horses and stock of every kind. From the trials I have made (under the disadvantages already mentioned) I am well satisfied that my crop of Corn in this way, will equal the yield of the same fields in the usual mode of cultivation, and that the quantity of Potatoes (proportionate to the number of Rows) will quadruple the Corn. I entertain the same opinion with respect to Carrots, but being more unlucky in the latter, I cannot speak with so much confidence, and still less can I do it with respect to Turnips.

From this husbandry, and statement then of what I conceive to be facts, any given number of acres will yield as much Corn in the *new* as they will in the *old* way, and will, moreover, with *little* or *no* extra labour produce four times as many Potatoes or Carrots, which adds considerably to the profit from the field but here it may be asked if the land will sustain these Crops, or rather the Potatoes in addition to the Corn. This is a question my own experience does not enable me to answer. The received opinion of many practical Farmers in England is, that Potatoes and Carrots are ameliorators, not exhausters of the Soil; preparing it well for other Crops. But I do not scruple to confess, that notwithstanding the profit which appears to result from the growth of Corn and Potatoes, or Corn and Carrots, or both, thus blended, my wish is to exclude Indian Corn altogether from my system of Cropping, but we are so habituated to the use of this grain, and it is so much better for negroes than any other, that it is not to be discarded; consequently to introduce it in the most profitable, or least injurious manner, ought to be the next consideration with the Farmer.

To do this, some are of opinion that a small spot, set apart *solely* for the purpose, and kept highly manured, is the best method. And an instance in proof, is adduced of a gentleman near Baltimore, who for many years past from the same ground has not made less than ten Barrels to the Acre in Drills, 6 feet apart, and (if I recollect rightly) 18 Inches in the rows. But quæry, where the Farmer has no other resource than the manure of his own Farm, will not his other crops be starved by this extra allowance to the Indian Corn? I am inclined to think it will; and for that reason I shall try the intermixture of Potatoes, Carrots and Turnips, or either (as from practice shall be found most profitable) with my Corn, which shall become a component part of some regular, and systematic plan best adapted to the nature of my soil.

To Societies which have been formed for the encouragement of agriculture, is the perfection to which husbandry is now arrived in England indebted. Why then does not this Country (Virginia I mean) follow so laudable and beneficial an example? and particularly why do not the gentlemen in the vicinity of Fredericksburg begin this Work? Your lands are peculiarly well adapted for it. There are more of you, in a small circle than I believe is to be found in the same compass almost anywhere. And you are well able to afford experiments; from which and not from theory are individuals to derive useful knowledge, and the Public a benefit. My love, to which Mrs. Washington's is joined, is presented to Mrs. Spotswood and I am, &c.[67]

To PETERSON & TAYLOR

Mount Vernon, February 15, 1788.

Gentn: I have received your letter of the 13 inst. and am sorry to find that my bill of Scantling has not yet been forwarded to the Eastern Shore. I should have thought, notwithstanding the communication by water was stopped, that it might have been conveyed by land. I am now, in a manner reduced to the necessity of depending upon you for Scantling, because I have, in expectation of being supplied by you,

---

[67] From the "Letter Book" copy in the *Washington Papers*.

employed my own Carpenters in other matters when they would have been preparing it.

As the River is now open I should imagine that it might be delivered much sooner than you mention in your letter; if it should not, I shall sustain a great injury, to say nothing of the disappointment. I am, etc.[68]

To WILLIAM IRVINE

Mount Vernon, February 18, 1788.

Sir: I have to acknowledge the receipt of your favor of the 27th. Ulto. and to thank you for the information contained in it. As a Communication between the waters of lake Erie and those of the Ohio is a matter, which promises great public utility, and as every step towards the investigation of it may be considered as promoting the general interest of our Country I need make [no] apology to *you* for any trouble, that I have given upon this subject.

I am fully sensible that no account can be sufficiently accurate to hazard any operations upon without an actual survey. My object in wishing a solution of the Quæries proposed to you, was that I might be enabled to return Answers, in some degree satisfactory, to several Gentlemen of distinction in foreign Countries who have applied to me for information on the subject in behalf of others who [wish] to engage in the fur trade, and at the same time to gratify my own curiosity and assist me in forming a judgment of the practicability of opening a communication should it ever be seriously in contemplation.

1st. Could a channel once be opened to convey the Fur, Peltry &c. from the lakes into the Eastern Country, its advantages would be so obvious as to induce an opinion that it would,

---

[68] From the "Letter Book" copy in the *Washington Papers*.

in a short time, become the channel of conveyance for much the greatest part of the commodities brot. from thence.

2d. The trade, which has been carried on between New York and that quarter is subject to great inconveniences from the length of the Commun. number of Portages, and at seasons from Ice; yet it has, notwithstanding, been prosecuted with success.

I shall feel myself much obliged by any further information that you may find time and inclination to communicate to me on this head. I am etc.[69]

*To JAMES WILKINSON

Mount Vernon, February 20, 1788.

Sir: I have received your letter of the 30th. of December,[70] written at George-Town. I am very sorry that your business was so pressing as to deprive me of the pleasure of seeing you at this place, while you was in the neighbourhood of it.

Doctor Stuart handed me the Indian fabricks which you did me the honor to send by him, and for which I beg you to accept of my warmest thanks. Altho' they are not novel to me, yet the sight of them will undoubtedly be highly pleasing to those who have never before had an opportunity of seeing work of this kind; and peculiarly gratifying to the curiosity of an European. I regret the loss of the Seeds, having long been endeavouring to possess myself of the curious shrubs of the Western Country, but sincerely congratulate you on your own fortunate escape.

I feel myself much obliged, Sir by the offer of your Services which you are so polite as to make me, and shall always retain a grateful remembrance of them. My compliments if you please to Mrs. Wilkinson. With much esteem I am etc.

[CH.H.S.]

---

[69] From the "Letter Book" copy in the *Washington Papers*.
[70] Not now found in the *Washington Papers*.

*To SAMUEL GRIFFIN

Mount Vernon, February 20, 1788.

Dear Sir: I have been duly honored and gratefully affected with the receipt of the Resolution of the Visitors and Governors of William and Mary College, appointing me Chancellor of the same; and have to thank you for your polite attention in the transmission. Not knowing particularly what duties, or whether any active Services are immediately expected from the person holding the Office of Chancellor; I have been greatly embarrassed in deciding upon the public answer proper to be given. It is for that reason I have chosen to explain in this private communication my situation and feelings; and to defer an ultimate decision until I shall have been favored with farther information on this subject.

My difficulties are briefly these. On the one hand, nothing in this world could be farther from my heart than a want of respect for the worthy Gentlemen in question; or a refusal of the appointment with which they have honored me, provided its duties are not incompatible with the mode of life to which I have entirely addicted myself. And on the other hand, I would not for any consideration disappoint the just expectations of the Convocation; by accepting an Office, whose functions I previously knew (from my pre-engagements and occupations) I should be absolutely unable to perform.

Although, as I observed before, I know not specifically what these functions are, yet, Sir, I have conceived that a principal duty required of the Chancellor might be a regular and indispensable Visitation once or perhaps twice a year. Should this be expected, I must decline accepting the Office. For, notwithstanding I most sincerely and ardently wish to afford whatever little influence I may possess, in patronizing the cause of

Science, I cannot, at my time of life and in my actual state of retirement, persuade myself to engage in new and extensive avocations.

Such being the *Sentiment* of a heart unaccustomed to disguise; I flatter myself the candid manner in which I have explained it, could not be displeasing to the Convocation; and that the intervening delay, between the *present* and the *moment* in which I shall have the pleasure of receiving such ulterior explanations as may enable me to give a *definitive answer* will not prove very detrimental to the Collegiate interests. With great esteem etc.[71]

To EMBREE & SHOTWELL

Mount Vernon, February 22, 1788.

Gentleman: I have received your letter of the 28th. Ulto. enclosing an Invoice of the Seeds shipped on board the Sloop Molly Beverly on my account which have since safety arrived.

The amount of your bill will be paid you by the House of Murray, Mountford & Bowen at New York.

The quality of the seeds cannot be determined till I have an opportunity of trying them, but let them turn out as they may, I dare say there has been nothing wanting on your part to procure those of the best quality for me. I am, etc.[72]

To CLEMENT BIDDLE

Mount Vernon, February 22, 1788.

Dear Sir: If this letter should get to your hand in time, I beg you would send me five bushels of good clean and fresh red Clover and likewise of Timothy seed by the [first?] Vessel

---

[71] From a photostat of the original kindly furnished by George A. Ball, of Muncie, Ind. (See Washington's letter to Samuel Griffin, Apr. 30, 1788, *post*.)

[72] From the "Letter Book" copy in the *Washington Papers*.

which you say would leave your Port for Alexandria after the Navigation would be open.

By a letter which I have just received from Mr. Smith of Carlisle dated the 5th. Inst. I am informed that he had at that time £200 of my money in his hands and would send it to you by the first safe conveyance. out of this please to pay yourself.

I will write more fully to you in a few days interim. I am etc.[73]

To REVEREND JOHN LATHROP[74]

Mount Vernon, February 22, 1788.

Sir: I have received your letter of the 28th. Ulto. accompanied by the three pamphlets which you did me the honor to send me. You will do me the favor, Sir, to accept of my best thanks for the mark of polite attention in forwarding your discourses to me.

The one delivered before the Humane Society is upon a subject highly interesting to the feelings of every benevolent mind. The laudable view of Institutions of this nature do honor to humanity. The beneficence resulting from them is not confined to any particular class or nation; it extends its influence to the whole race of mankind and cannot be too much applauded. I am etc.[75]

To MARQUIS DE CHARTIER DE LOTBINIÈRE

Mount Vernon, February 22, 1788.

Sir: I have been honored by the receipt of your letter of the 27th. Ulto. and am sorry to find, by it, that you have been so violently attacked by the tertium ague. I hope the bad effects

---

[73] From the "Letter Book" copy in the *Washington Papers*.
[74] Of Boston, Mass.
[75] In the writing of Tobias Lear. From a photostat of the original, through the kindness of Judge E. A. Armstrong, of Princeton, N. J.

of it are removed before this, and that you will not be afflicted by any returns of it.

I am very happy to find that matters have been adjusted between the Courts of Versailles and London without coming to an open rupture; for notwithstanding the exploits that may be performed or the eclat which may be acquired by military operations, yet the effects of war must be sincerely regreted by every humane and feeling mind.

I thank you, Sir, for your politness in offering me the services of the young Gentleman, your relation, who is at present with you, as my Aid de Camp; I have not the smallest doubt but his abilities and dispositions are such as would do him credit in any post, but, Sir, I must decline the honor which you would do me, for, at the close of the war, I resigned my military employments and quitted publick life, I have, therefore, no occasion for the services of an Aid de Camp, and I hope that a continuance of peace in this Country will render them unnecessary at any future period. I have the Honor etc.[76]

To THOMAS SMITH

Mount Vernon, February 22, 1788.

Sir: I have, at this late period, to acknowledge the rect. of your letter of the 22d. of May last. The reason of my not doing it in course, was not owing to any neglect or inattention on my part, but to the want of knowing that it was in my hands, for I received the Title papers of my land in Washington County which you sent to me in Philadelphia, and not expecting that anything was contained in the enclosure more than those, I delay'd opening it till a few days since.

---

[76] In the writing of Tobias Lear. From a photostat of the original kindly furnished by the Bostonian Society.

I have forwarded the letter to Mr. Bushrod Washington which was under the same cover with my papers; but I expect the contents of it have been anticipated by a letter from you since that time.

You have undoubtedly recd. a letter from me before this, requesting you to retain whatever you consider as a compensation for the trouble of yourself and Mr. Ross in prosecuting my land suit, out of the money which you may recover on my acct. from the bonds in your hands and transmit the residue to Clement Biddle Esqr. in Philadelphia. I am, etc.[77]

To SIR EDWARD NEWENHAM

Mount Vernon, February 24, 1788.

Dear Sir: I have been favored with your letter of the 10th. of Augt. and am very sorry to find, by it, that your intended voyage to this Country was prevented, and especially after you had made your arrangements and was upon the point of sailing; the cause of your detention must have made it still more displeasing to you, for, of all the vexations in life, that of a tedious and perplexing Lawsuit is the most disagreeable. I am, however, in hopes that your visit is not wholly given up, but only postponed.

You will be so good, my dear Sir, as to inform your friend Colo. Persse that I have a grateful sense of the favourable sentiments which he entertains of me, and present my best thanks to him for the Hay seed and Goosebury bushes which he is so polite as to propose sending me.

I must beg that you would not put yourself to any trouble or inconvenience in obtaining the wolf dogs for me, for however desirious I may be to procure a breed of them, I should

---

[77] From the "Letter Book" copy in the *Washington Papers*.

think they were too dearly purchased if you met with any difficulty in getting them.

At the same time you complain of having been deluged by incessant rains, we were, in this part of the continent, distressed by the opposite extreme. The drought, in this neighbourhood, was as severe last summer and fall as was ever known in the memory of man; The Grass and small grain were greatly injured by it; and the Indian Corn, in some places, almost entirely cut off. My farms were among the number of those which felt it in its greatest severity, but, happily, it was not general. The middle and eastern States had favourable seasons and food crops. A very severe winter has added to the inconvenience of short crops. We have since Christmas, experienced a series of cold weather which is very seldom felt in this climate, the navigation of our Rivers has been stopped by the frost since the first of January.

I thank you, my dear Sir, for your information upon the general State of politics in Europe; and would, in return, give you some account of our public affairs here had anything of importance transpired since my last letter to you of the   of   . I can only say that we are still in a state of expectation, waiting the result of the State Convention relative to the proposed plan of Government. Six States only have as yet decided upon it; they are favourable. The convention of new Hampshire is now in session. The most formidable opposition to it is expected to come from New York and Virginia; but as nine States will have determined upon it (and in all probability adopted it) before their Conventions take place, it is expected that its opponents in those States will not have sufficient influence to prevent its adoption there when it is found to be the general voice of the continent. Rhode Island has discovered some symptoms of recovering from her delirium; the papers mention the votes of several towns instructing their delegates in the legislature to have a convention of the People for the purpose of considering the proposed constitution.

Mrs. Washington joins me in Compliments to Lady Newenham and yourself. I am, etc.[78]

To BENJAMIN LINCOLN

Mount Vernon, February 28, 1788.

My dear Sir: I have to acknowledge the receipt of your three letters of the 3d. 6th and 9th inst. The information conveyed by the last was extremely pleasing to me, though I cannot say it was altogether unexpected, as the tenor of your former letters had, in some measure, prepared me for the event; but the conduct of the minority was more satisfactory than could have been expected. The full and fair discussion, which you gave the subject in your convention, was attended with the happiest consequences; it afforded complete information to all those who went thither with dispositions to be informed, and at the same time gave an opportunity to confute, and point out the fallacy of those specious arguments which were offered in opposition to the proposed Government. Nor is this all. The conciliating behaviour of the minority will strike a damp on the hopes which opponents in other States might, otherwise have formed from the smallness of the majority, and must be greatly influential in obtaining a favourable determination in those States which have not yet decided upon it.

There is not perhaps a man in Virginia less qualified than I am, to say from his own knowledge and observation, what will be the fate of the Constitution here, for I very seldom ride beyond the limits of my own farms, and am wholly indebted

---

[78] From the "Letter Book" copy in the *Washington Papers*.

to those gentlemen who visit me for any information of the disposition of the people towards it; but from all I can collect I have not the smallest doubt of its being accepted.

I thank you, my dear Sir, for the accounts which you have, from time to time, transmitted me since the meeting of your convention, nothing could have been more grateful or acceptable to me, I am also obliged by your promise to inform me of any important matters, that may transpire, and you know I shall, at all times be happy to hear of your welfare. Mrs. Washington joins me in compliments to Mrs. Lincoln and yourself. With the greatest esteem &c.[79]

To CALEB GIBBS

Mount Vernon, February 28, 1788.

Sir: I have received your letter of the 9th. inst. accompanied by the papers which you was so polite as to send me. I must beg you to accept my thanks for your attention in forwarding to me the pleasing decision of your convention upon the proposed Government. The candid and conciliating behavour of the minority places them in a more favourable point of view than the debates of the Convention gave room to expect, and sufficiently shews the good effects of the full and fair discussion which the subject met with.

The adoption of the Constitution in Massachusetts will, I presume, be greatly influential in obtaining a favourable determination upon it in those States where the question is yet to be agitated.[80]

No person can, at this moment pretend to say what *will* be its fate here, and I am perhaps less qualified to give an opinion

---

[79] From the "Letter Book" copy in the *Washington Papers*.
[80] The Massachusetts convention on Feb. 6, 1788, ratified the Constitution by a vote of 187 to 168.

upon it, from my own observation, than almost anyone, as I very seldom ride off my farms, and am indebted to Gentlemen who call upon me for any information which I have of the disposition of the people towards it, but from what I can collect, I have no doubt of its being accepted here. I am, etc.[81]

*To RUFUS KING

Mount Vernon, February 29, 1788.

Sir: I have received the letter with which you were pleased to honor me from Boston, and pray you to accept my thanks for and congratulations on, the important information it contains.

Happy, am I, to see the favorable decision of your Convention upon the proposed Government; not only on acct. of its adding an important State to the number of those which have already accepted it, but because it must be productive of good effects in other States, whose determination may have been problematical. The candid, and open behaviour of the minority, is noble and commendable. It will have its weight.

From my own knowledge, I cannot undertake to say what will be the fate of the Constitution in this State. I am altogether indebted to Gentlemen who visit me for information respecting the disposition of the people towards it, not having gone Six Miles beyond the limits of my own farms since my return from Philadelphia. From there accounts, no doubt, from the first, has been entertained in my mind of the acceptance of it here; notwithstanding the *indefatigable* pains which some very influencial characters take to oppose it.

I beg you to present me in respectful terms to Mrs. King, and to receive assurances of the esteem and regard with which I have the honor etc.   [N.Y.H.S.]

---

[81] From the "Letter Book" copy in the *Washington Papers*.

To EDMUND PENDLETON

Mount Vernon, March 1, 1788.

Sir: When Doctor Stuart was in Richmond I sent a number of public securities to him that he might receive the interest due upon them; among them was a Certificate for a Negro executed in the year with Interest due from the date, which he informs me he left in your hands to have the Interest paid thereon and transmitted to me as it could not be done while he was there. As I find, by the Revenue act, that the Interest drawn upon Certificates of this kind will be received in taxes for the year 1787, I shall be much obliged to you Sir, if you will take the trouble to have every thing which is necessary to be transacted respecting the matter done, and transmitted to me as I expect a visit from the Sheriff very soon. I am etc.[82]

To ANTHONY SINGLETON

Mount Vernon, March 1, 1788.

Sir: Two of the enclosed Certificates dated Jany. 4th. 1788 were received at the Auditors office on my acct. by Doctor Stuart when he was in Richmond, but as he was, by some means or other, prevented from having the necessary business respecting them transacted at the Treasurer's Office before he left that place, and has informed me that you will be so good as to do whatever is proper to be done respecting them, I have taken the liberty of sending them to you, requesting that you will be so kind as to return them to me compleated, as soon as possible, because I depend upon them for discharging a part of my taxes of the year 1787.

---

[82]From the "Letter Book" copy in the *Washington Papers*.

I have likewise enclosed to you five others recd. in the year 1786. as I see they are of the same tenor And I suppose require the same to be done with them as the above two. These last mentioned warrants have laid by me since their dates. I am so little acquainted with matters of this kind that I hardly know the use of them, much less the necessary forms they must pass before they are receivable in taxes. I am, etc.[83]

A DESCRIPTIVE LIST OF AUDITORS WARRANTS SENT TO TREASURERS OFFICE DIRECTED TO CAPTAIN SINGLETON [83]

March 1, 1788.

	£.	S.	d.
One dated—18th. Apl. 1786 for Interest due on a Loan office certificate—No. 237, dated 24 June, 1780 for	17	16	4
One dated—29 Novr. 1786 for sundry articles furnished for the use of the Mila. in the year 1774 allowed by the Court of claims in Fairfax County	20	0	0
One ditto ditto ditto for	20	0	0
One ditto ditto ditto for	20	0	0
One ditto ditto ditto for	27	16	6
One dated Jany. 4th. 1788 for Interest on a Lone Office Certificate, No. 252 dated 26th. March 1779 for	43	4	10
One dated Jany. 4th. 1788 for Interest on a lone office Certificate, No. 237, dated 24th. June 1780 for	6	9	0
	£155.	5.	8

To JAMES MADISON

Mount Vernon, March 2, 1788.

Sir: The decision of Massachusetts, notwithstanding its concomitants,[84] is a severe stroke to the opponents of the proposed

---

[83] From the "Letter Book" copy in the *Washington Papers*.
[84] Massachusetts accompanied her ratification with 9 proposed amendments.

Constitution in this State; and with the favorable determinations of the States which have gone before, and such as are likely to follow after, will have a powerful operation on the Minds of Men who are not actuated more by disappointment, passion and resentment, than they are by moderation, prudence and candor.[85] Of the first description however, it is to be lamented that there are so many; and among them, *some* who would hazard *every* thing rather than their opposition should fail, or have the sagacity of their prognostications impeached by an issue contrary to their predictions.

The determination you have come to,[86] will give pleasure to your friends. From those in your County you will learn with more certainty than from me, the expediency of your attending the election in it. With *some,* to have differed in sentiment, is to have passed the Rubicon of their friendship, altho' you should go no further. With others (for the honor of humanity) I hope there is more liberality; but the consciousness of having discharged that duty which we owe to our Country, is superior to all other considerations, will place small matters in a secondary point of view.

His Most Ch—n M—y speaks, and acts in a style not very pleasing to republican ears or to republican forms; nor do I think this language is altogether so to the temper of his own subjects at *this* day. Liberty, when it begins to take root, is a plant of rapid growth. The checks he endeavors to give it, however warrantable by ancient usage, will, more than probably, kindle a flame, which may not be easily extinguished; tho' for a while it may be smothered by the Armies at his command, and the Nobility in his interest. When the people are oppressed with Taxes, and have cause to suspect that there has

---

[85] The "Letter Book" copy reads: "who are are not more influenced by passion, Peak and resentment, than they are by candor, moderation and Judgement."
[86] To stand for election as a delegate to the convention for ratifying the Constitution.

been a misapplication of their money, the language of despotism is but illy brooked. This, and the mortification which the pride of the Nation has sustained in the affairs of Holland (if one may judge from appearances) may be productive of events which prudence will not mention.

To-morrow, the Elections for delegates to the Convention of this State commences; and as they will tread close upon the heels of each other this month becomes interesting and important. With the most friendly sentiments and affectionate regard &c.[87]

To THE SECRETARY FOR FOREIGN AFFAIRS

Mount Vernon, March 3, 1788.

Dear Sir: In acknowledging the rect. of your obliging favor of the 3d. Ult, permit me to thank you for the Rhubarb seed which accompanied it. To the growth of which, if food, a fair trial shall be given.

I have two imported female Asses from the Island of Malto; which, tho' not quite equal to the best spanish Jennies will serve to establish a valuable breed of these animals in this Country, besides, I have disseminated the breed of my spanish Jack to many of the still small kind of this Country, and if you have one of these or a better Jenny and should think the trouble of sending her here not too great she shall have the free use of the Jack and every necessary attention, and I shall have great pleasure in obliging you by it.

I was not unapprised of the treatment of letters in the post Offices of France but am not less obliged by the Friendly hint you have given me respecting this matter, mine contain nothing

---

[87] From the printed text in the sales catalogue of the *Washington-Madison Papers* (McGuire Collection, 1892).

which will be injurious to the receiver if the contents of them are inspected.

The decision of Massachusetts would have been more influencial had the majority been greater, and the ratification unaccompanied by the recommendatory Act. As it stands the blow is severely felt by the antifederalists in the equivocal States. This adoption added to the five States which have gone before it, and the three which more than probable will *next* follow, will (as there can be little doubt of Rhode Island following the example of her Eastern brethren) be too powerful I conceive for locality and sophistry to combat.

On this day, our elections of Delegates to the Convention of the State, commences, they will progress as our Court days in this month arrive, and form an interesting epocha in our Annals. After the choice is made, the probable decision on the proposed Constitution (from the character of members) can with more ease be conjectured; for myself I have never entertained much doubt of its adoption tho' I am a very incompetent Judge, never having been Six miles beyond the limits of my own Farms since my return from Philadelphia and receiving information of the sentiments of the people from visitors *only.*

It gives me much pleasure to hear that Mrs. Jays health is restored, and that you have the slight remains only of your long and painful indisposition, a little time and more moderate weather (if it should ever arrive, for at present there is no appearance of it) will, it is to be hoped, set you quite right again. In wishes for these, and offering compliments, I am Joined by Mrs. Washington with sentiments of the highest esteem and regard. I am, etc.[88]

---

[88] From the "Letter Book" copy in the *Washington Papers.*

To CLEMENT BIDDLE

Mount Vernon, March 3, 1788.

Dear Sir: If this should reach you before the sailing of the vessel which you informed me in your last was bound to Alexandria, I must request you to put on board her, on my acct. two good Linnen Wheels, one dozn. good strong wool Cards with [strong] teeth, and one hundred pounds of Clover seed in addition to the quantity which I have before desired you get. I am etc.

PS. Pray send me as soon as you conveniently can 40 yards of Lace, of the width and colour of the enclosed; that, or any other figure will do.[89]   [H. S. P.]

To HENRY KNOX

Mount Vernon, March 3, 1788.

My dear Sir: I pray you to accept my acknowledgments of your favors of the 10th. and 14th Ulto. and congratulation on the acceptance of the new Constitution by the State of Massachusetts. Had this been done without its concomitants, and by a larger Majority the stroke would have been more severely felt by the antifederalists in other States. As it is, it operates as a damper to their hopes, and is a matter of disappointment and chagreen to them all.

Under the circumstances enumerated in your letters, the favourable decision, which has taken place in that State, could hardly have been expected; Nothing less than the good sense, sound reasoning, moderation and temper of the Supporters of the measure, could have carried the question. It will be very influential on the equivocal States. In the two, which are next

---

[89] In the writing of Tobias Lear. The P. S. is in the writing of Washington.

to convene (New Hampshire and Maryland) there can be no doubt of its adoption and in So. Carolina but little, which will make nine States without a dissentient; the force of this argument is hardly to be resisted by local sophistry; candor and prudence therefore, it is to be hoped will prevail, and yet I believe there are some characters among us who would hazard *every* thing rather than cease their opposition or leave to the operation of the government the chance of proving the fallacy of their predictions of it, by which their sagacity and foresight might be impeached.

This day introduces the Elections for the Convention of this State, and they will progress regularly thro' the month as the Court days arrive. After which a more accurate opinion may be formed of the probable decision of the State.

From the last European intelligence, the Political state of affairs in France seem to be in a delicate Situation; what will be the issue is not easy to determine; but the spirit, which is diffusing itself may produce changes in that Government which a few years ago could hardly have been dreamt of. All these things, together with the importance assumed by G. B. on the occasion of her dispute with this power and the state of other powers on the Continent are strong additional motives for us to establish a well-toned Government. Mrs. Washington joins me in every good wish for you, Mrs. Knox and the family; and with sentiments of the most friendly and etc.[90]

To I. HUIBERTS [91]

Mount Vernon, March 3, 1788.

Sir: I have received your polite letter of the 22d. Ulto., and am much obliged to you for the kind tender of your services to

---

[90] From the "Letter Book" copy in the *Washington Papers*.
[91] Of Baltimore, Md.

execute any commissions for me in Holland; but as I have no business, at present in that quarter I cannot avail myself of your obliging offer, I have however, a no less grateful sense of it on that acct. You will please, Sir, to accept my best wishes for a safe voyage, a prosperous completion of your business in Europe, and a happy return to this Country. Mrs. Washington and the rest of the family Join in this wish. I am, etc.[92]

To RICHARD PETERS

Mount Vernon, March 5, 1788.

Sir: When I had the pleasure to be at your house last Summer you shewed me a triangular harrow with trowel tines for the purpose of cultivating your dell Crops. The appearance was prepossessing. But I forgot whether you spoke of its merits from theoretical, or practical knowledge. If the latter, will you permit me to request the favor of you to direct your workmen to furnish me with one, compleat in all its parts accompanied with lines or trowells sufficient for 4 more. Colo. Biddle will pay the cost, upon demand.

That you may be enabled to Judge of the proper sizes, I will inform you for what particular uses they are intended.

From the experience of two years, one the wettest, the other the dryest that ever was felt in *this* neighbourhood I am persuaded that as much (Indian) Corn can be raised in rows as in any manner which has yet been tried in such (midling) land and with such management as is usually allowed for this Grain and that by drilling Potatoes between, the quantity of the latter will at least quadruple that of the former. whether Potatoes in addition to the Corn will bear too hard upon the soil is a question, that has received an affirmative and negative answer. and both (it is said) from the experience of

---

[92] From the "Letter Book" copy in the *Washington Papers*.

Husbandry. I mean therefore to learn that which seems most profitable and in the practice of which I am already engaged. These Harrows then are to work the intervals between the Corn and Potatoes; which being 4 feet *only,* the dimensions of them must be proportioned to the space they are to operate in. But, notwithstanding the levelness of my land, the straitness and equi-distance of my rows, it would seem nevertheless dangerous to depend upon a *single* bout of this implement because if perchance the width between the Rows should exceed 4 feet the ground will not be broken, and if it falls short the plants will be cut up; twice therefore in each Row, seems necessary for safe and proper tillage. I mention it for your consideration only; my own opinion of the matter I must confess is (but it yields to experiance) that two feet from the center of the hindmost lines would be a proper Medium; this, with the outer lines of the trowel, will stir near, or quite 2½ feet of earth; and under certain circumstances may be sufficient without going twice in the same row, for cultivation of the plants; at all events, two bouts will give part of it a double stirring.

I will not trouble you with an apology for this request as it affords an opportunity to Mrs. Washington and myself to present our best wishes to Mrs. Peters and yourself and an occasion for me to assure you of the esteem with which I am, etc.[93]

To THOMAS SMITH

Mount Vernon, March 5, 1788.

Sir: Your letter of the 5th. Ulto. came duly to hand. The sum of £50 which you and Mr. Ross have received for bringing and prosecuting my Ejectments is perfectly satisfactory to me; I only wish it may be so to you, if it is not I must repeat my request that you will satisfy yourself.

---

[93] From the "Letter Book" copy in the *Washington Papers.*

I find that the greatest part of the money which you have received on my acct. has been paid without suits being brought as in this case you have all the trouble of a collector, without the benefit of a Lawyer, it is my wish that you would retain whatever is the customary commission for collecting, or receive a compensation for your trouble in some other way.

Major Freeman, in a letter to me before he left Fayette County, mentioned his having deposited in the hands of a Mr. Richd. Noble at Red-Stone about £30 for me and sundry papers which he was to forward to me. I have written to him twice upon the subject but have recd. no answer, I will, therefore, be much obliged to you, Sir, if you will get them from Mr. Noble whenever you are again in that part of the Country, and convey them to me. I am, etc.[94]

To CLEMENT BIDDLE

Mount Vernon, March 5, 1788.

Dear Sir: In your letter of the 3d of February you mentioned Messrs. Dunlap and Claypole having put into your hands a Vol. of their News Papers for the years 1785 and 86, which they desired might be forwarded to me and my acceptance thereof requested. I must now beg the favor of you to return them my best thanks for their politeness, and at the sametime, to inform them that I believe they misunderstood me in my application for their paper when I was in Philadelphia, for it was my intention to have taken it after my return home as well as in Philadelphia; they will, therefore, be so good as to forward them to me by every post, and at the end of each year I shall be glad to have a Vol. of them bound. I have, hitherto taken the Pensylvania Herald, but, from some cause or other, it has been discontinued for a number of weeks past; I will thank you to

[94] From the "Letter Book" copy in the *Washington Papers*.

discharge whatever may be due on my account for that paper, and inform the printers, in decent terms, that it need not be sent on to me in future, as I conceive one will be sufficient to give all the information that is necessary.

I have recd. a Letter from Thomas Smith Esqr. of the 5th ultimo, wherein he informs me that he has £200 in his hands for me, which he should forward to you by the first safe conveyance. Whenever you receive it you will please to discharge the balance which may be due to you for articles purchased on my acct. since our last settlement, and forward the remainder to me in the manner mentioned in a former letter, reserving in your hands about £20 to pay for any articles I may have occasion to procure in Philadelphia.

I must beg the favor of you to forward the enclosed letters to their respective addresses by the first conveyance that may offer after you receive them. I have, in the one to Mr. Peters, desired him to have a harrow made for me similar to one which I saw when I was [at his house] with some spare teeth; I will thank you to pay his bill for the same, and have them sent to me by the first Vessel bound to Alexandria, after the one which I suppose is now about sailing for that place, provided they cannot be compleated in time to be sent by her. I am etc.[95]   [H. S. P.]

To WILLIAM DEAKINS, JUNIOR

Mount Vernon, March 8, 1788.

Sir: This will be handed to you by my overseer who goes to George Town to procure a quantity of twine suitable for making a Sein, as there is none in Alexandria fit for that purpose. Should you have any such as he may chuse, I will thank you to let him have 150lb., and if the Balance of the Bond assigned

---

[95] In the writing of Tobias Lear. The words in brackets are in the writing of Washington.

to me by Mrs. Kirk has not yet been paid into the hands of Colo. Simms, you will please to retain that as part payment of the amount of the twine, and charge me with the surplus. Should you not have any yourself, you will oblige me by assisting Mr. Fairfax[96] in getting it, if to be sold in George Town, and, if the above mentioned Balance has been paid to Colo Simms, I will discharge the amount of the twine at the end of the fishing season. I am, etc.[97]

To BURWELL BASSETT

Mount Vernon, March 9, 1788.

Dear Sir: If my last letter to you, containing the Bond of the deceased Mr. Dandridge on which you were requested to bring suit, was not sufficiently explanatory of the intention, I now beg leave to inform you that my meaning is after Judgement shall have been obtained and execution levied on the Slaves belonging to the estate of the decd. Gentn. that you, or Mr. John Dandridge, in behalf of his Mother, wd. purchase for her use such as she may want, on my acct. In a word, as it is at the request of Mr. John Dandridge that suits are instituted, my wish is to accommodate the family as far as I can consistently, the mode of doing it I leave to you. being with very great esteem etc.[97]

To BENJAMIN LINCOLN

Mount Vernon, March 10, 1788.

My dear Sir: Your favor of the 20th ulto. and the papers accompanying it, came duly to hand. I believe none of your

---

[96] John Fairfax.
[97] From the "Letter Book" copy in the *Washington Papers*.

letters to me have miscarried, as I have recd. the papers containing the debates of your Convention very regularly.

I am sorry to hear that the issue of the Government in New Hampshire is, in any measure, dubious. Our concurrent accounts from that quarter have been favourable in the highest degree, they would have justified the expectation of unanimity in their Convention. The growing attachment of the people in your State to the proposed Constitution is certainly a strong proof of its general excellence. It shows that a due and impartial consideration of the subject will decide in its favor.

At the end of the present month we shall be able to form a tolerable judgment of what may be its fate here, as our returns for the delegates to the convention will be known at that time, and the characters chosen will be pretty generally decided in their opinions upon the matter before their delegation, and as that will determine the people in their choice. The general tenor of the information, which I derive from those Gentlemen who call upon me, seems to agree in the opposition losing ground. and that nothing is wanting to render the people so favourably disposed towards it as to put the decision beyond a doubt but proper information upon the subject. The opponents are indefatigable in their exertions, while the friends to the Constitution seem to rest the issue upon the goodness of their cause. There will undoubtedly be a greater weight of abilities against the adoption in this convention than in any other; we had a right to expect it from the characters who first declared against it here, but notwithstanding this, my own opinion is (as it has ever been) that it will be received. with great esteem and regard &c.[98]

---

[98] From the "Letter Book" copy in the *Washington Papers*.

To THOMAS CUSHING

Mount Vernon, March 10, 1788.

Dear Sir: Your letter of the 12th. Ulto. inclosing the recommendatory Amendments to the proposed plan of Government by your Convention, did not come to hand till last Saturday or it should have had an earlier acknowledgement.

The adoption of the Constitution by the State of Massachusetts will undoubtedly have a very happy influence upon the decision of those States which have yet to determine upon the important question. The respectability of your Majority, added to the candid and manly behaviour of the minority, will obviate any improper impressions which might have been made by its smallness. The full and fair decision which the subject met with in your Convention evidently shew the advantage of it by its effects, for, from every information which we could obtain here, it appears that there would have been a decided majority against the Constitution, had the matter been determined early in the session; nor will this be the only benefit derived from it, the publication of the debates will serve to remove objections in the minds of unprejudiced persons in other States who seek for information. It is not in the power of the best informed among us to say, at present, how it will terminate in this State; at the end of this month some judgement may be formed, as we shall then have a return of the delegates from the several Counties who are to compose the convention. There is perhaps no person less qualified than I am to give an opinion upon the matter from his own observation, as I am wholly indebted to those Gentlemen who visit me for any knowledge that I have of the dispositions of the people, not having been ten miles from home since my return from Philadelphia, but from every information, I have not a doubt of its being adopted here.

Mrs. Washington joins me in Compliments to Mrs. Cushing and yourself. I am, etc.[99]

To SAMUEL HANSON

Mount Vernon, March 18, 1788.

Sir: Your letter of the 16th. Inst. was handed me yesterday in Alexandria as I was going to dinner; previous to that I had seen my Nephew George Washington,[1] and asked him if he had heard of any suitable place for himself and Lawrence to board at after their quarter with Mr. McWhir expired; he told me that it was probable a place might be obtained at a Mrs. Sanford's; I desired him to inform himself of the terms &c. and let me know them; as I had not an opportunity of seeing him again before I left town to know the result of his enquiries, it is not, at this moment, in my power to give a decided answer to your offer of taking them again into your family.

Your candid and free communications respecting the conduct of my Nephews, while with you, meet my warmest approbation and deserve my best thanks, and I should think myself inexcusable, if, upon this occasion, I did not act a part equally open and candid, by informing you of general allegations which they have, from time to time, offered on their part, viz: They having been frequently detained from school in the morning beyond their proper hour, in consequence of not having their breakfast seasonably provided, and sometimes obliged to go to school without any. They have likewise complained of their not being permitted to dine with company at the House; and served indifferently in another place afterwards and, after being a short time with Mr. McWhir, they made application for

---

[99] From the "Letter Book" copy in the *Washington Papers*.
[1] George Steptoe Washington.

shirts, and upon being asked what they had done with those which were made for them not long before, they replied that the manner of washing them at Mr. Hanson's (in Lye without soap) had entirely destroyed them.

This communication, Sir, cannot, I think, be displeasing to a person of your candor. I do not state the above as *facts* but merely as the reports of the boys, and if they should live with you again it will undoubtedly have a good effect by shewing them that their reports will always be made known to you, and the truth or falsehood of them discovered.

The motive which first induced me to put the Boys with you, explained upon a former occasion together with the advantage of throwing them into company will still operate, and incline me to give a preference to your House upon terms nearly equal in other respects but I cannot decide upon the matter till I know the result of George's enquiries, and so soon as I do, you may depend upon hearing further from Sir, &c.[2]

To CAPTAIN NATHANIEL INGRAHAM

Mount Vernon, March 22, 1788.

Dear Sir: When I requested you to procure a Gardiner for me in Holland, which you was so obliging as to promise to do, I fear I was not explicit enough with respect to the terms &c. upon which I would wish to have him.

If one properly qualified for the business, could be obtained to come over in the nature of a redemptioner, or which will be more certain, who will indent himself for a certain term of years it would be most agreeable to me, because he would be much cheaper; but if one of a proper description cannot be procured in this way, I should be willing to give a good Gardener

---

[2] From the "Letter Book" copy in the *Washington Papers*.

£15 Sterling per annum. more than this I do not incline to offer, because I presume they might be obtained for that sum in this Country. I should prefer a single man, but have no objection to one who is married provided his wife understands spinning &c. and will indent as her husband does. and provided they have not a number of Children. A middle aged man will suit me best, as the necessary services cannot be expected from, or performed by, one advanced in years.

I should likewise be glad to procure a good coarse Weaver, and will be much obliged to you if you will endeavour to get one for me to come over on the terms mentioned above, I should give the preference to one who understands weaving both woollen and linen, but would be satisfied with one could do either well.

If it is necessary (or would be more convenient for you) for me to make any advance for defraying the charges &c. which may arise from this business, I will thank you to let me know it and will provide accordingly. As I also shall be for your telling me with the *utmost* candor if the request here made will be attended with the smallest inconvenience to you. It not being by any means, my intention to lay you under the most trifling difficulty by the request.

Wishing you a prosperous voyage and a speedy return. I am, etc.[3]

To CLEMENT BIDDLE

Mount Vernon, March 24, 1788.

Dear Sir: Your letter of the 16th. Inst. enclosing the Bill of Lading and Certificate of the Articles shipped on my Acct. came duly to hand. The Packet has not yet arrived unless she passed by here yesterday.

---

[3] From the "Letter Book" copy in the *Washington Papers.*

I thank you for your attention to the letters which I committed to your care. As I do not know whether you may have received the Interest due upon my Certificate in your hands, and some charges will arise from the harrow furnished by Mr. Peters, and the livery lace, I enclose you a Bank Bill for forty Dollars, which you will please to pass to my Credit. I am etc.[4]

[H.S.P.]

* To ELÉONOR FRANÇOIS ÉLIE, COMTE DE MOUSTIER

Mount Vernon, March 26, 1788.

Sir: I have received the letter wch. your Excellency did me the honor of addressing to me by the hand of Mr. Madison. While I am highly gratified with the justice you do me in appreciating the friendly sentiments I entertain for the French Nation; I cannot avoid being equally astonished and mortifyed in learning that you had met with any subject of discontent or inquietude since your arrival in America. Be assured, Sir, as nothing could have been more unexpected: so nothing can now give me greater pleasure than to be instrumental in removing (as far as might be in the power of a private citizen as I am) every occasion of uneasiness that may have occurred. I have even hoped, from the short time of your residence here, and the partial acquaintance you may have had with the characters of the persons, that a natural distance in behavior and reserve in address, may have appeared as intentional coldness and neglect. I am sensible that the apology itself, though it should be well founded, would be but an indifferent one, yet it will be better than none: while it served to prove that it is our misfortune not to have the same chearfulness in appearance, and facility in deportment, which some nations possess.

---

[4] In the writing of Tobias Lear.

And this I believe, in a certain degree, to be the real fact; and that such a reception is sometimes given by individuals as may affect a foreigner with very disagreeable Sensations, when not the least shadow of an affront is intended.

As I know the predilections of most of our leading characters for your Nation; as I had seen the clearest proofs of affection for your King given by the people of this Country, on the birth of the Dauphin; as I had heard before the receipt of your letter that you had been received at your public audience by Congress, with all the marks of attention which had ever been bestowed upon a Representative of any Sovereign Power; And as I found that your personal character stood in the fairest point of light; I must confess, I could not have conceived that there was one person in public office in the United states capable of having treated with indifference, much less with indignity, the representative from a Court with which we have ever been upon the most friendly terms. And confident I am that it is only necessary for such conduct to be known to be detested.

But in the mean, [time] so ardently do I wish to efface any ill impressions that may have been made upon Your Excellency's mind to the prejudice of the Public, by individuals; that I must again repeat, that I am egregiously deceived if the people of this Country are not in general extremely well affected to France. The prejudices against that Kingdom had been so rivetted by our English connection and English policy that it was sometime before our people could entirely get the better of them. This, however, was thoroughly accomplished in the course of the War, and I may venture to say that a greater revolution never took place in the sentiments of one people respecting another. Now as none of their former attachments have been revived for Britain, and as no subject of uneasiness has turned up with respect to France, any disgust or enmity to the latter would involve a mystery beyond my comprehension. For, I had always believed that some apparent cause, powerful in its nature and progressive in its operation, must be employed to produce a change in National sentiments. But no prejudice has been revived, no jealousy excited, no interest adduced, and, in short, no cause has existed (to my knowledge) which could have wrought a revolution unfriendly to your nation. If one or a few persons in New York have given a different specimen of thinking and acting, I rely too much upon your candor to apprehend that you will impute it to the American people at large.

I am happy to learn that your Excellency is meditating to strengthen the commercial ties that connect the two Nations: and that your ideas of effecting it by placing the arrangements upon the basis of mutual advantage coincide exactly with my own. Treaties which are not built upon reciprocal benefits, are not likely to be of long duration. Warmly as I wish to second your views, it is a subject of regret that my little acquaintance with commercial affairs and my seclusion from public life, have not put me in a state of preparation to answer your several questions with accuracy. I will endeavor to inform myself of the most interesting particulars and shall take a pleasure in communicating the result.

At present I can only remark that I think the taste for many articles of French merchandize is rather encreasing. Still there are three circumstances, which are thought to give the British merchants an advantage over all others. 1st. their extensive credit: (which, I confess, I wish to see abolished). 2dly. their having in one place Magazines containing all kinds of Articles that can be required: and 3dly. their knowledge of the precise kind of merchandize and fabrics which are wanted.

For my own part I could wish as I have just observed, to see the time when no credit should be given. Attention and experience in the American trade would enable the French merchants, I apprehend to accommodate our markets in other respects. Between this Country and England many causes of irritation exist: and it is not impossible but that the ill-policy of the British Court may accelerate the removal of our trade into other channels. With sentiments of the greatest respect etc.[5]

*To HENRY KNOX

Mount Vernon, March 30, 1788.

My dear Sir: Your favor of the 10th. came duly to hand, and by Mr. Madison I had the pleasure to hear that you had recovered from a severe indisposition, on which event I sincerely congratulate you.

The conduct of the State of New Hampshire has baffled all calculation, and happened extremely mal-apropos for the election of delegates to the Convention of this State; for be the *real* cause of the adjournment to so late a day, what it may, the antifœderal party with us do not scruple to declare, that, it was done to await the issue of this Convention before it would decide; and add, that if this State should reject it, all those which are to follow will do the same; and consequently, the Constitution cannot obtain, as there will be only eight States in favor of the measure.

Had it not been for this untoward event, the opposition in this State would have proved entirely unavailing, notwithstanding the unfair conduct (I might have bestowed a harder epithet without doing injustice) which has been practiced to rouse the fears, and to inflame the passions of the people. What will be the result *now,* is difficult for me to say with any degree of certainty, as I have seen but a partial return of the delegates,

---

[5]From a photostat of the original in the Paris Archives, *Aff. Etrang. Mems. et Docs., E. U.,* vol. 6.

and [am] not well acquainted with the political sentiments even of those few. In the Northern part of the State the tide of Sentiment, I know, is *generally* in favor of the proposed system. In the Southern part, *I am told,* it is the reverse. While [in] the middle, it is said, it is pretty much divided. The Kentucky district will have great weight in deciding this question; and the idea of its becoming an impediment to its seperation,[6] has got hold of them; while no pains is spared to inculcate a belief that the Government proposed will, without scruple or delay, barter away the right of Navigation to the River Mississippi.

The postponement in New-Hampshire will also, unquestionably, give strength and vigor to the opposition in New York; and possibly, will render Rhode Island more backward than she otherwise would have been, if *all* the New England States had *finally* decided in favor of the measure.

Mrs. Washington joins me in every good wish for Mrs. Knox, yourself and family, with Dear Sir Yr. Affecte. friend etc.

[MS. H. S.]

To BATTAILE MUSE

Mount Vernon, March 31, 1788.

Sir: I have received your letter of the 19th. inst. and Mr. Lear has, agreeable to your request therein, called upon Messrs. D.

---

[6]From Virginia.

On March 30 Washington wrote to a Captain Speak: "I cannot omit the occasion of communicating a piece of information I have received, to wit: that your Boat is engaged to meet passengers on this side to take them to the other by which I am deprived of the Ferriages. I hope the practice will not be continued except for yourself. I find the Ferry inconvenient, and unprofitable enough without this, to wish the discontinuance of it. A little matter more wo'd induce me to put it down and stop up the Road leading thereto." A copy of this letter is in the "Letter Book" in the *Washington Papers.*

On this same day (March 30) Washington also wrote to a Mr. O'Connor, in Alexandria, thanking him for a complimentary ticket to his lecture on "Eloquence." "Business (and indeed disinclination to leave my own bed when I am within a few miles of it) would not permit my attendence at the lecture last evening." A copy of this letter is in the "Letter Book" in the *Washington Papers.*

and I. McPherson and Wm. Hunter Junr. Esqr. who have informed him that the money shall be paid conformable to your advice.

It would have suited me exceedingly well to have discharged my proportion of the assessment on the Potomack Company in the manner mentioned in your letter, could I have received it previous to the 15th. Inst. as I paid Mr. Hartshorne on that day. As you say it will be more convenient for you to pay me the money which you have, or may receive on acct. of my Rents, in the first week in May than sooner, I have no objection to its being delayed till that time. I am, etc.[7]

To BENJAMIN LINCOLN

Mount Vernon, April 2, 1788.

My dear Sir: I have to acknowledge the reception of your favor of the 24th. of February which I have delayed answering till this time, in expectation of being able to give you some information of what will probably be the determination of this State upon the Constitution; but the proceedings of New Hampshire, so directly opposite to what we had reason to hope for from every Account, has entirely baffled all calculation upon the subject, and will strengthen the opposition in this State. The only ground upon which an opinion can be formed of what will be the decision here, is the return of the members for the Convention; of these I have as yet seen but a partial list, and of this list there are many who are unknown to me, so that I am not able to give you any more satisfactory information upon the subject than when I wrote last to you. This, however, I may say, that the Northern, or upper Counties are generally friendly to the adoption of the Government, the

[7]From the "Letter Book" copy in the *Washington Papers*.

lower *are said* to be generally unfriendly, the sentiments of the western parts of the State are not fully known; but no means have been left untried to prejudice them against the System; every art that could inflame the passions or touch the interests of men have been essayed; the ignorant have been told, that should the proposed Government obtain, their lands would be taken from them and their property disposed of; and all ranks are informed that the prohibition of the Navigation of the Mississipi (their favorite object) will be a certain consequence of the adoption of the Constitution. But notwithstanding these unfair and injust representations I have the fullest confidence in its being received in this State. With great regard, etc.[8]

To JOHN LANGDON

Mount Vernon, April 2, 1788.

Sir: Your letter of the 28th. of February came regularly to hand. The conduct of New Hampshire respecting the proposed government was a matter of general surprise in this, and I believe in every other part of the United States; for her local situation, unconnected with other circumstances, was supposed to be a sufficient inducement to the people of that State to adopt a general government, which promises more energy and security than the one under which we have hitherto lived, and especially as it holds out advantages to the smaller States equal, at least, to their most sanguine expectations.

Circumstanced as your Convention was, an adjournment was certainly prudent, but it happened very mal-apropos for this State, because the concurrent information from that quarter would have justified the expectation of a unanimity in the convention, whereas an account so opposite to every former

---

[8] From the "Letter Book" copy in the *Washington Papers*.

one having arrived at the very time when the elections were carrying on here, gave an opportunity to the opponents of the proposed Constitution to hold up to the people its not having been so generally approved of in other States as they had been taught to believe, and of consequence prepared them to receive other impressions unfriendly to the Government and tending to influence their votes in favor of antifederal characters. However I am still strong in the expectation of its being adopted here notwithstanding the unjust and uncandid representations, which have been made by the opponents to inflame the minds of the people and prejudice them against it. I am &c.[9]

To CALEB GIBBS

Mount Vernon, April 3, 1788.

Dear Sir: Your letter of the 24th. of Feby. and the enclosed news papers came duly to hand. The conduct of New Hampshire has I believe, been a matter of surprize in every part of the Country, and from what I can learn, wholly unexpected by a considerable part of the Convention themselves; The adjournment was, however, (circumstances as they were) a very prudent step, for it appears that the great question would have been lost if the sense of the convention had been taken upon it at that time.

It is still uncertain what the determination of this State will be; the Northern Counties are generally favourable to the adoption of the Constitution, the Southern are said to be unfavourable: and the Sentiments of the western parts of the State are not fully known; no pains, however, has been spared, and no art untried to inflame the minds of the people and prejudice them against the proposed system of Government. I am, etc.[9]

---

[9] From the "Letter Book" copy in the *Washington Papers*.

To RICHARD BUTLER

Mount Vernon, April 3, 1788.

Dear Sir: I have received your letter of the 13th Ulto. my acknowledging the reception of the printed Vocabulary must have been an omission, for it came safely to hand with the manuscript one. Your observation respecting the instability and inefficacy of our General Government is very just. They are not only apparent in the instance, which you mention, but have for a long time, strongly marked all our national transactions. This in my opinion, is a powerful argument, for adopting the proposed Constitution even if it were less perfect than it is, and while a constitutional door is left open for amendments whenever they may be found necessary.

I thank you, my dear Sir, for your information respecting the opposition to the proposed Government in the Country west of the Susquehanna. Notwithstanding the rancour and activity of the opponents in Pensylvania, I trust that they are generally speaking, persons of too little importance to endanger the general welfare of the Union by extending their influence to other States, or even any further in their own than to a few Counties, or over persons whose characters, dispositions, and situations are conformable to theirs.

How the important question will be decided in this State is yet uncertain. Opinions are various, and I can say nothing upon the subject from my own knowledge, as I but very rarely ride off my own farms, and am wholly indebted to the public papers and those Gentlemen who visit me for any information which I have; however from everything that I can collect, I am still confident of its adoption here. I am etc.[10]

---

[10] From the "Letter Book" copy in the *Washington Papers*.

To THOMAS SMITH

Mount Vernon, April 3, 1788.

Sir: Previous to the reception of your letter of the 11th. Inst. Colo. Biddle advised me of his having received from you £192.13.4. on my acct. he mentioned £200 having been brought to him by the Gentleman into whose charge you had given it but £7.6.8. being in bad gold, he did not incline to receive it, and had therefore returned it to the Gentleman by whom it was sent. I am, etc.

P. S. Since writing the above your letter of the 17th. Ulto. has come to hand. Mr. Smith of Baltimore transmitted to me the sum of £75.15.10. which you lodged in his hands, for me in October last.[11]

To SAMUEL CHAMBERLINE

Mount Vernon, April 3, 1788.

Sir: I have been favored with your letter of the 10 Ulto. and feel myself much obliged by the communication of your mode of cropping, which you have been pleased to make to me.

Every improvement in husbandry should be gratefully received and peculiarly fostered in this Country, not only as promoting the interest and lessening the labour of the farmer, but as advancing our respectability in a national point of view; for, in the present State of America, our welfare and prosperity depend upon the cultivation of our lands and turning the produce of them to the best advantage.

The method of treading out wheat with horses is certainly a very execrable one, and nothing but the necessity of getting it out by some means or other can justify the practice. Your mode of cropping (with the assistance of the Winlaw Thrasher)

---

[11] From the "Letter Book" copy in the *Washington Papers*.

claims the preference to every other if only considered as getting the wheat out so expeditiously as to preserve it from the ravages of the fly.

I wrote sometime in January last, to Arthur Young Esquire (Editor of the Annals of Agriculture) requesting him to send over to me one of Winlaw's thrashing Machines, if it was found, from the experience which it must have had in England, to possess that merit is ascribed to it in his Annals, I hope to receive it in time to prove it after the next harvest, and should its operation be as favourable as is represented, I shall conceive the cultivation of wheat to be infinitely more worthy of the farmers attention in this country than it is at present.

If, in the course of your farming, you should meet with anything further that is interesting and worthy of attention I shall be much obliged to you for a communication of it. I am, etc.[12]

To BARBÉ MARBOIS

Mount Vernon, April 4, 1788.

Sir: I have regularly received the letter you did me the honor to write to me on the 30th. of November last, accompanied by one from the Count de la Luzerne, respecting the claim of M. de Saqui des Tourts[13] to be admitted a member of the Society of the Cincinnati.

I should certainly find myself extremely happy in an opportunity of gratifying the wishes of so meritorious an officer as M. des Tourets; if I thought myself at liberty to take any part whatever in the premises. Recommended strongly as he is by the Count de la Luzerne and yourself I cannot have a doubt that he would be an acquisition and a credit to the Institution:

---

[12] From the "Letter Book" copy in the *Washington Papers*.
[13] Louis Charles Hilarion, Chevalier de Saqui des Tourès. He was a captain in the French Navy.

nor can I have a hesitation in believing that his pretentions are as good as those of some who have found admission into the Society. Yet as I have (amidst the almost innumerable applications that have been made to me) scrupulously avoided giving any decision and only referred the Documents I had received to the General Meeting I flatter myself I shall be considered as having done everything that was properly within my sphere, by making a similar reference in the present instance.

You will be sensible, I perceive Sir, that, from the Constitution of our Society, it would not have been right in me to have given a positive determination on the question. It would not be less proper than ever for me to take that upon myself. For, having by a circular letter to the several State Societies requested that I might not be re-elected President on account of my numerous avocations: the last Genl. Meeting was pleased so far to indulge me, as to make it a condition for inducing my acceptance, that I should be absolutely excused from all trouble and application incident to the office; and the whole business should devolve on the Vice President, viz, General Mifflin. As I shall not be present at the next General Meeting, I will transmit the application of M. des Tourets to Genl. Knox, the Secretary of the General Society.

The appointment of the Count de la Luzerne to the office of Minister of Marine and his *consequent removal to Europe,* will, I presume, supersede the expediency of my addressing him on this subject. Had that not been the case, I should have seized with eagerness the occasion of paying the tribute of my homage to his acknowledged talents and virtues. I am truly rejoiced to hear of the felicity of Madame de Marbois and yourself and hope you will be made still more happy *in the growing cement* of the two nations to which you allude. I am, etc.[14]

---

[14] From the "Letter Book" copy in the *Washington Papers.*

To CLEMENT BIDDLE

Mount Vernon, April 4, 1788.

Dear Sir: The articles which you shipped on my Acct. on board of the Charming Polly have arrived safe and in good order.

As I am under the necessity of purchasing, every year, a quantity of coarse Linen, Blanketings &c. for the clothing of my negroes, and sundry other articles for various purposes, and Goods of every kind being sold in Alexandria at a high advance, I am desireous of knowing if I could not supply myself from Philadelphia, or some other place, upon lower terms. I will therefore be much obliged to you if you would inform me of the price of the following articles, as soon as is convenient after you have received this, viz. German and British Oznaburgs of the best quality, suitable for making Negroes shirts and shifts. A kind of Rolls proper for summer Petticoats and Trousers, Dutch Blanketings, Nails from 6d. to 20d, and good ditching Spades by the dozen or single one.

I will thank you to be so good as to forward the enclosed letters to their respective addresses by the first safe conveyances and am, with great esteem etc.[15]   [H. S. P.]

To JAMES WILSON

Mount Vernon, April 4, 1788.

Dear Sir: You will please to accept of my best thanks for the copy of the debates of your late convention, which you have been so polite as to send me. That, together with your favor of the 11 Ulto. was handed to me by Mr. Madison. The violent proceedings of the enemies of the proposed constitution in your

---

[15] In the writing of Tobias Lear.

State are to be regretted as disturbing the peace of society; but in any other point of view they are not to be regarded; for their unimportance effectually precludes any fear of their having an extensive or lasting influence, and their activity holds up to view the general cast and character of them, which need only to be seen to be disregarded.

It is impossible to say, with any degree of certainty, what will be the determination of the Convention in this State upon the proposed plan of Government. I have no opportunity of gaining information respecting the matter, but what comes through the medium of the news papers or from those Gentln. who visit me, as I have hardly been ten miles from my farms since my return from Philadelphia. Some judgment may be formed when the members chosen by the several Counties to serve in Convention, are known, as their sentiments will be decided, and their choice determined, by their Attachments or opposition to the proposed System. A majority of those names I have yet seen are said to be friendly to the Constitution; but these are from the Northern parts of the State from whence less opposition was to be expected. It is however certain that there will be greater weight of abilities opposed to it here than in any other State. I am, &c.[16]

To CHARLES LEE

Mount Vernon, April 4, 1788.

Dear Sir: I am very sorry I have not yet been able to discharge my acct. with the James River Company for the amount of which you presented me with an order.

The almost total loss of my crop last year by the drought which has obliged me to purchase upwards of eight hundred

---

[16] From the "Letter Book" copy in the *Washington Papers*.

Barrels of Corn, and my other numerous and necessary demands for cash, when I find it impossible to obtain what is due to me, by any means, have caused me more perplexity and given me more uneasiness than I ever experienced before from the want of money. In addition to the disappointments which I have met with from those who are indebted to me, I have in my hands a number of indents and other public securities which I have received from time to time as the interest of some Continental loan office certificates etc. which are in my possession; as I am so little conversant in public securities of every kind as not to know the use or value of them, and hardly the difference of one species from another, I have kept them by me from year to year without having an idea that they would depreciate as they were drawn for interest, and never doubting but they would be received in payment of taxes at any time, till I have found by the Revenue Law of the last session, that only a particular description of them will pay the taxes of the year 1787; the others pay all arrearages of taxes and I am informed are not worth more than 2/6 in the pound. The injustice of this measure is too obvious and too glaring to pass unobserved; it is taxing the honest man for his punctuality, and rewarding the tardy or dishonest with the sum of 17/6 in every pound which is due from him for taxes. As you are now in Richmond I take the liberty of enclosing to you (in a letter from Mr. Pendleton) a Certificate for a negro executed in the year 1781 Amounting to £69. which I will thank you to negotiate for me there upon the best terms you can and pay the proceeds thereof in behalf of what is due from me to the James River Company. The principal for the negro, and three years interest thereon (which is all that was allowed) amounted to £138. which was divided into two Certificates, one receivable in the taxes now due, which I retain, to discharge part of my taxes for the year 1787 and the other you have with this. Upon what principle of justice interest is allowed on the above certificates from the 1st. of Jany. 1785 *only* my ideas are not sufficiently comprehensive to understand and if it should fall in your way to enquire should be glad to know; as also what will or is likely to be the final result of my holding the Certificates, which have been given to me for interest of the money I lent the Public in the day of its distress. I am well apprized that these are negotiable *things* as above, and when a person is *obliged* to part with them, he must, as with other commodities at market, take what they will fetch, but the object of my enquiry, is to know, as above, what the final end of them will be if retained in my chest. Strange indeed it seems, that the Public Officers should take in the original Certificates, issued new, by a scale of their own, reducing the money, as *they* say, to specie value, give warrants for interest accordingly, and then behold! these specie warrants are worth 2/6 in the pound. To commit them to the flames, or suffer this is a matter of indifference to me. there can be no justice, where there is such practices. You will pardon me for dwelling so long upon this subject. It is a matter which does not concern me *alone* but must affect many others. With great esteem etc.[17]

To CLEMENT BIDDLE

Mount Vernon, April 11, 1788.

Dear Sir: I have recd. your favor of the 31st Ulto. enclosing a letter and some seeds from Mr. Peters, and will thank you to send me, by the first Vessel bound this way, a good Wheat fan

---

[17] From the "Letter Book" copy in the *Washington Papers*.

On April 4 Tobias Lear wrote to Thomas Mahony, an house carpenter and joiner, giving the terms, by the year, at which Washington was willing to reemploy him. A copy of this letter is in the "Letter Book" in the *Washington Papers*.

On April 15 Mahony and Washington signed an agreement, as to terms, for one year. This agreement is in the *Washington Papers*.

(if there have been any late improvements on the common sort, which has been found useful, I shall prefer one with such improvements), and a steel-plated whip-saw of the best kind, seven and an half feet long; if you are not a competent judge yourself of the quality of the saw, I will thank you to get somebody to chuse one who is, as I wish it to be free from flaws and good in every respect.

You will oblige me by conveying the enclosed letter to Mr. Peters by the first good opportunity. I am etc.[18]   [H.S.P.]

To CLEMENT BIDDLE

Mount Vernon, April 14, 1788.

Dear Sir: Your favor of the 3d. inst. and the news papers accompanying it came to hand by the last mail.

In my letter to you of the 11th inst. I requested you to procure a wheat fan for me, but since that time I have found one more than I then knew of which compleated the number on my several farms and supersedes the necessity of your sending the one which I wrote for, provided this letter reaches you in time to prevent your procuring it.

I will thank you to inform me of the price of good Shad and Herring per Bbl. and if a quantity of them would meet with a ready sale in Philadelphia.

With great esteem etc.[19]

*To THOMAS JOHNSON

Mount Vernon, April 20, 1788.

Dear Sir: As well from report, as from the ideas expressed in your letter to me in December last, I am led to conclude that

---

[18] In the writing of Tobias Lear.
[19] From the "Letter Book" copy in the *Washington Papers.*

you are disposed (circumstanced as our public affairs are at present) to ratify the Constitution which has been submitted by the federal Convention to the People; and under this impression, I take the liberty of expressing a *single* sentiment on the occasion. It is, that an adjournment, (if attempted), of your Convention to a later period than the decision of the question in this State, will be tantamount to the rejection of the Constitution. I have good ground for this opinion, and am told it is *the blow* which the leading characters of the opposition in these two States have meditated, if it shall be found that a direct attack is not likely to succeed in yours. If this be true, it cannot be too much deprecated, and guarded against. The postponement in New-Hampshire, altho' made without any reference to the Convention of this State, and altogether from the local circumstances of its own, is ascribed by the opposition *here* to complaisance towards Virginia; and great use is made of it. An event similar to this in Maryland, would have the worst tendency imaginable; for indecision there wld. have considerable influence upon South Carolina, the only other State which is to precede Virginia, and submits the question almost wholly to the determination of the latter. The *pride* of the State is already touched upon this string, and will be raised much higher if there is an opening for it.

The sentiments of Kentucky are not yet known here. Independent of these, the parties with us, from the known, or presumed opinions of the members, are pretty equally balanced. The one in favor of the Constitution preponderates at present; but a small matter cast into the opposite scale, may make it the heaviest.

If in suggesting this matter, I have exceeded the proper limit, my motive must excuse me. I have but one public wish remaining. It is, that in *peace* and *retirement,* I may see this

Country rescued from the danger which is pending, and rise into respectability maugre the Intrigues of its public and private enemies.

With very great esteem &c.   [MD. H. S.]

To JOHN ARMSTRONG

Mount Vernon, April 25, 1788.

Dear Sir: From some cause or other which I do not know your favor of the 20th of February did not reach me till very lately. This must apologize for its not being sooner acknowledged. Altho' Colo Blaine forgot to call upon me for a letter before he left Philadelphia, yet I wrote a few lines to you previous to my departure from that place; whether they ever got to your hands or not you best know.

I well remember the observation you made in your letter to me of last year, " that my domestic retirement must suffer an interruption." This took place, notwithstanding it was utterly repugnant to my feelings, my interests and my wishes; I sacrificed every private consideration and personal enjoyment to the earnest and pressing solicitations of those who saw and knew the alarming situation of our public concerns, and had no other end in view but to promote the interests of their Country; and conceiving, that under those circumstances, and at so critical a moment, an absolute refusal to act, might, on my part, be construed as a total dereliction of my Country, if imputed to no worse motives. Altho' you say the same motives induce you to think that another tour of duty of this kind will fall to my lot, I cannot but hope that you will be disappointed, for I am so wedded to a state of retirement and find the occupations of a rural life so congenial; with my feelings, that to be drawn into public at my advanced age, could be a sacrifice that would admit of no compensation.

Your remarks on the impressions which will be made on the manners and sentiments of the people by the example of those who are first called to act under the proposed Government are very just; and I have no doubt but (if the proposed Constitution obtains) those persons who are chosen to administer it will have wisdom enough to discern the influence which their example as rulers and legislators may have on the body of the people, and will have virtue enough to pursue that line of conduct which will most conduce to the happiness of their Country; as the first transactions of a nation, like those of an individual upon his first entrance into life, make the deepest impression, and are to form the leading traits in its character, they will undoubtedly pursue those measures which will best tend to the restoration of public and private faith and of consequence promote our national respectability and individual welfare.

That the proposed Constitution will admit of amendments is acknowledged by its warmest advocates; but to make such amendments as may be proposed by the several States the condition of its adoption would, in my opinion amount to a complete rejection of it; for upon examination of the objections, which are made by the opponents in different States and the amendments which have been proposed, it will be found that what would be a favorite object with one State, is the very thing which is strenuously opposed by another; the truth is, men are too apt to be swayed by local prejudices and those who are so fond of amendments which have the particular interest of their own States in view cannot extend their ideas to the general welfare of the Union; they do not consider that for every sacrifice which they make they receive an ample compensation by the sacrifices which are made by other States for their benefit; and that those very things, which they give up operate to their advantage through the medium of the general interest.

In addition to these considerations it should be remembered
that a constitutional door is open for such amendments as shall
be thought necessary by nine States. When I reflect upon these
circumstances I am surprised to find that any person who is
acquainted with the critical state of our public affairs, and
knows the variety of views, interests, feelings and prejudices
which must be consulted in framing a general Government for
these States, and how little propositions in themselves so opposite to each other, will tend to promote that desirable end, can
wish to make amendments the ultimatum for adopting the
offered system.

I am very glad to find, that the opposition in your State, however formidable it has been represented, is, generally speaking,
composed of such characters, as cannot have an extensive influence; their fort, as well as that of those in the same class in
other States seems to lie in misrepresentation, and a desire to
inflame the passions and to alarm the fears by noisy declamation rather than to convince the understanding by sound arguments or fair and impartial statements. Baffled in their attacks
upon the constituion they have attempted to vilify and de-
base the Characters, who formed it, but even here I trust they
will not succeed. Upon the whole I doubt whether the opposition to the Constitution will not ultimately be productive of
more good than evil; it has called forth, in its defence, abilities
which would not perhaps have been otherwise exerted that
have thrown new light upon the science of Government,
they have given the rights of man a full and fair discussion,
and explained them in so clear and forcible a manner, as cannot fail to make a lasting impression upon those who read the
best publications on the subject, and particularly the pieces
under the signature of Publius. There will be a greater weight

of abilities opposed to the system in the convention of this State than there has been in any other, but notwithstanding the unwearied pains which have been taken, and the vigorous efforts which will be made in the Convention to prevent its adoption, I have not the smallest doubt but it will obtain here.

I am sorry to hear, that the College in your neighbourhood[20] is in so declining a state as you represent it, and that it is likely to suffer a further injury by the loss of Dr. Nisbet[21] whom you are afraid you shall not be able to support in a proper manner on account of the scarcity of Cash which prevents parents from sending their Children thither. This is one of the numerous evils which arise from the want of a general regulating power, for in a Country like this where equal liberty is enjoyed, where every man may reap his own harvest, which by proper attention will afford him much more than is necessary for his own consumption, and where there is so ample a field for every mercantile and mechanical exertion, if there cannot be money found to answer the common purposes of education, not to mention the necessary commercial circulation, it is evident that there is something amiss in the ruling political power which requires a steady, regulating and energetic hand to correct and control. That money is not to be had, every mans experience tells him, and the great fall in the price of property is an unequivocal and melancholy proof of it; when, if that property was well secured, faith and justice well preserved, a stable government well administered, and confidence restored, the tide of population and wealth would flow to us, from every part of the Globe, and, with a due sense of the blessings, make us the happiest people upon earth. With sentiments of very great esteem &c.[22]

---

[20] Dickinson College at Carlyle, in Pennsylvania.
[21] Dr. Charles Nisbet.
[22] From the "Letter Book" copy in the *Washington Papers.*

To JOHN VAUGHAN

Mount Vernon, April 27, 1788.

Sir: I have received your two letters of the 17th and 21st inst. and the papers containing the four numbers of Fabius which accompanied them.

I must beg you to accept my best thanks for your polite attention in forwarding those papers to me. The writer of the pieces signed Fabius, whoever he is,[23] appears to be master of his subject; he treats it with dignity, and at the same time expresses himself in such manner as to render it intelligible to every capacity. I have no doubt but that an extensive republication of those numbers would be of utility in removing the impressions which have been made upon the Minds of many by an unfair or partial representation of the proposed constitution, and would afford desirable information upon the subject to those who sought for it. I am happy to hear of your Father's safe arrival in Jamaica; you will please to tender my regards to him whenever you write. I am &c.[24]

To JOHN HOPKINS

Mount Vernon, April 27, 1788.

Sir: I received the enclosed Tax bill by the last post in a letter from Mr. Charles Lee who informed me that you had furnished him with it, and was so obliging as to offer to settle it with the Sheriff. I must beg you to accept of my best thanks for your kind offer, and shall take the liberty to trouble you upon the occasion.

The specie Tax for the years 1785 and 6 amounts to £107.11.9 which I find, by the Revenue act passed the last Session, may be

[23] He was John Dickinson.
[24] From a copy furnished by Mrs. Louis C. Madeira, of Philadelphia, Pa.

discharged in Certificates of a particular description, and for the payment of which I have enclosed you 8 Warrants amounting to £107.12.2.

To discharge the Certificate tax for the above mentioned years, amounting to £91.12.8. I have enclosed 305–53/90 Dollars in Indents, which, if I am rightly informed, will pay all arrears of the Certificate tax.

I shall endeavour to procure Tobacco notes to pay £71.14.6 due for the year 1787, and will forward them to you as soon as I can obtain them.

I observe that the Sheriff, of Green Briar has, in the enclosed bill, given in a tract containing 10,990 Acres which lies on the west side of the Great Kanawa, and has omitted one of 7276 acres patented in my name and that of George Muse but now my sole property laying on the East side of said River. If the Great Kanawa seperates the County of Green Briar from any other (as I conceive it does) this statement is erroneous; however I am not sufficiently acquainted with the bounds and divisions of those Counties to decide upon it; the Sheriff ought to know whether it is right or not, and I will thank you to mention the matter to him. The tract of 2000 Acres is also on the West side of the Great Kanawa, tho' by the tax bill it is placed in the County of Green Briar. Independently of the tracts here mentioned, I have 3 other lying on the Ohio, between the mouths of the Great and little Kanawa, but in what Counties they be or under what predicament they are, I know not [they may be]²⁵ *possibly sold;*²⁶ tho no application has ever been made to me, or any person in my behalf, to my knowledge, for the taxes, these contain 2314 Acres and 4395 Acres making together 9157 Acres. I have also, higher up the Ohio a small

---

²⁵ The words in brackets are inserted at a venture in an effort to clarify the careless copying.

²⁶ To satisfy the taxes(?).

tract of 587 Acres called the round bottom but how it is taxed, or what steps have been taken to collect it I know not.

Upon the reception of this you will be so obliging as to inform me if the warrants and Indents are such as will answer the purpose. I am, etc.[27]

---

[27]Immediately following this letter, in the "Letter Book" is a "List of Warrants and Indents sent to Mr. John Hopkins, to pay the taxes due upon my Lands in Green Briar County April 27, 1788" as follows:

	£	s	d
WARRANTS { One dated 29th Novr. 1786 for sundry articles furnished for the use of the Militia in the year 1774 allowed by the Court of Claims in Fairfax County for	20	0	0
One ditto .... ditto .... for	20	0	0
One ditto .... ditto .... for	20	0	0
One ditto .... ditto .... for	27	16	6
One issued to Thomas Swain for his Services in the militia of this State under Captain Sandford from Fairfax County dated Dec 8 1783 H. Randolph } J. Pendleton } signers .... for	4	16	0
One issued to Joshua Smolley for Do under Captn. Span from Louden County Augt. 5, 1782 B Clark } H. Randolph } Signers .... for	2	14	8
One payable to Mathew Whiting for Corn furnished the Continent dated 2d November 1783 allowed by the Court of Claims in Prince Wm. County M. Carrington } Saml. Jones } Signers .... for	9	0	0
One payable to Wm. Smith for waggon hire in Septr. 1781, dated 4 October 1783, Louden County M Carrington } Jams. Jones } Signers .... for	3	6	0
	£107	13	2

Green Briar taxes

2000 Acres .... at 6/ }
10,990 .... do .... at 6/ } Value £4782
2950 .... do .... at 6/ }

Tax on the above for the year 1785 ... £35..17..3.
Do .... 1786 ... 71..14..6
Do .... 1787 ... 71..14..6

£179.. 6..3.

Certificate tax .... 1785 ... 45..16..4
Do .... 1786 ... 45..16..4

£ 91..12..8

The receipts for these payments are in the *Washington Papers* under date of May 14, 1788.

To JAMES McHENRY

Mount Vernon, April 27, 1788.

Dear Sir: Not having sent to the Post office for several days, your favor of the 20th. inst. did not get to my hand till last night. I mention this circumstance as an apology for my not giving it an earlier acknowledgment.

As you are pleased to ask my opinion of the consequences of an adjournment of your Convention until the meeting of ours, I shall (tho' I have meddled very little in this political dispute less perhaps than a man so thoroughly persuaded as I am of the evils and confusions which will result from the rejection of the proposed Constitution, ought to have done) give it as my sincere and decided opinion that the postponement of the question would be tantamount to the final rejection of it, that the adversaries of the new Constitution Virginia and Maryland view it in this light, and they will press for the accomplishment of this measure as the denier resort. I have very good reason to believe to adduce arguments in support of this opinion is as unnecessary as they would be prolix. They are obvious, and will occur to you on a moments reflection.

Tho' the period to which the adjournment in New Hampshire was fixed, with no respect to the meeting of the Convention in this State, but was the effect, solely of local circumstances within itself, yet the opposition *here* ascribe it wholly to complaisance towards Virginia, make great use of it and undertake to pronounce that all the States thereafter whose Conventions were to precede hers will pursue the same line of Conduct, and of course that those which are to follow will receive their [direction] from it. Should Maryland fulfil this prognostic South Carolina may indeed be staggered and the prediction of the foes to the Constitution will thereby be realized, for the assertion so far as it respects North Carolina may with some truth I believe be applied while the opposition in New York it is well known will avail itself of every pretext for rejection.

The sentiments of the Western district of this State, are not yet brought to my view. Independently thereof the Majority, so far as the opinions of the Delegates are known or presumed, is in favor of the adoption and is encreasing; but as the parties from report are pretty equally poized a small matter cast into either scale would give it the preponderancy. Decisions, or indecisions then with you, will in my opinion, determine the fate of the Constitution, and with it, whether peace and happiness, or discord and confusion is to be our lot. The fœderalists here see and deprecate the idea of the latter, and their opponents doing all they can to encourage it as their last hope. Thus stands the matter in my eyes at present. with very great esteem etc.[28]

To DANIEL OF ST. THOMAS JENIFER

Mount Vernon, April 27, 1788.

Dear Sir: Accept my thanks for the obliging information contained in your letter of the 15th. inst.[29] The great, the important question must ere this, have received its first features in, if not the final of your Convention. If they are decisive and favourable, it will most assuredly raise the edifice. Seven affirmatives without a negative carries weight with them, that would almost convert the unbelieving Sister and yet, but in place of what I was going to add, I will say that, I am, etc.[2]

---

[28] From the "Letter Book" copy in the *Washington Papers*.

[29] Jenifer had written (April 15): "But three Counties in the State have chosen Members Antifederal to wit Ann Arundel, Baltimore and Harford and the Elections of these three will be controverted as to these Members to wit Mr. Saml Chase for Ann Arundel on account of being a Non resident the same objection to Mr Paca and Luther Martin in Harford. Baltimore a Double return 4 for and 4 against the Constitution. Tho' I am opinion when the ultimate decision happens that Mr Paca will vote for the proposed plann as it stands and recommend amendments, rather than risque a new Convention." Jenifer's letter is in the *Washington Papers*.

To CHARLES LEE

Mount Vernon, April 27, 1788.

Dear Sir: Your two favors of the 11th. and 17th. Inst. have been duly received. I am much obliged to you for the trouble which the negotiating the Certificate that I forwarded to you has given, and must further intrude upon you by requesting that you will dispose of the certificates which are in your hands to the best advantage and have the proceeds of them passed to my Credit with the James River Company. As I have already discharged my taxes here for the last year, I shall have no occasion for them on that score.

I thank you, my dear Sir, for your kind attention in forwarding the Acct. of my taxes due upon my lands in Green Briar, and as you inform me that Mr. Hopkins is so obliging as to offer to settle with the Sheriff for them, I shall write to him upon the subject, and enclose him Certificates to discharge all that is due previous to the year 1787, for the payment of which I shall endeavour to procure Tobacco notes, which shall be forwarded to him as soon as I can obtain them. With great regard etc.

P. S. Enclosed is a letter to Mr. Hopkins under a flying seal, which you will be so good as to close and deliver to him; you will see by the contents what steps I have taken to discharge the tax bill which you forwarded to me, and as it is probable that others of a similar nature will be rendered in (if the lands are not already sold) I think it would be best to lodge the Certificates which you have in the hands of Mr. Hopkins to pay that part of the tax which is due for 1787, and I will devise some other method to answer the demands of the James River Company.[20]

---

[20] From the "Letter Book" copy in the *Washington Papers*.

To COMTE DE ROCHAMBEAU

Mount Vernon, April 28, 1788.

My dear Count: I have just received the letter which you did me the honor to write to me on the 18th of January; and am sorry to learn that the Count de Grasse, our gallant coadjutor in the capture of Cornwallis, is no more. Yet his death is not, perhaps, so much to be deplored as his latter days were to be pitied. It seemed as if an unfortunate and unrelenting destiny pursued him, to destroy the enjoyment of all earthly comfort. For the disastrous battle of the 12th of April, the loss of the favor of his king, and the subsequent connection in marriage with an unworthy woman, were sufficient to have made him weary of the burden of life. Your goodness, in endeavoring to sweeten its passage, was truly commendable; however it might have been marred by his own impetuosity. But his frailties should now be buried in the grave with him, while his name will be long deservedly dear to his country, on account of his successful co-operation in the glorious campaign of 1781. The Cincinnati in some of the States have gone into mourning for him.

Altho' your nation and England have avoided, from prudential motives, going into a war, yet I fancy, their affections have not been much increased by the affair in Holland. The feeling occasioned to France by the interference of Prussia and Britain, may not pass away altogether without consequences. I wish, indeed, the affairs of France to be on a footing which would enable her to be the arbiter of peace to the neighboring nations. The poor Dutch Patriots seem, by some means or another, to have been left sadly in the lurch and to be reduced to a most humiliating condition. And as if the two Powers, who reinstated the Stadt Holder, had not done enough to set the middle nations together by the ears; they have embroiled, forsooth, all the north of Europe by bringing the Turks into hostility with the two Imperial Courts. Should France join with the latter, or even should she continue neuter, I can scarcely conceive that the Ottomans will be permitted to hold any of their possessions in Europe. The torch of hostility, being once kindled, commonly spreads apace; but it is beyond my prescience to foretell how far this flame will extend itself, before it shall be entirely extinguished.

Here, in America, we have not much news worth the trouble of communicating to you, my dear Count, though I know what is to ourselves often [a] matter of indifference, is to our friends at a distance a subject of curiosity. For that reason, I will subjoin, in one word, a State of affairs on this side of the water. All the public attention has been, for many months past, engrossed by a new Constitution. It has met with some opposition from men of abilities, but it has been much more ably advocated. Six States, that is to say, those of Massachusetts, Connecticut, Jersey, Pennsylvania, Delaware and Georgia have accepted it. The opinion is that Maryland and South Carolina will soon do the same. One more State, only, will be [then] wanting to put the Government into execution. And as the other Conventions are to meet early in the summer, we hope for the best. As to the intimation which your partiality for me has prompted you to make on my behalf: I need only say that every body knows that private life is my decided choice in preference to any thing the world can bestow. I am &c.[81]

To MARQUIS DE LAFAYETTE

Mount Vernon, April 28, 1788.

I have now before me, my dear Marqs. your favor of the 3d of August in the last year; together with those of the 1st. of

---

[81] From the "Letter Book" copy in the *Washington Papers*.

January, the 2d. of January and the 4th. of February in the
present. Though the first is of so antient a date, they all come
to hand lately, and nearly at the same moment. The frequency
of your kind remembrance of me, and the endearing expressions of attachment, are by so much the more satisfactory, as I
recognise them to be a counterpart of my own feelings for you.
In truth, you know I speak the language of sincerity and not
of flattery, when I tell you, that your letters are ever most welcome and dear to me.

This I lay out to be a letter of Politics. We are looking anxiously across the Atlantic for news and you are looking anxiously
back again for the same purpose. It is an interesting subject to
contemplate how far the war, kindled in the north of Europe,
may extend its conflagrations, and what may be the result before its extinction. The Turk appears to have lost his old and
acquired a new connection. Whether England has not, in the
hour of her pride, overacted her part and pushed matters too
far for her own interest, time will discover: but, in my opinion
(though from my distance and want of minute information
I should form it with diffidence) the affairs of that nation cannot long go on in the same prosperous train: in spite of expedients and in spite of resources, the Paper bubble will one
day burst. And it will whelm many in the ruins. I hope the
affairs of France are gradually sliding into a better state. Good
effects may, and I trust will ensue, without any public convul-
sion. France, were her resources properly managed and her
administrations wisely conducted, is (as you justly observe)
much more potent in the scale of empire, than her rivals at
present seem inclined to believe.

I notice with pleasure the additional immunities and facili-
ties in trade, which France has granted by the late Royal arret
to the United States. I flatter myself it will have the desired

effect, in some measure, of augmenting the commercial intercourse. From the productions and wants of the two countries,
their trade with each other is certainly capable of great amelioration, to be actuated by a spirit of unwise policy. For so surely
as ever we shall have an efficient government established, so
surely will that government impose retaliating restrictions, to
a certain degree, upon the trade of Britain. at present, or under
our existing form of Confederations, it would be idle to think
of making commercial regulations on our part. One State
passes a prohibitory law respecting some article, another
State opens wide the avenue for its admission. One Assembly
makes a system, another Assembly unmakes it. Virginia, in the
very last session of her Legislature, was about to have passed
some of the most extravagant and preposterous Edicts on the
subject of trade, that ever stained the leaves of a Legislative
Code. It is in vain to hope for a remedy of these and innumerable other evils, untill a general Government shall be adopted.

The Conventions of Six States only have as yet accepted the
new Constitution. No one has rejected it. It is believed that
the Convention of Maryland, which is now in session; and
that of South Carolina, which is to assemble on the 12th of
May, will certainly adopt it. It is, also, since the elections
of Members for the Convention have taken place in this State,
more generally believed that it will be adopted here than it
was before those elections were made. There will, however,
be powerful and eloquent speeches on both sides of the question in the Virginia Convention; but as Pendleton, Wythe,
Blair, Madison, Jones, Nicholas, Innis and many other of our
first characters will be advocates for its adoption, you may suppose the weight of abilities will rest on that side. Henry and
Mason are its great adversaries. The Governor, if he opposes
it at all will do it feebly.

On the general merits of this proposed Constitution, I wrote to you, some time ago, my sentiments pretty freely. That letter had not been received by you, when you addressed to me the last of yours which has come to my hands. I had never supposed that perfection could be the result of accommodation and mutual concession. The opinion of Mr. Jefferson and yourself is certainly a wise one, that the Constitution ought by all means to be accepted by nine States before any attempt should be made to procure amendments. For, if that acceptance shall not previously take place, men's minds will be so much agitated and soured, that the danger will be greater than ever of our becoming a disunited People. Whereas, on the other hand, with prudence in temper and a spirit of moderation, every essential alteration, may in the process of time, be expected.

You will doubtless, have seen, that it was owing to this conciliatory and patriotic principle that the Convention of Massachusetts adopted the Constitution in toto; but recommended a number of specific alterations and quieting explanations, as an early, serious and unremitting subject of attention. Now, although it is not to be expected that every individual, in Society, will or can ever be brought to agree upon what is, exactly, the best form of government; yet, there are many things in the Constitution which only need to be explained, in order to prove equally satisfactory to all parties. For example: there was not a member of the convention, I believe, who had the least objection to what is contended for by the Advocates for a *Bill of Rights* and *Tryal by Jury*. The first, where the people evidently retained every thing which they did not in express terms give up, was considered nugatory as you will find to have been more fully explained by Mr. Wilson and others: And as to the second, it was only the difficulty of establishing a mode which should not interfere with the fixed modes of any of the States, that induced the Convention to leave it, as a matter of future adjustment.

There are other points on which opinions would be more likely to vary. As for instance, on the ineligibility of the same person for President, after he should have served a certain course of years. Guarded so effectually as the proposed Constitution is, in respect to the prevention of bribery and undue influence in the choice of President: I confess, I differ widely myself from Mr. Jefferson and you, as to the necessity or expediency of rotation in that appointment. The matter was fairly discussed in the Convention, and to my full convictions; though I cannot have time or room to sum up the argument in this letter. There cannot, in my judgment, be the least danger that the President will by any practicable intrigue ever be able to continue himself one moment in office, much less perpetuate himself in it; but in the last stage of corrupted morals and political depravity: and even then there is as much danger that any other species of domination would prevail. Though, when a people shall have become incapable of governing themselves and fit for a master, it is of little consequence from what quarter he comes. Under an extended view of this part of the subject, I can see no propriety in precluding ourselves from the services of any man, who on some great emergency shall be deemed universally, most capable of serving the Public.

In answer to the observations you make on the probability of my election to the Presidency (knowing me as you do) I need only say, that it has no enticing charms, and no fascinating allurements for me. However, it might not be decent for me to say I would refuse to accept or even to speak much about an appointment, which may never take place: for in so doing, one might possibly incur the application of the moral resulting from that Fable, in which the Fox is represented as inveighing against the sourness of the grapes, because he could not reach them. All that it will be necessary to add, my dear Marquis, in order to show my decided predilection, is, that, (at my time of life and under my circumstances) the encreasing infirmities of nature and the growing love of retirement do not permit me to entertain a wish beyond that of living and dying an honest man on my own farm. Let those follow the pursuits of ambition and fame, who have a keener relish for them, or who may have more years, in store, for the enjoyment.

Mrs. Washington, while she requests that her best compliments may be presented to you, joins with me in soliciting that the same friendly and affectionate memorial of our constant remembrance and good wishes may be made acceptable to Madame de la Fayette and the little ones. I am &c.

P. S. May 1st. Since writing the foregoing letter, I have received Authentic Accounts that the Convention of Maryland have ratified the new Constitution by a Majority of 63 to 11.[32]

*To PIERRE CHARLES L'ENFANT

Mount Vernon, April 28, 1788.

Sir: I have been duly favoured with your letter of the 15 Instt., enclosing a Memorial to the General Meeting of the Cincinnati; and, agreeably to your request, shall transmit the Enclosure to the Secretary, to be laid before the meeting.

As your embarrassments have been a source of long and severe inquietude, I should be truly happy in knowing that they were removed. But, as it was the express condition of my accepting the Presidency of the Society, "that I should be exempted from all applications and cares respecting it: I trust when this stipulation shall be generally known that all addresses will be made to the Vice-President or Secretary.

---

[32] From the "Letter Book" copy in the *Washington Papers*.

While I sincerely condole with you on the loss of your good father; you will permit me to remind you, as an inexhaustible subject of consolation, that there is a good Providence which will never fail to take care of his Children: and be assured, Sir, it will always give me real satisfaction to find that prosperity and felicity have been attendant on all your steps.

With sentiments of great esteem etc.[33]

To DOCTOR BENJAMIN RUSH

Mount Vernon, April 28, 1788.

General Washington presents his best compliments and thanks to Doctor Rush, for the polite attention manifested in forwarding the elegant engraving[34] from the Right Hble. the Earl of Buchan. The General takes the liberty of requesting that the Doctor (whenever an occasion may happen) will have the goodness to make his most grateful acknowledgments to that patriotic Nobleman, for so flattering a token of his esteem and friendship.[35]

To SAMUEL GRIFFIN

Mount Vernon, April 30, 1788.

Dear Sir: I am now to acknowledge the receipt of your letter of the 15th. of April, in which you did me the favor to enclose an extract from the original Statute, designating the duties of the Office to which I had been appointed.

Influenced by a heart-felt desire to promote the cause of Science in general, and the prosperity of the College of William

---

[33] From a microfilm of the original in the Hayes Memorial Library, Fremont, Ohio.

[34] This was "a print of the celebrated Mr Napier," who was John Napier, or Neper, laird of Merchiston, inventor of logarithms, the present notation of decimal fractions, etc.

[35] From the "Letter Book" copy in the *Washington Papers*.

and Mary in particular, I accept the office of Chancellor in the same; and request you will be pleased to give official notice thereof to the learned Body, who have thought proper to honor me with the appointment. I confide fully in their strenuous endeavours for placing the system of Education on such a basis, as will render it most beneficial to the State and the Republic of letters, as well as to the more extensive interests of humanity and religion. In return, they will do me the justice to believe, that I shall not be tardy in giving my cheerful concurrence to such measures, as may be best calculated for the attainment of those desirable and important objects. For the expressions of politeness and friendship blended with your communications, you are desired to receive my best acknowledgments. I am &c.[36]

To JOHN PORTER

Mount Vernon, April 30, 1788.

Sir: I have received your letter of the 9th. instant by the Post and have found myself not a little at a loss to know how to answer it.

While rivetted to the toils and perplexities inseperable from the Commission of Commander in Chief; I sought not to avoid trouble, I shunned not to enter into the minutest investigation of innumerable disagreeable subjects, for, unfortunately, in our army, they were but to numerous and too troublesome to my repose. But to rip open again the disagreeable subjects that seemed to be forever closed with the war and my retirement, I could not think of doing it, unless I would first consent to give up all the prospects of tranquility, which, I flattered myself, awaited the last years of a life, that had been devoted almost invariably to the services of others. The sacrifice would be too

---

[36] From the "Letter Book" copy in the *Washington Papers.*

great, and the expectation unreasonable. All that I can be expected to do in your case is to observe upon the state of it (not
from a recurrence to papers which are packed away but according to the best of my recollection) that your absence from the
Army appeared to be rather the effect of an unaccountable in-
discretion than of a premediated criminality; and that, altho'
precedent and the good of service made your dismission indispensable on account of your having gone beyond Sea without a
regular permission, your character in other respects stood unexceptionable: insomuch that considerable interest was made in
your behalf by Officers of good reputation.

Upon this State of facts; although it would be highly improper for me to give any opinion to Congress, yet so far am I
from wishing to prejudice an impartial examination into the
Justice of your applications, that I cannot have the least objection to their investigating and determining the matter, in whatsoever manner may seem most proper to them. In whatsoever
manner the business may result, I cannot ever with propriety
say anything more on the subject. I am, etc.[87]

To MARQUIS DE CHASTELLUX

Mount Vernon, April 25[–May 1], 1788.

My dear Marquis: In reading your very friendly and acceptable letter of 21st. December 1787, which came to hand by the
last mail, I was, as you may well suppose, not less delighted
than surprised to come across that plain American word "my
wife." A wife! well my dear Marquis, I can hardly refrain
from smiling to find you are caught at last. I saw, by the eu-
logium you often made on the happiness of domestic life in
America, that you had swallowed the bait and that you would

---

[87] From the "Letter Book" copy in the *Washington Papers*.

as surely be taken (one day or another) as you was a Philosopher and a Soldier. So your day has, at length, come. I am glad of it with all my heart and soul. It is quite good enough for you. Now you are well served for coming to fight in favor of the American Rebels, all the way across the Atlantic Ocean, by catching that terrible Contagion, domestic felicity, which time like the small pox or the plague, a man can have only once in his life: because it commonly lasts him (at least with us in America, I dont know how you manage these matters in France) for his whole life time. And yet after all the maledictions you so richly merit on the subject, the worst wish which I can find in my heart to make against Madame de Chastellux and yourself is, that you may neither of you ever get the better of this same domestic felicity during the entire course of your mortal existence.

If so wonderful an event should have occasioned me, my dear Marquis, to have written in a strange style, you will understand me as clearly as if I had said (what in plain English, is the simple truth) do me the justice to believe that I take a heartfelt interest in whatever concerns your happiness. And in this view, I sincerely congratulate you on your auspicious Matrimonial connection. I am happy to find that Madame de Chastellux is so intimately connected with the Dutchess of Orleans, as I have always understood that this noble lady was an illustrious pattern of connubial love, as well as an excellent model of virtue in general.

While you have been making love, under the banner of Hymen, the great Personages in the North have been making war, under the inspiration, or rather under the infatuation of Mars. Now, for my part, I humbly conceive, you have had much the best and wisest of the bargain. For certainly it is more consonant to all the principles of reason and religion (natural and revealed) to replenish the earth with inhabitants, rather than to depopulate it by killing those already in existence, besides it is time for the age of Knight-Errantry and mad-heroism to be at an end. Your young military men, who want to reap the harvest of laurels, don't care (I suppose) how many seeds of war are sown; but for the sake of humanity it is devoutly to be wished, that the manly employment of agriculture and the humanizing benefits of commerce, would supersede the waste of war and the rage of conquest; that the swords might be turned into plough-shares, the spears into pruning hooks, and, as the Scripture expresses it, "the nations learn war no more."

Now I will give you a little news from this side of the water, and then finish. As for us, we are plodding on in the dull road of peace and politics. We, who live in these ends of the earth, only hear of the rumors of war like the roar of distant thunder. It is to be hoped, that our remote local situation will prevent us from being swept into its vortex.

The Constitution, which was proposed by the fœderal Convention, has been adopted by the States of Massachusetts, Connecticut, Jersey, Pennsylvania, Delaware, and Georgia. No State has rejected it. The Convention of Maryland is now sitting and will probably adopt it; as that of South Carolina is expected to do in May. The other Conventions will assemble early in the summer. Hitherto there has been much greater unanimity in favour of the proposed government than could have reasonably been expected. Should it be adopted (and I think it will be) America will lift up her head again and in a few years become respectable among the nations. It is a flattering and consolatory reflection, that our rising Republics have the good wishes of all the Philosophers, Patriots, and virtuous men in all nations: and that they look upon them as a kind of Asylum for mankind. God grant that we may not disappoint their honest expectations, by our folly or perverseness.

With sentiments of the purest attachment &c.

P. S. If the Duke de Lauzun is still with you, I beg you will thank him, in my name, for his kind remembrance of me, and make my Compliments to him.

May 1st. Since writing the above I have been favoured with a duplicate of your letter in the hand-writing of a lady, and cannot close this without acknowledging my obligations for the flattering Postscript of the fair Transcriber. In effect, my dear Marquis, the Characters of this interpreter of your sentiments are so much fairer than those through which I have been accustomed to decypher them, that I already consider myself as no small gainer by your Matrimonial connection. Especially, as I hope, your amiable amanuensis will not forget, at sometimes, to add a few annotations of her own to your original text.[88]

To WILLIAM STEPHENS SMITH

Mount Vernon, May 1, 1788.

Dear Sir: I consider myself the more indebted to your obliging care in transmitting the letter of the Marquis de la Fayette, as by that means you have given me the double advantage of hearing from two of my distant, military friends at once.

It is so long since I have had the satisfaction of holding any immediate intercourse with you, that I may be allowed to touch on a subject rather obtrusive [*sic*] indeed, but not (I presume) the less pleasant on that account: I mean your entrance upon the road of connubial life. Permit me, then, to wish that it may be strewed with flowers, and that every possible happiness may

---

[88] From the "Letter Book" copy in the *Washington Papers.*

attend you and the partner[39] of your Journey, who, (if I am not egregiously misinformed by those who are well acquainted with her) is worthy of that distinguished lot of felicity. Mrs. Washington wishes that her compliments may be presented with mine to yourself and Lady. You may ever count upon my sincere regard, and believe me to be, Dear Sir, etc.[40]

*To MARY MORRIS[41]

Mount Vernon, May 1, 1788.

Madam: With infinite pleasure Mrs. Washington and myself received from Mr. Morris the News of your intended visit to Mount Vernon, and that you will be accompanied by Miss Morris and the young Gentlemen who are lately returned to you (on which happy event we sincerely congratulate you). We have only to wish, further, that you could make it convenient to bring the other Children; for with much truth we can assure you of the pleasure it would give us to see them all under this roof with you and Mr. Morris.

Being engaged in my mornings ride when John came, and he anxious to proceed, I detain him no longer than I can unite Mrs. Washingtons best wishes and compliments to mine, for you, and the family, in a particular manner I beg you to assure the young Gentlemen of the cordial reception they will meet from Madam, Yr. etc.

PS. Mr. Morris in his letter to me says, you will be so obliging as to bring (sending it to Colo. Biddle if it is the least inconvenient will do equally well) muslins agreeably to the inclosed Memorandum.[42]

---

[39] Smith married Abigail Adam, daughter of John Adams.
[40] From the "Letter Book" copy in the *Washington Papers*.
[41] Wife of Robert Morris and sister to Bishop William White.
[42] From a photograph of the original kindly furnished by Frederick E. Atwood, of Boston, Mass.

To BENJAMIN LINCOLN

Mount Vernon, May 2, 1788.

My dear Sir: I have now to acknowledge the receipt of your favor of the 29 of March which should have been done at an earlier period had any thing transpired in these parts that was worth communicating.

I can now with pleasure, inform you that the State of Maryland adopted the proposed Constitution last Monday by a very great majority; this you will undoubtedly have announced by the public papers before this letter reaches you but that State will not receive the sole benefit of its adoption, it will have a very considerable influence upon the decision in Virginia, for it has been strongly insisted upon by the opponents in the lower and back counties in this State that Maryland would reject it by a large majority; the result being found so directly opposite to this assertion will operate very powerfully upon the sentiments of many who were before undecided and will tend to fix them in favor of the Constitution, it will if I am not misinformed, have this effect upon many who are chosen to the Convention and who have depended in a great measure upon the determination of Maryland to confirm their opinion. But, exclusive of this influence, the most accurate returns of the members of the Convention, with their sentiments, so far as they were known, annexed, gave a decided majority in favor of the Constitution, and the prevailing opinion is, that it gains advocates daily. I never have, for my own part once doubted of its adoption here, and if I have at any time been wavering in my opinion the present appearances and concurrent information would have compleatly fixed it.

I am very sorry to find by your letter that there is so much of the spirit of insurrection yet remaining in your State, and that it discovered itself so strongly in your Assembly. but I hope the influence of those Gentlemen who are friendly to the proposed constitution, and the conciliatory disposition which was shown by many of the minority in your Convention will so far pervade the States as to prevent that factious spirit from gaining ground.

Mrs. Washington and the Children thank you for your kind remembrance of them and unite with me in the best wishes for your happiness. With sentiments of the highest esteem etc.

P. S. Enclosed is a letter from your young friend.[43]

To REVEREND JOHN ETTWEIN[44]

Mount Vernon, May 2, 1788.

Reverend Sir: I have received your obliging letter of the 28th of March, enclosing a copy of some remarks on the Customs, Languages &c. of the Indians, and a printed pamphlet containing the stated rules of a Society for propagating the Gospel among the Heathen,[45] for which tokens of polite attention and kind remembrance I must beg you to accept my best thanks.

So far as I am capable of judging, the principles upon which the society is founded and the rules laid down for its government, appear to be well calculated to promote so laudable and arduous an undertaking, and you will permit me to add that if an event so long and so earnestly desired as that of converting the Indians to Christianity and consequently to civilization, can be effected, the Society of Bethlehem bids fair to bear a very considerable part in it. I am, Reverend Sir, with sentiments of esteem, &c.

---

[43] From the "Letter Book" copy in the *Washington Papers*.

[44] A Moravian bishop.

[45] The remarks on the customs and languages of the Indians, by David Zeisberger, is in the *Washington Papers*. The printed pamphlet will be found in the *Washington Papers* under date of Nov. 1, 1787.

To GOUVERNEUR MORRIS

Mount Vernon, May 2, 1788.

Dear Sir: Your letter of the 29th. Ulto. reminds me of an omission which I should have been ashamed of, did I not conceive that my apology will be as Satisfactory as it is Just. The omission I allude to is not acknowledging the receipt of your favour which accompanied the Books,[46] and thank you for your care of the latter. The apology is the hourly expectation of seeing you at this place on your return to Philadelphia. Whether the latter is adequate to the former you are to Judge of, be this as it may, it is the best I can offer.

I have not at any moment, despaired of this States acceptance of the new Constitution and less since the ratification of Maryland by so large and decided a Majority; the *fury* of the opposition, I believe is spent, the grand push was made at the Elections and failing of success therein the hopes of its leaders begin to flag and many of them or I am mistaken wish the business was to commence de novo; in which case a different line of March would be taken up by some of them.

It was with very singular pleasure I received information of the intended visit from Mrs. Morris &c. I take it for granted, tho' Mr. Morris has not said as much, that he will add to our happiness by becoming one of the Party, to repeat the same to you is, I hope unnecessary, as you cannot doubt of the pleasure it would give me. Mrs. Washington offers her compliments to you, and with sentiments of sincere esteem and regard I am, etc.

P. S. Colo. Humphrey's who is here, thanks you for your kind remembrance of him, and prays you to accept his best wishes.[47]

---

[46] Morris's letter, which is in the *Washington Papers,* makes no mention of books.
[47] From the "Letter Book" copy in the *Washington Papers.*

To JAMES MADISON

Mount Vernon, May 2, 1788.

My dear Sir: Your favor of the 10th. ult. came duly to hand, and the enclosure for Mr. D. Carroll[48] was forwarded the next day by a direct and safe conveyance. That Gentleman however was not of the Convention; but the body, of which you supposed him a member by a large (of sixty odd to twelve) and decided majority have ratified the new Constitution. A thorn this is in the sides of the leaders of opposition in this State; should South Carolina give as unequivocal approbation of the system the opposition here must become feeble for eight affirmatives without a negative carries *weight* of argument if not eloquence with it that would cause even the unerring sister to hesitate. Mr. Chace, it is said, made a display of all his eloquence. Mr. Mercer discharged his whole artillery of inflamable matter; and Mr. Martin did something; I know not what, presume with vehemence, but no converts were made, no, not one. So business after a very short Session, ended; and will if I mistake not render yours less tiresome. I am, etc.[49]

To ROBERT MORRIS

Mount Vernon, May 2, 1788.

Dear Sir: Permit me to assure you in unequivocal terms, that the proposed visit of Mrs. Morris, and such parts of your family as are mentioned in your letter of the 29th. Ulto. will give sincere pleasure at Mount Vernon. Mrs. Washington and myself only wish that you had not confined it to Miss, and the

---

[48] Daniel Carroll, of Rock Creek.
[49] The text is from the sales catalogue of the *Washington-Madison Papers* (McGuire Collection, 1892).

two Mr. Morris; of this I have taken the liberty to inform Mrs. Morris in a letter, hoping that she may find it convenient to bring the other parts of your family along with her. I hope you will not (tho' you are silent on the head) let us not want the pleasure of your Company to make the party perfectly happy.

On the safe arrival of your Sons I heartily congratulate you as I hope I may do on the recovery of your finger from the severe blow we are told it received in your tour to Norfolk. Mrs. Washington joins me in every good wish for you, and with Sentiments of very great esteem and regard I am, etc.[50]

To GEORGE STEPTOE WASHINGTON

Mount Vernon, May 5, 1788.

Dear George: I yesterday received a letter from Mr. Hanson, informing me that you slept from home three nights successively, and one contrary to his express prohibition. Complaints of this nature are extremely painful to me, as it discovers a degree of impropriety in your conduct, which, at your time of life your good sense and discretion ought to point out to you and lead you to avoid. Although there is nothing criminal in your having slept with a companion of good manners and reputation as you say you have, yet your absenting yourself from your own lodgings under that pretence may be productive of irregularities and disagreeable consequences; and I now insist upon it, in the most pointed terms, that you do not repeat it without the consent and approbation of Mr. Hanson.

One strong motive for my placing you in your present lodgings was that you might, in your conduct out of school, be guided by Mr. Hanson's advice and directions, as I confide

---

[50] From the "Letter Book" copy in the *Washington Papers*.

very much in his discretion and think that he would require nothing of you but what will conduce to your advantage; and at the age to which you have now arrived you must be capable of distinguishing between a proper and improper line of conduct, and be sensible of the advantages or disadvantages which will result to you through life from the one or the other.

Your future character and reputation will depend very much, if not entirely, upon the habits and manners, which you contract in the present period of your life; they will make an impression upon you which can never be effaced. You should therefore be extremely cautious how you put yourself into the way of imbibing those customs which may tend to corrupt your manners or vitiate your heart. I do not write to you in this style from knowing or suspecting that you are addicted to any vice, but only to guard you against pursuing a line of conduct which may imperceptibly lead on to vicious courses. Mr. Hanson has done you and Lawrence justice in saying, that your behavior since you have been last with him has been unexceptionable except in this instance and one more which he has not mentioned, and I hope this is the last complaint I shall ever hear while you remain in your present situation at least, as it will prevent me from using means to regulate your behaviour, which will be disagreeable to us both. I am your sincere friend and affectionate uncle.[51]

To SAMUEL HANSON

Mount Vernon, May 5, 1788.

Sir: Your letter of yesterday was handed to me last evening. I am sorry that the conduct of one of my Nephews has been such as to render a complaint to me necessary, but I am

---

[51] From the "Letter Book" copy in the *Washington Papers*.

extremely obliged to you for the communication. George has now advanced to that time of life when it is absolutely necessary that his conduct should be regulated by some means or other. Coercion would be extremely painful to me, but if advice, remonstance and gentle methods will not answer the purpose others must be taken. Enclosed is a letter to him which I have left open for your perusal.

I am glad to find that Lawrence has behaved so well, I rather suspected that trespasses would have commenced on his part than on that of George. I am, etc.[52]

To JOHN FITZGERALD AND GEORGE GILPIN

Mount Vernon, May 6, 1788.

Gentn: If you have fixed upon Monday next for the meeting of the Directors of the Potk. Company at the Falls of the Shanandoah, have given Messrs. Johnson and Lee notice of it, and informed Mr. Stuart[53] and his accusers thereof you will please to let me know it, (having heard nothing yet of the determination) In these cases, and that I may have nothing to retard my speedy return after the business of the meeting is finished I shall set off on thursday, take the great and Seneca Falls in my way up, make a visit or two in Berkeley, and be at the place of meeting by ten oclock on Monday. I am, etc.[52]

*To JAMES McHENRY

Mount Vernon, May 8, 1788.

Dear Sir: To a letter which I wrote you some days ago, I beg leave to refer you. I congratulate with you on the happy

---

[52] From the "Letter Book" copy in the *Washington Papers*.
[53] Richardson Stewart.

decision of your Convention; having no doubt of its weight on those States which are to follow.

In a letter (just received) from Colo. Spaight[54] of North Carolina he informs me of his having sent a small bag of Pease to your care, for me. Have you received them? If so, be so good as to forward them by the Stage (the Cost of which I will pay; without dispatch they will come too late) to Alexandria.

A Monsr. Campion who brought over my Asses, says he is in distress, and has written to me for money. Pray what is his character in Baltimore, and what has he been employed about this year and half, in that place? Though he had no demand upon me for the service he performed, yet, I gave him a sum of money as an acknowledgment of my sense of the proper discharge of the trust reposed in him. He told me at that time (fall was twelve months) that he should spend the winter in Baltimore and Sail for France in the Spring. In the Spring (as I was going to Phila. he told me he should sail in the Fall. In the fall, as I returned from thence, he assured me he should Sail in a fortnight. Since which I have heard nothing from, or of him till now, his application to me for money. Your answer (soon) to this part of my letter will be very acceptable to Dear Sir Yr. etc.[55]

To DOCTOR BENJAMIN RUSH

Mount Vernon, May 10, 1788.

Sir: Your favour of the 26th. ulto. together with the seeds of the manget werzel[56] and the Pamphlet respecting the cultivation and use of this valuable plant, came safe and claims my particular acknowledgments. I thank you for both, and shall

---

[54] Richard Dobbs Spaight.
[55] From a photostat of the original kindly furnished by Judge E. A. Armstrong, of Princeton, N. J.
[56] The root of scarcity.

endeavor to propogate the former with care and attention: Mrs. Washington joins me in compliments to Mrs. Rush. I am, etc.[57]

To PETERSON & TAYLOR

Mount Vernon, May 10, 1788.

Gentn: Enclosed is a Bill of the Scantling which you sent me according to the measurement of it. There is a deficiency of 21 pieces, as you will see by the bill annexed which is a copy of the one sent to you last winter; you will see the dimensions of the deficient pieces by comparing the two bills. There are 15 pieces among those sent which are not conformable to any mentioned in the original bill, and of course are useless to me, unless 7 of them, which are 12 ft. long, 6 by 4, should be included with the studs 10 ft. long 6 by 4, of which you will observe there is a deficiency of 19. I would wish to be informed whether you could supply those pieces which are wanting immediately because if you cannot I must get them myself.

Should you have any doubts respecting the proper measurement of the Scantling they can easily be removed (and it is my wish that they may) by being measured by yourselves or by a person of your own appointing as the pieces are now stacked and can be run over in a few hours. I am, etc.[58]

To VICTOR MARIE, CHEVALIER DU PONT

Mount Vernon, May 12, 1788.

Sir: I have lately had the honor of receiving your polite letter of the 22d. of April enclosing one from the Marquis de la Fayette, which would have given me a double pleasure to have

---

[57] From the "Letter Book" copy in the *Washington Papers*.
[58] Following this letter in the "Letter Book" is a copy of the scantling sent for and the scantling received.

received from your own hands by informing me of the welfare of that much esteemed character and giving me an opportunity of paying a proper attention to a person recommended by him: this pleasure however I flatter myself I shall yet receive by your visiting Mount Vernon.

You will please, Sir, to accept of my best wishes that your tour to this Country may be perfectly pleasing and conformable to your expectations, and that you may return to your native land with impressions favourable to America and its Citizens. I have the honor, etc.[59]

To MISS JAMES JAMIMA JACOBINA DOUGLAS[60]

Mount Vernon, May 12, 1788.

Miss: I have received your letter of the 26th. of November and have lately had an opportunity, (by a Gentleman of this neighbourhood who was in Richmond) of making the enquiries which you desired. He informs me that he was the Gentleman mentioned in your letter which acknowledges there is a balance in his hands due to your father but says the sum is not so large as you mention, some part of it having been already paid.

It will readily occur to you that the only method of recovering the money will be to invest some person on the spot with proper power to act on your behalf and receive it for you. The necessity of appointing some person living in the neighbourhood of the Gentleman from whom the money is due is so obvious that you cannot but be sensible of it. And permit me to observe here that my agency in this business thus far has been no ways inconvenient or disagreeable to me, but my various avocations which require an unremitting attention would

---

[59] From the "Letter Book" copy in the *Washington Papers.*
[60] Of Edinburgh.

compel me to do an injury to my feelings by declining to take any part in recovering or receiving the money if it should be proposed. I am, etc.[61]

*To BEZALEEL HOWE

May 12, 1788.

I do hereby certify and make known to all to whom the presents shall come that Mr. —— Howe, late a Lieutt. in the New-Hampshire line of the Continental Army, was an Officer of a fair and respectable character, that he served some part of the last year of the War as an auxiliary Lieutenant with my own Guard, that he commanded the Escort which came with my baggage and Papers to Mount Vernon at the close of the War, and that in all my acquaintance with him I had great reason to be satisfied with his integrity, intelligence and good dispositions.

To CLEMENT BIDDLE

Mount Vernon, May 12, 1788.

Dear Sir: I have received your two letters of the 29 of April and 4th of May. Since my application to you for the prices of Linen and Blankets I have had an opportunity of supplying myself with both, upon pretty reasonable terms, but am no less obliged to you for the trouble of your inquiries respecting them.

The Philadelphia Packet has not yet arrived, but if she sailed at the time you mention she may be expected very soon.

I will thank you to inform me whether you have received the Interest due upon my Certificate in your hands, as there is a balance due to you in consequence of those articles last purchased on my Acct. which shall be remitted if it is not adjusted by the above Interest.

---

[61] From the "Letter Book" copy in the *Washington Papers*.

Will you be so obliging as to let me know in your next what the price of dble and single refined Sugar is with you?

Nails from 8d to 20d can be purchased cheaper in Alexandria than in Philadelphia. 20d can be had in the former place at 10/2 per M allowing 20 lb to the M; whereas 20 lb at 9d would amount to 15/ Pensylvania Currency; but I believe all under 8d would come cheaper at 9d per pound. With great esteem, I am etc.

PS. Pray forward the Letter to Genl. Armstrong when a good conveyance offers.[62]   [H.S.P.]

To THE SECRETARY FOR FOREIGN AFFAIRS

Mount Vernon, May 15, 1788.

Dear Sir: I am indebted to you for your favors of the 20th and 24th Ult, and thank you for your care of my foreign letters; I do the same for the Pamphlet you were so obliging as to send me.[63] The good sense, forcible observations, temper and moderation with which it is written cannot fail, I should think of making a serious impression, even upon the antifœderal mind where it is not under the influence of such local views as will yield to no argument, no proofs. If you could conveniently furnish me with another of these Pamphlets I would thank you, having sent the last to a friend of mine.

Since the Elections in this State little doubt is entertained of the adoption of the proposed Constitution with us (if no mistake has been made with respect to the sentiments of the Kentucky members). The opponents to it I am informed are *now* also of this opinion. Their grand manœuvres were exhibited at the Elections, and some of them if reports be true were not

---

[62] In the writing of Tobias Lear. The P. S. is in the writing of Washington.
[63] Jay's letter of Apr. 20, 1788, which is in the *Washington Papers,* merely mentions but does not give the title of the pamphlet.

much to their credit. Failing in their attempt to exclude the friends to the new government from the Convention, and baffled in their exertions to effect an adjournment in Maryland, they have become more passive of late; should South Carolina (now in session) decide favourably, and the Government thereby (nine States having acceded) get in motion I can scarcely conceive that any one of the remainder, or all of them together were they to convene for the purpose of deliberation, separated from each other as they then would be, in a geographical point of view would incline to with draw from the Union of the other nine. Mrs. Washington unites with me in Compliments and good wishes for you and Mrs. Jay, and I am etc.[64]

To THOMAS LEWIS

Mount Vernon, May 19, 1788.

Sir: Enclosed is the duplicate of a letter I wrote to you agreeably to the date, but having heard nothing from you since, I am apprehensive it may have met with a miscarriage and therefore send this copy by your Brother who will endeavor to contrive it safe to you.

I have been called upon for Taxes, and threatened at the sametime with a Sale of the land after June, if the money is not paid before, by the Sheriff of Green brier County. As I have been suffering loss after loss for near ten years while I was in the public Service and have scarcely had time to breathe since. this proceedure seems to me to be a little hasty, no regular application been made to me, nor I might add any application at all but by these threats indirectly sent. to be threatned with a Sale when I cannot upon enquiry find that others who have

---

[64] From the "Letter Book" copy in the *Washington Papers*.

lands in the same County have been treated in that rigorous manner seems to carry with it singular appearance. I am however, endeavouring to provide for the payment but wish to meet with that measure and indulgence which is shewn to others.

I have heard also, that People, under some other authority than mine, are settling in the point of a Fork between Cole River and the Great Kanhawa; as I have a tract of two thousand Acres which includes this spot these persons should be informed thereof to prevent deception to themselves, or trouble to me. The authority (if you incline to act under it) with which you are invested will enable you to settle this matter with them and to continue them thereon if you can agree on terms. I am, etc.[65]

*To RICHARD DOBBS SPAIGHT

Mount Vernon, May 25, 1788.

Sir: The letter with which you honored me the 25th. of last month, and the Pease (by way of Baltimore) are safe at hand. I pray you to accept my thanks for them. I shall cultivate the Pease with care, this year in hills, to accumulate Seed, next year in broadcast, for a crop.

I am sorry to find by your letter that the State of North Carolina is so much opposed to the proposed Government. If a better could be agreed on, it might be well to reject this; but without a prospect (and I confess none appears to me) policy I think must recommend the one that is submitted. The sentiments of this State will soon be known. The second day of June the Convention is to meet. Since the election of delegates to it, the prevailing opinion is, that a majority of the members are in favor of the Constitution, but as they are soon to speak

---

[65] From the "Letter Book" copy in the *Washington Papers.*

their own sentiments it would be imprudent to anticipate them, even, if they were reduced to certainty. Maryland has ratified by a very large Majority; Sixty three to Eleven. With great esteem etc.[66]

To JOHN COWPER

Mount Vernon, May 25, 1788.

Sir: I have been duly favored with your letter of the 12th. Inst. In answer thereto I beg leave to inform you that I am not disinclined to part with my moiety of the land purchased (by the deceased Colo. Fielding Lewis and myself) in North Carolina, provided a reasonable and adequate price can be obtained for it.

For this land, that Gentleman and myself paid (to the best of my recollection) a pistole an Acre 20 odd years ago, and expended considerable Sums in ditching to reclaim the low parts thereof. If under this information you should feel disposed to give a sum that would in some measure make us whole, I would in order to accomodate the Executors of Colo. Lewis who are desirous of selling his moiety, part with mine also; and will as soon as Mr. John Lewis can be consulted communicate the terms to you. Without such disposition on your part, it would be useless to fix on any price or the credits because I am not inclined to sell my part at any considerable loss being fully convinced that if a good government is established and property thereby secured that Land *generally,* will again be in demand and consequently rise, and those which are situated as *this* is will command almost any price, if the Cut between Elizabeth River and Pasquetant (to make which nothing in my opinion is easier) should be effected. I am, etc.[67]

---

[66] From the original in the North Carolina Historical Commission.
[67] From the "Letter Book" copy in the *Washington Papers.*

*To COMTE DE ROCHAMBEAU

Mount Vernon, May 28, 1788.

My dear Count: I take the liberty of introducing to your acquaintance Mr. Barlow,[68] the person who will have the honor of handing this letter to you. He is a Gentleman of liberal education, respectable character, great abilities, and high reputation for literary accomplishmts. He is peculiarly and honorably known in the Republic of Letters both here and in Europe, for being the Author of an admirable Poem, in which he has worthily celebrated the glory of your Nation in general and of yourself in particular. Attended, as he is, with so many interesting circumstances and under so many unusual advantages, I need add no more than just a recommendation to your attention and civilities.

Since I had the pleasure of writing to you by the last Packet, nothing worthy of notice has happened in America, except the adoption of the Constitution in Maryland by a very great Majority. I embrace you, my dear Count, with all my heart; and have the honor, etc.[69]

To MARQUIS DE LA LUZERNE

Mount Vernon, May 28, 1788.

Sir: As not anything which is interesting to your happiness and glory can be indifferent to me, I have a sincere, pleasure in congratulating you on your appointment as Ambassador from the most Christian King to the Court of London.

Altho your Excellency may possibly have had some knowledge of Mr. Barlow (the gentleman who will put this letter

---

[68] Joel Barlow.
[69] From the original in the *Rochambeau Papers* in the Library of Congress.

into your hands and of whom it is recommendatory) during your residence in America; yet his celebrity as a writer was not then so great as to have attracted the same admiration and applause, which he hath since merited and obtained by the publication of his celebrated Poem entitled the Vision of Columbus. That Work is dedicated by permission to the King of France, and is intended as an honorable testimony of America's gratitude and affection for the French nation. I observe that it has been republished in London, and that the Critical Reviewers have treated that Author, in their Strictures upon it, as a person possessed of a very distinguished and sublime Genius. I will only trespass on your time to add that Mr. Barlow's character and talents are such as authorize me to commend him to your particular notice: and to assure you, my dear Marquis, with how great personal consideration and esteem. I have the honor, etc.[70]

*To REVEREND FRANCIS ADRIAN VANDERKEMP[71]

Mount Vernon, May 28, 1788.

Sir: The letter which you did me the favor to address to me the 15th. of this instt. from New York has been duly received, and I take the speediest occasion to well-come your arrival on the American shore.

I had always hoped that this land might become a safe and agreeable Asylum to the virtuous and persecuted part of mankind, to whatever nation they might belong; but I shall be the more particularly happy, if this Country can be, by any means, useful to the Patriots of Holland, with whose situation I am

---

[70] From the "Letter Book" copy in the *Washington Papers*.
[71] A Menonite minister from Holland.

peculiarly touched, and of whose public virtue I entertain a great opinion.

You may rest assured, Sir, of my best and most friendly sentiments of your suffering compatriots, and that, while I deplore the calamities to which many of the most worthy members of your Community have been reduced by the late foreign interposition in the interior affairs of the United Netherlands; I shall flatter myself that many of them will be able with the wrecks of their fortunes which may have escaped the extensive devastation, to settle themselves in comfort, freedom and ease in some corner of the vast regions of America. The spirit of the Religions and the genius of the political Institutions of this Country must be an inducement. Under a good government (which I have no doubt we shall establish) this Country certainly promises greater advantages, than almost any other, to persons of moderate property, who are determined to be sober, industrious and virtuous members of Society. And it must not be concealed, that a knowledge that these are the general characteristics of your compatriots would be a principal reason to consider their advent as a valuable acquisition to our infant settlements. If you should meet with as favorable circumstances, as I hope will attend your first operations; I think it probable that your coming will be the harbinger for many more to adventure across the Atlantic.

In the meantime give me leave to request that I may have the pleasure to see you at my house whensoever it can be convenient to you, and to offer whatsoever services it may ever be in my power to afford yourself, as well as to the other Patriots and friends to the rights of Mankind of the Dutch Nation.[72] I am etc.   [H. S. P.]

---

[72] Vanderkemp visited Mount Vernon July 29–30, 1788.

To MARQUIS DE LAFAYETTE

Mount Vernon, May 28, 1788.

My dear Marquis: I have lately had the pleasure to receive the two letters by which you introduced to my acquaintance M. Du Pont and M. Vanderkemp and altho' those gentlemen have not as yet been to visit me, you may be persuaded that whensoever I shall have the satisfaction of receiving them, it will be with all that attention to which their merits and your recommendations entitle them.

Notwithstanding you are acquainted with Mr. Barlow in person, and with his works by reputation, I thought I would just write you a line by him, in order to recommend him the more particularly to your civilities. Mr. Barlow is considered by those who are good Judges to be a genius of the first magnitude; and to be one of those Bards who hold the keys of the gate by which Patriots, Sages and Heroes are admitted to immortality. Such are your Antient Bards who are both the priest and door-keepers to the temple of fame. And these, my dear Marquis, are no vulgar functions. Men of real talents in Arms have commonly approved themselves patrons of the liberal arts and friends to the poets of their own as well as former times. In some instances by acting reciprocally, heroes have made poets, and poets heroes. Alexander the Great is said to have been enraptured with the Poems of Homer and to have lamented that he had not a rival muse to celebrate his actions. Julius Cæsar is well known to have been a man of a highly cultivated understanding and taste. Augustus was the professed and magnificent rewarder of poetical merit, nor did he lose the return of having his atcheivments immortalized in song. The Augustan age is proverbial for intellectual refinement and elegance in composition; in it the harvest of laurels and bays was wonderfully mingled together. The age of your Louis the fourteenth, which produced a multiude of great Poets and great Captains, will never be forgotten: nor will that of Queen Ann in England, for the same cause, ever cease to reflect a lustre upon the Kingdom. Although we are yet in our cradle, as a nation, I think the efforts of the human mind with us are sufficient to refute (by incontestable facts) the doctrines of those who have asserted that every thing degenerates in America. Perhaps we shall be found, at this moment, not inferior to the rest of the world in the performances of our poets and painters; notwithstanding many of the incitements are wanting which operate powerfully among older nations. For it is generally understood, that excellence in those sister Arts has been the result of easy circumstances, public encouragements and an advanced stage of society. I observe that the Critics in England, who speak highly of the American poetical geniuses (and their praises may be the more relied upon as they seem to be reluctantly extorted,) are not pleased with the tribute of applause which is paid to your nation. It is a reason why they should be the more caressed by your nation. I hardly know how it is that I am drawn thus far in observations on a subject so foreign from those in which we are mostly engaged, farming and politics, unless because I had little news to tell you.

Since I had the pleasure of writing to you by the last Packet, the Convention of Maryland has ratified the federal Constitution by a majority of 63 to 11 voices. That makes the seventh State which has adopted it, next Monday the Convention in Virginia will assemble; we have still good hopes of its adoption here: though by no great plurality of votes. South Carolina has probably decided favourably before this time. The plot thickens fast. A few short weeks will determine the political fate of America for the present generation and probably produce no small influence on the happiness of society through a long succession of ages to come. Should every thing proceed with harmony and consent according to our actual wishes and expectations; I will confess to you sincerely, my dear Marquis; it will be so much beyond any thing we had a right to imagine or expect eighteen months ago, that it will demonstrate as visibly the finger of Providence, as any possible event in the course of human affairs can ever designate it. It is impracticable for you or any one who has not been on the spot, to realise the change in men's minds and the progress towards rectitude in thinking and acting which will then have been made.

Adieu, my dear Marquis, I hope your affairs in France will subside into a prosperous train without coming to any violent crisis. Continue to cherish your affectionate feelings for this country and the same portion of friendship for me, which you are ever sure of holding in the heart of your most sincere, &c.[73]

To SAMUEL HANSON

Mount Vernon, June 8, 1788.

Sir: Your letter of the 4th. instant,[74] which was delivered to me on my return from my late journey, is now before me; and requires that I should say something in reply on a subject, in which I feel myself more embarrassed and more awkwardly situated than ever I have been before.

It is but justice to my own feelings to observe, that I am conscious I have never been indisposed to do whatever might be in my power in favor of those whose misfortunes had been

---

[73] From the "Letter Book" copy in the *Washington Papers.*

On May 29 Washington sent a bill of lading to Clement Biddle, for 10 barrels of shad and 40 barrels of herrings "which you will please dispose of on Commission to the best advantage." A copy of this letter is in the "Letter Book" in the *Washington Papers.*

[74] In the *Washington Papers.*

unavoidably brought upon them, without any fault of their own. In this predicament, I doubt not, I was not a little concerned at an application for employment under a Government which does not yet exist, and with the Administration of which (in case it should be adopted and carried into execution) it is *much more* than possible I may never be concerned. The chaos of uncertainty in which we are involved, and the impropriety of my anticipating events or hazarding opinions, would scarcely permit me to touch, however slightly, on these delicate topics.

These circumstances, I observe, had not entirely escaped your attention, you will not, therefore, think it hard that I should mention the subject as peculiarly distressing and perplexing to me. Delicacy forbids that I should enlarge as to myself; as to yourself, I will only add that I know nothing but that your character stands in the fairest possible point of light, and consequently cannot be actuated by any prejudice against your pretentions.

I beg, Sir, that the candour and freedom which I have used on this occasion may not be misinterpreted to give you any unintended and unnecessary anxiety; or to induce you to believe that I have taken in ill part the application, although I thought it to be altogether untimely and improper.

On the contrary you may rely upon my protestation, that I am in every personal consideration, with real esteem and Friendship. Sir, Your, etc.[75]

To JOSEPH BARRELL[76]

Mount Vernon, June 8, 1788.

General Washington, having lately received with great satisfaction the medal which the Owners of the adventure to the

---

[75] From the "Letter Book" copy in the *Washington Papers*.
[76] Of Boston, Mass.

Pacific Ocean have been pleased to transmit to him, begs leave to return his best acknowledgments to those Gentlemen for the very acceptable Compliment, and to assure them that his hearty wishes for success attend their enterprise, he hopes and even flatters himself that the day will arrive (at no very distant period) when the sources of commerce shall be enlarged and replenished; and when the new Constellation of this Hemisphere shall be hailed and respected in every quarter of the terraqueous globe![77]

To JAMES MADISON

Mount Vernon, June 8, 1788.

My dear Sir: I am much obliged by the few lines you wrote to me on the 4th, and though it is yet too soon to rejoice one cannot avoid being pleased at the auspicious opening of the business of your Convention. Though an ulterior opinion of the decision of this State on the Constitution would, at any time previous to the discussion of it in the Convention, have been premature yet I have never yet despaired of its adoption here. What I have mostly apprehended is that the insidious arts of its opposers to alarm the fears and inflame the passions of the Multitude, may have produced instructions to the Delegates that would shut the door against argument and be a bar to the exercise of judgment. If this is not the case I have no doubt but that the good sense of this Country will prevail against the local views of designing characters and the arrogant opinions of chagreened and disappointed men.

The decision of Maryland and South Carolina by so large Majorities and the moral certainty of the adoption of the proposed constitution by New Hampshire will make *all*, except

---

[77] From the "Letter Book" copy in the *Washington Papers*.

desperate men look before they leap into the dark consequences of rejection. The Ratification by eight States without a negative. By three of them unanimously. By six against one in another. By three to one in another. By two for one in two more; and by *all* the weight of *abilities* and *property* in the other is enough to produce a cessation of opposition. I do not mean that numbèrs alone is sufficient to produce conviction in the Mind, but I think it is enough to produce some change in the conduct of any man who entertains a doubt of his infalibility.

Altho' I have little doubt of your having received a copy of the enclosed pamphlet,[78] yet I send it. It is written with much good sense and moderation. I conjecture, but upon no certain ground, that Mr. Jay is the author of it. He sent it to me some time ago, since which I have received two or three more copies.

With sincere esteem and affectionate regard.[79]

To JONATHAN TRUMBULL

Mount Vernon, June 8, 1788.

My dear Sir: Although a multitude of avocations, joined to a recent Journey which I have been obliged to make in order to visit the works on the Potomac, have occasioned me to postpone giving an answer to your letter in favor of Lieut. Howe; yet I delayed not to forward the necessary Certificate for that Gentleman so that it might come to him, before the time fixed for his departure. I have at length found a moment's leisure to take up my pen and to tell you, in few words, the state of Politics in this part of the Union.

Our Convention has been assembled about a week, and so far as I am advised of their proceedings seem to have made as

---

[78] Probably Jay's "Address to the People of the State of New York on the subject of the Constitution."

[79] The text is from the sales catalogue of the *Washington-Madison Papers* (McGuire Collection, 1892), which is palpably more accurate than the "Letter Book" copy.

auspicious a beginning as could have been expected. Mr. Henry and Colo. Mason are at the head of the opposition; in favour of the Constitution are many very able men: among these we count Messrs. Pendleton, Wythe, Blair, Madison, Nicholas, Innis, Marshall and a long train of other worthies. Governor Randolph, (in answer to a speech in which Mr. Henry had insinuated that the federal Convention had exceeded their Powers and that nothing forbade us to live happy under the old Confederation with some alterations) described pathetically our perilous situation as a full Justification of the proceedings of the federal Convention and declared since so many of the States have adopted the Constitution without alterations, that he should vote for it in its present form. Upon the whole (though great and unwearied artifices have been practiced to prejudice the people in many parts of the State against the new government) I cant avoid hoping and believing, to use the fashionable phrase, that Virginia will make the ninth Column in the federal Temple. May all things turn out for the best; in respect to this highly favored Continent, is the constant and unfeigned prayer of Yours, etc.[80]

To THE SECRETARY FOR FOREIGN AFFAIRS

Mount Vernon, June 8, 1788.

Dear Sir: By the last Mail, I had the pleasure to receive your letter of the 29th. of May, and have now the satisfaction to congratulate you on the adoption of the Constitution by the Convention of South Carolina. I am sorry to learn there is a probability that the majority of members in the New York Convention will be Antifederalists. Still I hope that some event may turn up before they assemble, which may give a new complexion to the

---

[80] From the "Letter Book" copy in the *Washington Papers*.

business. If this State should, in the intermediate time, make the ninth that shall have ratified the proposed government, it will, I flatter myself, have its due weight. To shew that this event is now more to be expected than heretofore, I will give you a few particulars which I have from good authority and which you might not, perhaps, immediately obtain through any public channel of conveyance.

On the day appointed for the meeting of the Convention a large proportion of the members assembled and unanimously placed Mr. Pendleton in the Chair. Having on that and the subsequent day chosen the rest of their officers and fixed upon the mode of conducting the business, it was moved by some one of those opposed to the Constitution to debate the whole by paragraphs, without taking any question until the investigation should be completed. This was as unexpected as acceptable to the federalists: and their ready acquiescence seems to have somewhat startled the opposite party, for fear they had committed themselves.

Mr. Nicholas opened the business by very ably advocating the system of Representation. Mr. Henry in answer went more vaguely into the discussion of the Constitution, intimating that the federal Convention had exceeded their powers and that we had been and might be happy under the old Confederation with a few alterations. This called up Govr. Randolph, who is reported to have spoken with great pathos in reply: and who declared, that, since so many of the States had adopted the proposed Constitution, he considered the sense of America to be already taken, and that he should give his vote in favor of it without insisting previously upon amendments. Mr. Mason rose in opposition and Mr. Madison reserved himself to obviate the objections of Mr. Henry and Colo. Mason the next day. Thus the matter rested when the last accounts came away.

Upon the whole the following inferences seem to have been drawn: that Mr. Randolph's declaration will have considerable effect with those, who had hitherto been wavering; that Mr. Henry and Colo Mason took different and awkward ground, and by no means equalled the public expectation in their speeches; that the former has probably receded somewhat from his violent measures to coalesce with the latter, and that the leaders of the opposition appear rather chagreened, and hardly to be decided as to their mode of opposition.

The sanguine friends of the Constitution counted upon a majority of twenty at their first meeting, which number they imagine will be greatly increased: while those equally strong in their wishes, but more temperate in their habits of thinking speak less confidently of the greatness of the majority, and express apprehensions of the arts that may yet be practised to excite alarms with the members from the Western district (Kentucky). All, however, agree that the beginning has been auspicious as could possibly have been expected. A few days will now ascertain us of the result. With sentiments of the highest esteem etc.[81]

To OLIVER POLLOCK

Mount Vernon, June 8, 1788.

Sir: I received your letter of the 11th. of May, at the moment when I was setting out on a preconcerted Journey to meet the Directors of the Potomac Company, on business of importance, at the Shanandoah Falls, that circumstance has necessitated me to defer giving an acknowledgment untill this time.

It would be with peculiar pleasure that I should write to his Excellency the Governor of Louisiana, on your behalf; if I did not think that there would be a glaring impropriety in my

---

[81] From the "Letter Book" copy in the *Washington Papers*.

assuming that liberty with that Representative of the Spanish King. Especially as I have never had the honor of a personal acquaintance or any correspondence with the Governor, and as I do not feel myself authorised to take a greater latitude of freedom in this respect, than any other unknown, private citizen. These motives of delicacy on my part, I hope will be considered, in the same point of light and of the same weight by you, as they have appeared to me. I am, etc.[82]

To THOMAS PLEASANTS, JUNIOR

Mount Vernon, June 8, 1788.

Sir: I have been duly favored with your letter of the 2d. inst. containing an extract from Mr. Didsbury's letter to you. In addition to what he has there recited, I can only inform you that the tract in which Major Vanbraam[83] holds or held a share, lays on the *little* Kanhawa, but in what County (whether Greenbrier, Ohio, or Harrison) I am not sufficiently acquainted with the boundaries of them to decide. nor can I say whether or in what manner the tract of 28,400 has been divided or give the least information with respect to the *quality* of the land; consequently can say nothing as to the value of it. The natural situation of it is exceedingly advantageous for it is not only a part of the highest survey on the Ohio (that was made under the Proclamation of 1754) but it lays on the Communication which is opened, or opening under the authority, and at the expence of the State from Morgan Town (Harrison Court House) to the Ohio. From Judge Mercer you may, possibly, get a more particular acct. of this matter for if my memory does not deceive me, his brother Colo. George Mercer (for whom he was

[82] From the "Letter Book" copy in the *Washington Papers.*
[83] Jacob Van Braam.

acting Attorney) either by purchase, or by the advance of his (Vanbraams) quotas of the expence of Surveyd. Patenting &c. is involved in this business. I am, etc.[84]

To WILLIAM SMITH AND OTHERS

Mount Vernon, June 8, 1788.

Gentlemen: Captain Barney has just arrived here in the miniature ship called the Federalist;[85] and has done me the honor to offer that beautiful *Curiosity* as a Present to me on your part. I pray you, Gentlemen, to accept the warmest expressions of my sensibility for this *specimen of American ingenuity:* in which the exactitude of the proportions, the neatness of the workmanship, and the elegance of the decorations (which make your Present fit to be preserved in a Cabinet of Curiosities) at the same time that they exhibit the skill and taste of the artists, demonstrate that Americans are not inferior to any people whatever in the use of mechanical instruments and the art of ship-building.

The unanimity of the agricultural State of Maryland in general, as well as of the commercial Town of Baltimore in particular, expressed in their recent decision on the subject of a general Government, will not (I persuade myself) be without its due efficacy on the minds of their neighbors, who, in many instances, are intimately connected not only by the nature of their produce, but by the ties of blood and the habits of life.

---

[84] From the "Letter Book" copy in the *Washington Papers.*

[85] The *Federalist* was a miniature ship, 15 feet long and perfect in every detail. It had been mounted on wheels and drawn by 4 horses in the procession with which Baltimore celebrated the adoption of the Constitution by Maryland. After the procession the merchants and shipowners of Baltimore sent it to Mount Vernon as a present to Washington. Capt. Joshua Barney navigated it down Chesapeake Bay and up the Potomac, where it was moored to the Mount Vernon wharf for several weeks until blown from its moorings and sunk in a high wind which did much damage to the trees and shrubberies of Mount Vernon.

Under these circumstances, I cannot entertain an idea, that the voice of the Convention of this State, which is now in session, will be dissonant from that of her nearly-allied sister, who is only separated by the Potomac.

You will permit me, Gentlemen, to indulge my feelings in reiterating the heart-felt wish, that the happiness of this Country may equal the desires of its sincerest friends; and that the patriotic Town, of which you are Inhabitants (in the prosperity of which I have always found myself strongly interested) may not only continue to encrease in the same wonderful manner it has formerly done; but that its trade, manufactures and other resources of wealth may be placed permanently in a more flourishing situation than they have hitherto been. I am &c.[86]

*To HENRY KNOX

Mount Vernon, June 17, 1788.

My dear Sir: I received your letter of the 25th. of May, just when I was on the eve of a departure for Fredericksburgh to pay a visit to my mother from whence I returned only last evening. The information of the accession of South Carolina to the New Government, since you letter, gives us a new subject for mutual felicitations. It was to be hoped that this auspicious event would have considerable influence upon the proceedings of the Convention of Virginia; but I do not find that to have been the case. Affairs in the Convention, for some time past, have not worn so good an aspect as we could have wished: and, indeed, the acceptance of the Constitution has become more doubtful than it was thought to be at their first meeting.

---

[86]From the "Letter Book" copy in the *Washington Papers.*

The purport of the intelligence, I received from my private letters by the last nights mail, is, that every species of address and artifice has been put in practice by the Antifederalists to create jealousies and excite alarms. Much appears to depend upon the final part which the Kentucke members will take; into many of whose minds apprehensions of unreal dangers, respecting the navigation of the Mississipi and their organization into a separate State, have been industriously infused. Each side seems to think, at present, that it has a small majority, from whence it may be augered that the majority, however it shall turn, will be very inconsiderable. Though, for my own part, I cannot but imagine, if any decision is had, it will be in favor of the adoption. My apprehension is rather that a strenuous, possibly, successful effort may be made for an adjournment; under an idea of opening a corrispondence with those who are opposed to the Constitution in other States. Colo. Oswald[87] has been at Richmond, it is said with letters from Antifœderalists in New York and Pensylvania to their Coadjutors in this State.

The Resolution, which came from the Antefederalists (much to the astonishment of the other party) that no question should be taken until the whole Plan should have been discussed paragraph by paragraph; and the remarkable tardiness in their proceedings (for the Convention have been able as yet only to get through the 2d. or 3d. Section), are thought by some to have been designed to protract the business until the time when the Assembly is to convene, that is the 23d. instant, in order to have a more colorable pretext for an adjournment. But notwithstanding the resolution, there has been much desultory debating and the opposers of the Constitution are reported to

[87] Eleazer Oswald.

have gone generally into the merits of the question. I know not how the matter may be, but a few days will now determine.

I am sorry to find not only from your intimations, but also from many of the returns in the late Papers, that there should be so great a majority against the Constitution in the Convention of New York. And yet I can hardly conceive, from motives of policy and prudence, they will reject it absolutely, if either this State or New-Hampshire should make the 9th. in adopting it; as that measure which gives efficacy to the system, must place any State that shall actually have refused its assent to the New-Union in a very awkward and disagreeable predicament.

By a letter which I have just recd. from a young Gentleman[88] who lives with me, but who is now at home in New-Hampshire, I am advised that there is every prospect that the Convention of that State will adopt the Constitution almost immediately upon the meeting of it. I cannot but hope then, that the States which may be disposed to make a secession will think often and seriously on the consequences. Colo. Humphreys who is still here, occupied with literary pursuits, desires to be remembered in terms of the sincerest friendship to you and yours.

Mrs. Washington and the family offer, with me, their best Compliments to Mrs. Knox and the little ones. You will ever believe me to be, with great esteem etc.   [MS. H. S.]

To RICHARD HENDERSON

Mount Vernon, June 19, 1788.

Sir: Your favour of the 5th. instant was lodged at my house, while I was absent on a visit to my Mother. I am now taking the earliest opportunity of noticing its contents, and those of

---

[88] Tobias Lear.

its Enclosure. Willing as I am to give satisfaction so far as I am able, to every reasonable enquiry (and this is certainly not only so, but may be highly important and interesting,) I must however, rather deal in general than particular observations: as I think you will be able, from the length of your residence in the country, and the extensiveness of your acquaintance with its affairs, to make the necessary applications and add the proper details. Nor would I choose that my interference in the business should be transmitted, lest, in a malicious world, it might be represented that I was officiously using the arts of seduction to depopulate other countries, for the sake of peopling our own.

In the first place it is a point conceded, that America, under an efficient government, will be the most favorable Country of any in the world for persons of industry and frugality, possessed of a moderate capital, to inhabit. It is also believed, that it will not be less advantageous to the happiness of the lowest class of people because of the equal distribution of property the great plenty of unoccupied lands, and the facility of procuring the means of subsistence. The scheme of purchasing a good tract of freehold estate and bringing out a number of able-bodied men, indented for a certain time appears to be indisputably a rational one.

All the interior arrangements of transferring the property and commencing the establishment you are as well acquainted with as I can possibly be. It might be considered as a point of more difficulty, to decide upon the place which should be most proper for a settlement. Although, I believe that Emigrants from other countries to this, who shall be well-disposed, and conduct themselves properly, would be treated with equal friendship and kindness in all parts of it; yet, in the old settled States, land is so much occupied, and the value so much enhanced by the contiguous cultivation, that the price would, in general be an objection. The land in [the] western country, or that on the Ohio, like all others, has its *advantages and disadvantages*. The neighborhood of the Savages and the difficulty of transportation were the great objections. The danger of the first will soon cease by the strong establishments now taking place; the inconveniences of the second will be, in a great degree, remedied by opening the internal Navigation. No Colony in America was ever settled under such favorable auspices, as that which has just commenced at the Muskingum. Information, property and strength, will be its characteristics. I know many of the settlers personally and that there never were men better calculated to promote the welfare of such a community.

If I was a young man, just preparing to begin the world or if advanced in life, and had a family to make a provision for, I know of no country where I should rather fix my habitation than in some part of that region, for which the writer of the quæries seems to have a predilection. he might be informed that his namesake and distant relation, Genl. St. Clair, is not only in high repute, but that he is Governor of all the Territory westward of the Ohio, and that there is a gentleman (to wit Mr. Joel Barlow) gone from New York by the last French Packet, who will be in London in the course of this year, and who is authorized to dispose of a very large body of land in that Country. The author of the quæries may then be referred to the "Information for those who would wish to remove to America:" and published in Europe in the year 1784, by the great Philosopher Dr. Franklin. Short as it is, it contains almost every thing, that needs to be known on the subject of migrating to this Country. You may find that excellent little Treatise in "Carey's[89] American Museum, for September, 1787."

---

[89] Mathew Carey.

It is worthy of being republished in Scotland, and every other part of Europe.

As to the European Publications respecting the United States, they are commonly very defective. The Abbe Raynal is quite erroneous.[90] Guthrie,[91] though somewhat better informed, is not absolutely correct. There is now "an American Geography preparing for the press by a Mr. Morse[92] of New Haven in Connecticut" which, from the pains the Author has taken in travelling through the States and acquiring information from the principal characters in each, will probably be much more exact and useful. of books at present existing, Mr. Jefferson's "Notes on Virginia" will give the best idea of this part of the Continent to a Foreigner: and the "American Farmer's Letters," written by Mr. Crevecœur (commonly called Mr. St. John) the French Consul in New York (who actually resided twenty years as a farmer in that State) will afford a great deal of profitable and amusing information, respecting *the private Life* of the Americans; as well as the progress of agriculture, manufactures, and arts in their Country. Perhaps the picture he gives, though founded on fact, is in some instances embellished with rather too flattering circumstances. I am, &c.[93]

To MARQUIS DE LAFAYETTE

Mount Vernon, June 19,[94] 1788.

I cannot account for your not having received some of my letters, my dear Marquis, before you wrote yours of the 18th of

---

[90] Guillaume Thomas François, Abbé Raynal's *A Philosophical and Political History of the British Settlements and Trade in North America*, published in Edinburgh, in 1779.
[91] William Guthrie. His *New Geographical, Historical and Commercial Grammar* was published in London in 1777.
[92] Rev. Jedidiah Morse.
[93] From the "Letter Book" copy in the *Washington Papers*.
[94] Both Ford and Sparks print this under June 18.

March, as I have been writing to you, at short intervals, constantly since last autumn. To demonstrate the satisfaction I enjoy on the receipt of your favours; I always answer them almost as soon as they arrive. Although, on account of my retirement from the busy scenes of life and the want of diversity in the tenour of our affairs, I can promise to give you little novelty or entertainment in proportion to what I expect in return. Were you to acknowledge the receipt of my letters, and give the dates of them when you write to me, I should be able to ascertain which of them had reached you, and which of them had miscarried. I am left in doubt whether the Indian Vocabularies &c. &c. have got to you or not.

There seems to be a great deal of bloody work cut out for this summer in the North of Europe. If war, want and plague are to desolate those huge armies that are assembled, who that has the feelings of a man can refrain from shedding a tear over the miserable victims of Regal Ambition? It is really a strange thing that there should not be room enough in the world for men to live, without cutting one anothers throats. As France, Spain and England have hardly recovered from the wounds of the late war, I would fain hope they will hardly be dragged into this. However, if the war should be protracted (and not end in a campaign as you intimate it possibly may) there seems to be a probability of other powers being engaged on one side or the other. by the British papers (which are our principal source of intelligence, though not always to be relied upon, as you know) it appears that the Spaniards are fitting out a considerable fleet and that the English Ministry have prohibited the subjects of their Kingdom from furnishing transports for the Empress of Russia. France must be too intent on its own domestic affairs to wish to interfere, and we have not heard that the King of Prussia, since his exploits in Holland, has taken it into his head [not to] meddle with other people's business. I cannot say that I am sorry to hear that the Algerines and other piratical powers are about to assist the Porte, because I think Russia will not forget and that she will take some leisure moment, just to keep her fleets in exercise, for exterminating those nests of Miscreants.

I like not much the situation of affairs in France. The bold demands of the parliaments, and the decisive tone of the King, shew that but little more irritation would be necessary to blow up the spark of discontent into a flame, that might not easily be quenched. If I were to advise, I would say that great moderation should be used on both sides. Let it not, my dear Marquis, be considered as a derogation from the good opinion, that I entertain of your prudence, when I caution you, as an individual desirous of signalizing yourself in the cause of your country and freedom, against running into extremes and prejudicing your cause. The King, though, I think from every thing I have been able to learn, he is really a good-hearted tho' a warm-spirited man, if thwarted injudiciously in the execution of prerogatives that belonged to the Crown, and in plans which he conceives calculated to promote the national good, may disclose qualities he has been little thought to possess. On the other hand, such a spirit seems to be awakened in the Kingdom, as, if managed with extreme prudence, may produce a gradual and tacit Revolution much in favor of the subjects, by abolishing Lettres de Cachet and defining more accurately the powers of government. It is a wonder to me, there should be found a single monarch, who does not realize that his own glory and felicity must depend on the prosperity and happiness of his People. How easy is it for a sovereign to do that which shall not only immortalize his name, but attract the blessings of millions.

In a letter I wrote you a few days ago by Mr. Barlow (but which might not possibly have reached New York until after his departure) I mentioned the accession of Maryland to the proposed government, and gave you the state of politics to that period. Since which the Convention of South Carolina has ratified the Constitution by a great majority: that of this State has been setting almost three weeks; and so nicely does it appear to be ballanced, that each side asserts that it has a preponderancy of votes in its favour. It is probable, therefore, the majority will be small, let it fall on whichever part it may; I am inclined to believe it will be in favour of the adoption. The Conventions of New York and New Hampshire assemble both this week; a large proportion of members, with the Governor at their head, in the former, are said to be opposed to the government in contemplation: New Hampshire it is thought will adopt it without much hesitation or delay. It is a little strange that the men of large property in the South, should be more afraid that the Constitution will produce an Aristocracy or a Monarchy, than the genuine democratical people of the East. Such are our actual prospects. The accession of one State more will complete the number, which by the Constitutional provision, will be sufficient in the first instance to carry the Government into effect.

And then, I expect, that many blessings will be attributed to our new government, which are now taking their rise from that industry and frugality into the practice of which the people have been forced from necessity. I really believe, that there never was so much labour and economy to be found before in the country as at the present moment. If they persist in the habits they are acquiring, the good effects will soon be distinguishable. When the people shall find themselves secure under an energetic government, when foreign nations shall be disposed to give us equal advantages in commerce from dread of retaliation, when the burdens of war shall be in a manner done away by the sale of western lands, when the seeds of happiness which are sown here shall begin to expand themselves, and when every one (under his own vine and fig-tree) shall begin to taste the fruits of freedom, then all these blessings (for all these blessings will come) will be referred to the fostering influence of the new government. Whereas many causes will have conspired to produce them. You see I am not less enthusiastic than ever I have been, if a belief that peculiar scenes of felicity are reserved for this country, is to be denominated enthusiasm. Indeed, I do not believe, that Providence has done so much for nothing. It has always been my creed that we should not be left as an awful monument to prove, " that Mankind, under the most favourable circumstances for civil liberty and happiness, are unequal to the task of Governing themselves, and therefore made for a Master."

We have had a backward spring and summer, with more rainy and cloudy weather than almost ever has been known: still the appearance of crops in some parts of the country is favorable, as we may generally expect will be the case, from the difference of soil and variety of climate in so extensive a region; insomuch that, I hope, some day or another, we shall become a storehouse and granary for the world. In addition to our former channels of trade, salted provisions, butter, cheese &c. are exported with profit from the eastern States to the East Indies. In consequence of a Contract, large quantities of flour are lately sent from Baltimore for supplying the garrison of Gibraltar. With sentiments of tenderest affection etc.[95]

---

[95] From the "Letter Book" copy in the *Washington Papers*.

INDEX

INDEX

By David M. Matteson

Accounts, claims, and warrants, Washington and warrants, interest, depreciation, 5, 430, 460, 461; Washington's English, 65; warrants and taxes, 469. *See also* Estates.

Adams, Abigail, marriage, 487*n*.

Adams, John, marriage of daughter, 487*n*.

Advice and admonitions, nephew's prodigality, 101; agent's dereliction, 143, 144; new legislator, 313; public use of private letter, 380, 387, 390, 404; nephew at academy, conduct, 492.

Agriculture, Virginia system, evils, 298, 299, 388; benefit of new government, 351; need of experimentation in restoration, 388; life, 414; societies, 417; American dependence, 455; progress, 526. *See also* Animals; Fertilizers; Implements; Mount Vernon; products by name.

Alexander, ——, Samuel Washington's estate, 157.

Alexander, Gerard, as security, 241.

Alexander, Robert, letter to, 61; debt to Washington, 61, 398; Custis estate, 62; bill of exchange, 212; as security, 241.

Alexandria, Va., as fur-trade depot, 211, 218–222.

Alexandria Academy. Washington and affairs, 347; Washington's nephews, 347, 443, 444.

Allen, William, daughter, 276*n*.

Altamont, John Denis Browne, *earl* of, Irish wolf hounds, 402.

Alton, Elizabeth, account, 255.

American Antiquarian Society, material from, 166*n*.

Anderson, Harriet Rebecca, Colvill estate, 102, 391, 392.

Andrews, ——, shipmaster, 361.

Animals, price at Pittsburgh, 135. *See also* animals by name.

Annapolis Convention, meeting, 4; failure of delegations, 123, 127, 138.

Anstey, John, introduction, 175.

Anterroches, Chaunae, *comtesse* d', appeal for son, 170*n*.

Armistead, John, letter to, 133; father's estate, debt to Washington, 133.

Armstrong, Edward A., letters possessed by, 53*n*, 109*n*, 140*n*, 174*n*, 178*n*, 324*n*, 422*n*, 495*n*.

Turkey, Russia, 185, 259, 350, 375, 406, 412, 475, 476.

Turner, George, letter to, 207; Cincinnati, 207.

Turner, *Lieut.* Thompkins Hilgrove, Huddy reprisal, 3.

Turnips, culture, experimentation, 244, 332, 333, 337, 414.

Tuttle, Timothy, Washington's New York land, 246.

Umbrella, Washington's, 235.

Union, crisis, disturbances, 26, 33–35, 51, 52, 59, 61, 68, 77, 108, 122–124, 128, 130, 153, 166, 169, 229; effect of Mississippi River navigation question, 133*n*; Washington and participation in crisis, 126; need of strengthening, coercive power, 138, 139, 190, 260; Washington on Knox's plan, 153; public and reform, 171, 173, 176; obstacles to reform, basis, 176, 245; or monarchy, 190; commerce and West, 192, 250; effect of state sovereignty, 238, 239; McIntosh's plan, 364; strengthening, and foreign relations, 435; economic effect of strengthening, 467; expected effect of new government, 485, 508, 520, 525. *See also* Annapolis Convention; Confederation; Continental Congress; Federal Convention; Organization; Ratification.

Union, 80*n*.

Vail, Robert W. G., acknowledgment to, 166*n*.

Van Braam, Jacob, frontier land, 515.

Vanderkemp, *Rev.* Francis Adrian, letter to, 504; welcome to America, 504; Mount Vernon, 505; Lafayette, 506.

Varnum, James Mitchell, Ohio Company, 412.

Vass, Ephraim, fort, Washington's adventure, 47.

Vaughan, John, letter to, 468.

Vaughan, Samuel, letters to, 6, 70, 313; Mount Vernon, 6; gift, 70; plan of Mount Vernon, 313; Washington on relations, 314.

Vermont, admission, 192.

Vetch, seed, 414.

Vigournere du Plessis. *See* Du Plessis.

Virginia, paper money, 50, 129; calling of Federal Convention, 51, 52; Potomac Company legislation, 53, 129, 300, 301, 335; taxation in kind, 68, 115, 312, 324; conduct of legislature, 71, 73, 75, 122, 129; delegates to Federal Convention, Washington, 71–73, 76, 115, 119, 120, 122, 151, 171–173, 177, 180, 187, 188, 191, 193, 194, 197, 198, 208, 209, 211, 213, 229; military certificates and warrants, depreciation, payment of taxes, 82, 129, 460, 468–470; Mississippi River navigation, 113*n*, 122, 250; Cincinnati, 134, 328; trade regulations,

Washington, George Steptoe, education, expenses, 267, 280, 320, 347, 443, 444; letter to, 492; admonished on conduct, 492–494.

Washington, Hannah (Bushrod), bereavement, 141, 142.

Washington, Hannah (Fairfax), brother's bequest, 306.

Washington, John Augustine, Pennsylvania land, 97, 142; death, brother and estate, 141, 160, 185, 186, 209.

Washington, Lawrence, Cartagena expedition, 37.

Washington, Lawrence Augustine, education, expenses, 267, 280, 320, 347, 443; conduct, 494.

Washington, Lund, French land, 16; Colvill estate, 109; Mercer estate, 118; Washington's affairs, 188 n; letter to, 212; Washington's debt, 212, 242, 251.

Washington, Martha, health, 200; and Federal Convention, 211.

Washington, Mary, letter to, 158; financial needs, plantation, son's comment, 158–160, 162; plans for residence, and Mount Vernon, 160–162; illness, son summoned, 209, 210; son's visit, 517.

Washington, Samuel, estate, embarrassment, 157.

Washington, Warner, letter to, 306; Fairfax estate, 306.

Washington, William, letter to, 275 n; coach, 275 n.

Washington Bottom, Pa., disposal of land, mill, 9, 11, 12, 86, 87, 93, 97, 140, 141, 202, 274.

Washington County, Pa., Washington's land, 11, 12, 85–88, 90, 91, 96, 274.

Washington-Humphreys Copies, material from, 166 n.

Washington-Madison Papers, material from, 52 n, 373 n, 404 n, 432 n, 491 n, 511 n.

Water. *See* Wells.

Watson, Josiah, (and Co.), letter to, 109; Colvill estate, 109; bill of exchange, 167.

Weather, drought, 284, 288, 294, 325, 336, 425; extreme cold, 401, 404, 425.

Weaving. *See* Cloth.

Webster, Noah, letter to, 301; ratification, 301.

Weedon, George, letters to, 134, 182, 328, 340; Cincinnati, 134, 328; Jerusalem artichokes, 182; willow cuttings, 328, 340.

Weissenfels, Frederick, letter to, 371; office-seeker, 371.

Welch, Wakelin, Washington's affairs, 65, 69, 356, 361, 362; letters to, 65, 361.

Wells, Mount Vernon, pump, 264.